SPIRAL DYNAMICS

Developmental Management

General Editor: Ronnie Lessem

Charting the Corporate Mind
Charles Hampden-Turner*

Greening Business
John Davis

Ford on Management
Henry Ford*

Managing Your Self
Jagdish Parikh

Conceptual Toolmaking
Jerry Rhodes

Integrative Management
Pauline Graham

Total Quality Learning
Ronnie Lessem

Executive Leadership
Elliott Jaques and Stephen D. Clement

Transcultural Management
Albert Koopman

The Great European Illusion
Alain Minc

The Rise of NEC
Koji Kobayashi

Organizing Genius
Paul Thorne

European Strategic Alliances
Sabine Urban and Serge Vendemini

Intuition
Jagdish Parikh, Fred Neubauer and Alden G. Lank

Spiral Dynamics
Don Beck and Chris Cowan

Managing in Organizations that Learn
Steven Cavaleri and David Fearon

*For copyright reasons this edition is not available in the USA

Spiral Dynamics

Mastering Values, Leadership, and Change

Don Edward Beck and Christopher C. Cowan

Exploring the New Science of Memetics

First published 1996

Reprinted 1996 (twice), 1999 (twice), 2000

Blackwell Publishers Inc
350 Main Street
Malden, Massachusetts 02148, USA

Blackwell Publishers Ltd
108 Cowley Road
Oxford OX4 1JF, UK

Library of Congress Cataloging in Publication Data
Beck, Don (Don Edward)
Spiral Dynamics: Mastering Values, Leadership, and Change/Don Edward
Beck and Christopher C.Cowan
p. cm.
Includes index.
ISBN 155786–940–5 (Hbk.: alk. paper)
1. Values – Psychological aspects. 2. Typology (Psychology)
3. Leadership – Psychological aspects. 4. Personality and social
intelligence. I. Cowan, Chris.
II. Title.
BF778.B34· 1995   95–22494
158–dc20   CIP

British Library Cataloguing in Publication Data
A CIP catalogue record for this book is available from the British Library

Commissioning Editor: Richard Burton
Desk Editor: Paul Stringer
Production Controller: Pam Park
Illustrations: Elaine Moore

Typeset in 10 on 12pt Ehrhardt
at the Spartan Press Ltd, Lymington, Hants
Printed and bound in Great Britain byMPG Books Ltd, Bodmin, Cornwall

This book is printed on acid-free paper

Contents

Section 4: Global Order and Chaos on the Dynamic Spiral

Resources for Spiral Wizards

Authors Don Edward Beck and Christopher C. Cowan have designed a series of learning experiences around the principles of Spiral Dynamics to apply it directly in business and organizational life, as well as in societies at large. These include applications in leadership systems and styles, the *Streams* Technology for aligning and integrating entities, community development, large-scale systems transformations, health and wellness, sports values, education, public safety, and, of course, management supervision.

In addition, they have developed a number of assessment systems, media packages, and customized versions of this point of view. Many of these items are now available in Spanish, Dutch, and Portugese, as well as English.

Finally, The National Values Center offers tailored in-house work with clients and an extensive series of public workshops in both the theory and practice of Spiral Dynamics. These events occur on a regular basis in Dallas, Texas, with introductory sessions (SD-I) every January/February and the advanced seminars (SD-II) each June.

Don Edward Beck and Christopher C. Cowan
PO Box 797, Denton, Texas 76202–0797, USA
Telephone (817) 383–1209 and (817) 382 6103
Fax (817) 382–4597
E-mail 70731.303@CompuServe.com

INTRODUCTION

Spiral Dynamics presents a new framework for understanding the dynamic forces at work in human affairs – business, personal lives, education, and even geopolitics.

It is not another hard-edged and simplistic 'types of people' model nor a soft, 'everybody's beautiful' egalitarian approach. Based in decades of research, real-world applications, and the latest findings of both organizational theorists and neurobiology, this book lays out a very specific Tool Kit for managing the deepest differences in people. These core intelligences exist like *strange attractors* below our values, beliefs, and ethical structures. By applying the right tools at this base level rather than to surface symptoms, any bright, curious human being can, quite simply, change the world.

In the next few pages I will survey the principles of Spiral Dynamics.

Ronnie Lessem, Series Editor

Spiral Wizardry:
Managing Spiral Dynamics

'Spiral Wizards instinctively roam over vast landscapes seeing patterns and connections others do not notice because their old paradigm, "first tier" filters do not allow them to. They can move through the spine of the Spiral awakening, unblocking, empowering or repairing each of the 'MEMEs (genetic or cultural codes) of an organization. Such a Wizard appreciates chaos and thinks more like a creative designer than a reengineer. The process links functions, people and ideas into new, more natural flows that add precision, flexibility, rapid response, humanity and fun to getting the work done. That is the power of new paradigm, "second tier" thinking, to constantly survey the whole while tinkering expertly with the parts. Monitoring the full Spiral is especially vital during periods of large-scale turbulence and change, like right now.'

Introduction

This book on 'Spiral Dynamics' represents the culmination of forty years of research and development, aimed at global managers specifically and citizens of the globe generally. Having been initiated by an American Professor of Psychology, Clare W. Graves, in the sixties, it has since been developed by his two dedicated followers, Don Beck and Chris Cowan, based on their extensive work in North America and South Africa.

In more recent years the work of the British biologist Richard Dawkins (*The Selfish Gene*) and the Polish-American psychologist Mihaly Csikszentmihalyi (*The Evolving Self*) has been incorporated to bring the fresh language of 'memes' (rhymes with themes) to what has been popularly called 'value systems' or 'levels of psychological existence' theory. The net result is one of perhaps the three major breakthroughs in approaches to managing complexity – the other two being 'systems' and 'chaos' theory – of this century.

In the course of their book, Beck and Cowan begin in Section 1 with a 'spiral overview' before introducing us to the intricacies of Spiral Dynamics. Within it they set the context for the different managerial minds arising out of different times, introduce us to the so-called ^vMEME (values-attracting meta-meme) systems that underlie such different managerial eras, and outline the diverse structural attributes of the Spiral mind. What biochemical genes are to cellular DNA, ^vMEMEs are to our psycho-social and organizational 'DNA.' In section 2, they take us through the fascinating dynamics of spiraling human systems. These include the dynamics of change, leadership, complexity, alignment and integration.

This may be, in fact, as far as you may need to go in order to improve your ability to manage diversity and complexity. Should you want, however, to deepen your understanding of the underlying Spiral structure – that, is the individual, organization or societal ^vMEMEs themselves – you will proceed on to Section 3. Therein you will discover, in turn, the precise ^vMEMEs of *Survival, Kinship, Power, Purpose, Achievement* and *Consensus* orientations (the old paradigm), as well as *Integrative* and *Holistic* (new paradigm) orientations which personalities, companies and societies are just now undergoing. The authors project that the Spiral's dynamics will give rise to further integrated 'global awakenings,' which will, in turn, lead to still more new ^vMEMEs since the process of elaborating human systems seems to be open-ended.

Spiral Overview

Different Minds

In the first chapter of their book, Beck and Cowan refer to the current destabilization of belief structures and loosed anchors in a diverse but not yet interdependent world. 'Like migrating tectonic plates, several core ways of thinking – paradigms, if you will – are grinding against each other. Ancient tribal and ethnic sores are belching fire while transnational companies linked by satellites conduct their business above.'

^vMEME Systems

Worldviews In the second chapter, the two authors go on a so-called "^vMEME hunt'. Such a ^vMEME reflects a world view, a valuing system, a level of psychological existence, a belief structure, an organizing principle, a way of thinking or a mode of adjustment. It represents, firstly then, a *core intelligence* that forms systems and directs human behavior. Secondly, it *impacts upon all life choices* as a decision-making framework. Thirdly, each ^vMEME can manifest itself in both *healthy and unhealthy* forms. Fourthly, such a ^vMEME is a discrete *structure* for thinking, not just a set of ideas, values or cause. Fourthly, it *can brighten and dim* as the **Life Conditions** (consisting of historic

Times, geographic *Place*, existential *Problems*, and societal *Circumstances*) change.

Systems The eight landmark ᵛMEMEs which make up the Spiral's central core and developmental process are represented in terms of different colors. The first six of these make up 'old paradigm' business, management, education, and community. The **BEIGE** ᵛMEME is structured in loose bands and underpinned by survival processes. The **PURPLE** ᵛMEME is structured in tribe-like groups and is underpinned by circular processes. The **RED** ᵛMEME is structured in empires and underpinned by exploitative, power-seeking processes. The **BLUE** ᵛMEME is structured in pyramidal form, and underpinned by purposeful, controlling or even authoritarian processes. The **ORANGE** ᵛMEME is structured in delegative forms, underpinned by achievement-oriented, autonomy-seeking, and strategic processes. The **GREEN** ᵛMEME is structured in an egalitarian fashion, underpinned by processes that are both experiential and consensual. The two ᵛMEMEs, finally, that constitute the beginnings of a 'new paradigm' are **YELLOW** and **TURQUOISE**. **YELLOW** is flexible, integrative, and knowledge-based, both as a structure and in its processes, while **TURQUOISE** is holistic and global in structure, flowing and multidimensional in its processes.

In chapter 3, thereby completing their overview, Beck and Cowan enter into the 'Spiral mind', outlining the seven principles that underlie it. Firstly, human nature includes a **capacity for new** ᵛMEMEs to awaken without eliminating old ones. Secondly, shifting **Life Conditions activate** ᵛMEMEs which may emerge, surge, regress or fade in response. Thirdly, the overall Spiral is forged by a **pendulum-like alternation** between the Self-Expressive, internally controlled 'me' -ᵛMEMEs (*Survival, Power, Achievement, Flexibility*), and the Self-Sacrificing, externally anchored 'we' -ᵛMEMEs (*Kinship, Purposeful, Consensual, Global*). Fourthly, **each** ᵛMEME **comes in phases**, either in personal passage or historic epoch, like waves on a beach, ENTERing as a surge, dominating the scene as a strong PEAK, and then EXITing from prominence to be replaced by another. Fifthly, the emergence of thinking systems along the Spiral is from **lesser to greater complexity**. Sixthly, ᵛMEMEs **coexist as mixtures** such that a generally consensual **GREEN**-oriented character may activate his or her power seeking **RED** aspect in sports, and call up an **ORANGE** achievement orientation in marketing meetings. Seventhly, and finally for Beck and Cowan, the ᵛMEMEs **cluster in tiers of six**. The old paradigm (which the authors refer to as 'First Tier') clusters together our 'Subsistence' level concerns with starvation (**BEIGE**), of magical spirits (**PURPLE**), of aggressors (**RED**), of disruption to law and order (**BLUE**), of loss of autonomy (**ORANGE**), and of social disapproval (**GREEN**). The new paradigm 'Being' series recontextualizes the old in terms of an information rich, highly mobile, 'Global village' where all the ᵛMEMEs are active at once (**YELLOW**) and

(TURQUOISE) as they resonate with compassionate strength for the enhancement of both one and all.

The Dynamics of Change

Change Potential

In the five chapters that follow their overview, Beck and Cowan enter into the heart of 'Spiral Dynamics'. In chapter 4, on Change, they refer to Clare Graves' finding that people vary in terms of their 'MEME systems' potential to change along an 'OPEN–ARRESTED–CLOSED (OAC) continuum. Beck and Cowan then identify the Six Conditions that have to be met if an individual or organization is to experience lasting change. Firstly, the *potential* for change must be there. Secondly, if there are still *unresolved problems* from a lower order, you cannot expect to effect change at higher Spiral levels. Thirdly, there needs to be felt *dissonance* within the current 'MEME system before change will be welcomed in. Fourthly, there needs to be sufficient *insight* into the causes of the dissonance, and awareness of alternative approaches to their resolution. Fifthly, the specific *barriers* to change need to be concretely identified, and then eliminated, bypassed, neutralized or reframed into something else. Sixthly and finally, when significant change occurs you can expect periods of confusion, false starts, long learning curves and awkward assimilation while *consolidation* of the new thinking occurs. If there is no culture of nurturing *support* during the transformation, new 'MEMEs rarely germinate, much less bloom.

When all of these Six Conditions are met, new 'MEMEs may awaken, and movement along the Spiral may occur. But you must establish where you are before setting a course for where you want to be. That leads Beck and Cowan to cite five critical landmarks which mark the Sequence of Change. Just as you probably have a mixture of 'MEMEs within, you are also likely to be at different points along the way in different aspects of your work and life.

ALPHA, phase 1, is a state where individual, organization or societal 'MEMEs are in a healthy dynamic tension with surrounding *Life Conditions*. With Phase 2, BETA, doubts arise as a person enters a new phase of his or her life or a company loses key personnel and market share. As we leave ALPHA for BETA we first try 'more of the same,' refocusing our efforts with a view to working harder and smarter. Frequently that accelerates movement into even deeper BETA. If things get bad enough we move from anxious BETA, phase 2, through degrees of turbulence toward chaotic GAMMA, phase 3. We may find a 'Reform Option' escape route and bypass the trauma. If not, things become terrible but there is seemingly no place left to go. This is the GAMMA Trap! Phase 4 heralds escape from the trap with a DELTA surge toward a new system. This vibrant phase, however is also full of dangers.

Getting rid of what you do not like does not mean you have captured what you do want. It is phase 5, the new ALPHA, which brings about the consolidation of the ideas and insights from BETA and GAMMA through DELTA. For a while, things are again in balance, congruent, and 'all is right with the world.'

Finally, in their consideration of the dynamics of change, Beck and Cowan identify seven distinct Variations. They propose that Change^1 ≠ Change^2, but instead that each Variation represents an approach which fits particular circumstances. These spread across an arc from 'Horizontal' through 'Oblique' and then 'Vertical' change directions. Horizontal Change of the 1st and 2nd Variations is the norm when First Tier 'MEMEs are solidly in control during ALPHA or early BETA phases, and when only a few of the above mentioned Six Conditions for change can be met. Horizontal forms include Fine-TUNE and Expand-OUT from base systems which remain essentially the same.

The Oblique forms, Change of the 3rd and 4th Variations, Stretch-DOWN and Stretch-UP, modify the base 'MEME systems while adding or subtracting elements of other nearby 'MEMEs. Such Oblique change often represents a practical limit for First Tier 'old paradigm' thinking. In fact the quality movement is possibly the best example of such Oblique change, though half-hearted attempts at reengineering run a close second. Only Second Tier intervention makes large-scale transformation across 'MEMEs possible.

Vertical Change of the 5th, 6th, and 7th Variations – Break-OUT, UP-Shift, and Quantum – involve the awakening of new 'MEMEs, though it may also resurrect ones that were thought to be buried and gone. In any case this represents 'change through the Spiral, which may be revolutionary (5th) or evolutionary (6th) or in multiple 'MEMEs at once, Quantum Change of the 7th Variation.' Vertical change entails meeting all Six Conditions and often requires a direct assault on both internal and external barriers.

The Dynamics of Leadership

Leadership dynamics, beginning with chapter 5, describe what Beck and Cowan term System Wizards, Change Wizards, and Spiral Wizards. System Wizards understand a given 'MEME thoroughly, knowing intuitively how to 'lead' people within that particular 'MEME's sphere of influence. Change Wizards understand the transitional cusps between 'MEMEs and how to move between one and the next.

Chapter 6 describes the ability to consider broad spectrum views and respond to many systems at once. This is the realm of the Spiral Wizard. Spiral Wizardry is constructed out of the Second Tier dynamics that begin with the **YELLOW** and **TURQUOISE** 'MEMEs. The former provides the inner directed, individualistic viewpoint that connects particles and sub-systems into natural sequences. The latter introduces a focus on others and spiritual reawakening that brings those things into harmony.

Spiral leadership firstly involves establishing positive relationships through three universal principles: **Politeness**, **Openness** and, an idea surprising to some, decisive **Autocracy** (P-O-A). Secondly the Spiral Wizard recognizes and honors individual 'MEMEs at a personal and institutional level. Thirdly, effective Spiral leadership adapts different people and different situations with these different 'MEMEs.

In the final analysis, Spiral Wizardry involves management of the whole 'MEME spectrum. Taking respective account of people and work, for example, entails all of the following at once.

TURQUOISE
- spiritual bonds pull people and organizations together
- work must be meaningful to the overall health of life

YELLOW
- people enjoy doing things that fit who they are naturally
- workers need free access to information and materials

GREEN
- people want to get along and feel accepted by their peers
- sharing and participating are better than competing

ORANGE
- people are motivated by the achievement of material rewards
- competition improves productivity and fosters individual growth

BLUE
- people work the best when they are told how to do things the right way
- doing duty and being punished when failing to do so gives meaning to life

RED
- people need to be dominated by strong leadership that gives rewards
- workers will put up with a lot if their basic needs are met regularly

PURPLE
- people are 'married' to their group – nepotism is normal
- workers owe their lives and souls to the parent-like organization

Spiral Alignment – *Streams*

Spiral Alignment, chapter 7, is a comprehensive design process that obliges managers to align future visioning, strategic thinking, long- and short-term planning into a single stream-like flow. There are ten elements in such a streaming process. First, *decide what business you are in*, asking such questions as why does your enterprise exist, what work do you do, and what do you want to become? Second, *chart big picture patterns* and flows, initially investigating downstream through hypothetical plots and movie scripts and subsequently upstream, tracking the deepest currents, the wellsprings of change. Third, *take an inventory* of resources, functional capacities and life-cycle stages. Only now, that is fourthly, are you ready to develop and propagate a *strategic vision*, ensuring that you communicate it throughout your organization's Spiral, in all its languages, not only to yourself or your peers.

In establishing, fifthly, your specific *strategy for change* you will need to pay particular attention to the respective 'MEMEs. **PURPLE** will want you to embody change in rituals, traditions and symbols. **RED** will require heroic leaders and storytellers to forge a new mythology. **BLUE** strategy will need to be 'carved in stone', in the shape of a mission statement and new rules. **ORANGE** will be looking for specific signs of 'how this is getting me ahead', while **GREEN** defines ends and means in distinctly humanistic terms. **YELLOW**'s approach revolves around keeping the whole Spiral healthy through necessary and aligned outputs. Sixthly, then, it is *connect everything to everything else.*

'Bureaucracies take care of themselves, not the flow of work.' At this seventh point, according to Beck and Cowan, you *create a hypothetical model* of your ideal organization that fits with the six elements already outlined, and that is congruent with the flow of work itself. In the eighth process, *realignment,* whereby you reshape current systems to fit the new model, managers need to pay particular attention to the forces of resistance. Change ceremonies need to accommodate **PURPLE**; change mandates, accompanied by tangible rewards, need to appeal to **RED**; **BLUE** needs to be able to espouse a new cause.

The ninth element involves the selection of *the right person for the job.* If the job is competitive and high-risk, seek out an **ORANGE**-oriented leader; if you require tough-minded, cold-blooded decisions in times of crisis, look for some **RED**; if you are needing to involve people in teams along the way, choose for more **GREEN**; if complexity and diversity is the name of the game, lean toward **YELLOW** or even **TURQUOISE** criteria. Finally, element number ten, build in an *ongoing realignment process* in recognition that change is constant, not a closed loop nor even cycles, but an open-ended Spiral requiring continuous adjustment through ALPHA, BETA, GAMMA, and DELTA towards a new ALPHA.

Spiral Integration – *Templates*

Spiral Integration, chapter 8, completes the dynamics of the Spiral. It incorporates what Beck and Cowan refer to as *Templates*. These templates, three of them in all, are designed to accommodate the full Spiral. Instead of being rigid, permanent cutouts, Spiral Templates are organic, living layers that fuse together, stretch, adjust and mesh, like interdependent layers of our skins. There are in fact three kinds of template.

Workflow – the X Template On the X Template, every variable that influences the job to be done is included in the *workflow*. Such terms as value analysis, value chain, enterprise networking, and horizontal management are pertinent here. The intent of this template is to link together all of the variables that impinge on the job to be done so that they are handled in a coordinated and logical manner. The payoff is that the ultimate output will be clean, focused, strategic and lean.

Management – the Y *Template*   People and resources operating through the Y Template support, facilitate, assist, enhance and improve X Template procedures and performance. Thereby, the healthy Y Template is flexible, apolitical, demands P-O-A, changes and reconstitutes itself as the X need arises. This is where many conventional functions of management, supervision, and strategic planning are incorporated, but always with an eye to the Spiral and its ᵛMEMEs.

Command Intelligences – the Z *Template*   The unique insight and wisdom of the Z Template, for Beck and Cowan, is the combination of *executive core* and *focused intelligences*. The executive core monitors the whole process like the CPU in a computer. It is a small group chosen for its competence, experience and maturity, representing a microcosm of what is required to coordinate X and Y Templates, and to maintain a lookout to enable the organization to thrive in the milieu-at-large. The second function of the Z Template is to bring Focused Intelligences to bear upon problems. Knowledge, skills and informed perspectives transcend rank in making decisions.

Some clusters drawn to Z from all the Templates may include a *wild duck pond* where bright, non-conformists can explore off-the-wall ideas; a *nursery* or development track where neophytes can be exposed to mainline functions in each of the three templates at low risk to the organization; a *war room* that displays the vital signs of the company, including models of the environment and profiles of competitors; a *play pen*, that is a loose and creative environment for renewal and change; a *crisis team* of rapid response experts who can be quickly deployed for damage prevention and control; and a *Wizard's tree house*, or periodic convention of Spiral Wizards who can scan for new trends and opportunities, and feed them into the Command Intelligences. Such Spiral Wizards, as we may recall, are able to span the full ᵛMEME spectrum, in their awareness if not also in their leadership activity.

The Spiral's ᵛMEME Structure

The First Tier

In the third part of their book, Beck and Cowan provide us with a 'Spiral Wizard's Field Manual' that directly applies Spiral Dynamics to day-to-day events and experiences. It includes in-depth analyses of each of the individual

'MEMEs, starting with the six that belong to the First Tier, or 'old management paradigm'. In each case the authors are concerned not only with the 'MEME itself – its implications for you, for people around you, and for your organizations – but also with the way you enter, engage with, and exit from that particular 'MEME's influence. As a preview, these are activated as follows:

- **BEIGE** requires subsistence needs be met in order to remain alive
- **PURPLE** is nurtured through observing rituals, finding reassurance, and by expressing a sense of enchantment in life's mystery
- **RED** is excited by stories of company heroes, by celebrating feats of conquest, and by evidence of respect
- **BLUE** is reinforced through appeals to traditions, fair treament for all, and by honoring length of service and loyalty
- **ORANGE** is exercised by displaying symbols of success, individuals being recognized for their achievements, and challenges for improvement
- **GREEN** is enhanced by stressing the importance of the people, responsiveness to feelings, and a caring socially responsible community

The Second Tier

In chapter 15 we enter the systemic, FlexFlow 'new paradigm' world of the Beck and Cowan Second Tier. The focus now is on competence and functionality and qualities of being, not having or even doing, within the context of flexible and open systems that can for the first time take the full Spiral into account without the 'blinders' of First Tier 'MEMEs. The prevailing worldview is information-rich, and multidimensional, part of a complex interactive system. Chaos driven subsystems interact within the physical, economic and social environments as **YELLOW** seeks to find natural ways of living that focus energies. (The reader will discover that Section 2 was an application lesson in this perspective.)

Clare Graves' theory predicts that, with the move to **TURQUOISE** heralded in chapter 16, the great questions first raised with **YELLOW** can begin to be answered in this new global, holistic order of being. The independent self now becomes part of a larger, conscious whole, both as individual and as organization. Networking, on a whole Earth basis, is routine as the expanded use of mind tools and competencies becomes a global reality. The focus, then, is on the good living of all entities as integrated systems. We become supremely conscious of energy fields and holographic links in all walks of work and life, using collective human intelligence to work on large-scale problems without sacrificing individuality.

Spiral Chaos – *Global Awakenings*

In their final chapter, Beck and Cowan expose us to some applications of their new Spiral Dynamics perspective to world orderliness and disorders. To deal with the many levels of the complex 'global awakenings' as a Spiral Wizard, Spiral congruence is required. For example, if the culture that surrounds you is at a lower range of 'MEME development, goals must be more immediate and specific; at a higher level they can be more abstract and distant. Since cultures' 'MEMEs evolve, each social universe is an interactive moving picture rather than a still frame.

Spiral Order – *Scanning the Environment for Patterns*

In scanning geopolitical currents, therefore, the Spiral Wizard needs to look out for:

- *FLASHPOINTS*, that is crises caused by collisions between different 'MEMEs
- *HOTSPOTS*, that is areas bubbling below the surface that could soon erupt
- *DIASPORAS*, involving the spread or migration of people with shared 'MEMEs
- *REGRESSIONS*, that is a Spiral downshift, due to worsening life conditions
- *HARMONICS*, that is the simultaneous movement of two or more 'MEME systems
- *GRIDLOCK*, as two strong 'MEME systems oscillate back and forth in conflict
- *CUTTING EDGES*, representing the first flash of new 'MEMEs awakening

Establishing your Geo-Templates

The Template that prevails at a given time in a given place will be determined by: the functional needs of life on Earth (**TURQUOISE**); the Spiral levels that are active in this time and place (**YELLOW**); the needs of people as a human community (**GREEN**); the prevailing spheres of economic and political influence (**ORANGE**); authority assigned through national treaties or religious dictates (**BLUE**); where the 'big me' leaves his personal mark (**RED**); where the spirits and the ancestors walk(ed) (**PURPLE**); and finally by the space currently occupied by a particular band of people (**BEIGE**).

Sounding for Geo-currents

National and international 'geo-currents' can be identified in Spiral terms: **PURPLE-RED** ethnicity, tribalism, and dictatorship; **RED-BLUE** nationalism, ideology and theocracy; **BLUE-ORANGE** free market and multiparty democracy; or **ORANGE-GREEN** social democracy, communitarianism, and egalitarian humanism. In macro-managing the planet, whether from a political or a commercial vantage point, the Spiral Wizard must necessarily adopt a Second Tier **YELLOW-TURQUOISE** standpoint. Firstly, within such a perspective, Spirals are viewed as healthy when each of the 'MEMEs is expressing itself from a positive, additive perspective. The Wizard must always ask the question 'Will this expression of a given 'MEME add to or take from the life of the Spiral as a whole and the life of each individual riding on it?' In other words, will other 'MEMEs remain free to express themselves and develop their own trajectories?

Secondly, therefore, a human Spiral is healthy when avenues are open for movement on towards the more complex bands of thinking. Forced blockages cause the Spiral to stagnate or even to implode. The trap must be unlocked and barriers broken down before all hell breaks loose! For example, for Beck and Cowan, **PURPLE** and **RED** must establish effective **BLUE** authority before **ORANGE** enterprise can sprout. **BLUE** stability and **ORANGE** entrepreneurism must be present before **GREEN** social transformation is feasible. At the same time it takes an overarching **YELLOW** to macro-manage the whole process.

In quoting, finally, the work of their mentor Clare Graves from some twenty years ago, Beck and Cowan refer to his statement that 'the present moment finds our society attempting to negotiate the most difficult, but at the same time most exciting, transition the human race has faced to date'. The future presents, Graves wrote in 1974, three distinct possibilities:

- A massive regression back to our stone-age beginnings if we fail to stabilize our world's weapons and endangered resources
- A version of George Orwell's *1984*, embodied in forms of **BLUE-ORANGE-GREEN** tyrannical, manipulative government with glossed over communitarian overtones
- The emergence of a Second Tier approach to business and society which would be fundamentally different from the one we know today, equipped to act locally and plan globally while acting globally and planning locally at the same time.

The choice, inevitably they say, is ours.

SECTION 1

Overview of Spiral Dynamics

This first section introduces to you the powerful concepts of 'memes' and ᵛMEMEs, the evolution of dynamic human systems, the thinking of Dr. Clare W. Graves, and the form that brings it all together, the Dynamic Spiral.

One of the chief beauties of the spiral as an imaginative conception is that it is always growing, yet never covering the same ground, so that it is not merely an explanation of the past, but it is also a prophecy of the future; and while it defines and illuminates what has already happened, it is also leading constantly to new discoveries.

Theodore Andrea Cook, *The Curves of Life*, Dover Publications, New York, 1979.

At each stage of human existence the adult man is off on his quest of his holy grail, the way of life he seeks by which to live. At his first level he is on a quest for automatic physiological satisfaction. At the second level he seeks a safe mode of living, and this is followed, in turn, by a search for heroic status, for power and glory, by a search for ultimate peace, a search for material pleasure, a search for affection-ate relations, a search for respect of self, and a search for peace in an incomprehensible world. And, when he finds he will not find that peace, he will be off on his ninth level quest.

As he sets off on each quest, he believes he will find the answer to his existence. Yet, much to his surprise and much to his dismay, he finds at every stage that the solution to existence is not the solution he has come to find. Every stage he reaches leaves him disconcerted and perplexed. It is simply that as he solves one set of human problems he finds a new set in their place. The quest he finds is never ending.

Clare W. Graves

I

Different Times Produce Different Minds

While these are chaotic and turbulent times, they are hardly crazy ones. There is rhyme to both the reason and the unreason. Order lurks in the chaos; a deeper chaos still lurks in the order. Those who have eyes to see, ears to hear, and spirals in their minds to understand, will rest easier knowing the sky is not falling, after all. These Wizards in our midst do not live in Edwin Abbot's two-dimensional *Flatland*. Their thinking is not trapped in repetitive cycles, either. Values, complexity, and change have new meanings in Spiral space, the best place to live and conduct business in the twenty-first century.

Late twentieth century folk are caught in a storm of conflicting values. Ethnic eruptions, crises *du jour*, and ecological uncertainties cloud the future. Like clashing weather fronts, political, technological, economic, and social forces are spawning windshears and tornadoes over the global marketplace. Most executives, like airline pilots using yesterday's technology, have been caught by surprise in the downdrafts. Neither our business gurus nor our social forecasters had prepared us for the turbulence. Nothing has arrived to set our altimeters or true our compasses, much less equip us with a means for regaining control.

Captains of both the private and public sectors are restructuring, downsizing, reengineering, and playing catch-up with the change curve, only to fall further out of trim. Gridlock is everywhere. At many levels, we are flying through turbulent storms of severity and complexity never even mocked-up in our simulations. Why is this?

For one thing, we are entering a period of millennium hysteria. Back in the tenth Century – the close of the last thousand-year phase on the Gregorian calendar – western Europe fell into turmoil. Near-panic gripped the Christian community as many believed the year AD1000 would bring the end of the world at the hand of a wrathful, decimal Deity.

Even the hundred-year transitions shake up societies. The French have the term *fin de siecle* for crazy periods like these when mystics, soothsayers, and prophets engage in end-time predictions. No wonder David Koresh and the Branch Davidians near Waco, Texas, attracted so much attention in 1993 with their apocalyptic beliefs. Likewise, it should come as no surprise when guru-seeking executives grasp at the reorganizational flavor-of-the-month so desperately.

This cycle sickness does not infect Eurocentrics or the business community alone, though. It spreads all over the planet. Regardless of which calendar you use, today's world is chaotic, crisis-filled, and complex almost beyond belief. Whether you are among the corporate suits, in priestly garb, in a military uniform, or just hanging out doing your thing in a pair of jeans, you are living the Chinese 'curse' of very interesting times.

Second, deep-seated and fundamental belief structures have been tilted, causing us to question everything. In the past we were isolated by physical distance and smoke-signal communications. Now we know too much, too soon. When one place is upset, it reverberates globally within the hour. Like migrating tectonic plates, several core ways of thinking – paradigms, if you will – are grinding against each other. These deep rubs echo in major eruptions at the surface. The shock waves rock cultural groupings, redraw national boundaries, redefine markets, and rewrite futurists' scenarios. The quakes reverberate in geopolitics, race relations, ethnic conflicts, religious schisms, gender relations, education, business, the environment, criminal justice, and our ongoing questions about morality and what is right.

Third, we inhabit a polyglot, diverse, but not yet interdependent world. All of the stratified human life forms, from tribal societies to info-techies, are in daily conflict over niches and resources. The end of the bipolar world dominated by super-powers brought a resurgence of old mindsets, surprising intruders from the dark and violent history of our kind. At the same time, fresh approaches to living on Earth are being liberated. We are going back to the future and forward to the past, engaging all of history's villains and saints in quick time.

The complications of this diversity can be overwhelming. Ancient ethnic sores are belching fire while transnational companies linked by satellites conduct their business oblivious to the feudal past below. Virtually any social, environmental, or spiritual cause with PR savvy can get down-center-stage media exposure on global TV. When in the spotlight, people at every level of development – from pre-literate indigenous people living on a once-remote island to terrorists espousing some fundamentalism to the cyber-nerds hacking about along the 'information superhighways' – show up as essentially the same. It is as if every human mindset that has ever lived is returning to demand a place in the sun and a piece of the pie.

Finally, our expanding sciences and technologies have shrunk all of those good folks into global villagers. No one can hide. Ted Turner's CNN and Boeing's 7X7s collapse both time and distance. The World Wide Web concentrates knowledge. What happens anywhere is instantly known everywhere. Both the good news and media sharks' frenzies over the bad spread on the wind. Volatile ideas run like wildfires on the prairie, burning over stable institutions and fragmenting them.

If a 'psychograph' could register on a Richter-type scale for social upheaval, what level of human quakes are we presently experiencing? 4.5? 5.7? 7.2? Even worse? Imagine some consequences.

- What if there are no jobs for the thousands of professionals whose mid-management positions are disappearing because of 'right-sizing,' flattening, layoffs in anachronistic Cold War industries, and the silicon-based new-hires who demand no benefits package?
- What if there are not enough niches for the millions of intelligent Third World 'have-nots' being drawn like moths to the developed nations by the bright lights of a 'better life' in the cities?
- What if the next Attila shows up on global television with the threat of unleashing pocket-sized nuclear weapons built from Black Market surplus by laid off physicists and acquired in exchange for bread?
- What if a malignant version of some fear-laced "-ism" – "this Truth is the *only* Truth and will prevail at any cost" – suddenly rears its head for conquest and domination? Can the glass fiber infrastructure of the global village withstand terrorists fighting holy wars or self-righteous crusades?
- What if a bioengineered beasty slips into the oceans and spreads to threaten all carbon-based life like a home-grown Andromeda strain? Or a superbug like the Ebola virus or even a descendant of some more common disease like tuberculosis decides to thumb its nose at our antibiotics and evolves to plague us while the cure is burning up in a rain forest's pyre?
- What if a leading cause of human death continues to be fellow humans? Will the predatory, nothing-to-lose, life-is-cheap violence of desperation continue to put what little civilization we agree upon further at risk?
- What if a radio telescope searching for extraterrestrial intelligence suddenly finds a clear signal from a remote galaxy proving we are not alone as Masters of the Universe? A calling card left by someone whose 'pure research' budget was not axed by politicians?

Great Ideas are Forged in Chaotic Times

It seems that we are at a break point, a shift in psycho-tectonics of profound significance. In the April 1974 issue of *The Futurist*, Clare W. Graves warned that mankind was preparing for a 'momentous leap' and we should pay heed. His quarter century of research had disclosed pending changes in human nature which were about to impact American culture and the world to the core.

This phenomenon of deep change is not unique. Human history is filled with intervals of turbulence and diasporas. Sometimes retuning and mild adjustments of the *status quo* restore balance. But occasionally major chaos erupts to trigger order-of-magnitude, epochal changes. This seems to be one of those times.

Social analysts Heidi and Alvin Toffler caution that 'the old world map is obsolete – we are undergoing the deepest rearrangement of global power since the birth of industrial civilization.' (*New York Times*, October 31, 1993, p. E-17)

What are some implications of all of this? First, we need the flexibility to deal with clans, tribes, empires, ideologies, enterprise zones, human communes, and villages of lone eagles which cover the planet. It is imperative to work constructively with 1st through 4th World human groupings and their ranges from have-a-lots to have-nots, can-dos to cannots. It is no longer possible to deny the long-term impacts of our technologies and the costs of our 'success,' nor to shirk the responsibilities of our potential.

Second, we must get to the bottom of what it is in human nature that causes so much chaos. In earlier times when harmony was essential to survival it seems we could settle major conflicts with compromise or Chieftains' edicts. When we could only resort to bows and arrows, even the very worst decisions had only a limited, local significance. Today's squabbles have intercontinental implications. Everybody is impacted, like it or not. Something about us – not just our tools – has become less ordered but vastly more powerful.

The Humpty Dumpty Effect

The complex times in which we find ourselves are stretching our capacities for self-management; sometimes Earth seems to be rocking out of control. We have encountered 'The Humpty Dumpty Effect.' As described in the familiar nursery rhyme, the fat-and-happy Humpty Dumpty falls from his perch upon a wall. In fact, he has a great fall. In Lewis Carrol's version, he even becomes fractured into many chunks. That is bad enough but there is worse news to come. All of the King's horses and men – resources maximized! – cannot restore poor Humpty Dumpty to his vaunted perch. Doing their best is not enough. There is no glue strong enough to put him together again. The dedicated efforts of the most prestigious consultants and respected pundits are inadequate. Entropy wins.

There are clear signs of an impending Humpty Dumpty condition. A catalogue of quick-fixes, flavor-of-the-month training packages, and snake-oil salespeople appear on the scene. Large-scale regressions into the past – nostalgic trips into corporate history and ' . . .Give me that old time

Humpty Dumpty sat on a wall
Humpty Dumpty had a great fall
All the king's horses
And all the king's men
Couldn't put Humpty together again

religion . . .' managerial approaches become popular. Debates over conflicting 'Truths' force everyone to draw lines in the moral sand and defend their grounds. Shrill voices replace calm ones. Zealots make grand claims for simplistic and narrow cures. Trendiness sets in, causing everyone to scurry about copying what others are doing, regardless of price or evidence of efficacy. Then come the gridlocks and stalemates. Corporate ladder climbers reach dead-ends. Stress goes up as trust sinks down. An 'every man for himself' mentality sets in, whether for individuals, departments, or the whole titanic enterprise. The brittle hopelessness of the Humpty Dumpty Effect crashes into obstacles and turns the world upside down, like *Titanic* into an iceberg.

Why did the Big Egg fail to anticipate his plight? Why did his own experience, academic theories, and training let him down so hard? Was he so arrogant he thought himself unsinkable? Why did the forecasters and lookouts fail to warn him of impending danger, even though colleagues had close calls already? Were his messengers afraid to deliver bad news? Did the guardians of the *status quo* keep word from getting to the top of the wall? Might they actually have enjoyed his tumble?

No doubt poor Mr Dumpty would like to have known. Business executives and others in leadership roles all around the world are feeling off balance without understanding why. As they look from their own walls, Humpty Dumpty seems to have splattered everywhere – in corporate suites and financial centers; in academic ivory towers and think tanks; in state capitols and city halls; in churches, cathedrals, mosques, and synagogues; at the U.N. and Canadian Parliament; in 'democratic' nations and eyes-open dictatorships. Yet the iceberg warnings go largely ignored.

Like unsinkable *Titanic*, we are at-risk because we are prisoners of our own paradigms. Our successes, like the Big Egg's girth, have overwhelmed us. We thought our worlds would continue forever along the same trajectories. We thought it was safe to 'drive change' down from our lofty perches. Little did we know how limited and distorted our views had become, and how much we were not seeing because of our walls.

Distortions in Cycleland

In his book *Cycles*, Samuel A. Schreiner, Jr., invites the reader to discover 'Cycleland,' claiming that 'cycles are at work everywhere and in everything. It is more than a possibility that the study of cycles will one day reveal the long-sought-after unifying principle that will enable man to understand how the universe really works.' (p. 2)

Pendulum swings and S-curves do explain a lot, from life-cycles (birth, growth, maturity, decline, and death) to seasonal, cosmic, economic, population, long-wave, and generational shifts. The oil industry uses them constantly to track their markets. But even these patterns may be illusory and deceptive, especially if one believes the pendulum always returns, given enough time to the same place. If trapped in Cycleland's back-and-forth, up-and-down rhythms and patterns, we miss uniqueness, quantum change, and evolutionary flows.

Arthur Schlessinger, Jr., the noted north American historian, claimed for years that the average pendulum swing from liberal to conservative, and vice versa, occurs every 30 years. He has been forced to recant in light of the overwhelming Republican Party victory in November of 1994. There was only a two-year period between that landslide and more liberal Bill Clinton's victory in 1992. You can forget about reliable 30-year cycles; and you will if you understand spirals.

Great awakenings break from the past, thus interfering with the pendulum's predictable arc. Ray Grenier and George Metes observe in *Enterprise Networking: Working Together Apart* that '. . . in the past, we were able to work in and manage change because we could predict cycles. Cycles are obscure, "mutant", or discontinuous. Evolutionary changes obviate trend planning.' (p. 34). They break cycles and introduce new dimensions.

This is disturbing news to people who depend on framing problems in terms of the solutions they know how to deliver. That includes those who rely on the back and forth swing of the reliable pendulum. The Humpty Dumpty Effect is devastating to established orders, but essential to what must come next.

Minds Change With the Times

Different times force us to think differently. The first harbingers of change are often 'Old Testament'-type prophets who show up with cries of alarm, predictions of doom and gloom, demands for penitence, and threats of fire and brimstone. Next come visionaries with messianic hopes and dreams who point to Nirvana just ahead. They offer to lead us to sweetness, salvation, and bliss – though usually for a price. Then the more pragmatic pathfinders emerge without fanfare or hubris to scout through the chaos and confusion and to set about the task of planting the seeds of a new way.

It is in our nature to solve problems, but then to create new ones. Human beings love to engage in quests of one kind or another. The long list includes: the Holy Grail, the lost city Atlantis, the Messiah, Peace, Shangri La, the Unified Field, Self-Actualization, Nirvana, Life Everlasting, the Golden Bough, and the chosen king who could pull Excalibur from its stone.

Today, a new chapter begins in the never-ending saga as we try to breach another rock and unlock the nature of human thinking. With this Rosetta Stone-like translation, bright people – ordinary people – can pull forth answers for the paradoxes and problems that will set our course into the years ahead. Wizards of all kinds will arise. But what message will they read etched on this tablet? What psychological languages do humans speak? Why have there been so many different worlds on Earth?

The historic evidence is clear: New times produce new thinking.

- In an early age we found refuge in clans and safety in a threatening world by awakening the capacity to sense the spirits and placate them through magic. *New times, new thinking.*
- When the magic and ritual become stifling, we escaped by asserting a raw sense of self and slaying the dragons that lurk in the dark. The powerful individual sought to dominate kith, kin, and nature. *New times, new thinking.*
- When chaos and anarchy then reigned supreme, we sought meaning and found peace of mind in the absolute and unquestioned order of a Higher Power or rightful authority, the organizing principle greater than any individual or group *New times, new thinking.*
- When that absolute order became oppressive and repressive and we grew weary of waiting for future rewards, individualists challenged the authorities and tried to create the abundant 'good life' here and now. *New times, new thinking.*
- When this progress-oriented materialism failed to bring happiness, we became lonely. Then we wanted to rediscover human feelings, recapture spirituality, and find 'ourselves.' *New times, new thinking.*

From our earliest upright steps as Homo sapiens we have trekked from one awakening to another, becoming a slightly different being with every one. New times produce new thinking as new theories of everything are spawned, history is revised, priorities and values are reordered-stacked, and people marvel that they did not see it all so clearly before.

The Shifting Views of Tom Peters and the Tofflers

Few management gurus have been as celebrated over the last decade as ex-McKinsey & Company consultant Tom Peters, author, columnist, and television personality. He initially made his name and fame in 1982 by preaching the virtue in 'pursuing excellence' and of MBWA – 'management by walking around.' A decade later he seemed to recant a bit, deciding the whole 'excellence' theme was 'about wacky ideas' and the companies he selected as 'excellent' were not that, after all. They just did some 'excellent' (does that also mean 'wacky'?) things.

His 1992 book, *Liberation Management*, was reviewed less than glowingly in the *Wall Street Journal* by Jack Falvey (December 31, 1992, p. A5) who chose to quote Mr Peters:

> 'My objective in this final Markets and Innovation chapter is to confuse you, not to help you sort things out. It's my belief, in these turbulent times, that anyone who is not thoroughly confused has no chance of success.'

To his credit, Tom Peters was forthright enough to suggest he did not have a clue as to what was really happening. Apparently, by his own admission, he did not know in 1982 either. But, like so many of us who have done 'wacky' things in our pasts, he was not being dishonest. He was doing his best. He reported as he saw and understood. He could not know what he did not know; and he knew that.

If you carefully examine the six books Tom Peters has produced as a case study in Spiral Dynamics (and you should), you will get a clue as to what we are suggesting. Note the shifts from his *In Search of Excellence* (with Robert H. Waterman, Jr.) and *A Passion for Excellence* (with Nancy Austin), to *Thriving on Chaos*, and then to *Liberation Management*. He could not have written these books in a different sequence. In fact, you get a distinct feeling some kind of pattern is evolving. It seems that Peters begins to recognize it in his 1994 compendium of interesting thoughts, *The Tom Peters Seminar*. He concludes that since 'crazy times call for crazy organizations,' a fresh approach to thinking about corporate beings is required.

As you will discover shortly, what Peters (with tongue in cheek) now calls ' . . .weird enough,' is simply a next developmental step on a Spiral of thinking systems. You will also come to recognize that the organizing principles that Peters (and Peter Senge, Edwards Deming, Stephen Covey, and many others) advocate are never *the* solution, but *a* solution set that lies at a particular region within a whole spectrum of organizational forms.

Alvin and Heidi Toffler's popular trilogy – *Future Shock, The Third Wave,* and *Power Shift* – also maps a pattern of change. But even their 1993 book, *War and Anti-War: Survival at the Dawn of the 21st Century,* still does not uncover the deep forces that drive major transformations. While the symptoms make for interesting and entertaining reading, we are left with the unanswered question: Why do these changes occur – what causes new social waves to form?

Tom Peters and the Tofflers are not alone in avoiding this difficult question. You can watch it being skirted in the latest business 'fashion, magazines' on airport book racks or in executive waiting rooms, their promising covers beckoning anyone seeking the latest in competitive advantage, cutting-edge ideas, and profiles of role-models who have made it to the top. The more inspirational selections offer paths to growth, 'becoming,' peace of mind, healthy families, and harmonious lives among the stresses of an uncertain world.

All beg the question – Why? It is as if we are blessed with elegant tiles for a mosaic but have no design. There are mounds of great ideas, insightful bits, and clever pieces, but no artist with a plan for turning the whole assortment into an elegant, integrated picture and no grout to hold it together.

How might the chunks connect? What is it in our DNA, in how our brain makes a mind, that produces new perspectives, new thinking? Something invisible, intangible, yet powerful drives these changes and transformation sequences. What is it? A powerful force? A scientific pattern? A mystical Spirit? A cosmic law? Pure happenstance? The roll of God's dice, after all?

The Wonderful World of Spirals

'There is a theory that history moves in cycles. But, like a spiral staircase, when the course of human events comes full circle it does so on a new level. The 'pendulum swing' of cultural changes does not simply repeat the same events over and over again. Whether or not the theory is true, it serves as a metaphor to focus our attention. The topic of this book [and *Spiral Dynamics*, as well!] represents such a spiral cycle: chaos gives way to order, which in turn gives rise to new forms of chaos.' Stewart, Ian, *Does God Play Dice? The Mathematics of Chaos,* Basil Blackwell, Cambridge (MA) 1989.

Behold the eloquence of the spiral. Consider the internal integrity, the elegant architecture. Everything connects to everything else. In your mind's eye picture the beauty of a sea shell; with your mind's ear listen to its roar. Now imagine a Thanksgiving banquet table. Out from the spiraling cornucopia, the mythical horn of plenty, pours the abundance of harvest. Next, think of the night sky. Look out into the cosmos and imagine Earth's place in it, a little hanger-on following one of the billions of swirling spots in the Milky Way, itself a swirling blob among billions.

Spirals exist from the sub-atomic to the interstellar realms as a dominant universal fractal. Deep within the cell nucleus are the long, spirally wound ribbons of DNA on which rest life's genetic code. At the other extreme, distant spiral galaxies send us greetings from the past. Spirals are alive, magical, power-ful, and multidimensional. They can be as fearful and destructive as a tornado or as seductive and haunting as a whirlpool. You ignore them at your peril.

Ralph Waldo Emerson described life on a spiral staircase: 'We wake and find ourselves on a stair; there are stairs below us which we seem to have ascended, there are stairs above us which go out of sight.' Life's spiral is expansive, open-ended, continuous, and dynamic. All of the whorls are alive at once. Yet there is also an inner intelligence that draws them together in a hierarchical structure, the curvatures of life.

Cometh the Thinking: Spiral Dynamics

This book is about the forces inside the human spirals that wind through individual minds, drive organizations to new plateaus, and push societies to evolve through layers of complexity. It is also about a body of knowledge that draws together practically everything that has come before in leadership, management, and organizational design. Finally, it is about the next epoch's King's Horses, Men, and Women. Arriving in the nick of time like the cavalry in an old western movie, we will call them the Spiral Wizards. Be ready: they may decide that Humpty the Egg is a lost cause and look for a Super Chicken to lay a fresh one.

In any case, their task is a big one. Again from *Enterprise Networking,* Grenier and Metes conclude that:

> 'To prevail in this new environment – this maelstrom of complexity – we must aim beyond the mark. We can't just plot the trend, frame the problem in familiar terms, then design and deliver the solution. We'll never be able to react to the next level of complexity demanded of us.'

The problems that come at us in transition to the twenty-first century can only be resolved by solutions that they, themselves, create. The pattern repeats itself: New times demand New Thinking. Only this time, the 'new thinking' must be more than the next regular step on Emerson's staircase. It must be well 'beyond the mark.' When Vaçlav Haval, President of the Czech Republic, accepted the Philadelphia Liberty Medal at Independence Hall on 4 July 1994, he remarked:

> 'There are good reasons for suggesting the modern age has ended. Many things indicate that we are going through a transitional period, when it seems that something is on the way out and something else is painfully being born. It is as if something were crumbling, decaying and exhausting itself, while something else, still indistinct, were arising from the rubble.'

The Construction of Spiral Dynamics

Each time we experience the New Times, New Thinking sequence, a controversial if not altogether revolutionary view of human nature evolves. The resulting synthesis of ideas, perspectives, and theories yields a compelling restatement of what it means to be human.

We are now in the seventh expression of the Times–Thinking sequence. Again, the search is on again for the core mechanism that shapes human nature; but this one will be revolutionary. We suggest that knowledge and insight crucial to uncovering it exist in two related tributaries of thought. The first is the expansive *Levels of Human Existence* framework laid out by developmentalist Clare W. Graves, formerly Professor Emeritus Psychology,

Union College, New York. The second is the concept of 'memes' introduced by British biologist Richard Dawkins and later amplified by psychologist Mihaly Csikszentmihalyi. Together, they combine lessons from molecular biology and the neurosciences with more traditional psychological research.

The Pathfinder on the Mohawk

Our friend and mentor, Clare W. Graves, lived and worked in the upper Hudson Valley, only a few miles from the historic Mohawk River and the Erie Canal. Graves was a relatively obscure professor of psychology in the years following World War II. As often seems to happen, wartime energy and post-war euphoria served as breeding grounds for visionary thinking and bold, new break-throughs in human knowledge. Such was the case with Graves. Rather than rehash older psychological constructs or participate in the debates between the conflicting theories of the day, he decided to start afresh by searching the reasons behind shifting views of human nature.

Graves sought to get to the mind of the matter and explore why people are different, why some change but others don't, and how better to navigate through the emerging and often chaotic versions of human existence. As he put it:

> 'Briefly, what I am proposing is that the psychology of the mature human being is an unfolding, emergent, oscillating spiraling process marked by progressive subordination of older, lower-order behavior systems to newer, higher-order systems as man's existential problems change.'

Damn it all, a person has the right to be who he is.
Clare W. Graves

In other words, human thinking evolves in recognizable packages as the world around us gets more complicated and we try to keep up. At the same time, we are constantly altering our world because we are clever. Graves was one of the first psychologists who understood that we live, act, make decisions, and undergo change through complex systems. His informal drawings and illustrations would be familiar to any serious student of quantum physics, general systems, and chaos theory.

Graves' orientation was to integrate 'bio-,' 'psycho-,' and 'socio-,' thus meshing human knowledge and breaching the walls of academia that separated disciplines and fields. As early as 1973 he was pointing to the critical importance of mind/brain research with a focus on how the mind is shaped by neurological structures and networks, and how it is activated by chemical agents and life's conditions. Such speculations amounted to heresy in those golden years of the humanistic views that led to today's political correctness and egalitarian orthodoxy, but Graves held fast.

He would often summarize his point of view in the following constructs:

1. Human nature is not static, nor is it finite. Human nature changes as the conditions of existence change, thus forging new systems. Yet, the older systems stay with us.
2. When a new system or level is activated, we change our psychology and rules for living to adapt to those new conditions.
3. We live in a potentially open system of values with an infinite number of modes of living available to us. There is no final state to which we must all aspire.
4. An individual, a company, or an entire society can respond positively only to those managerial principles, motivational appeals, educational formulas, and legal or ethical codes that are appropriate to the current level of human existence.

A Spiral vortex best depicts this emergence of human systems as they evolve through levels of increasing complexity. Each upward turn of the spiral marks the awakening of a more elaborated version on top of what already exists. The human Spiral, then, consists of a coiled string of value systems, world views, and mindsets, each the product of its times and conditions.

Clare Graves was a man out of his time. In the late 1970s Canada's *MacLean's Magazine* referred to his concept as 'the theory that explains everything.' While he would personally cringe at such a claim, his work is massive and elegant – a comprehensive thinking process, systems package, and action strategy whose time had not yet come two decades ago.

But time has a way of sifting the wheat from chaff when it comes to ideas. Constructs with greater explanatory power and practical application tend to prevail. Only now, a full decade after his death in 1986, are Graves' contributions becoming widely known and recognized. The theory of human emergence, change and transformation he proposed has been richly fleshed out and validated rather than replaced by contemporary research. Once you start thinking 'like a Gravesian,' you will find this point of view has the power and precision to deal with people and social forces of all kinds, from hostile warlords and virulent '-isms' to the relief agencies caring for their victims and peace-keepers befuddled by the mess.

The same principles of Spiral Dynamics apply to a single person, an organization, or an entire society. Since it describes human nature in a universal sense rather than through personality types or racial, gender, and ethnic traits, the model provides a common language for grappling with both local and global problems. It offers a unifying framework that makes genuinely holistic thinking and actions possible.

While Graves was involved in research as a social scientist, a large portion of his work was actually reported in the business sector. His article, 'The Deterioration in Work Standards,' appeared in the *Harvard Business Review* of November 1967. Not only did he predict the erosion of America's productivity, but he laid the foundation for the current interest in total quality and reengineering. As you will discover, the Graves conceptual system provides the human factors component that the followers of Edwards Deming have been seeking and others do not yet realize they lack. His framework maps out how to transform a company or a culture to make it healthy and receptive for the introduction of complex technologies and rapid change.

Genes and Memes: Circuit Riders on the DNA

In *The Evolving Self* (HarperCollins, 1993), Mihaly Csikszentmihalyi uses the expression 'memes' to contrast with 'genes' in identifying the origins of human behavior as opposed to physical characteristics.

The term itself was first introduced a number of years ago by Richard Dawkins who abbreviated the Greek root, 'mimeme.' He and others have used it to describe a unit of cultural information such as a political ideology, a fashion trend, language usage, musical forms, or even architectural styles. In the March 1994 issue of *Wired* magazine, John Perry Barlow states that Dawkins' idea involves

> ' . . . self-replicating patterns of information that propagate themselves across the ecologies of mind, a pattern of reproduction much like that of life forms . . . They self-reproduce, they interact with their surroundings and adapt to them, they mutate, they persist. They evolve to fill the empty niches of their local environments, which are, in this case, the surrounding belief systems and cultures of their hosts, namely, us.'

Thus, what biochemical genes are to the DNA, memes are to our psycho-cultural 'DNA.' Genes are the information units of our physical nature derived from genetic contributions of mom and dad and properties inherited from our species. Memes are born, Csikszentimihalyi notes, 'when the human nervous system reacts to an experience.' (*Evolving Self*, p. 120) They are the information units in our collective consciousness and transport their views across our minds.

A meme contains behavioral instructions that are passed from one generation to the next, social artifacts, and value-laden symbols that glue together social systems. Like an intellectual virus, a meme reproduces itself through concepts like dress styles, language trends, popular cultural norms, architectural designs, art forms, religious expressions, social movements, economic models, and moral statements of how living should be done.

Memes act much like particles. Spiral Dynamics proposes the existence of another kind of wave-like meta-meme, a systems or 'values meme' ('MEME). These 'MEMEs are organizing principles that act like attractors for the content-rich memes Dawkins and Csikszentimihalyi describe. Big 'MEMEs are the amino acids of our psycho-social 'DNA' and act as the magnetic force which binds memes and other kinds of ideas in cohesive packages of thought. While they are initially shaped in each human mind, 'MEMEs are so vital they reach across whole groups of people and begin to structure mindsets on their

The ᵛMEME Attractor*

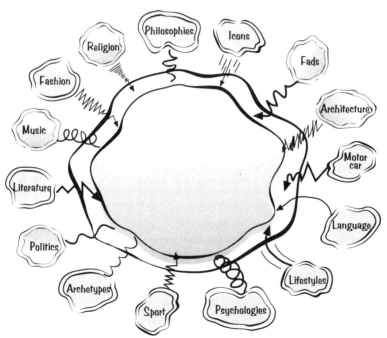

* Each ᵛMEME is an organizing principle, centre of gravity, geometric fractal, self-replicating force, and magnetic field that attracts content-rich little memes

own. ᵛMEMEs establish the pace and process for gathering beliefs. They structure the thinking, value systems, political forms, and world views of entire civilizations. ᵛMEMEs are linchpins of corporate cultures that determine how and why decisions are made. Our individual ᵛMEME stacks are central to our personalities and set the tone for relationships and whether we are happy campers or restless souls.

While genes evolve slowly, the decision systems formed by ᵛMEMEs are always on the move. ᵛMEMEs can be so dominant they seem like archetypes and are easily misinterpreted as 'types' of people. When several are in harmony, ᵛMEMEs resonate like the notes in a musical chord. However, ᵛMEMEs in conflict lead to troubled individuals, dysfunctional families, corporate malaise, fractured churches, and civilizations in decline and fall. Since they are 'alive,' ᵛMEMEs can ebb and flow, intensify and soften like a string of Christmas tree lights on a dimmer. Several different ones may line up in support of a specific issue, idea, or project because they share the values contents. At other times, people with essentially the same ᵛMEME decision-making frameworks may disagree violently over details of beliefs and what is 'the good,' degenerating into holy and un-civil war.

We can have toxic, dangerous genes that predict physical troubles ahead. (How to deal with this knowledge may be the single biggest issue confronting medical ethicists today.) We can have nasty, unpleasant memes nestled among our attitudes, beliefs, and behaviors. Likewise, you may find misfit ᵛMEMEs in control of individuals, organizations, or cultures. The forces that enable us to respond to new problems in the environment can also block successful adaptation if the ᵛMEMEs are unhealthy. Any strength, taken to the extreme, becomes a weakness. No wonder so many great cultures fade into historical footnotes. Their ᵛMEMEs wore down long before their monuments.

The ᵛMEMEs encode instructions for our world views, assumptions about how everything works, and the rationale for decisions we make. To clarify with an illustration, think about a fast-track, highly competitive, self-directed and status-sensitive Yuppie you have known. He or she strongly expresses what we will color-code as the **ORANGE** ᵛMEME. It often attracts things like dressing for success, driving the prestigious motor car, being seen in the right places, displaying the upscale spouse or partner, making the right career moves, and seeking autonomy along with the pot of gold.

As long as that ᵛMEME flashes and repeats its messages, the pattern will continue. It may be passed right on to the children who translate it into their own special music, fashion statements, and attitudes at the mall. The ᵛMEME's processes may be dominant throughout a neighborhood and central to the politics of a community. It may often, remain steady, or become even more intense. **ORANGE** is only one of eight principle ᵛMEMEs attached to the Spiral.

ᵛMEMEs are like a parallel life form. We are barely aware of their power because we can only infer their existence from behavioral displays and the artifacts swirling around them. But like the intestinal *compadre*'s that digest our food for us, 'MEMEs assist the wetware of our minds to sort out what the world is 'really' like. *Spiral Dynamics* describes how they act at three different but clearly interrelated levels:

- **Individuals** possess dominant 'MEMEs which shape their life priorities and values, from most basic survival to global villager and beyond. Child development involves the awakening, guidance of, and learning to express 'MEMEs in healthy forms at appropriate times. The appearance of new 'MEMEs often provokes a personal crisis in family and work relationships. Executive careers are highly vulnerable to these conflicts and overloads.
- **Organizations** have the 'MEMEs that will determine their success or failure in the competitive marketplace or the court of social responsibility at their basic cultural 'DNA' level. While the task of O.D. (organization development) has long been to refine or realign the nuts-and-bolts of what companies do, it is quickly coming to include the awakening of new 'MEMEs. Memetic change is a greater challenge by far than just 'working harder and smarter.'
- **Societies**, whether local or national, toss to and fro unless firmly grounded in the critical 'MEMEs which are congruent with the kind of worlds they occupy. Both upheaval and stability are products of 'MEMEs on the move, though few analysts manage to look through the fog of confusing ideas to see them.

These are only a few manifestations of the core 'MEMEs in action. The dynamic Spiral is the framework on which 'MEME awakenings and expressions hang. It is the organizing principle that pulls the 'Why?' from apparent chaos and translates our values languages. Instead of categorizing behavior or classifying people – there are plenty of other models that do that – Spiral Dynamics will guide your search for the invisible, living 'MEMEs that circulate far deeper within human systems and pulsate at the choice-making center in the core intelligences of every person, organization, or society.

2

The Nature of ᵛMEME Systems

Like genes, memes do not operate in solo, but interlock in the mosaics that form weltanshauungs, *worldviews.*
Howard Bloom, *The Lucifer Principle*, The Atlantic Monthly Press, New York, 1995, p. 131.

Get your passport. We are about to go hunting on the Spiral. During the journey you will interview some very different people across time, space, and cultures. You will ride on a magic carpet within your virtual reality mind. (How is that for meshing mythology with high technology – Aladdin meets Steven Jobs thanks to Walt Disney?) Your assignment is to find an answer to one question in everybody you encounter: 'What is life all about?' Though you may have your own answer already, we assume you want to know what others think since their perspectives are fundamental to management, religion, education, and politics. Now, let us take off on a ᵛMEME hunt.

Interviews with Six People

Songoma

The magic carpet first touches down in rural KwaZulu in southern Africa. 'I seek the answer to "What is life all about?"' you inform a middle-aged songoma. (A songoma casts and removes hexes, weaves spells, dispenses potions, and sells concoctions of *muti* (magic medicine) to protect the users from evil ones and/or enlist the good powers to their side.) 'To please the spirits,' the songoma says cautiously, uncertain as to who you are and which clan you are from. 'We live to honor our ancestors,' the songoma continues while rubbing a smooth amulet, 'for they are still with us. And we live for our tribe.' 'Thank you very much,' you say, 'and may good fortune shine on you and yours.' As you leave you recall seeing just such a person in the film Shaka Zulu and reading about similar memes in Tony Hillerman novels about the Navajo.

Street Kid

Faster than a speeding bullet you fly to New York's South Bronx and onto a subway. You now find yourself face-to-face with a remorseless-looking street kid in a dirty graffiti-filled car. The young tough's cold, piercing stare sends a chill up your spine. In spite of the macho swagger, you ask the question, hanging close to the get-away carpet. 'It's none of your goddamn business' the kid sneers, all the while checking you out to see if you're carrying and to be sure you're not an undercover cop or a stooge from the dreaded Green Dragon gang uptown. You don't appear dangerous or worth mugging, so the kid says, 'OK, since you asked, I'll tell you. But, you'd better listen, hear me? Life's a bitch. You gotta watch your backside 'cause nobody else will. Everybody's on the take, and they all got a price. If you want something you gotta get it yourself. Might be dead tomorrow, so do it now or never. Anybody gets in your face, they pay for it. That's just the way it is. Anybody says otherwise is a fool. All I want from other people is respect.' 'Thank you, sir,' you say, breathing a sigh of relief that your magic carpet is whisking you away, another ᵛMEME in hand. The kid's world was depressing, but he had adapted to it. Could you? Anyway, your spirits are lifted by the sounds of a bright Sousa march as you fly up the Hudson River toward the fabled 'Plains of West Point,' the U.S. Military Academy.

West Point Cadet

You glide down beside a clean-cut, clear-eyed plebe at the Academy standing before the General Douglas McArthur monument close to the famous West Point 'plain.' After the two of you review the 'Duty, Honor, Country' quotation etched in the stone, you ask your question. The cadet's answer is full of certainty and conviction: 'There is a higher calling that transcends everything else in importance. It's on that marble. It's in my religion. I learned it from my parents. It's part of our nation's heritage. And I've taken an oath to defend it and the flag that represents it. I'm prepared to die for these sacred principles. This is the only way we can guarantee our way of life for future generations. It is God's will that we spread freedom and democracy across the Earth.' The cadet salutes smartly and walks away, leaving his ᵛMEME with you. You pack it into your memory.

'Quite a commitment,' you think to yourself as you wonder what your strange odyssey will bring you next. The magic carpet selects a polar route to Singapore. As you fly over Inuit villages in the Arctic you think back to the Songoma – similar – and the street kid – what a difference in world views. The reverie ends as the carpet drops you off in front of Raffles Hotel. As you land, an Asian Yuppie exits his BMW and hands the keys to the valet. This is your interview.

Entrepreneur

Sipping 20-year-old Scotch at the bar, this elegantly dressed entrepreneur offers a very different answer to your question. 'The way I look at it,' he replies, 'the world is my oyster. The challenge in life is to win the biggest and finest pearls one can, then sell them and grow bigger ones. One can't take it with one, you know. We'd just as well enjoy the best this life has to offer since it may be all there is. I've worked hard, and I know how to play the game well. There are always risks, but that's what keeps us players at it. Now, you must pardon me; I've got to take this call from my Hong Kong office. All the best, though, and I wish you prosperity and good joss in your travels.'

Scotch sipped and another 'MEME in hand, you remount the carpet. Apparently, it's an Anglophile since you depart Raffles and head straight to London. As you fly across the mid-East, you think of what the street kid might be like with oil money, and how similar the straight-ahead thinking of the West Pointer actually is to some of the mullahs whose Islamic beliefs at first appear so distant.

Social Activist

Presently you hear Big Ben chiming in the distance, bringing you back to the question as you marvel at the human diversity in your virtual travels. Now, here you are, standing next to an intense young woman with a protest sign on the steps of Trafalgar Square. Her knapsack is covered with political buttons and packed with organically grown snacks and textbooks on international affairs. After you've engaged in some requisite small-talk about the pigeons, tourists, and current geopolitical hot-spots, you pose the question: 'What is life really about?' 'Ohhhh,' coos your respondent, 'what a marvelous question. I shall answer first, but then you must share your own views with me. I feel life's all about people and belonging – you know – an understanding of our need for harmony and community. I suppose it boils down to love. We must move away from the materialism and competitiveness of this age before we lose our humanity. There are so many in need, yet governments do so little to help. We just ended a human rights demonstration at the Parliament and we'll be back tomorrow. Everyone must do all they can to promote justice and peace, everywhere. Don't you think? It's your turn, now.' Tacky carpet! Before you can even begin framing an appropriately sensitive answer, it's whisked you off your feet and back across the equator.

Parks Ranger

This time you find yourself in an African game reserve, sitting beside a camp fire with a game ranger. Making tea, the warden is dressed in the usual khaki bush working attire. Nothing with designer labels; nothing fancy, only functional. You sense an instant openness and promise of candor, so you do not hesitate to pose 'the question.' The ranger remains silent a moment before answering: 'Well, I've given that some thought and don't have anything spectacular to offer – but as I see it, I get a great deal of personal satisfaction out of working here to reclaim and preserve our natural habitat. So I guess my answer should be that I believe we should celebrate and respect life as it is. Even more than that, I think we should seek to understand how everything relates to everything else, and how nature has its own tempo and flow of which we are only a small part.'

You bid farewell as the carpet picks you up and brings you back to your virtually real reality, a sack of ᵛMEMEs in hand. You have interviewed six people, all of whom offered radically different responses to the question: 'What is life all about?' Which one had the right answer, the best response? Why do you think so? Are they all of equal value? Which ᵛMEME comes the closest to your own conception?

The Same Six People (Ten Years Later)

Since we are in command of this virtual reality, let us make things even more complicated. We shall use the time-travel feature of the carpet to look in on these six people ten years in the future.

Songoma (+10 years)

Our friend the songoma has expanded his operation. He now owns a small chain of pharmacies which sell both traditional folk remedies and First World medicines. Many of the mystical, animistic beliefs appear to have been left behind, but you're not so certain what goes on in the back room. You sense that, for a hefty fee, shamanistic services might be available to you along with Alka-Seltzer.

Street Kid (+10 years)

Surprise (or not)! The tough Street Kid has become a militant urban evangelist, preaching a hellfire-and-brimstone message which demands a Puritanical strictness in lifestyle and adherence to his unique version of Islam from his converts. Several of 'that old gang of his' are now bodyguards who ride along in the stretch limo. He really believes he has been called by a Higher Power to deliver the Truth and fight against any who oppose it.

West Point Cadet (+10 years)

The Cadet graduated and fulfilled his obligation, but has now left the Army. He didn't go far, though, and has become the academic dean of a small military prep school in Virginia. The stiffly-braced Cadet is now less rigid and more realistic. He appears to have lost some of the flag-waving zealotry but has maintained his discipline and crusader spirit. His devotion to high principles is also intact.

Entrepreneur (+10 years)

The Singapore entrepreneur has been working as a volunteer in a poor section of Cebu, in the Philippines, on a major human rights project. A former business competitor ran into the ex-Yuppie in the Manila Hotel and was startled at such a laid back, easy-going appearance. No more self-promotion. Fast track ambitions and compulsiveness had disappeared. 'How's business?' the associate had asked. 'Well, I'm not into that anymore. I'm a different person now – I'm discovering what it means to be a human being. That bypass surgery really opened my eyes; you can't buy the peace of mind I have now.'

Social Activist (+ 10 years)

And what happened to the social activist in London who, a decade ago, was finding a new cause around every turn? Our sensitive friend's hand-crafted posters were noticed by an art director. She has now become an account executive for a prosperous public relations firm and thoroughly enjoys the Mercedes, fashionable clothes, and prestigious address. Former activist colleagues feel betrayed that such an 'enlightened' person sold out to the materialistic establishment. She's handled the rejection well and now has a new circle of more *simpatico* friends. The knapsack has been replaced with a Gucci bag.

Parks Ranger (+10 years)

The parks ranger died two years ago. Per his wishes, he was buried in a simple, unmarked grave beneath a baobab tree on a hill deep into the reserve. His colleagues all say the ranger stayed pretty much the same, totally committed to the idea of natural ecological systems while thriving on a much simpler life style. He had lived the way he relished, true to his principles. People from all walks of life – the different tribes, jobs, and cultures around the park – attended a farewell ceremony out of genuine respect for the ranger's contributions.

Why Differences? Why Change?

Now you are again circling back to the present on the magic carpet, thoroughly confused. One person – the ranger – stayed the same. Another – the cadet –

developed greater maturity and perspective but within the same world view. Four changed significantly: One – the street kid – from a foul-mouthed sinner to a fundamentalist saint; another – the Entrepreneur – from a focus on competing for self to a genuine concern for others. Yet, the former social activist changed from a life of demanding equality for all to making personal profits and living 'the good life' herself. The songoma became a successful merchant as well as a mystic. It is clear that ᵛMEMEs move and that there may even be a pattern to it.

Re-enter Clare W. Graves

Let us take one more trip on our magic carpet. We will travel back in time to the late 1970s and drop in on a relatively obscure professor. He is working in a dull, gray building that houses the Department of Psychology at Union College, in Schenectady, New York. Pose your question to Professor Clare W. Graves, a tall, lean, provocative man with dancing eyes and a deep oratorical voice. 'Dr Graves,' you ask, 'why do the people we've interviewed have different answers when asked, "What is the meaning of life?" And why did some change their conceptions after ten years, yet others remained basically the same?'

'Good questions,' he chortles while scanning his mind for some way to make a complex topic clear for us. 'It's in our nature. Without being too technical, may I suggest that human existence contains numerous, probably infinite, modes of being, precisely rooted in the multifold potentially of mankind's hierarchically structured brain. What you have encountered is simply evidence of the emergence of different modes of being in people and, under certain conditions, changes to other levels of existence.'

He continues. 'I confronted that same problem in the early 1950s when I became frustrated teaching different psychological theories in my classes. Though they kept asking, I was unable to tell students which theory was "right." I was about ready to leave the profession entirely because it was in such a mess. That's when I decided I would launch a major research project. I wanted to find out why people like the ones you interviewed see the world so differently, yet are not necessarily locked into those views. To make a long story short, my data supported the conclusion that human nature is such that modes of being can ebb and flow. New ones can replace old ones, yet the old ones don't disappear. They still exist within us. Furthermore, there are potentially new modes of being on the horizon that we have not experienced.'

Qualities of ᵛMEMEs

This section will describe the characteristics of those invisible core intelligences (ᵛMEMEs) that were impacting our friends without their knowledge.

ᵛMEME flow

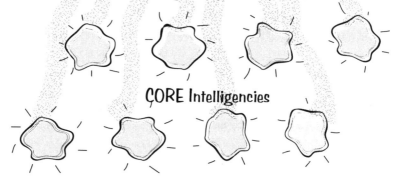

CONCRETE Actions, Behaviors, Attachments
CONCEPTS Systems, Beliefs, Schemes

CORE Intelligencies

Then we will look into the laws, codes and principles that influence the shifts, elaborations, and arrangements in these evolving modes of being as described by our friend Clare W. Graves. This is the Spiral's intelligence.

A ᵛMEME transposes itself into a world *view*, a value *system*, a *level* of psychological existence, a belief *structure*, organizing *principle*, a *way* of thinking, and a *mode* of living.

ᵛMEMEs possess the following qualities:

1. ᵛMEMEs manifest the core intelligences that form systems and impact human behavior: A ᵛMEME contains the basic package of thought, motives, and instructions that determine how we make decisions and prioritize our lives. Each has its own sending and receiving channel, organization design, intensity level, code of conduct, and set of assumptions regarding the way the world works.

A ᵛMEME occupies a human mind much like a parasite moves into the body and reorders the neurological equipment to fit its way of thinking. Each has a directional compass that makes it predatory and expansive or passive and cooperative. They all contain antibodies to fend off attacks from competing ᵛMEMEs.

ᵛMEMEs shape our basic life priorities which, in turn, result in surface level decisions and behaviors others can observe. Television characters Arch

Bunker and Murphy Brown are ᵛMEMEs apart. Alas, one cannot detect the operating ᵛMEME in a person simply by observing behavior – *what* someone does. Only recognizing *why* a person is doing or saying certain things will lead to the ᵛMEME. An unscrupulous character may attempt to convince you that he is speaking from the very sensitive **GREEN** ᵛMEME that focuses on human well-being and social causes when, in fact, he is driven by a quite selfish form of the **ORANGE** ᵛMEME that wants to talk you out of your money to support his 'charitable' expense account.

Here is a quick preview of the eight landmark ᵛMEMEs that have appeared to date around which ideas and beliefs gather. You will find a more extensive summary of the eight core ᵛMEMEs at the end of this chapter and a narrative discussion of all their phases in Section 3.

ᵛMEME	Popular Names	Basic Motives
BEIGE	*SurvivalSense*	staying alive through innate sensory equipment.
PURPLE	*KinSpirits*	blood relationships and mysticism in a magical and scary world.
RED	*PowerGods*	enforce power over self, others, and nature through exploitive independence.
BLUE	*TruthForce*	absolute belief in one right way and obedience to authority.
ORANGE	*StriveDrive*	possibility thinking focused on making things better for self.
GREEN	*HumanBond*	well-being of people and building consensus get highest priority.
YELLOW	*FlexFlow*	flexible adaptation to change through connected, big-picture views.
TURQUOISE	*GlobalView*	attention to whole-Earth dynamics and macro-level actions.

2. ᵛMEMEs impact all of life's choices: ᵛMEMEs are self-organizing entities which elaborate themselves into consistent packages that impact virtually everything in our lives. Like powerful viruses, they attach themselves to those ideas, people, objects, and institutions that allow them to reproduce and radiate their core messages. Each contains its own framework for religion, politics, family life, education, mental health, work and management, social order, and law. The identical ᵛMEMEs may flow over athletic fields, through the media, in legislative cloak rooms, executive suites, cathedrals, and classrooms.

ᵛMEMEs act like magnetic fields that bind entities together or cause them to repel. Racial divisions are often ᵛMEME divides. Churches flail around and split when new ᵛMEMEs awaken in a portion of their membership. Major ᵛMEME shifts are occurring in business, causing severe turbulence and demands for restructuring. The current plague of 'broken homes' and fractured families is, in large measure, a function of ᵛMEMEs in collapse.

A well-entrenched ᵛMEME will have built a powerful supporting structure around itself. Change often requires a painful uprooting before a new ᵛMEME can take hold and grow. Societies shifting from Marxism into free market democracies are in that condition, as are bureaucracies seeking to privatize and dictatorships on the verge of theocracy.

ᵛMEMEs develop minds of their own. They possess the capacity to launch religious crusades, explore the outer limits of space, follow Pied Pipers into the sea, endanger our natural habitat, or stand up for human rights. No power on Earth can stop a ᵛMEME whose time has come, not talk radio, a Papal encyclical, or a U.N. resolution.

3. ᵛMEMEs express both healthy (*for-better*) and unhealthy (*for-worse*) qualities: ᵛMEMEs themselves are neither good nor bad, healthy nor unhealthy, positive nor negative. For example, the same ᵛMEME that produces Navajo mysticism, Aboriginal dream travels, or Walt Disney-inspired fantasy trips can also be cursed by superstitions or influenced to drink Jim Jones' suicidal purple Kool Aide in Guyana. The ᵛMEME that liberates the imagination and dedication of millions on behalf of noble causes and brings ordered purpose to their lives may lock others into militant, fanatical, holy-warfare and ethnic terrorism.

Healthy ᵛMEMEs are those that allow or even facilitate the positive expression of other ᵛMEMEs on the evolving Spiral, even though they may be in competition for influence. Often ᵛMEMEs become malignant, lacking the internal regulation system to tell them when to stop growing. Others become closed, locked-in, and repressive, imposing a guardian mentality.

4. ᵛMEMEs are structures of thinking: ᵛMEMEs determine *how* people think or make decisions in contrast to *what* they believe or value. Graves referred to them as *schemas*, containers in which contents (*themas* and memes) could be poured. A dyed-in-the-wool zealot who champions one religion as 'the only true way' has the same ᵛMEMEs as another dyed-in-the-wool zealot who advocates a different one. Their conflict is contentual rather than within the ᵛMEME's core intelligence.

Other examples might include:

- Two street gangs in China Town in New York City are competing for shakedown, 'protection' racket niches on overlapping turf in the same **RED** ᵛMEME zone.
- Two religious '-isms' locked in a holy war over the rights to erect one's temple over what both believe to be 'holy ground' in Northwest India also live in the same **BLUE** ᵛMEME zone.

- Republicans and Democrats compete for political privilege and economic power with different candidates, but within the same politics-as-usual **ORANGE** zone game.
- Union and management officials are locked in competition for power inside a dying company while it loses market share and moves toward overall collapse, an *impasse* within the **RED** to **ORANGE** zone.

Conflicts occur between ᵛMEMEs when they overlap in limited space, either physical or conceptual, and seek to influence the same people. For example:

- An ideology-based **BLUE**-zone society armed with Truth is at war with an **ORANGE**-dominated secular movement. Attempts to replace a fundamentalist religious Communal/Collective system with Individual/Elite 'Westernized' values prematurely may trigger a regression to feudal barbarism.
- An affluent, growth-and-development-oriented **ORANGE** segment of a community is caught in political warfare with an ecology conscious, anti-growth element more in the **GREEN** zone for control of the city council.
- A **BLUE/red** segment willing to fight for stability and order is at odds with a risk-taking and expansionist **ORANGE/blue** mass. For example, the Sooner farmers and open-space ranchers in the musical *Oklahoma* competed for dominance in 'the territory' and which memes would prevail.

5. ᵛMEMEs can brighten and dim as *Life Conditions* change: ᵛMEMEs have strong cybernetic (able to read the feedback and adjust) capacities and are driven to preserve their core intelligences and proliferate their influence wherever they find open minds. Each has a dimmer switch to allow it to turn up or turn down as it receives instructions from its own 'DNA' or signals from changing *Life Conditions* in the milieu. Rather than being static and rigid, ᵛMEMEs have the capacity to shift their focus, intensity, and field of operation. A "ᵛMEMEologist' would think of them as active, persistent, and often aggressive thought cells that can spread like wild fires across generations, continents, and professions.

The Songoma's ᵛMEME shift vacated animistic **PURPLE** while awakening entrepreneurial **ORANGE**. The West Point cadet's thinking expanded from a less to more mature version of the **BLUE** ᵛMEME. The street kid was converted from wild **RED** into a hard-line **BLUE**. The London activist found humanistic **GREEN** to be a bad trip and settled into materialistic **ORANGE**. The Park Ranger found satisfaction in completing his life within the **YELLOW** ᵛMEME's zone.

You will find different ᵛMEMEs at work in different functions in a company. They often clash at staff meetings over whatever the issue of the day happens to be. You may have a friend who is suffering through ᵛMEMEetic change over family matters, or may be going through a major life passage.

Downsizing will cause a ᵛMEME shift as those who remain suffer the pangs of guilt. Many high-visibility change efforts fail becaue they miss entirely the anchor ᵛMEMEs that cause people to resist.

What are the dynamics, however, that determined the action of the respective ᵛMEMEs? Are there detectable patterns or was everything the result of pure chance, the independent actions of unrelated particles, or the unbridled self-interest of audacious ᵛMEMEs? Consider these characteristics:

BEIGE   If the thinking is **automatic**; the structures are **loose bands**; the process is **survivalistic**.

PURPLE   If the thinking is **animistic**; the structures will be **tribal**; the processes will be **circular**.

RED   If the thinking is **egocentric**; the structures are **empires**; the process is **exploitative**.

BLUE   If the thinking is **absolutistic**; the structures are **pyramidal**; the process is **authoritarian**.

ORANGE   If the thinking is **multiplistic**; the structures are **delegative**; the process is **strategic**.

GREEN   If the thinking is **relativistic**; the structures are **egalitarian**; the process is **consensual**.

YELLOW   If the thinking is **systemic**; the structures are **interactive**; the process is **integrative**.

TURQUOISE   If the thinking is **holistic**; the structures are **global**; the process is flowing and **ecological**.

A Quick ᵛMEME Overview

The evolution (rolling out) of the ᵛMEMEs follows several trajectories:

From less complex   **To** more complex
          natural, technological, and human **environments** . . .

From surviving   **To** surfing beyond
in the bush   the Internet
          through the awakening of new **minds** and consciousness levels . . .

From a small   **To** the global village
piece of land   and cyberspace
          via migrations across land and information terrain

The FIRST TIER   'Subsistence ᵛMEMEs'

BEIGE *'Survivalistic'* ᵛMEME   1st Awakening   Graves Code: A-N
Basic theme: Do what you must just to stay alive
Characteristic beliefs and actions:

- Uses instincts and habits just to survive
- Distinct **self** is barely awakened or sustained
- Food, Water, Warmth, Sex, and Safety have priority
- Forms into survival **bands** to perpetuate life

Where seen: The first peoples, newborn infants, senile elderly, late-stage Alzheimer's victims, mentally ill street people, starving masses, bad drug trips, and 'shell shock.' Described in anthropological fiction like Jean Auel's *Clan of the Cave Bear*.

PURPLE *'Magical'* ᵛMEME   2nd Awakening   Graves Code: B-O
Basic theme: Keep the spirits happy and the 'tribe's' nest warm and safe
Characteristic beliefs and actions:

- Obey the desires of spirit beings and mystical signs
- Show allegiance to chief, elders, ancestors and the clan
- Preserve sacred objects, places, events, and memories
- Observe rites of passage, seasonal cycles, and tribal customs

Where seen: Belief in guardian angels and Voodoo-like curses, blood oaths, ancient grudges, chanting and trance dancing, good luck charms, family rituals, and mystical ethnic beliefs and superstitions. Strong in Third-World settings, gangs, athletic teams, and corporate 'tribes.'

RED *'Impulsive'* ᵛMEME   3rd Awakening   Graves Code: C-P
Basic Theme: Be what you are and do what you want, regardless
Characteristic beliefs and actions:

- The world is a jungle full of threats and predators
- Breaks free from any domination or constraint to please self as self desires
- Stands tall, expects attention, demands respect, and calls the shots
- Enjoys self to the fullest right now without guilt or remorse
- Conquers, out-foxes, and dominates other aggressive characters

Where seen: The 'Terrible Twos,' rebellious youth, frontier mentalities, feudal kingdoms, James Bond villains, epic heroes, soldiers of fortune, 'Papa' Picasso, wild rock stars, Atilla the Hun, William Golding's *Lord of the Flies*, and Mighty Morphin Power Rangers.

BLUE '*Purposeful*' 'MEME   4th Awakening   Graves Code: D-Q
Basic Theme: Life has meaning, direction, and purpose with predetermined outcomes

Characteristic beliefs and actions

- One sacrifices self to the transcendent Cause, Truth, or righteous Pathway
- The Order enforces a code of conduct based on eternal, absolute principles
- Righteous living produces stability now and guarantees future reward
- Impulsivity is controlled through guilt; everybody has their proper place
- Laws, regulations, and discipline build character and moral fiber

Where seen: Rev. Billy Graham, Frank Capra's *It's a Wonderful Life*, Puritan America, Confucian China, Hassidic Judaism, Dickensian England, Singapore discipline, codes of chivalry and honor, charitable good deeds, the Salvation Army, Islamic fundamentalism, Garrison Keillor's Lake Wobegon, Boy and Girl Scouts, patriotism.

ORANGE '*Achievist*' 'MEME   5th Awakening   Graves Code: E-R
Basic Theme: Act in your own self-interest by playing the game to win
Characteristic beliefs and actions:

- Change and advancement are inherent within the scheme of things
- Progress by learning nature's secrets and seeking out best solutions
- Manipulate Earth's resources to create and spread the abundant good life
- Optimistic, risk-taking, and self-reliant people deserve their success
- Societies prosper through strategy, technology, and competitiveness

Where seen: The Enlightenment, 'success' ministries, Ayn Rand's *Atlas Shrugged*, Wall Street, Rodeo Drive, The Riviera, emerging middle classes, the cosmetics industry, trophy hunting, Chambers of Commerce, colonialism, TV infomercials, the Cold War, DeBeers diamond cartel, breast implants, fashion, J. R. Ewing and *Dallas*.

GREEN '*Communitarian*' 'MEME   6th Awakening   Graves Code: F-S
Basic Theme: Seek peace within the inner self and explore, with others, the caring dimensions of community
Characteristic beliefs and actions:

- The human spirit must be freed from greed, dogma, and divisiveness
- Feelings, sensitivity, and caring supersede cold rationality
- Spread the Earth's resources and opportunities equally among all
- Reach decisions through reconciliation and consensus processes
- Refresh spirituality, bring harmony, and enrich human development

Where seen: John Lennon's music, Netherlands' idealism, Rogerian counseling, liberation theology, Doctors without Borders, Canadian health care, ACLU, World Council of Churches, sensitivity training, Boulder (Colorado), GreenPeace, Jimmy Carter, Dustin Hoffman in *The Graduate*, animal rights, deep ecology, Minneapolis-St Paul social services, the music of Bruce Cogburn, Ben & Jerry's Ice Cream company.

The Second Tier   'Being' ᵛMEMEs

YELLOW *'Integrative'* ᵛMEME   7th Awakening   Graves Code: G-T
Basic theme: Live fully and responsibly as what you are and learn to become
Characteristic beliefs and actions:

- Life is a kaleidoscope of natural hierarchies, systems, and forms
- The magnificence of existence is valued over material possessions
- Flexibility, spontaneity, and functionality have the highest priority
- Knowledge and competency should supersede rank, power, status
- Differences can be integrated into interdependent, natural flows

Where seen: Carl Sagan's astronomy, Peter Senge's organizations, Stephen Hawking's *Brief History of Time*, W. Edwards Deming's objectives, Paul Newman's version of stardom, chaos theory, appropriate technology, eco-industrial parks (using each other's outflows as raw materials), early episodes of TV's *Northern Exposure*, Fel-Pro, Inc. (a gasket manufacturer), Fred Alan Wolf's 'new physics,' Deepak Chopra's *Ageless Body*.

TURQUOISE *'Holistic'* ᵛMEME   8th Awakening   Graves Code: H-U
Basic Theme: Experience the wholeness of existence through mind and spirit
Characteristic beliefs and actions:

- The world is a single, dynamic organism with its own collective mind
- Self is both distinct and a blended part of a larger, compassionate whole
- Everything connects to everything else in ecological alignments
- Energy and information permeate the Earth's total environment
- Holistic, intuitive thinking and cooperative actions are to be expected

Where seen: Theories of David Bohn, McLuhan's 'global village,' Gregory Stock's *Metaman*, Rupert Sheldrake and morphic fields, Gandhi's ideas of pluralistic harmony, Ken Wilber's 'Spectrum of Consciousness,' James Lovelock's 'Gaia hypothesis,' Pierre Teilhard de Chardin's 'noosphere.'

CORAL, for these authors, is still unclear.

3

The Mind of the Spiral

In summer of 1984 we joined with Clare Graves in a presentation of his theory at a major conference of the World Future Society in Washington, D.C., not realizing that this was to be his last public forum. We still have fond memories of him bounding out of the taxi at the hotel following his flight from Albany. He had suffered the ill effects of a series of heart attacks and other medical problems for a decade, severely curtailing his activities and short-circuiting the popularization of his work. But his energy level was high on this trip, and he relished the opportunity to let his visionary mind speak once again.

After the usual introductions, the stage was set. Graves rose up in a majestic pose and in his deep, still resonant voice bellowed out, 'I call my point of view The Emergent, Cyclical, Double-Helix Model of Adult Biopsychosocial Systems Development.' This audience of futurists did what most other groups over the years had done when he spoke those words. Some sighed, others muttered, a few giggled, and many exclaimed 'uh', 'wow' or 'oh, no' to indicate they knew their minds were about to be invaded by a powerful new ^{v}MEME or that they were about to encounter a stream of complicated gibberish they would probably not understand.

Typically, Graves paused to let the murmur die down – he knew what it was about – before he retorted, with a twinkle in his eyes: 'Well, damn it, that's what it is!' The crowd roared, then relaxed as he then explained his point of view with a lucidity and force that left his listeners asking 'Why have we not thought of this before? Why is something which makes so much sense not more widely known? This is the key to unlocking some of our most difficult riddles.' Too bad Humpty Dumpty was not in attendance.

They could not know how poor health and a scholar's rigorous need to fill in theoretical gaps had combined to delay the complete presentation of Graves' framework. He fully expected, but was unable to experience, the revolution in brain/mind research that has fleshed-out his thinking during the last decade.

^vMEME "DNA" Spiral

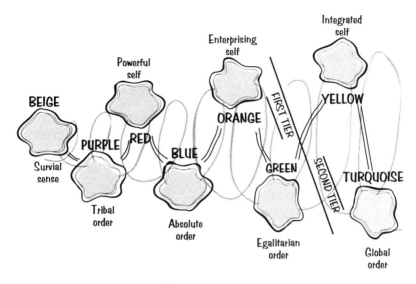

A psychological map

Living Systems-Within

While the name given by Clare Graves to his conception of human nature is imposing, it can be reduced to a few essentials. In the previous section we described the core intelligence of a single ^vMEME (a Gravesian 'biopsychosocial system') as it replicates across society at-large, just as genes send their chemical messages throughout the body. Now we will describe the core intelligences within the Spiral itself – the organizing principle that awakens new ^vMEMEs, regulates their balances, causes regressions back into previous zones, and sets chaotic shifts in motion.

As we suggested with the 'New Times, New Thinking' sequence, each major societal upheaval has spawned a different view of life itself – why we are here, what is our nature, what is our ultimate destination? Each ^vMEME develops its own views of the rules that should govern social systems, who should make decisions regarding what, the forces that drive the evolutionary surge toward complexity, and why different people are passing through different levels of development at the very same time.

Recognize that you will think about this Spiral intelligence through the ^vMEMEs that are presently active in your own mind, and that will produce the metaphors and perspectives that fit for you. Someone else will see aspects of the model differently, have preferences for different ^vMEME stacks in friends, and filter the Spiral through their own colored glasses. They will locate its core wisdom – the *elan vital* – in various places. Perhaps the guiding force rests with the Creator, God, or Allah; in the way of Confucius or teachings of the Buddha; the materialistic Machine or scientific Truth; even an amorphous higher power, nature, or the goddess. However you locate it, a living intelligence is at work, carried in both our genetic DNA and our ᵛMEMEetic 'DNA.'

Seven principles describe this core intelligence of the spiral and frame the emergent patterns of new paradigms, management theories, and even purchasing habits in the globalizing marketplace. They uncover the deepest trend that generates trends; the most basic dynamics that give birth to gurus; and the global generator of 'new' or next world orders. They also explain how and why ᵛMEMEs appear and behave in networks or assemblages.

Principle 1: *Humans possess the capacity to create new ᵛMEMEs*

A critical piece in Graves' perspective is that humans possess within themselves the capacity to exist at different levels of psychological development and even add a new level. These are not inherently 'better-than' or 'worse-than' states, but they do reflect different perspectives on what the world is like and the complexity one finds in it.

This variability in levels of existence underlines our capacity to escape the tyranny of lethargic genes. While genes take their own sweet time to bring about change, human ᵛMEMEs have the capacity to leap up an evolutionary Spiral virtually overnight.

'[The development of] the human being,' Graves once noted, 'is an unfolding or emergent process marked by the progressive subordination of older behavioral systems to newer, higher order behavioral systems.' Clearly, we have a powerful and dynamic mind, one that can recalibrate itself, form new ᵛMEME systems in response to changing *Life Conditions*, and even create new organizational designs and functions in global arrangements unheard of only a decade ago.

Are there more latent capacities in our mind/brain as yet untapped? Is Homo Sapiens[1995] the evolutionary end of our species, or only 'the state of the art' for our contemporary world? Look back at what the cutting-edge thinkers might have been discussing when the *Life Conditions* were different. Let us say, roughly:

100,000 years ago	Homo Sapiens *survivalus*	**BEIGE**
	To be human beings, not just animals	
50,000 years ago	Homo Sapiens *mysticus*	**PURPLE**
	Forming tribes, magic, art, spirits	
10,000 years ago	Homo Sapiens *exploiticus*	**RED**
	Warlords, conquest, discovery	

5000 years ago	Homo Sapiens *absoluticus*	BLUE
	Literature, monotheism, purpose	
1000 years ago	Homo Sapiens *materialensis*	ORANGE
	Mobility, individualism, economics	
150 years ago	Homo Sapiens *humanisticus*	GREEN
	Human rights, liberty, collectivism	
50 years ago	Homo Sapiens *integratus*	YELLOW
	Complexity, chaos, interconnections	
30 years ago	Homo Sapiens *holisticus*	TURQUOISE
	Globalism, eco-consciousness, patterns	
Today?	Homo Sapiens ———————	CORAL

In an early presentation of his findings to the National Institutes of Mental Health in Washington, D.C., in 1973, Graves warned that he was about to 'crawl forth on a fragile limb.' Human systems, he would argue, reflect different activation levels of our dynamic neurological equipment, i.e., our brains' chemical wetware, complex cell assemblages, and billions of potential neuron connections. 'As man solves the problems of existence at a level,' Graves contended, 'new brain systems may be activated and, when activated, change his perceptions so as to cause him to see new problems of existence.' Instead of beginning only as passive hardware without content (Locke's *tabula rasa* or blank slate view), it turns out the normal human brain comes with potential 'software'-like systems just waiting to be turned on – latent upgrades!

Thanks to the recent revolution in the neurosciences we mentioned earlier, what Graves half-jokingly referred to as 'a fragile limb' in 1973 has grown into a strong branch of knowledge in the mid-1990s. This new information base provides us far greater insight into our systems-seeking, problem-solving nature and only continues to add support to his 'Levels of Psychological Existence' theory.

For this remarkable process of an open systems, awakening brain to function within us, three conditions must be met:

A. A set of instructions, probably encoded in our DNA, that equip us to awaken new systems which add to or even replace old ones: As University of Syracuse (New York) physicist Erich Harth put it in *Dawn of a New Millennium: Beyond Evolution and Culture* (New York: Penguin Books, 1991, p.x.),

> 'We might as well assume that there existed in the brain of prehistoric man, like the invisible images on an undeveloped film, the latent abilities to carry out functions that would not find expression for many thousands of years. By what strange principle of evolution did they get there?'

B. Dynamic forces generated in both nature and nurture that trigger specific systems: Michael S. Gazzaniga, the highly-respected neuroscientist who co-discovered the 'split brain' (left–right hemisphere) theory, suggests that brain systems interact to shape a person. In applying what biologists call Selection Theory to psychology, he proposes that a massive inventory of possibilities exists within the brain. Gazzaniga notes that 'What looks to be learning is in fact the organism searching through its [built in] library of circuits and accompanying [behavioral and cognitive] strategies that will best allow it to respond to the [environmental] challenge.' (*Nature's Mind*, New York: Basic Books, 1992, p. 200.)

Writing on the evolution of consciousness in the brain in his popularization, *Bright Air, Brilliant Fire*, neurobiologist Gerald Edelman comments:

> 'In this book I have maintained that mind has arisen in a very definite way through the workings of evolutionary morphology. I have attempted to show that consciousness has arisen, at least in this little speck of the cosmos, at a particular historical time. That it emerges from definite material arrangements in the brain does not mean that it is identical to them, for, as we have seen, consciousness depends on relations with the environment and, in its highest order, on symbols and language in a society.' (Basic Books, 1992, p. 198).

C. The capacity of the human brain to house a number of subsystems, all at the same time, with some active and others relatively passive: Contemporary research into the nature of Multiple Personality Disorder (MPD) – popularized in *Dr Jeckel and Mr Hyde*, *The Three Faces of Eve*, or *Sybil* – has pointed toward such a capacity. The conventional view was the personality can split, fragment, or shatter into lesser individuals. Now, the emerging view ' . . .conveys the idea of layering, of different ways of being that are embedded within a whole' (*The Sciences*, November/December, 1992, p. 32). It is within our nature, then, as human beings to possess the potential to awaken an unlimited number of ᵛMEMEs and allow them to coexist within our conceptual libraries.

Principle 2: *Life Conditions awaken ᵛMEMEs which may emerge, surge, regress, or fade in response*

ᵛMEMEs are a product of the interaction of the equipment in our nervous systems with the *Life Conditions* that we face. This interface of existence *conditions-without* (from nature and human activity) and latent *capacities-within* is what Graves called the 'double-helix' aspect of his theory.

ᵛMEMEs do not emerge at inevitable stops on a train track through time nor are irrevocably scripted within human biology. Rather, the primary driving force that has sculpted the Spiral is activated in the dynamic interaction between our internal states and our external worlds. A pattern will appear when conditions factors are cyclic, and disappear when they are not.

There are four important aspects of these *Life Conditions*: Times, Place, Problems, and Circumstance.

Historic Times: Location along the overall line of human development, the particular culture's stage of emergence, and phases in the individual's life passages.

Key notions: Epochs, dispensations, generations, periods, cycles, dates, time-frames, personal histories, phases, senses of past/present/future.

At any point in chronological Time, and within virtually any community, you can find people who are living in the same year but whose thinking is rooted in very different eras. At any given period in your life you will have evolved a unique ᵛMEME package designed to fit that Time and the cultural themes it presents. For many people in Western cultures, the 1940s were quite different from the 1950s, or the 1960s, the 1980s, or the mid-1990s. For some Third-World societies, however, the Times have been remarkably steady for generations.

When the passage of Time does change external conditions, our internal potentials are awakened by the stress so we may add (or rearrange) ᵛMEMEs in response. This sequential layering of human adaptive intelligences is something like growth rings on a tree. Each ring reflects the environmental conditions during its season. While the duration of human seasons varies, ᵛMEME systems leave rings of culture and psycho-social development that are much the same. Who you are today, were yesterday, and will be tomorrow is shaped in large part by the conditions you experience at different times of your growth. We are not locked into our Times, but we are certainly influenced by them.

In September of 1992 the body of an 'Iceman,' a Neolithic wanderer from two millennia BC, was discovered frozen in an Alpine glacier. The Austrians named him 'Oetzi.' His unwitting gravesite yielded pieces of woven clothing, weaponry and other equipment to suggest his technology was hardly crude or primitive. It was apparently state-of-the-art for Europe of 4000 years ago. At that time, the continent was a quiet agricultural backwater. Poor Oetzi would have been a crude bumpkin by the standards of societies flourishing elsewhere – in Egypt, Mesopotamia, and China.

Suppose we had the technology to bring the Iceman's mind alive by growing his DNA? What kind of mind would it be? What ᵛMEMEs had emerged in him? Assuming his immune system could handle the bacteria and viruses that hunt us down, would he regress down the Spiral to a more primitive system still, overwhelmed by the shock from our complex, higher technology world? Or might he adapt quickly, awakening new ᵛMEMEs, and sell the rights to his story for a TV movie?

Humans live in different Times at the same time. When the agricultural age dawned, many people still lived by the code of hunting and gathering society; but many (like Oetzi?) did not. When the steam engines of the Industrial Age chugged to life, the bulk of humanity was still walking behind teams of plow horses or water buffalo, keeping to their 'rightful' places, but not everybody. When the Information Age exploded onto the scene, billions of us were still rising in the morning and retiring in the evening to the rhythms of the farm and the fading whistles of mills only just beginning to rust, but not all. George Orwell remarked that '. . .any epoch always contains a great deal of the last epoch.' Now, as we move beyond the age of bits and bytes, what new silicon cock will sound the dawn, alerting us to the next era ahead? What of these times will be carried forward to the next, and what abandoned? Who among us will remain in these Times, and who will move on to discover new ˅MEMEs?

Geographic **Place**: The physical conditions, both natural and man-made ecology, within the perception of the individual or group.

Key notions: Atmospheric conditions; electromagnetic flux; natural habitat (ice, desert, rain forest, urban sprawl, rural spread); architecture; population density; amount and kinds of external stimulation; chemicals and minerals in air, soil, and food; light sources and types; climatic variations.

In *The Power of Place*, Winifred Gallagher identifies many of the factors in our geographic location that greatly impact our social values and interactions. Being an isolated island race produces different collective behaviors from migratory folk in icy mountains or cultures evolving in a warm fertile valley. While she notes a differentiated influence of these factors, Gallagher observes:

> 'Throughout history, people of all cultures have assumed that environment influences behavior. Now modern science is confirming that our actions, thoughts, and feelings are indeed shaped not just by our genes and neurochemistry, history and relationships, but also by our surroundings.' (*The Power of Place: How Surroundings Shape Our Thoughts Emotions and Actions*, Simon & Schuster, 1993, p. 12).

Gallagher's 'surroundings' include everything from nature's broad theatre of influences (geomagnetic fields, Earth's topography, sky, weather, seasons, etc.) to man-made environments such as rooms, work places, buildings, cities, and living spaces. She refers to the Chinese concept of *feng shui*, an eclectic discipline that combines 'bits of art, geophysical observation, psychology, religion, folklore, and plain common sense' (p. 143). *Feng shui* describes the process of harmonizing people and their settings. Clearly, harmony or dissonance with these settings will shape how and why different kinds of thinking emerge in some people, cause misfitness in others, and create havoc in populations when the environmental backdrop suddenly changes. It is amazing how much effort is often required to re-'discover' ancient wisdom.

Human **Problems**: Priorities, needs, concerns, and requirements for existence facing a particular individual or group, some of which are common to all humans and others unique to a culture, community, or personality.

Key notions: Survival issues like food and water; availability and richness of niches; perceived levels of threat or safety; cultural norms and requirements; communication and languages; dominant temperaments, natural wanderlust, and thrill-seeking personalities; technologies; social memories, unresolved historic issues, icons and relics from the past; disease and epidemics; wild cards that disturb the previous social order

---

Existence problems such as these overwhelm the coping mechanisms within the prevailing order and trigger the necessary equipment in the brain that can (1) perceive the conditions more accurately, and then (2) free up the resources and conceptual power to deal with them appropriately. Each core ^{v}MEME on the Spiral has its own unique collection of problems that must be addressed. When a number of them are surging at the same time and in the same place, the degree of turbulence and conflict will increase accordingly. Many of the world's 'hot-spots' are heated by the friction of simultaneous ^{v}MEME awakenings, but also by problems overpowering existing resources.

Social **Circumstance**: Individual, group, and cultural placement within hierarchies of power, status, and influence.

Key notions: Social roles; positioning in the resource flow; socioeconomic 'class'; educational level; opportunities and access to niche pathways; appearances and physiognomy; interpersonal dynamics; political systems; family lineage; racial, age, and gender factors.

No two people share identical Circumstances, even in the same times, in a nearby Place, and with similar Problems. Birth orders, social position, genetic inheritance, family privilege, intellectual or physical endowments, and the plain old luck-of-the-draw will differ. The same can be said regarding any given group, collection of people, or social stratum. Whether we like it or not, these unequal *Life Conditions* have a significant impact in human affairs. No two people can inhabit identical conceptual worlds or share the same experiences in the same way. Even identical twins have their differences. Obviously, much of what goes on in politics, religion, and therapy are closely related to this aspect of the Spiral.

The Circumstances define boundaries, either open or blocked, for us. They must be recognized in dealing with both 'minority' and 'majority' groups, 'advantaged' and 'disadvantaged' persons. The Circumstances are like a set of blinders that can keep any of us from seeing the whole Spiral as someone else might. As one of the four elements in *Life Conditions*, the Circumstances also frame which ᵛMEMEs are likely to become acceptable, appropriate, and justifiable in a given context. Confusion regarding effective schools, appropriate hiring and promotion practices, and fragmented neighborhoods all relate to Circumstances.

To summarize the *Life Conditions* (Times, Place, Problems, and Circumstances):

. . .if the Life Conditions are heavily . . .	. . .then 'sensible' people will . . .
BEIGE – a state of nature	act much like other animals.
PURPLE – mysterious and frightening	placate spirits and join together for safety.
RED – tough and dangerous like a jungle	fight to survive in spite of what others want.
BLUE – directed by a higher power	obey higher authority and be faithful to the Truth.
ORANGE – full of viable alternatives	pragmatically test for advantages to succeed.
GREEN – shared habit of all humanity	join community to experience shared growth.
YELLOW – at risk of chaotic collapse	learn how to be free but also principled.
TURQUOISE – a single living entity	seek the order beneath Earth's apparent chaos.

Principle 3: ᵛMEMEs zig-zag between Express-self and Sacrifice-self themes

The overall Spiral is forged by the pendulum-like shift between a focus on 'me' and concerns with 'we,' orientations somewhat akin to the *yin* and *yang* of Chinese philosophy or Martin Buber's 'I:Thou.' Psychologist Mihaly Csikszentmihalyi summarizes this idea when he says:

> 'Social scientists (Abraham Maslow, Lawrence Kohlberg, Jane Loevinger, and James Fowler) describe a dialectical motion between differentiation and integration, between turning attention inward and then outward, between valuing the self and then the larger community. It is not a circular motion that returns to where one started, but rather, it resembles an ascending spiral, where concern for the self becomes steadily qualified by less selfish goals, and concern for others become individualistic and personally meaningful.' (Mihaly Csikszentmihalyi, *The Evolving Self*, HarperCollins, 1993, p. 235)

Hence, each core ᵛMEME falls closer to one side or the other of a pendulum's arc within the Spiral. One family is designated with warm colors (**BEIGE,**

RED, ORANGE, YELLOW) which represent Express-self, 'I'-oriented 'MEMEs. The other group is assigned cool colors (PURPLE, BLUE, GREEN, TURQUOISE) and are the Sacrifice-self, 'we'-oriented set.

Individuals and societies tend to tilt from one magnet-like pole to the other. Whenever this human pendulum approaches the far side of its force-field, it generates the new *Life Conditions* that can only be addressed with solutions from the other. If too much 'me'-ism is the problem, then a form of 'we'-ness will then be required to restore balance. If the 'we' is excessive, then liberation of some 'me' becomes attractive if harmony is desired.

When the swing begins, the brain must activate the equipment to deal with messages from or about the upcoming 'MEME family. The shift toward Communal/Collective 'coming to peace within' requires a radar-like sense so external messages can be picked up quickly and accurately, magnified, and feedback incorporated to insure compliance. The shift toward Individual/ Elite 'move against and take control' requires an internalized gyroscope-like intelligence, the self-directed compass needed to explore new territories, sail into uncharted waters, and break with the safety of tradition.

INDIVIDUAL/ELITE POLE	COMMUNAL/ COLLECTIVE POLE
I : me : mine	*We : us : ours*
Take charge, make changes, move against nature, control the external world, rely on the power of the self.	Accept the inevitable, live within nature's constraints, focus on coming to peace with who one is, seek authority from outside.
Task: Explore the outside. *Locus of Control:* Inside	*Task:* Fix the inside. *Locus of Control:* Outside

The Individual/Elite 'MEME family is focused on the external world (outside the self) and how to gain power over it, to master it, to change it. Control is located within the particle-like individual who strives to bend things in his/her direction. The Express-self systems it forms are more loosely bound, less constrained, more accepting of change, willing to take more risks, and markedly increase our degrees of behavioral freedom when awakened. They tend to break shackles to free up more expansive views, but they also unlink chains that keep parts organized into wholes. As the free-standing, 'special' individual becomes more centralized; demands for personal rights and liberties, perks and prerogatives, and empowerment for every-'one' surges. The family crest says, 'I am the captain of my fate . . . the master of my soul.'

The other pole is home to the radar-like Communal/Collective ('us/we')

^vMEME family. In this self-sacrificing zone, control is anchored in something more powerful than any individual – the kin and folk, the unifying Higher Power, the community of mutual interest, or Earth's living system. Yet, just as the Express-self group focuses energy on impacting the world 'out there,' the Sacrifice-self person's deep concerns are inside – efforts to come to grips with who, or what, or why one is and find peace with that. Because of this emphasis, thinking within this ^vMEME group tends to be more conservative of the *status quo* (whatever its politics) and order-seeking. The Communal/Collective energy promotes consolidation, acceptance of the external world as it is, and surrender of immediate self-interest for what is in the best interest of one's reference group(s). While there is some enlargement of conceptual space as the pendulum swings across the Spiral into this range, more energy goes to building trustworthy structures, finding stability, and building uniform consistency into living – 'Duty, Honor, Country;' ' . . .Thrifty, Brave, Clean, and Reverent.'

Warm color ^vMEMEs always divide entities into hierarchies. With **BEIGE**, the fastest runner or highest reach. With **RED** it is power. With **ORANGE**, status. With **YELLOW**, knowledge and competency. Cool ^vMEMEs gather people into groupings which flatten hierarchies, equalize entities, and redistribute resources. With **PURPLE** it is kith and kin. For **BLUE** it is the congregation of believers. With **GREEN** it is the assembly of common interests and sensitivities. This dynamic also causes the appearance of a cyclic pattern within the Spiral.

Perhaps a mind experiment can illustrate the oscillation of the ^vMEMEs. Assume that you are holding a Spiral sea-shell by its tip. Now, imagine that you could swing a weight on a cord inside that form. Begin with the weight high up at the small end of the shell and, while your pendulum is swinging, slowly release the string. You are now combining the effects of both a cycle and a spiral.

In terms of ^vMEME, you release your pendulum at the **BEIGE** beginning ('I survive') and gradually extend the string. Watch the pendulum swing across the peak **BEIGE** system to Exiting sub-system **BEIGE/purple**, then Entering **beige/PURPLE** and on to Peak **PURPLE** ('we, the clan'). It then swings across and down the Spiral through the sub-systems to the next landmark, **RED** ('I, the powerful'), over and down some more to Peak **BLUE** ('we, the True Believers'), back to the **ORANGE** zone ('I, the capable'), over to **GREEN** ('we, the accepting'), to **YELLOW** ('I, the knowing'), then to **TURQUOISE** ('we, the becoming'). You could continue this process so long as the Spiral grew and you had enough string.

Like voyagers in a sea shell, we travel the Spiral among these Individual/Elite and Communal/Collective zones, mixing them together in our minds and refining our personal blends in our ^vMEME profiles. The proportion of 'me' to 'we' ^vMEMEs sets the tone for generations ('Yuppie Baby Boomers' versus 'Depression-Era,' the 1980s versus the 1950s, or the 'Roaring

Twenties' versus the Civil War), establishes stereotypes of national character (the free-wheeling Italians vs. the accurate and orderly Swiss), and marks phases in individual development (the upstart 'Terrible Twos' vs. trend-conscious and desperate to fit-in puberty). Recognizing and managing these ever-changing ᵛMEME stacks is at the heart of Spiral Dynamics.

To summarize this Principle, keep these primary swings in mind:

- swings in focus from an Internal ('me') to an External ('we') locus of control and then back again
- swing in centrality of the self between a free-standing individual and a person defined primarily in terms of the group
- swing in reliance on external inputs and feedback from others to trusting internal judgments
- swing from attempting to explore the external world and master it to a need for repair of the inner world and coming to peace with it

Principle 4: *ᵛMEMEs emerge along the Spiral in a wave-like fashion*

Awakenings along the Spiral occur after pressure builds up leading to a spurt to the next system, usually up, but sometimes down. Although the shift may appear to be sudden and chaotic (Graves used the term 'saccadic'), undetected movement is occurring beneath the surface all along.

New ᵛMEME systems come in like waves to a beach. Each has its own ascending surge, designed to fathom the *Life Conditions* of its world. At the same time, each also overlaps the receding waves of the previous systems as they fade. Sometimes the interference generated as new systems compete in their ascendancies slows the overall Spiral's momentum, even shoving it backwards. At other times, the ᵛMEME waves resonate and reinforce one another to speed the evolution of thinking along.

Each wave carries the seeds of its birth and death, residues from previous systems fading and the first glimmers of new ways of being just ahead. The active life of a ᵛMEME has three phases. (1) **Entering**: When first awakening there is a period of preparation and energy increase. This includes the initial formation and refinement of a system, as well as the 'Eureka!' period of discovery and exploration. If you think of a sine curve, this is the upside. (2) **Peak**: Next comes an interval of dynamic tension and *apparent* stability around the pinnacle. The *Life conditions* and ᵛMEMEs are in sync, congruent, and balanced. Graves always argued that this was largely a theoretical state since pure, isolated tones are rare in nature. However, it is also the easiest to talk about – there are only eight Peak ᵛMEMEs thus far – if one is willing to accept for the moment simplicity that is not there. (3) **Exiting**: That interval of apparent stability is followed by a period of disintegration, a confusing time when the system is becoming imbalanced and ineffectual as more complicated

A ᵛMEME's Life Cycle

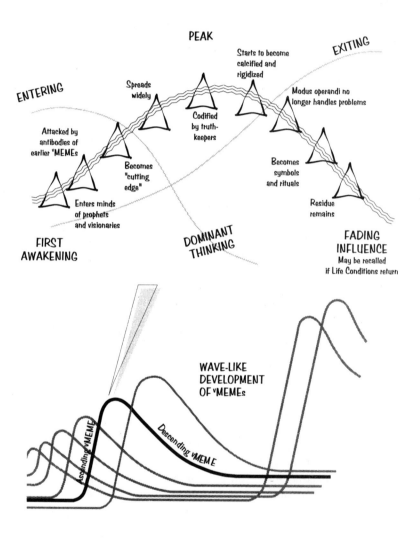

Problems outstrip its capacities. We are now on the slippery slope downward and, if we have untapped potential and available resources, getting ready for the next wave.

The Dynamic Spiral is always a process in process but without guarantees of movement or change. Graves was always careful to point out that:

> 'Neither change nor lack of change is the rule. If there is no disturbance to the dynamic tension [no matter where along the curve], no change will appear to be the rule. If there is disturbance and imbalance, then change will appear to be the rule.'

You will understand this even better when we discuss how ^{V}MEMEs change in detail in Section 2.

Principle 5: ^{V}MEMEs spiral up and down through levels of complexity

The emergence along the Spiral is from lesser to greater complexity; from the mode of living necessary at one stratum of problems to the mode of living essential for the complications of the next layer of *Life Conditions*. Survival favors those who 'fit in' to those conditions, whatever that takes, not necessarily those who are 'the fittest,' either physically, mentally, or emotionally.

This is not to say that everyone or every group within a social system rides the identical crest of emergence. In fact, many will persist in maladaptive behaviors, ill-conceived, incongruous, and destined to destroy the society's chances at survival. Robert B. Edgerton, Professor of Anthropology and Psychology at UCLA, makes that point crystal clear in his book, *Sick Societies: Challenging the Myth of Primitive Harmony*. He notes:

> 'Adaptation, then, may sometimes take place rapidly in response to environmental demands, but it need not, and often does not, lead to predictable changes in economic practices and is even less likely to do so in social organization or culture. Once again, it must be reiterated that beliefs and practices that developed in response to earlier, and presumably different, environmental pressures tend to persist, and the result may come to be far less than efficient utilization of an environment' (pp. 194–5).

Just because someone wields power gives absolutely no assurance the thinking is up to the complexity of issues ahead. Often, the reverse is true and the comic strip character Pogo was right: 'We is met the enemy and they is us.' The number of significant variables in the *Life Conditions* is not infrequently beyond the capabilities of the leadership's existing ^{V}MEME stack. Revolutions often fail to meet their leaders' promises because in the act of revolt the critical minds and resources necessary to meet expectations of 'the people' are destroyed. Until new ^{V}MEMEs are introduced or activated, things can only stagnate and, more likely, deteriorate. We will explore how to avoid this situation in Section 2.

Recognize that appropriateness of ᵛMEMEs is a matter of perspective. You will find illustrations of these 'Healthy' and 'Unhealthy' characteristics with each of the ᵛMEMEs which are described in detail in Section 3. Given the extent to which this is a judgment call based on the evaluator's own position on the Spiral, it is no wonder that churches split and splinter, that juries become deadlocked, that whole cultures rise and become extinct, and that one person's freedom fighter can be another's terrorist. Like Goldilocks' porridge, the complexity of what is 'just right' at one Spiral zone is 'too hot' someplace else, 'too cold' for another.

Although each new ᵛMEME builds on the foundation of those which came before and adds new factors of complexity, the pattern of ᵛMEMEs' emergence does not blindly follow a predetermined script in a mechanistic, step-by-step fashion. The systems which have evolved thus far are but the mind-prints of our psychological 'DNA' at work. Different segments of the human population, living on different psychological strata, will be moving simultaneously to their own different futures along the Spiral.

There is an intelligence in the awakenings, an internal logic like that within the snail's shell for why different ᵛMEME systems appear. You can begin to reason it out, but understand that one of the laws of Spiral Dynamics is that we humans do not necessarily act in a rational fashion. Much of what we do, for good or bad, to help or hinder our success in adapting to our environment, is pure happenstance. The luck-of-the-draw, trial-and-error, and hit-or-miss also characterize our life choices. However, the links across the *Life Conditions* and the ᵛMEMEs within us, like the amino acid sequence in DNA, encode the flow of the future.

Still, because our knowledge and experiences are additive, movement along the Spiral is in the direction of greater complexity. Again from Csikszentmihalyi, 'Complex skills are built up by complex activities . . . evolution is the history of the complexification of living matter' (*Evolving Self*, p. 170). In terms of Spiral Dynamics, that overall flow has four characteristics:

- *expansion of psychological space* – toward more multifaceted personalities, diverse organizational forms, and a much more complicated planet
- *expansion of conceptual space* – toward bigger picture views, wider span of influence, and extended time frames
- a *progressive increase of alternatives* – toward more choices to make from a broader menu of ways to do a thing
- a *progressive increase in degrees of behavioral freedom* – toward more possibilities in terms of how to be, ways to display emotions, acceptable kinds of human interrelationships

This process is rather like the evolution of Intel Corporation's line of computer chips from the once-astonishing 8086 through '286, '386, '486 to the '586 christened 'Pentium' in hopes of breaking set, so sand will sound more sophisticated.

Principle 6: 'MEMEs coexist within our 'onion'-like profiles

If we were to slice a transparent human Spiral from the top of the funnel down to the tip, we would see an asymmetrical, onion-like profile of 'MEMEs. Properly labeled, this form would display the relative strength of each colored layer regarding specific issues. Since 'MEMEs are types of thinking nested *in* us rather than types *of* us, and since we think about many things – religion, family, work, sports, politics – it follows that we can also host several ways of thinking which may mix-and-match to the subject areas.

'MEME Stacks - Systems in People

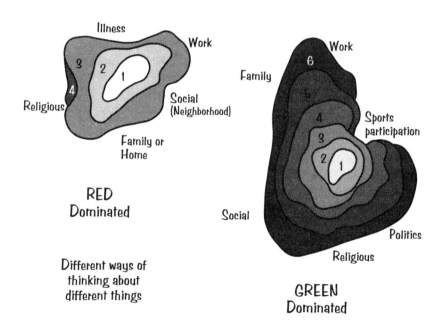

For example, these two profiles illustrate the relative strength and priority of the eight core 'MEMEs within two individuals. One is centered around the **RED** zone, the other more in the **GREEN** range. Note that the '**RED**' person thinks about religion through the **BLUE** 'MEME and how close **PURPLE** is to the surface regarding family and homelife. On the other hand, the '**GREEN**' character activates **RED** when engaged in sports and retains a strong **ORANGE** regarding business. As you go through Section 3, keep this graphic in mind and think about your own ᵛMEME onion. Ask which ones take hold, when, and why. In Section 2 we will discuss how to do that for a business group and an entire society in Section 4.

If you could look at the great 'onion' of humanity, you would quickly see that millions of people are at different levels along the Spiral simultaneously. In spite of the population bulge toward its middle, the blessings and curses of each ᵛMEME's awakening have been twisted around on a global Rubik's Cube. Television sees to it that we experience all of these systems, albeit vicariously, on the evening news. In this real-time, interactive, cellular world every human problem seems to be present on all sides. Under such twisted conditions, fresh brains as well as concentrated brawn will be necessary to straighten out the puzzle. Many of today's young people are in distress because they can see the enormity of our existence problems but have not a clue as to the solutions which lie, of course, along the Spiral.

Principle 7: ᵛMEMEs cluster in Tiers of Six along the Spiral

Thus far, it appears that ᵛMEMEs live most happily in groups of six. The six systems in the First Tier of the human odyssey were ascending steps away from our more animalistic nature and our subsistence problems. Think of them as the first stage of a rocket that blasts off with its rush of raw power. In Graves' own language from *The Futurist*:

> 'In human existence, our species begins by stating in the simplest way those themes which will preoccupy us through thousands of variations. At this point in history, the societally effective leading edge of man in the technologically advanced nations is currently finishing the initial statement of the sixth theme of existence and is beginning again wtih the first theme of an entirely new and more sophisticated variation.'

If you recall the chart on pages 50–1, in which we rather capriciously ordained 'The Leading Edge of Thinking' through history, you may have been left wondering what happened in the past 30 years. Well, now you know. It appears that something happens at this threshold which markedly elaborates our thinking and enlightens what some wistfully call 'Homo lucens,' man the enlightened. This is the human rocket's second stage burn, one that benefits from the first but now adds refinement, fine-tuning, and more precision to our trajectory. With its thrust are born the new king's horses, women, and men.

Many other thinkers have described important aspects of the First Tier and even suggested the transition. To Csikszentmihalyi's list of Maslow, Kohlberg, Loevinger, and Fowler should be added notables O. J. Harvey and Jean Piaget. With all due respect, however, to these and many other illustrious scholars, Graves' theory is the only framework we have found which puts both the entire developing flow – from survival through the socialized, actualized self rediscovering the spirit – and the impetus behind the process – the

The Emerging Spiral of ᵛMEMEs

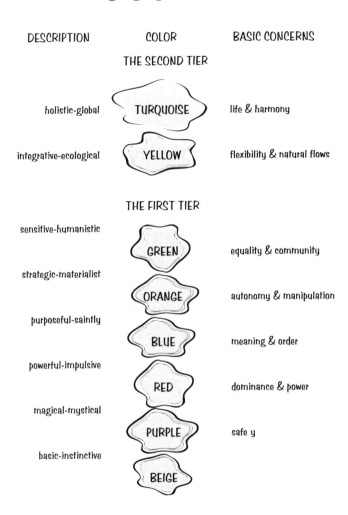

DESCRIPTION	COLOR	BASIC CONCERNS
	THE SECOND TIER	
holistic-global	TURQUOISE	life & harmony
integrative-ecological	YELLOW	flexibility & natural flows
	THE FIRST TIER	
sensitive-humanistic	GREEN	equality & community
strategic-materialist	ORANGE	autonomy & manipulation
purposeful-saintly	BLUE	meaning & order
powerful-impulsive	RED	dominance & power
magical-mystical	PURPLE	safe y
basic-instinctive	BEIGE	

– PsychoSocial "DNA"– MEMEs (passed from mind to mind)

Biological DNA-
GENES (passed from GENE pools)

- temperament-texture
- raw intelligences
- mind styles
- body shape and change
- disease potentials
- racial characteristics

Basic Biology -   impacted by environment, nutrition, experiences, and time.
Gene patterns vanish through 3rd or 4th generation.

systems-producing interaction of *Life Conditions* with 'MEMEs – into perspective. What that offers is an open-ended trajectory into the future which the average 'Joe' and 'Joan' can actually use at work tomorrow.

It is open-ended because the human Spiral is only beginning. We are presently in the midst of transition from the First Tier of six 'MEMEs onto the Second Tier of Spiral development. Clare W. Graves describes such a point of demarcation:

> 'After being hobbled by the more narrow animal-like needs, by the imperative need for sustenance [BEIGE], the fear of spirits [PURPLE] and other predatory men [RED], by the fear of trespass upon the ordained order [BLUE], by the fear of his greediness [ORANGE], and the fear of social disapproval [GREEN], suddenly human cognition is free. Now with his energies free for cognitive activation, man focuses upon his self and his world [YELLOW, TURQUOISE, etc.].'

Besides the notable dropping away of fears, other significant differences between the First and Second Tiers include a marked increase in conceptual space, dropping away of compulsion, an ability to learn a great deal from many sources, and a trend toward getting much more done with much less energy or resources.

Yet, what we find in the process, Graves warns, is not necessarily pleasant. While each ascending step along the Spiral solved some problems of existence, it created others in their place, the residues of successful living. Today many people feel exhausted from already having experienced three or four wrenching transformations during their lifetimes. Some encountered **BLUE**'s-TruthForce early on and embraced noble causes as faithful followers. But then the pragmatism of **ORANGE**'s StriveDrive shifted their focus to individual materialistic goals and fiscal games. 'Let the others sacrifice and settle for later; not *moi*,' they said. Then, as those worlds of material success began to unravel, now-frustrated Baby Boomers found themselves contemplating their aging navels through a **GREEN**-tinted crystal. 'Surely this is not all there is?' they asked. 'My, man, it's even less than you said,' replies an intelligent but angry and increasingly **RED**-dominated Generation X from all around the globe.

At the very same time that the **RED** 'MEME's egocentric dragons and **PURPLE**'s demons continue to haunt us and draw off energy from one end of the Spiral, people at the other end are also perplexed and in quest of a way of being that can include self respect and close involvement with others in a complicated world. There is much to sort out inside our hearts and minds as we contemplate the step from the First Tier toward the Second.

YELLOW, the first 'being' (rather than subsistence) level, starts off this 2nd Tier of 'MEMEs with a reprise of the six basic themes in our history – survival once again, but now in context of an information-rich, highly mobile, global village. The eighth (**TURQUOISE**) system is a repeat of the second, but an order of magnitude more complex – Mega-Tribes, Mega-Trends, and Mega-Shocks – fleshed-out by all that has happened in the 1st Tier. If this curious six-on-six aspect of the theory holds up, the ninth (**CORAL**) will be a version of the **RED** third level. That has awesome implications for geopolitics, the marketplace, and us individual human beings. Rush Dozier calls this a leap into the 'Thought Era' in that we may soon alter biological evolution through bioengineering. He concludes: 'The intelligence that enabled science to fathom the quantum code of matter and the genetic code of life is beginning to fathom the synaptic code of the mind.' (*Codes of Evolution*, Crown Publishers, New York, 1992, p. 264) And some people wonder why the Spiral becomes more complex.

A Final Note: The Matter of Labels

Graves originally labeled his Levels of Existence with pairs of letters. The first half of the alphabet (A, B, C, etc.) designated *Life Conditions* in the milieu and the second half (N, O, P, etc.) awakened capacities in the mind. Thus, the first ᵛMEME system would have the rather complicated designation A-N, then B-O, and so forth. (Graves' illustration of the development of psychosocial systems, which is shown in chapter 4, demonstrates how these designations were derived.) A few of our colleagues use numbers, although we believe that tends to 'stack the deck' since many people conclude that higher numbers must be inherently superior to lower ones. Where ᵛMEMEs are concerned, appropriateness and congruence are the key words, not placement in the hierarchy.

In the mid-1970s we made up a color-code for the ᵛMEMEs and use it for simplicity. The advantage of the colors is that it is hard to say that 'BLUE' is invariably better or worse than 'RED.' They are different; one will match better at times than another which could even clash violently. Again, here are the ᵛMEME colors and some memory aids:

1 **BEIGE** A-N (savanna grasslands),
2 **PURPLE** B-O (the royal color of tribal chiefs and monarchs),
3 **RED** C-P (hot blooded emotions and the 'fire in your eyes'),
4 **BLUE** D-Q (the sky, the heavens, and the True (blue) believer),
5 **ORANGE** E-R (radiating energy of steel in an industrial furnace),
6 **GREEN** F-S (green politics, forests, and ecological consciousness),
7 **YELLOW** G-T (solar power and alternative technologies),
8 **TURQUOISE** H-U (the color of oceans and Earth as viewed from space),
9 **CORAL** I-V (life deep within the seas).

The convention for designating Entering, Peak, and Exiting states is case-sensitive. We use the upper-case color alone – **GREEN** – for the Peak.

Because it carries elements of the previous ᵛMEME on its back, the Entering phase would be **orange/GREEN**. The Exiting phase is **GREEN/yellow** because the next more complex problems are awakening just ahead of their strong predecessor. When more than one ᵛMEME is involved – and that is usually the case – we list them in order of relative influence in the situation – **BLUE-RED** or **purple/RED-ORANGE**, for example. As you apply Spiral Dynamics, use whichever symbols work best for you.

A ᵛMEME Lexicon

ᵛMEME MALIGNANCY – A virus-like condition where a ᵛMEME grows out of control.

ᵛMEME MATES – The pairing to two (or more) ᵛMEMEs which coexist and may even synergize under particular *Life Conditions*. (A warm color individual/elite ᵛMEME often pairs with a cool communal/collectivist ᵛMEME in synergy.)

ᵛMEME MIGRATION – The pattern of ᵛMEME movement as they flow over the planet and proliferate through education, immigration and travel, economic transitions, entertainment and the mass media.

ᵛMEME SCAPE (*horizontal*) – The distribution of ᵛMEMEs over social and geographic landforms such as families, companies, communities, regions, and societies.

ᵛMEME SHIFT – When one ᵛMEME supplants another to become dominant from either higher or lower on the Spiral.

ᵛMEME STACK (*vertical*) – The specific ᵛMEMEs which are active within an individual, organization, or society, which form themselves into a hierarchy for priorities, and which are arranged in response to specific issues and circumstances.

ᵛMEME ZONE – Locales where a specific ᵛMEME(s) clearly dominates at a particular time because of specific *Life Conditions*.

SECTION 2

The Dynamics of the Spiral's 'MEMEs

This section explores the dynamics of the Spiral's 'MEMEs. It begins with the principles of 'MEME Change. Next, we meet the Spiral Wizard and start building a Tool Kit for Leadership and organization tailored to the 'MEMEs. Finally, you will learn Spiral Alignment to put systems right and Spiral Integration to make them work effectively.

4

Change and the Spiral

Former Congressperson Barbara Jordan from Texas raised the issue of change in her address before the 1992 Democratic National Convention in New York when she said, 'Yes, it is time to change. But, I ask, change from what to what?' She repeated it for effect: 'Change *from* what, *to* what!'

More than anything else, today's business and political gurus are talking about change. The interest is justified. The 1990s is an era of transitions. The word 'change' is glibly tossed around and programs to 'manage change' are everywhere, usually offered at considerable expense. Why do so many books about change end up gathering dust on the shelves of business executives and change agents? Why do so many change efforts fail despite very good intentions?

The central theme of *Spiral Dynamics* is that we are suffering from the Humpty Dumpty Effect because we are missing the key mechanisms that impact human dynamics in the first place. This is especially the case when it comes to facilitating the transformation of corporate cultures or addressing the critical issues around race, crime, education, societal imbalances, and large-scale systems in transition. In our collective defense, like Humpty Dumpty's handlers, we have all been doing the very best we know how to do.

The major challenges that confront leaders in the 1990s are the result of impasses, failures, log jams, cul-de-sacs, grid locks, and surface level solutions that stem from the behavioral, authoritarian, and systems-thinking schools of thought. Certainly there are situations where the simple manipulation of carrots and sticks can alter behavior, especially over the short term. The recent focus on a total systems perspective as represented in the work of

Wave-like Development of ᵛMEME Systems

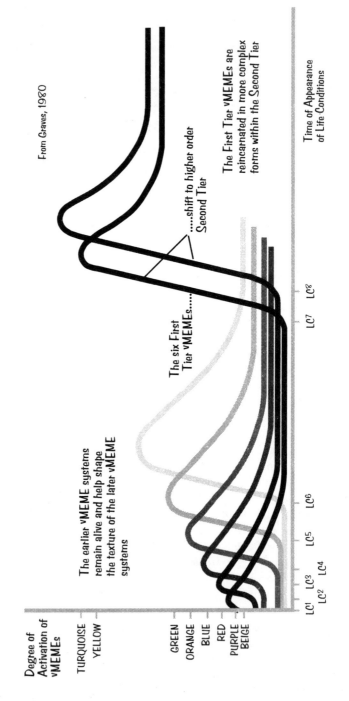

From Graves, 1980

Degree of Activation of ᵛMEMEs

The earlier ᵛMEME systems remain alive and help shape the texture of the later ᵛMEME systems

TURQUOISE
YELLOW

GREEN
ORANGE
BLUE
RED
PURPLE
BEIGE

The six First Tier ᵛMEMEs.......

.....shift to higher order Second Tier

The First Tier ᵛMEMEs are reincarnated in more complex forms within the Second Tier

LC¹ LC² LC³ LC⁴ LC⁵ LC⁶   LC⁷ LC⁸

Time of Appearance of Life Conditions

Peter Senge and the MIT group has added significantly to many organizations. Yet, all three of these approaches fail to address the deepest human dynamics that remain so hidden and elusive. They stop short of the deepest change factors, the evolutionary ᵛMEMEs.

- Concrete Actions, Behaviors, and Attachments – *Carrots and sticks might work here*
- Concepts, Systems, Beliefs and Schemes – *Programs to influence systems or beliefs might work here*
- *Core Intelligences (ᵛMEMEs)* – *Changes in* **how** *people think will naturally impact* **what** *people think and* **why** *they behave*

Scientists are exploring the possibilities of altering the arrangements of over 100,000 genes on our biological DNA. Their interest is to produce healthier bodies and lives. Our interest, here, is to describe how to influence the emergence and expression of the eight core ᵛMEMEs presently sequenced in our psychological 'DNA.' The plan is to increase your odds for the development of healthy minds, organizations, communities, and societies.

ᵛMEMEtic Strategies for Change

As ᵛMEMEs change, so do thinking and behavioral choices since the ᵛMEMEs' intelligences are at the core of both. Attempts to change how people think or what they do, while ignoring the role of ᵛMEMEs, are both naive and ineffective. If it truly matters whether thinking priorities change and certain behaviors are eliminated, altered, or modified, then one must pay attention to and deal with the underlying ᵛMEMEs of the matter.

This discussion about change will deal directly with the ᵛMEMEs through these essential questions:

1. How and under what conditions are new ᵛMEMEs awakened and placed online?
2. How can you increase or decrease the power of specific ᵛMEMEs in influencing beliefs and behaviors in a particular situation?
3. Why are some ᵛMEMEs amenable to influence while others seem to resist any attempt at change?
4. How can you recognize, understand, and in some cases influence the processes of natural ᵛMEME change and transition?
5. How do the various ᵛMEMEs on the Spiral impact on each other, especially when profound change is occurring in many of them all at the same time.

These and other change related matters can be addressed by rephrasing Barbara Jordan's basic question into the following: 'Change from what ᵛMEMEs to what ᵛMEMEs?' The practical solutions to many of our social problems and conflicts will flow from the answer. Please note this word of caution, though. Minds under the exclusive control of the **RED, BLUE, ORANGE,** or **GREEN** ᵛMEMEs may have difficulty accepting the assumptions behind this approach to change dynamics since each of the First Tier ᵛMEMEs is convinced it already has *the* answer.

That said, Spiral Dynamics is based on these perspectives regarding ᵛMEMEs:

- The SIX necessary conditions for ᵛMEME change.
- The FIVE stepping stones along the path of ᵛMEMEs in transition.
- The SEVEN variations of the degree of change.

Principles of Spiral Change

The Spiral is best viewed as a moving picture, not a snapshot (unlike so many quadrant models and personality typologies). From a Spiral Dynamics perspective, change is a given since neither *Life Conditions* nor human capacities are fixed. Alterations in either can awaken new ᵛMEMEs because they offer more explanatory power and more degrees of freedom to act in a increasingly complex *milieu*. However, as Graves always pointed out: 'Change is not the rule; lack of change is not the rule.' There are no guarantees.

Several technologies for change are active in First World cultures. The **BLUE** school relies on doctrine, mandates from authorities, and revival of traditional rules, although it sometimes resorts to **RED** force when thwarted. The behaviorist school attempts to buy change through **ORANGE** manipulation of carrots and sticks, a tactic that does not work with **YELLOW** and may trigger antibodies in **GREEN**. None of these approaches to change works for the whole Spiral. Always remember that what is appropriate and 'next' for you and your thinking will be too far out for some, too simplistic for others.

Each core ᵛMEME on the Spiral has characteristics which dictate the strategies required to subdue or soften it, check it, reframe it, or 'change its mind' and alter the contents. At **PURPLE** one finds diminishing fear, weakening bonds, and emerging ego; with **RED**, questioning of personal power and a need for structured discipline; with **BLUE**, hunger for autonomy, lack of purpose or paralyzing guilt; with **ORANGE**, a need for significance, contribution, and positive achievements; with **GREEN**, feelings of alienation from the group and internal discord; with **YELLOW**, a sense of knowing the great questions but needing coordinated action to implement answers.

Since the Spiral is a complex living system, change in one ᵛMEME alters the constellation. Lewis Thomas, famous for his contributions to *The New England Journal of Medicine*, warned in *The Fragile Species*:

> 'Making well-thought-out changes in living systems is a dangerous business. Fixing one part, on one side, is likely to produce new and worse pathological events miles away on the other. The most dangerous of all courses is to begin doing things without recognizing the existence of a system . . . '
> (p. 82)

And, when a person experiences 'change' by repairing old systems, strengthening others, or even awakening new ones, the total social atom will be disturbed. No wonder leaps forward are often preceded by desperate regressive steps backward. Many corporate training staffs forget that 'changing' people at work also impacts their home lives. Thomas is right; human systems interact precipitously.

While there is no sure correlation between ᵛMEMEs and temperament, the cool colors are generally more authoritarian; the warm colors more flexible. Rigidity is high in **BLUE** and **GREEN**. Dogmatism passes from a High in **BLUE** to its Low in **YELLOW**. Guilt surfaces in **BLUE**; disappears in **ORANGE**; resurfaces in **GREEN**; drops away again in **YELLOW**. 'Don't fence me in!' demands for freedom are the highest in **RED**; somewhat mollified into a quest for autonomy at **ORANGE**; and become unemotional individualism without isolation in **YELLOW**.

BEIGE experiences distress and delight based on biological satisfaction; **PURPLE** lives with fear and superstition; **RED** is caught up with anger and avoiding shame; **BLUE** deals with an almost perpetual guilt burden; **ORANGE** is manic in its competitive urges to win in this life; and **GREEN** carries great responsibility for others and the burden of caring so much. What emotionality there is in **YELLOW** is based in feelings about one's own performance and failures of systems to function as needed. **TURQUOISE** seems to reactivate outer-focused spirituality and Zen-like emotions based in liberation of consciousness without ceremony or groupiness. Keep these points in mind and you can avoid many of the personality-based pitfalls change presents.

The Six Conditions for ᵛMEME Change

These Six Conditions apply throughout the Spiral. Which ones are met and to what extent sets the limits for the seven Variations which complete this chapter. You should always evaluate them fully before attempting change interventions. Miss one and the odds of lasting change are slim. Skip more than one and you are spinning your wheels at best, raising the specter of serious regressions at worst. On the other hand, help an organization realize which Conditions are incomplete and how to meet them and then watch the break-throughs happen once all six are met.

Condition 1 – POTENTIAL . . .

. . . in the Individual or the Collective brain syndicate. All people are not equally open to, capable of, or prepared for change. You may know some individuals who are altogether different persons today compared with 5 or 10 years ago. But you probably know many others who talk about changing yet never quite get around to it. Every community has its crusty old souls who are perennial 'agin'-ers.' Sometimes called CAVE people (Citizens Against Virtually Everything), they have been consistently the same for decades, flag-bearers for a worldview that has worked for them and which they have never doubted.

The human normally lives in a *potentially* open system of needs, values, and aspirations. We tend, however, to settle into what appears to be a closed state wherein we operate in a consistent, enduring steady way. Once reached, we tend to stay in these zones of comfort – 'I y'am what I y'am,' quoth Popeye – unless powerful forces induce turbulence. (In his popular video series, Morris Massey calls this 'a significant emotional event.' Jim Payne of the University of Mississippi refers to 'a poke with a pointy stick' as an impetus for change. Others refer to it as 'a whop up the side of the head to get your attention,' 'a wake-up call,' or 'a tipping point.')

Even with an attention-getter, change is not assured because still-mysterious internal nervous system dynamics are also at work. We do not bring the same raw materials to the table, though no one understands why the differences or how to recognize them easily. So, before launching into a change initiative, you should first assess the capacity of the person or group to change in the intended direction. This is often the make-or-break Condition. You will have difficulty with that if your own thinking flows out of either traditional behaviorist (the brain begins as an empty vessel) or humanistic (everybody is born with the same potential) assumptions. If either is the case, beware of making the same mistake 99% of change agents do – applying the techniques of change that work on you to your clients. Step through the looking glass and try the Spiral, instead.

Estimating the Potential for Change: OAC Status
Graves' experiences in business and clinical research convinced him that people vary in terms of their change potentials along a continuum from OPEN to ARRESTED to CLOSED (OAC). Effective interventions require not only that you identify the ᵛMEME profile in a person or group, but that you also be quite sensitive to these states.

OPEN: potential for more complex level functioning
- healthiest form with most possibilities for adjustment
- history and capacities conducive to movement
- Open state thinking changes as conditions/realities change
- deals effectively with barriers
- doesn't present as sharp a picture of the level as Closed does

ARRESTED: caught by barriers in self/situation
- possibility for change only if barriers are overcome
- may lack insights that explain what is happening
- will require more dissonance be created to spark change
- makes excuses and rationalizes the *status quo*

CLOSED: blocked by biopsychosocial capacities
- may lack neurological equipment or necessary intelligences
- historic traumas may have triggered closure
- unable to recognize barriers, much less overcome them
- threatened by change and fights to stay put or else

ARRESTED
Movement to future
ᵛMEMEs is blocked
by barriers though
previous ways of
being remain
available

CLOSED
Psychological blindness
keeps the person from
seeing alternatives, either
in the past or future ways
to be

OPEN
Centralized in a ᵛMEME
system but can move freely
in any direction as shifting
Life Conditions
may require

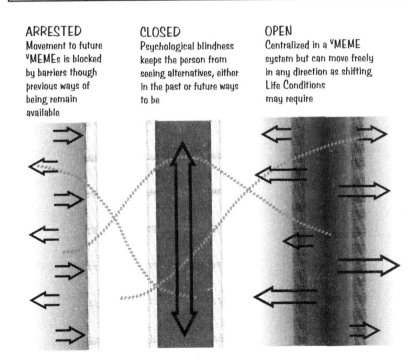

If you can discern someone's OAC status on a topic, you know the probabilities for overall ᵛMEME change, how to modify the contents of attitudes, the degree of change that is appropriate, the amount of energy it will require, and the stress it will produce. When working with attitudes and beliefs, heed the advice from Kenny Rogers in his song *The Gambler*: ' . . .[you must] know when to hold 'em and when to fold 'em and when to just walk away.' Such an educated guess is essential to mastering change and avoiding time wasted in hopeless arguments and projects doomed from the onset. Why pour good money (and time, energy and emotions) after bad?

If you can assess the OAC status of an individual or organization's ᵛMEME profile, you can predict the likelihood of movement and what would need to be done to facilitate it. The more OPEN the ᵛMEME systems, the more capable the entity will be of responding to shifts in the milieu. The more CLOSED, the greater the stress of dealing with change, the higher the resistance, and the stronger the denial that anything significant is even going on. If you push against a CLOSED system, know that you are asking for real trouble because it will push back.

The OPEN State: Readiness to Accept New Modes of Being

- OPEN thinking strives to remove barriers to allow for the expression of individual differences without getting locked into habitual patterns or unexamined assumptions.
- OPEN thinking anticipates that change is inevitable and shows considerable elasticity without always jumping on bandwagons.
- OPEN thinking acknowledges the role the external conditions play in making change easy or difficult for people.
- OPEN thinking is often displayed in the ability of a person to engage a number of Spiral sub-systems – from celebrating **PURPLE** in ethnic festivals to contemplating **TURQUOISE** on Earth Day.
- OPEN thinking is usually displayed in good listening skills, a non-judgmental approach to life, tolerance of differences, and a lack of closed-mindedness.

When in the OPEN state, we function in ways that remove restraints and allow us to step around or through the barriers to change. We work to change negative circumstances and revise conditions that are obstacles, either within the self or in the *milieu*. So long as sufficient energy is available, the healthy person changes when alterations in the *Life Conditions*, (**LCs**) demand the use of different coping means. This realigns ᵛMEMEs to congruence with circumstances. Such terms as 'rolling with the flow,' 'dealing with whatever comes down the pike,' 'keeping all my options open' or 'getting myself sorted out' suggest Openness.

When OPEN, issues are re-framed, premises revised, and entirely new givens adopted. The OPEN state should be thought of in respect to an issue, not necessarily a global style of living. One might be OPEN in business; ARRESTED in family relations; and CLOSED in thinking about religion.

The ARRESTED State: Reluctance to Rock the Boat

In the ARRESTED state one tries to live within the barriers life has imposed and come to grips with the *status quo*. As Doris Day advised musically, '*Que sera, sera. Whatever will be will be.*' The goal here is to make the most of what is and to do one's best under the circumstances, adapting to fit the **LCs** that are. The barriers may be adjusted a bit, but basic assumptions remain unaltered. Change efforts are directed to refine, polish, and work harder-and-smarter. (We will refer to these as Change of the First Variation.) While a person still has access to earlier ᵛMEMEs, there is little movement along the Spiral toward more complex systems.

Other common ARRESTED themes are: coming to peace with that which is, restoring balance to a rocky world, living with the establishment, and fitting serenely into one's niche in life. People speak of changing 'one of these days.' ARRESTEDness is common for most of us unless major alarm bells go off in our lives or we work deliberately to remain OPEN.

New **LCs** produce anxiety and uncertainty when we are ARRESTED. Some contents of our beliefs are challenged but, like a Styrofoam cup, the container will only bend so far before it cracks. Like Gorbachev and others of their generation, President Bush was ARRESTED at **blue/ORANGE** during his 1992 campaign. The steady criticism that 'he just doesn't get it' was *prima facie* evidence. When ARRESTED, we may sense difficulties but believe there is nothing for it since 'that's just the way the cookie crumbles' and 'you can't fight city hall.' That inability to adapt and change things leads to frustration, denial, anger, resentment and a leading malady of our age – 'stress.'

- ARRESTED thinking leads to attempts to live within life's barriers and adjusts to them the best way possible.
- ARRESTED thinking is evidenced in undue stress, gastro-intestinal disorders, passive-aggressive behaviors, and other forms of personal and social frustration.
- ARRESTED thinkers reject transformational models of change focusing instead on fixer-uppers within the tried-and-true.

The CLOSED State: This Is All There Is

In the OPEN state it is possible to entertain thinking from new ᵛMEMEs on-the-rise and access previous systems when appropriate. The OPEN Spiral is like a computer-monitored automatic transmission. ARRESTED is like a standard shift; we have fixed speeds to adjust to conditions as they are, but not to make them different. CLOSED is on or off; the thinking lacks the flexibility even to envision alternatives and instead locks-up, hunkers-down, and tries to make the world fit what it can do according to the values and beliefs it defends.

CLOSED state thinkers often exhibit a core ᵛMEME at its peak, shutting the door to both past and future ᵛMEMEs on the rest of the Spiral. Frenzied zealots, political extremists, workaholics, bleeding-heart social workers, and hard core criminals are typically CLOSED. Alternative perspectives are rejected, even cursed and demonized. 'My way is the only way a rational person could think,' they believe. Those standing elsewhere on the Spiral are seen as heretics, idiots, renegades, criminals or fools.

If pushed too far on the CLOSED issue, these individuals may have breakdowns, show panic and manic behaviors, fits of rage, violence, suicide, severe depression, or psychotic incidents. Theirs is a tight little world which, given enough time, tends to collapse unless enabled and supported by others who share the pathology. If you must share a common roof, beware the falling timbers.

CLOSEDness can spring from two sources – the outside **LCs** which activate the ᵛMEMEs or one's genes and 'wiring' within. Thus far, there is no sure way to tell which dynamic triggers the CLOSED condition. If it is from the **LCs** and situational, the CLOSEDness may be alterable. The person might be captive of a lifetime's experiences and only able to escape once seared-in memories have been processed and unhealthy instructions counter-manded in therapy. Such a person may open up once the world seems different.

If the CLOSEDness is within the person's biologic structure, it may well be unalterable. The person may have a limited palette, restricted to certain ᵛMEMEs because of biological damage or developmental deficiency. If the neurological equipment necessary for certain complex modes of thinking is simply not accessible, the person will be CLOSED. Until more is discovered about how brains and minds function, there is not much to be done.

In organizations, the collective brain syndicate may be deficient. This is often the case in executive suites where senior managers (or union leaders) have simply cloned themselves with associates who see the world just as they do. Until 'fresh blood' (access to new ᵛMEMEs and the alternative ideas they attract) is introduced, the capacity to do things differently may simply not exist and efforts to implement change will be wasted or downright destructive.

Signs of CLOSED thinking are:

- INAPPROPRIATENESS – lack of adaptability to a changing milieu;

every idea is washed in the same color, regardless. Laughter, anger, conversational topics are out of context. Behavior appears awkward and contrived.

- INSATIABILITY – There is never enough. The person's urges are never satisfied. The CLOSED individual always needs more and makes incessant demands: 'Do you love me?' But there are never enough 'Yes, I love you.' There is always doubt. 'Tell me again; I don't believe you.'
- EXCLUSIVITY – There is no other position, no other way to be. Any other view is rejected out of hand. Only a few people are in the inner-circle; everybody else, even those slightly removed, are in the 'them' group.
- UNDUE RESPONSE TO FRUSTRATION – Reactions to barriers or being blocked are extreme, far beyond what is called for in the situation. Flies off-the-handle at even minor difficulties. When stressed, the CLOSED person becomes irritable quickly. One may even faint, become physically ill, or appear traumatized. You should anticipate sudden or extreme reactions to unexpected stimuli (blowups).
- FULFILLS TASKS TO EXTREMES – A perfectionist; compulsive. A person who constantly checks and rechecks to be certain it is 'right,' 'in line with,' or 'true to form.'
- BUILDS A SHELL – Avoids exposure to other positions or views. Hides or destroys information that runs counter to one's own position. Demands censorship and thought control. 'Don't confuse me with the facts, my mind is already made up.'

To summarize Condition 1, the mind/brain must have the potential for further development and expansion of conceptual space. That includes OPENness (or at least alterable ARRESTEDness) and the necessary intelligences to handle the new LCs. No matter how often you attempt to jump-start change along the Spiral, it cannot happen unless the necessary raw material is present. For example, Stalin's purges made free-market 'democracy' difficult for generations of Russians who still waffle between hard-nosed controls and entrepreneurism. Significant corporate change usually requires new minds at the top, not just training and development interventions. And most human beings do seem blessed with 'talents' – latent capacities that can be stimulated, but we do not have the same ones.

So, the stipulations for meeting Condition 1 are:

- The thinking is not CLOSED, but is OPEN or at least ARRESTED. The person or group has not reached the limit of available capacities, whatever the reasons for that ceiling may be.
- The requisite intelligences are present to deal in the more complex *milieu*. These may be within the individual or the cumulative knowledge/skill base of the social system. Howard Gardner's Theory of Multiple

Intelligences includes seven which should certainly be considered for Spiral Potential and to which we will refer again later.

- The person, organization, or society is free from restrictive pathologies, unresolved 'sink-holes,' and historical baggage.

Condition 2 – SOLUTIONS . . .

. . . for Current (and Previous) Existence Problems. Do not expect change into new levels if serious, unresolved problems or threats still exist within the present state. Sensible people put first things first by concentrating on issues appropriate to their current level of existence. If you raise the threat of 'Huns at the gates' with the expectation that more complex thinking will emerge, do not be surprised if the walls go up instead and the person or group retreats into a psychological fortress of denial. If you resurrect even older *Life Conditions* and reawaken the ᵛMEMEs calibrated to resolve those archaic problems, growth up the Spiral is unlikely and a regression may be the result.

Instead of threats, satiate the ᵛMEMEs that are active. Read the problems and solve them at the present level. If stability is the key issue, bring order. If Black Market corruption is rampant, flood the market with merchandise. If fear is draining productivity, deliver the bad news quickly and then make things safe. To satisfy Condition 1, be certain that:

- Problems of the ᵛMEMEs at the current Spiral level are being adequately managed.
- A zone of comfort has been reached and relative balance achieved.
- Excess energy is available to explore the next more complex system.

Condition 3 – DISSONANCE . . .

. . . is present within the current ᵛMEME system. Change does not occur unless the boat rocks. The turbulence is produced by movement of its conceptual cargo or by waves generated elsewhere which impact on the heretofore steady-state system. Relationship problems get individuals' attention. Unexpected feedback from corporate attitude surveys shake up executive suites. Drops in sales, lower productivity, and quality declines get the attention of manufacturers. Escalations in crime, broken homes, divided churches, and frustration with the political status quo prod communities.

Often, the task of consultants, counselors, and parents is to inject dissonance so people 'get off their backsides' and act before things get really bad. If you know Meredith Wilson's *The Music Man* you recall how Professor Harold Hill shook River City, Iowa, with his song announcing that 'You've got trouble, right here in River City . . . '. Like many too clever (**ORANGE**) consultants, his solution was the one he alone could provide – namely, a

(BLUE) boys' band with instruments and uniforms to get the at-risk youth out of (RED) P-O-O-L halls.

What factors produce the sensation of dissonance?

- Awareness of the growing gap between *Life Conditions* and current means for handling those problems.
- Enough turbulence to create a sense that 'something is wrong' without so much chaos that the whole world seems to be coming apart.
- Abject failure of old solutions to solve the problems of new *Life Conditions* may stimulate fresh thinking, release energy, and liberate the next ᵛMEME(s) along the Spiral.

Condition 4 – INSIGHT . . .

. . . into probable causes and viable alternatives. By 'insight' we mean there is an understanding of (1) what went wrong with the previous system and why, as well as (2) what resources are now available for handling the problems better. Until people have a rationale for understanding why the prior system was embraced initially and why it was eventually undermined, lasting change into the next order is fitful. Insight keeps the old problems in focus and clarifies the new ones. Meeting this condition is central to taking the next steps in addressing the volatile race/ethnicity issue in the United States, South Africa, Europe, and elsewhere. Few 'leaders' possess Spiral Insight because most are still focused on superficial types of people instead of the thinking systems within.

Different patterns and models, as well as step-by-step processes for implementing them, are essential to moving into a new system. These alternative scenarios must be active in the collective consciousness before they can be considered. Too often, they are guarded in the minds of an elite few 'planners' or 'decision makers.' People need mental pictures of what things might be like for them in their own real *Life Conditions*, not for some distant Hollywood stars or textbook case-studies.

Some ways to initiate change in patterns and models include:

- Greater insight into how systems form, decline, and reform – particularly one's own. People must accept the possibility of change as well as the means.
- Put a stop to wasteful regressive searches into out-moded answers from the past which simply cannot address greater complexity of the present.
- Consider optional scenarios, fresh models, and experiences from applicable sources. Scout the competition and demonstrate concretely what alternatives look like.
- Quickly recognize the appearance of new *Life Conditions* and the ᵛMEMEs required to shift into congruence. Custom tailor for best fit.

Condition 5 – BARRIERS . . .

. . . to Change *Identified* and *Overcome*. Barriers can make change difficult, if not impossible. They must be recognized (no more denial) and identified concretely (name names), and then (a) eliminated, (b) bypassed, (c) neutralized, or (d) reframed into something else. These barriers are first identified as part of the external field and the *Life Conditions*, then later purged from the mindset of the person or group.

In step one, the recognition phase, barriers are usually seen to be external. 'It's their fault!' 'We are oppressed and they will pay!' 'If it were not for you (management, spouse, children), I could be a real person!' 'The bloody establishment holds us down.' As the barriers are identified concretely in step two, the reasons they are effective obstacles show up in one's self as well as the external environment. The greatest barriers are often those of our own making which exist because, like the Krel monster in the classic film *Forbidden Planet*, our thoughts bring them to life and our anger only makes them stronger. Many prominent African Americans have recently begun to discuss purging these mind monsters, just as the reunited Germans have started an introspective quest into alienation in their culture.

- The barriers, either historic or current, must be identified and targeted. Clean up both the world outside and the world inside.
- Risks, consequences, and the pain of barrier removal must be calculated. Bridges may need to be burned to replace *for-worse* with *for-better* relationships. Energy should not be wasted on suicidal assaults on barricades or ill-fated attempts to regain the mythical 'glorious days of yesteryear.'
- Excuses and rationalizations for not implementing change should be exposed. Then full-court press strategies and tactics are employed in undermining and removing barriers. Be sure there is again a solid foundation before starting to rebuild.

Condition 6 – CONSOLIDATION . . .

. . . and *Support* during the transition. As in the Parable of the Sower, the seeds of change often fall on thin or hostile soil, infested with weeds and difficulties. Lacking a supportive culture, the new ᵛMEMEs barely germinate, much less bloom. Even when they do, new awakenings are usually characterized by high-energy but also high-*klutziness*. Exciting discoveries have not yet become mature expressions and so appear half-baked and clumsy. It takes a while for the new systems to blend into the profile. This period of adjustment is volatile and takes some shaking-out. After all, the individual brain is reconnecting itself and the corporate brain syndicate is making new acquaintances.

When significant change occurs, you can expect a period of confusion, false starts, long learning curves, and awkward assimilation. Those who change – either as individuals or organizations – may be punished by those who do not understand what is happening and now find themselves left out, misaligned and threatened. Old barriers may be rebuilt in the form of punitive rules, turf battles, and power tests. New obstacles might be set up. Sometimes, you will have to go around, let the bridge burn and not look back.

When all of the Six Conditions are met, new 'MEMEs *may* awaken and movement along the Spiral *may* occur. (There are other Variations on change within systems even if all Six are not met.) Consider the Six as you observe everything from national politics to discussions of global ecology to schisms within religious movements. The Spiral principles are the same. To summarize:

```
1  POTENTIAL in the mind/brain
2  SOLUTIONS to current problems
3  DISSONANCE and uncertainty
4  INSIGHT and alternatives
5  BARRIERS identified and resolved
6  CONSOLIDATION and support
```

The Five Steps in the Pathway of 'MEME Change

Again, to Barbara Jordan's question – 'from what, to what?' you must establish where you are before setting course for where you want to be. It is crucial to assess where the individual, the organization and/or its components lie with regard to the five landmarks along the Pathway of Change. Graves assigned Greek letters to the five phases: ALPHA, BETA, GAMMA, DELTA, and New ALPHA. The ALPHA step is stable and balanced; BETA is a time of uncertainty and questioning; GAMMA is full of anger and confusion; DELTA is inspired enthusiasm; and Next ALPHA is stability in the next system(s) up or even down the Spiral. The simple graphic that follows explains the five stepping stones in the path.

Since the Spiral is about ways of thinking about things, not types of people, you can stand in several places on the pathway at once. You might be at ALPHA in regard to a twenty-year marriage, trapped at desperate GAMMA on the job, a lost soul wandering around BETA at church, and be living in a town that is experiencing a DELTA of growth and renewed sense of community. Someone else's existence might concentrate around just one of the landmarks concerning practically everything, a life dealing with the unique conditions at that junction in the change pathway.

Stages of Vertical Change
variations 5, 6, and 7

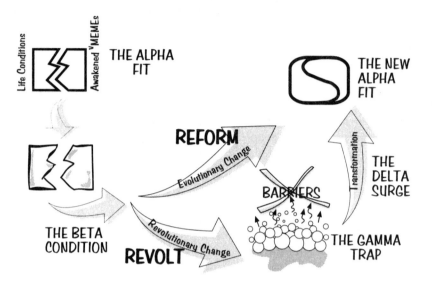

Phase 1: The ALPHA Fit

ALPHA is a place where individual, organizational, or cultural ᵛMEME systems are in sync with and relatively successful at addressing the *Life Conditions*. Think of ALPHA as a state of dynamic tension, much like pre-stressed concrete structures. The controlled pulls stabilize the form and gives it strength. Since the *Life Conditions* along the Spiral describe different levels of complexity, the ᵛMEME must match those colors. When they do, there is ALPHA balance and stability.

- An individual 'has it together' in his or her personal world and believes it will be relatively smooth sailing for awhile.
- The company is doing well in its 'niche' in terms of the primary indices – market share, return on investment, worker satisfaction, etc.
- The society is meeting the needs of its citizens as challenges and opportunities are matched by resources and people.
- Human systems are in a state of equilibrium, homeostasis, and integration. In a symbolic sense, 'God's in His heaven and all's right with the world.'

Leaving the ALPHA Phase for BETA and GAMMA: ALPHA is often illusory. What appears stable is not; what seems at rest is in motion just beneath the surface. BETA and GAMMA represent conditions of instability, turbulence, and chaos. Since change is inherent within the nature of things, two developments challenge ALPHA's stability. First, the external world itself changes in response to natural phenomena (climate, pestilence, plagues, earthquakes, etc.) and human-engineered events (wars, economic fluctuations, improved health care, social unrest, environmental alterations, etc.). Second, meeting the needs of people at the ALPHA stage may well awaken or imbalance other *Life Condition*–'MEME system links, thus upsetting the ALPHA calm. The act of successful living introduces new and unforeseen elements. Sometimes boredom sets in once the mountain has been conquered and there is no apparent frontier. Even a football team with two Super Bowl wins can lose the hunger for the three-peat. ALPHA States are both temporary and transitory even though to many they give an illusion of stability, of permanence. Solutions sow the seeds of next-order Problems.

Phase 2: The BETA Condition

A Time of Uncertainty, Questioning, and Frustration. BETA is a place of doubts. Something is wrong, but what is it? The older ways of living no longer quite work. A person's world begins to come unglued. A marriage shows evidence of stress and strain; the family becomes dysfunctional. A company begins to lose key people, productivity drops, or other signs of deterioration appear without clear reasons. A service club loses membership or falls prey to factional turf battles and divisive empire building. A once-healthy community experiences political scandals and racial stress as the crime rate mounts and citizen morale suffers.

- In the **BEIGE** world, the habitat can no longer support the bands as food becomes more difficult to find.
- In the **PURPLE** world, the offerings and rituals fail to fend off the evil spirits as the tribal order begins to collapse.
- In the **RED** world the have/have-not contract begins to erode as the powerful haves are 'weighed in the balance and found wanting.'
- In the **BLUE** world the Truth no longer guarantees order and the future as doubt, skepticism, and new options appear.
- In the **ORANGE** world, 'the good life' is frayed and tarnished by consumptiveness as the search for inner peace flourishes.
- In the **GREEN** world, warm, human aspirations wear thin as the realities of complex societal problems and limited resources are laid bare.
- In the **YELLOW** world, the reliance on individual choices and freedom fails to provide the cooperative action necessary for overall survival.

BETA problems are better felt than told. We experience the frustration and the discomfort in our hearts more than our minds. Things feel shaky. We sense the turmoil but cannot get a handle on the causes. We know something is amiss. We can see it, touch it, taste it, and smell it but not explain it. And we can't explain why we cannot. Graves reported the onset of neurotic systems at this stage – changes in eating habits, alcoholism and other addictions, and mindless rituals with more form than substance. And how do we typically respond to BETA symptoms?

As we first leave ALPHA for BETA, we try 'more of the same' in the naive belief that there is nothing wrong with existing ALPHA systems. We 'focus,' 'rededicate our lives,' purge 'negativity,' or get people to work 'harder and smarter.' We put more resources into the ALPHA systems, train people to implement those systems more effectively, or nail down the rules and run a tighter ship. We have failed to recognize that aspects of the *Life Conditions* ALPHA was handling have changed, making the operating systems incongruent or irrelevant. In fact, as we sharpen the edge of the ALPHA systems, we generally make things worse, not better. Frequently, this accelerates movement into deeper BETA and that may not be a bad thing.

- When parents overly constrain their children at the first signs of independence just to maintain parental control (and ALPHA stability), they may transform the child's anger into rebelliousness, endangering future relationships.
- When the South African police and military establishment imposed draconian control measures in the Black townships in the 1980s, they simply poured petrol on the fires, actually escalating both the internal and external pressures that led to profound change.
- When a company attempts to retain key people by simply enhancing the financial rewards and perks (**ORANGE**), they may be repeating the very behavior that motivated those employees to search for working relationships elsewhere where trust and imtimacy are more highly valued (more **GREEN**).

On first reaching BETA we look around for ways to reform, fine-tune, or adjust the ALPHA systems while keeping their main features. Continuous improvement is the watchword. Think like an airplane. Rather than just trimming the tabs to restore balance in flight, we might upgrade our flap assemblies and overhaul our piston engines, firmly believing we are still living within the same ALPHA *Life Conditions*. If that is so, things will get better. However, if we are actually struggling with altogether different circumstances, then forcing our best 1950s' DC-3 solutions onto 1990s' jet-powered Problems only makes things worse.

In BETA we may experience a nostalgia for the good old days when everything seemed to work. Recently the music of the 1950s and 60s has returned, as well as dress styles and other cultural expressions. We forget that we rejected the Old ALPHA systems formed back then, along with bongo drums, huge chrome tail fins, and *in loco parentis* control of everything by middle-aged white males. 'Gimme that ol' time religion' sounds hauntingly comfortable until we face the realities of new Problems that *Ozzie and Harriet* never confronted and a lifespace far from the world of *Lassie*.

Phase 3: The GAMMA Trap

A State of Anger, Hopelessness, and Revolution. If things get bad enough, the entity moves from BETA on down toward GAMMA. Here one is trapped by barriers that seem insurmountable. The denial and foggy thinking of BETA give way to stark reality. There is now a clear vision of how bad things are. Whether the perception is accurate or not, it produces a very real sense of knowing what went wrong and why.

Before the Trap, the Reform Option. The trip to full-fledged GAMMA is not inevitable. Often at this juncture the *Reform Option* is still ahead and offers a detour around the Trap for those quick enough to take it. If most of the Six Conditions are being met and the rest are nearly so, individuals can take charge of their lives and bypass the depths of GAMMA. Companies can recognize the dangers looming ahead and do something before collapse. Whole societies can turn things around before infrastructures become irreparable and the fabric of civilization frays beyond mending. Locating the Reform Option usually requires that someone flag us down and point it out. Actually taking the Reform road demands a willingness to pro-act rather than react, a sincere commitment to take some risks, and the energy to turn away from a slippery path and head cross-country. (We will revisit the Reform Option shortly in Change of the 6th Variation.) Most people wait to see for themselves that the next bridge is out, and then it is too late because they are in the GAMMA Trap.

Deep GAMMA is a difficult time because part of the perception is a near-total lack of power to do anything about it. Often, the accessible ^{v}MEME system is itself the barrier. The person knows too much for his or her own good. Like the American doughboys in World War I, 'how're you gonna keep 'em down on the farm after they've seen Paree?'

The emotions of frustration and confusion at BETA give way to deep anger and hostility in GAMMA. Even the past does not fit anymore. Imagine the feelings of being locked in the trunk of an automobile, unable to get free. No one can hear your desperate pleas for help. No more breathing space. Can you sense the panic, the fear? You are living on an emotional roller coaster. There are frantic attempts to break out, to find a simple moment of peace in a chaotic and tumbling world. The patience in BETA to 'wait and see' or 'hope things will work out OK' is supplanted by impatient demands for action, and action now. There is nothing left to lose.

Once systems move into the GAMMA phase, without realizing it they have turned away from the old ALPHA ways for good. There is no turning back to how it used to be, yet there is no place to go. Such is the GAMMA Trap. One can detect it in individuals who are down-Spiraling, anxiously searching for the trail to Nirvana. Organizations and entire societies can, likewise, find themselves in a free fall, not knowing whether they will survive beyond tomorrow or not. At every turn they feel blocked. The BETA options no longer exist. The trunk has been slammed shut.

All available energy goes to existing one day at a time. Nightfall brings moments of reflection and despair. Daybreak only awakens primordial survival instincts – flee or fight. But, what good is it for the moth to dart into the open flame? What is the use? Forget the future. To hell with the past. Other people will have to look after themselves. The pain penetrates into the depth of the soul. The wolf is at the door. If you have lived life in harm's way, you have been there. If you listen to the mournful tones in country and western music, the angry guitars in Grunge, or can hear the hopeful pain in the Blues, you understand the GAMMA Trap. If you are lucky, you do not have to spend a long time caught in its emotional doldrums; the winds of change carry you on. If unfortunate, the GAMMA Trap can become a lifestyle.

Confronting GAMMA Barriers: GAMMA produces an assault on the barriers (Condition 5). The barriers come in all shapes, sizes, and intensity levels. Whether they are 'real' or 'imaginary' makes little difference; one's actions will logically flow from those perceptions. Some walls exist outside of us such as the lack of access to education; limited job opportunities; racial, gender, ethnic, or nationalistic boundaries; relationship or marriage traps; and authoritarian, despotic control structures. Alternatively internal blockages such as unresolved psychological wounds and grudges, even connected to child rearing experiences; personal doubts, low self-concepts and lack of personal power; guilt from past failings and betrayals; and our finite talents and intelligences all form boundaries. GAMMA is a time of wanting to escape, run away, break-out, and be free of the bonds that entrap us. Watch how a friend goes through a mid-life crisis or struggles through a divorce and you can often sense the erratic nature of GAMMA.

When confronted with powerful and pervasive barriers, each of the Spiral's ᵛMEMEs will respond in particular ways. Because GAMMA is rarely much fun, anticipate the dark side or unhealthy expression of the system during the rapid down-shift:

- When **BEIGE** confronts the barriers, it will curl up in a fetal position and die. San Bushmen who are imprisoned by the police are often dead in the morning.
- When **PURPLE** confronts the barriers, it will descend into a fearful, superstitious existence, totally surrounding the self with altars, rituals, and omens. The shaman and chieftain are empowered against the gods.

- When **RED** confronts the barriers it will go (a) 'damn the torpedoes; full speed ahead' or (b) fight tooth and nail and take no prisoners. Get down and dirty.
- When **BLUE** confronts the barriers, it will sink into a righteous crusade, sponsor inquisitions and witch-hunts, and demonize the enemy while deifying the true patriots.
- When **ORANGE** confronts the barriers it will engage in sleazy and shady deals, blackmail and bribery, and other under-the-table tactics. Whatever it takes to win.
- When **GREEN** confronts the barriers, it will descend into a rigid, holier-than-thou, politically correct stance, arrogantly questioning everybody else's motives.
- When **YELLOW** confronts the barriers, it will evaluate the scene and depart or not after analysis of whether the cards are stacked against positive actions.

If the barriers are profound enough, you will see full-scale retrenchment into the previous level down the Spiral. **BLUE** shifts toward **RED**, **RED** toward **PURPLE**, **GREEN** toward **ORANGE**. These regressions are difficult at best. The GAMMA Trap spawns psychopathic rather than neurotic behaviors, ranging from forms of self-destructiveness (wild-and-crazy acting out and even suicide) to morbid anti-social acts (crime, vicious personal attacks, homicide, and terrorism.) Riots break out, post offices are shot-up, and airplanes are bombed from within the GAMMA Trap.

Phase 4: The DELTA Surge

When the GAMMA Trap is finally unsprung the restrictive walls are breached, the constraints released, and the DELTA Surge is ignited. This is a yeasty time, a period of excitement and rapid change where the barriers are overcome and previous restraints drop away. People prepare to take charge of their own destinies. The past no longer controls the present. The DELTA energy rush is often raw, enthusiastic, and indelicate. 'Eureka!', 'Ah, ha!' and 'At last!' are heard everywhere as the thrill of liberation mobilizes people in search of the new Utopia, the glorious New ALPHA ahead.

The DELTA Surge is full of dangers, however. The grass may look greener on the other side but, after crossing the divide, one often discovers it was made so by spray paint. Only when the cheering stops does reality creep back in, and that sometimes leads to a shift back toward GAMMA. The victory over the deadly obstacles may be illusory, a set-up. The keepers of the orthodoxy may want you to think you have escaped; once you celebrate and expose yourself, you look up only to realize you have been manipulaated. The barriers are still standing, just repainted to look different.

Breaking free of the GAMMA barriers is not the same thing as reaching the

New ALPHA. Getting rid of what you do not like (the hated barriers) does not mean you have captured what you want. Sometime celebrations are premature. Often people break free from one tyrant only to become the captive of a bigger one. This first-stage DELTA rocket of change is raw power and lacks the sophisticated technology to insert the payload accurately into orbit. Highly emotional revolutionary elements may become so preoccupied with the barriers they turn the rocket back on themselves as a final coup. They haul down the statues of the previous order. They seek out the intelligentsia and take them to the guillotine or gallows. They send the engineers packing. They discredit everything from the past, even the founders of the revolution in the belief that the magical phoenix can (and will) rise from the ashes of the previous system. Often they get a vulture instead, and the trains do not even run, much less on time.

Phase 5: The New ALPHA

The New ALPHA reflects the consolidation of the ideas and insights from BETA and GAMMA through the DELTA Surge. The Change Variations that stream from the BETA Condition are softer and more pliable than the hard, anger-driven upsurges out of the GAMMA Trap. The individual returns to a steady state as the world is once again in sync. The organization is congruent with its marketplace or professional niche. Society itself appears to be in stride with its environment. Balance is restored between *conditions- without* and ᵛMEME *systems-within*. Many come to believe the ultimate has been reached; the world will stay thus forever. Of course, just over the horizon, around the bend, or up the road lies the next BETA Condition.

Seven Variations on the Theme of Change

The word 'change' signifies too many different things to too many different people for it to have any specific meaning for anyone. Everyone assumes others understand what *they* mean when the word is used. Based on such erroneous assumptions leaders may unknowingly apply a perfectly valid CHANGE SOLUTION, except to the wrong CHANGE PROBLEM.

These approaches to change fall along an arc which extends from two HORIZONTAL Variations in which the Spiral itself remains stable; through the two OBLIQUE Variations where there is some inter-ᵛMEME turbulence; then to the three VERTICAL Variations where there are shifts from ᵛMEME to ᵛMEME. Summarizing the seven variations of change:

The 7 VARIATIONS	CHARACTERISTICS
7th Quantum Vertical	Useful when there is movement in a number of 'MEMEs at the same time. Integral to successful nation-building, community integration, and functioning in a global marketplace. Seen in era-shifts like the Industrial Revolution or Information Age.
6th UP-Shift Vertical	Describes the shift in the critical mass from one 'MEME level to the next on the Spiral. Key concept is EVOLUTION as a new layer is added. Seen in the DELTA Surge.
5th Break-OUT Vertical	Describes an assault on the GAMMA-like barriers. Characterizes REVOLUTIONS, but is useful whenever something needs to be blown away and reformed anew. Risk of regressions.
4th Stretch-UP Oblique	Dominant thinking stays in original 'MEME position but incorporates elements of some more complex 'MEMEs. Useful from BETA to avoid the GAMMA Trap and when potential is limited.
3rd Stretch-DOWN Oblique	Stay in base 'MEME position while reawakening earlier 'MEME systems on a temporary basis in an attempt to deal with a pressing situation. A frequent first response from BETA conditions.
2nd Expand-OUT Horizontal	Elaborate basic 'MEME system to include more contents and flesh out its repertoire. Form of enrichment, enhancement, and development. Useful in early BETA and ALPHA Fit.
1st Fine-TUNE Horizontal	Adjustment of an existing 'MEME system within the ALPHA fit to keep it in sync and running smoothly. Thinking and assumptions remain essentially the same, but techniques and information improve.

Change of the 1st Variation – 'Fine-TUNE' for Horizontal Change

The basic system of big ᵛMEMEs is unchanged, but particular contents are fine-tuned and even replaced. Change efforts aim to restore balance and harmony, to adjust, and to improve within the givens. Organizations shuffle titles and try to work more efficiently – 'harder and smarter.' Motivational seminars, 'hot' new books, and training interventions to introduce fresh paradigms are popular when Horizontal change is underway. Sometimes, this sort of stirring-up is all that is required to enliven a troubled system. It is all that is possible when the dominant ᵛMEMEs are Closed or tightly Arrested.

So, for many people, this first Horizontal Variation is the practical limit. Yet business seldom honors it. One of the contemporary **ORANGE** pathologies is the belief that movement UP is the only important shift, either higher in the organization or along the Spiral. Sideways development – doing the current job better – is only to be expected (within the **ORANGE/ blue** work ethic) and therefore no big deal. Winners are supposed to aspire to more power, transfer up the organization, or extend the span of control. Heaven help those who are happy as they are.

Variation 1 'Fine-Tune'			
	NO	*SOME*	*YES*
1 Potential	x		
2 Problems solved		x	
3 Dissonance		x	
4 Insights	x		
5 Barriers found	x		
6 Consolidation	x		

Change of the 2nd Variation – 'Expand-OUT' for Horizontal Development

The second horizontal Variation of Change involves enhancement and elaboration of the existing ᵛMEME system. Expand-OUT Change adds to content, increases skills, or broadens a knowledge base. It may involve modifications of ideas, attitudes and beliefs, although the core framework (the big ᵛMEMEs) is unchanged. This is the frequent outcome of training where people learn more about what they are doing, move toward mastery of a subject, or improve the operation of a system. This is like the evolution of Microsoft's DOS through many interactions – 1.1, 2,0, 3.3, 5, then 6.22. The changes within DOS have been Variation 2 steady improvements and enhancements. (Bill Gates offered Vertical change with Windows 95.)

Organizations frequently convince themselves they are involved in dramatic, fundamental Vertical change when they boldly begin strategic planning or quality initiatives. At the end of the process many come to discover that they were actually in Variation 2. The activity may have changed corporate

Variation 2 – 'Expand-OUT'			
	NO	SOME	YES
1 Potential	x		
2 Problems solved		x	
3 Dissonance		x	
4 Insights		x	
5 Barriers found	x		
6 Consolidation	x		

vocabulary, but it never reached the company's 'MEMEs. Horizontal enhancement of the givens and some nifty new *Vision-Mission-Goals* statements is about all they have accomplished. Unless untapped Potential is available and located, the Barriers are dealt with, and a supportive framework for Consolidation of the new system is in place, Expand-OUT will be the limit, though it may also be enough.

Ways to Adjust the Content of Each 'MEME   Change of the 2nd Variation may be exactly what the person or organization needs. It is frequently the objective of marketing and public relations efforts. If adjustment of contents is your objective, here are some approaches:

COMMUNAL/COLLECTIVE – In the Sacrifice-self, Outside-Control Cool-Colored zones . . .
PURPLE – 'Sacrifice now to the ways of the ancestors'

- word of elders (or opinion leading relatives) conforming to traditional, ancestral ways
- ritualized and ceremonial announcements from shaman, elders, chieftains of new views
- messages from the spirit realm – signs, omens, and spells

BLUE – 'Sacrifice self now for reward to come later'

- pronouncements from proper kind of higher authority (It must be the right authority, though; i.e., a respected Catholic for a Catholic, a Rabbi for an Orthodox Jew, a ranking 'sworn officer' for a cop, a fellow extremist for a radical. In **BLUE**, only certain people possess authority; others are discounted or *contrasted* from moderate positions over to the non-believer enemy camp.)
- documented instructions delivered in a timely fashion through the chain-of-command or as citations in the 'holy' book(s)

GREEN – 'Sacrifice now for rewards now for self and others'

- pressure from the valued reference group's consensual opinion and/or persuasion by significant other(s) within that circular community (Change is derived from peer authority. The community threatens rejection of those who are not 'team players.' Valued members pass judgment on which information to use, which to ignore.)

- benefits accrue to serve interests of one's own collective instead of niche rivals

TURQUOISE – 'Sacrifice self so that all life, not just my life, endures'

- sensation from own instincts and intuitions plus any other information sources
- perceived threats to survival of large-scale natural systems
- the long-range health of the Spiral (in an individual, organization, or society)

INDIVIDUAL/ELITE – In the Express-self, Inside-Control, Warm-Colored zones . . .
RED – 'Express self impulsively (as self desires) without shame or guilt'

- perceived immediate benefits for 'me' to look good, feel good, gain face, get what 'I' want
- sense of advantage and increased power to control others and dominate situations
- repetition under pressure with meaningful, tangible prizes as reinforcement
- coercion and offers one cannot refuse without fear of pain or even death

ORANGE – 'Express self calculatedly with little shame or guilt'

- new information procured by one's own right-thinking mind or through one's own direct experience (There must be a sense that ideas are self-procured and of the person's own discovery if they are to be accepted. Facts are facts only when supported by personal observations. New ideas are only useful if by their creation, at their own initiative. **ORANGE** scoffs at 'higher' authority and disregards others' views, so clever others simply convince them that alternatives are their own original thoughts.)
- research data and 'scientific' facts derived from prestigious sources one has hired (especially when they lend support to pre-existing hunches)
- leads to gains of status, prestige, and position within a competitive hierarchy

YELLOW – 'Express self, but never at the expense of others or the Earth'

- new information, regardless of the source (**YELLOW** may change due to respected authority, others' opinions, or what self does/thinks alone. Variability does not stress this ᵛMEME and absolute certainty is not an objective.)
- increased functionality of outcomes – things work more naturally
- getting more done with high quality, high acceptance, and low costs in human energy and Earth's resources

Change of the 3rd and 4th Variations – Oblique 'Stretch-DOWN' and 'Stretch-UP'

The Oblique Variations fit when things have gone beyond the ALPHA Fit toward the BETA Condition, when there is some OPENness, more Potential is available, and there is enough Insight to see alternatives. In Variations 3 and 4, the base 'MEME system takes on some aspects of neighbors on the Spiral. Like a crab, the thinking forays out, gets its fill, then scurries back into its zone of comfort. This is 'talking the talk without walking the walk.' New titles, activities, and buzz-words are commonplace. Experiments with altered organization forms and managerial techniques, plus acquisition of the hottest speakers and gimmicks are typical when oblique change is underway. While the base system does take on some characteristics of adjacent systems, the anchors are still holding fast to the Spiral and will not permit a wholesale transition.

Stretch can be UP or DOWN the Spiral. Variation 3, Stretch-DOWN, is the more troubling. It is commonplace when economies are in trouble, families come under stress, and over-extended companies struggle to survive. Cults and drill instructors use it to initially 'program' new recruits.

During **Change of the 3rd Variation**, expect nostalgic, sometimes desperate, down-Spiral searches for 'the good old days,' 'back to basics,' and 'fundamentals revisited.' Once they are found and the needs met (or the threats removed), a person may snap back to the base profile. Decision systems are likely to turn down toward the previous level, whatever it might have been. **GREEN** stretches back toward more **ORANGE** 'investment' and economic concerns; **ORANGE** resurrects **BLUE**'s absolute righteousness when the new-fangled reforms appear to be in trouble; and **BLUE** gets down-and-dirty into **RED** when times are tough, the holy cause is at risk, and 'the Enemy' is at the gates.

Some triggers for Change of the 3rd Variation include:

- **PURPLE** – evil forces and sudden unexplained changes in milieu
- **RED** – potential shame, loss of control, and disrespect
- **BLUE** – ambiguity, weak authority, disorder, and opposing -isms
- **ORANGE** – loss of autonomy and freedom or incompetence
- **GREEN** – disharmony and fragmentation of once-accepting group
- **YELLOW** – no access to knowledge and pointless regimentation

Change of the 4th Variation is Stretch-UP. TQM, most corporate development efforts, government privatization initiatives, and the perpetual buzz in education for the next new and improved teaching method are generally of this Variation. These oblique stop-gaps placate, enhance appearances, and layer on fresh paint. The efforts may be sincere, but they will not effect systemic change beyond the First Tier. If the experimentation with new ways of thinking prove too risky, a person will be likely to slide back to the safety of the base.

For example, an airline might have bought some new airplanes and hired a fresh advertising agency, but its management structure and service will be basically the same. Old union vs. management grudges will be unresolved. The company will *appear* different. When the hoopla is over the directors will congratulate themselves on their progress and even give each other bonuses. If the entire airline industry is in trouble and our company's competitors rely on horizontal change techniques of the 1st or 2nd Variation, then Variation 4 may be quite enough to prevail in the market.

Variations 3 and 4 'Stretch-UP/DOWN'			
	NO	SOME	YES
1 Potential	x		
2 Problems solved	x		
3 Dissonance			x
4 Insights	x		
5 Barriers found	x		
6 Consolidation			x

Unfortunately those who cannot handle Change of the 4th Variation are often the same people who laid the foundations of companies. They still work 'where the rubber meets the road' doing essential tasks. But these old-time participants are ignored or pushed out in the throes of oblique Stretch-UP just to get in fresh, young faces or save on benefits, especially when **ORANGE** is in control of the transition. The wisdom, experience, and insight thus lost in change games is often incalculable. You will see in Section 2 that it is always best to have command intelligences based in the Second Tier when large-scale systems are on the move.

As we pointed out, one of the best illustrations of the oblique change Variations has been the Quality movement. Many executives took up the mantle of Deming and Total Quality, investing huge sums in programs that never had the power to work because the bolts holding the organization to its place on the Spiral were never loosed and there was little room for Stretch, much less full Vertical change. New wine is dumped into the very same old wine-skins; only the labels are attractively reengineered.

Change of the 5th, 6th, and 7th Variations – Vertical Change

Vertical change generally breaks patterns and awakens new ᵛMEMEs, although it may resurrect previous ones that were thought to be buried and gone in the process. Different ᵛMEMEs take charge and/or the ᵛMEME stack is rearranged. For individuals, these are major life transitions. For organizations, vertical change is transformational and leads to new approaches to the business they thought they were in. Back to the computer metaphor, it is like a switch from an early version of DOS to Windows 95 or even UNIX or a Mac.

There are three Variations of vertical change – Break-OUT (5th Variation), UP-Shift (6th Variation), and Quantum (7th Variation). Break-OUT assaults the barriers, but sometimes leads right into the GAMMA Trap if the attack fails. The more controlled UP-Shift takes an evolutionary approach which awakens new ᵛMEMEs while bypassing GAMMA. Finally, there is the most complex 7th Variation in which a number of ᵛMEME transitions are under-way simultaneously, Quantum change.

Change of the 5th Variation – 'Break-OUT'   Break-OUT occurs once the instability and turbulence have driven the entity into the depths of a GAMMA Trap – frustration, anger, desperation. On the way out of BETA either nobody noticed the Reform Option (Change of the 6th Variation) in time to move gently from BETA across to DELTA or the requisite conditions simply could not be met. Instead, the slide into GAMMA went right to the bottom. This time of emotional loading is when all hell breaks loose, symbolically or literally. Such transformational change is tumultuous; it marks life passages and 'significant emotional events.' Variation 5 change is a turning point in corporate histories, sometimes under the flag of Chapter 11 bankruptcy, and topples governments.

Variation 5 'Break-OUT' (Revolutionary)		
	NO SOME	YES
1 Potential		X
2 Problems solved		X
3 Dissonance		X
4 Insights	X	
5 Barriers found	X	
6 Consolidation		X

When Break-OUT change is approaching, you will probably recognize BETA and GAMMA signals from several ᵛMEMEs at once. The whole system is at risk. It may be marked by a general shift in focus from Communal/Collective to more Individual/Elitism or the reverse, and is often noted as a sea-change for entities already in motion. By this time the pressure has built to the point that talking is futile and the 'call to arms' is sent to mobilize warriors, partisans, patriots, and the union faithful.

- Fundamental change is demanded in the prevailing structures and systems. Compromise is neither desired nor sought after.
- An unrelenting 'all or nothing' assault on the barriers/obstacles is launched. Change it or destroy it.
- Those former friends and 'moderates' who refuse to mount the barricades are defined as Quislings, Uncle Toms, sell-outs, and traitors. They are worse than the enemy.
- Actions are defended and justified by abstracting noble purpose into 'the cause' – one is fighting for freedom, the flag, or to 'make the world safe for . . .' whatever.

For example, many people speaking as African-American 'leaders' are now reframing the long Oblique civil rights movement into revolutionary Vertical terms. For them, Malcolm X has replaced Martin Luther King, Jr., as historic role model and mentor. Instead of being viewed as a 'riot,' the 1992 disturbances in South Central Los Angeles became a GAMMA rebellion, a justifiable attempt by African-Americans to throw off the yoke of colonial oppression imposed by a European establishment. The risk is that such a Break-OUT redefinition may trigger antibodies in white supremacist elements, igniting a counter-revolutionary response since the opposing belief sets are still within the same ᵛMEME region on the Spiral.

Surviving Break-OUT undamaged requires Second Tier thinking. We will address how to do that in Section 4. For now, just keep these two principles of congruence in mind:

(1)   If a large group of people is fairly homogeneous and at lower levels on the Spiral, change efforts must be more narrow, concrete, and immediate than if they are at higher levels. In like-thinking entities centered in the higher ranges, more abstract, broader and distant goals are viable.

(2)   If the entity is heterogeneous, the communicated goals must be both concrete and abstract, immediate and remote. They must be simulcast on all the ᵛMEME frequencies to which the parties are listening.

Vertical Change is implemented through the Spiral level(s) of a population, just as it is for an individual. A civilization centered around **RED** requires operant and respondent conditioning – concretely meeting people's needs with tangible stuff – not abstract persuasion or promises. **GREEN** requires consensus building and shared reasoning. **BLUE** needs doctrinaire authoritarianism during the transition and **ORANGE** must sense opportunities for individual growth. During this revolutionary time anticipate the symbols and songs of liberation, the enthusiasm of the righteous, and the glorious heroes who open the GAMMA Trap and lead into the freedom of DELTA. Caution them to keep their bags packed since revolutionary leaders are often dethroned and replaced as evidence of restabilization into the next ALPHA.

Change of the 6 Variation – 'UP-Shift'   Rather than falling into the depths of the GAMMA Trap, an Open system with untapped potential and insight that 'the' way of being is only 'a' way has the possibility for the Reform Option, an evolutionary change which virtually bypasses the GAMMA crisis in favor of DELTA and a new ALPHA. This is feasible because, even when drastic change is afoot, a few people see the light before all hell breaks loose and recognize the need for fundamental change without having to hit the barriers head-on. Such morphing (smoothly changing shape and gracefully altering course) can occur a number of times in a company's or culture's history without its falling into deep GAMMA. Finding this alternative course requires that: (a) the people involved must be largely in OPEN rather than ARRESTED or CLOSED thinking; (b) there is plenty of raw material for fresh thinking; (c) they have clear insight as to what the next ALPHA can be like; and (d) the rest of the Six Conditions for Change are being met. If such is the case, a relatively peaceful, evolutionary transformation from the current BETA condition to the New ALPHA is possible. If not, expect some degree of a Revolutionary process.

Variation 6 'UP-Shift' (Evolutionary)			
	NO	*SOME*	*YES*
1 Potential			X
2 Problems solved			X
3 Dissonance			X
4 Insights			X
5 Barriers found			X
6 Consolidation			X

When evolutionary Vertical change occurs, there are new wineskins for the new wine, not just cosmetic fixes. Vertical transitions from one ᵛMEME arrangement to another are like shifting gears; a different power ratio is engaged. But as in the gear-box, there is no need to destroy what was in order to shift toward what will be. If extra power is needed, a brief regressive trip into previous systems may be part of the package.

Effective Vertical change pays attention to both the *Life Conditions* and the ᵛMEME stack as a package. It is astounding how much energy in criminal justice and at-risk intervention goes into modifying behavior and attitudes without due attention to the *Life Conditions* that make the distasteful aspects of the **PURPLE** and **RED** ᵛMEMEs seem necessary for survival. Change is unlikely to endure when people go back into the same circumstances, confronting the same barriers, that engendered their difficulties in the first place.

Altering the *milieu* is not enough to insure Vertical change. While some people meet all Six of the Conditions, others cannot. They will lack the Potential or Insight or Dissonance or something. A few will be CLOSED in a ᵛMEME profile. Intervention efforts are not failures just because the change does not 'take' for everyone. Those who are unready for change should not destroy the possibilities for everyone else.

You cannot change people, but people can change and you may facilitate the process or stand in its way. Altered *Life Conditions* stimulate the awakening of new ᵛMEMEs. If you know the principles of change on the Spiral, if you can really alter the Conditions of Existence, and if the person(s) are sufficiently OPEN, you may be able to ease their shift toward more elaborated, or at least more appropriate, thinking. This is the intent of many drug counselors, parents, penologists, teachers, and therapists. If they would first uncover the ᵛMEMEs it becomes fairly easy to link treatment with the client's Spiral level. That this is not done is generally apparent in the failure rates of most drug treatment programs and the growth of the prison industry.

Change of the 7th Variation – 'Quantum' In Change of the 7th Variation, many ᵛMEME systems are in transition throughout a whole society. These are the Quantum shifts underway in Eastern Europe, Africa, South America, and even in the U.S. Second Tier thinking is necessary to contemplate, much less manage, multi-systems change.

Quantum shifts are risky because both Break-OUT (Revolutionary) and UP-Shift (Evolutionary) tracks are possibilities, but may not be readily compatible. In the resulting turbulence the Spiral becomes wobbly and vulnerable to ᵛMEME collisions. There are major shake-outs and desperate struggles for survival as people find themselves competing for niches. Many find themselves again close to the GAMMA Trap. Those who survive the pain (and most do) or bypass it are redeemed, renewed, reborn. But communal GAMMA is a stressful and very dangerous time because there is so much complexity and so much must change at once. The airline industry, big oil, telecommunications, and American autos have all seen GAMMA and are now feeling the pressure for Vertical change.

Section 4 describes a process for managing large systems along the Evolutionary track. It is a relatively simple means for dealing with simultaneous diversity and a plan for integrating the myriad elements into a seamless flow. The ultimate goal is the overall health of the Spiral and the well-being of each of us that are riders on it together.

Variation 7   'Quantum' Vertical

1 POTENTIAL throughout the Spiral to move to what's next for them
2 PROBLEMS at many levels are being adequately resolved
3 DISSONANCE pervades the system in appropriate ways for all levels
4 INSIGHT is shared and alternatives fit the whole structure
5 BARRIERS are resolved both vertically and horizontally across levels
6 CONSOLIDATION builds interdependency in mutually-supportive layers

---

ASSESS Before Trying to Implement Change

Before leaving this discussion of change, here is a final cautionary note. In trying to understand change in someone or a company, always ask, 'In what way does the person operate in respect to this issue?' Ask not, 'At what level is this person and how do the rules indicate I should be?' Graves always instructed that the latter approach is looking for simplicity that is not there. People are not types; they think about things in their lives in different ways. Different parts of organizations have personalities all their own, too, and you should ask the same question of social movements. Keep Barbara Jordan's question ever in mind: ' . . .change from what, to what?'

- Before you commit yourself to a personal or business relationship with someone, assess both the 'MEME profile and OAC potentials: Tough CLOSED **RED/blue**, 'Politically Correct' CLOSED **GREEN/orange**, or scrupulously honest OPEN **BLUE**? (How many times have you heard a person say he or she will be able to change a partner 'once we're married,' only to divorce a year or two later?)
- Before you acquire or merge with a company, be certain you look beyond the bottom-line numbers or products. You should assess the corporate Spiral and what futures are accessible because of it. What dominates the 'MEME stack: ARRESTED **ORANGE**, too much tradition-bound **BLUE**, healthy **RED** ready to work, heavy on the **GREEN**, or untapped **YELLOW**?
- Before sending either troops or nation-builders into 'warlord' territory like Somalia or 'rebellious' Chechnya be certain to take a Spiral reading. When nations attempt to export their homefront solutions and impose them unmodified onto someone else's problems, everyone usually suffers for the effort. Even 'humanitarian' excursions must be aligned to fit the *Life Conditions* as the U.N. belatedly discovered in Bosnia.

To begin to get a picture of the Spiral profile, you must examine the personality (or corporate culture) in repect to a number of issues and the reactions in terms of response to those issues. This becomes a 'MEME profile, not a categorical place on the continuum. Then, in making strategic decisions for managing, educating, or helping, the most effective approach is very simple: Read the Feedback. If we listen through the Spiral, people are constantly saying why they act as they do, why they believe as they do, and how we can be most effective in our dealings with them. They tell us whether they are ready for change and which Variation is appropriate. Put most simply, as Clare Graves was fond of saying,

'If he purrs, continue;
if he growls, back off.'

5

The Dynamics of Leadership

Most textbooks on managerial leadership, as well as the instruction manuals for leaders, need to be rewritten. The helpful contributions of Steven Covey and others who are wrapping the **ORANGE** 'MEME between **BLUE** and **GREEN** bookends do not go far enough. They are still relying on the First Tier, rather than the entire Spiral.

Lee Cullum, *Dallas Morning News* columnist and PBS (public broadcasting) commentator, refers to the present time as 'The Age of Limbo.' By this she means we are trapped in a twilight zone between the death and decay of an old order that is ceasing to work and the full emergence of a new paradigm which can fill the gap. Cullum is not simply describing the interlude between 'MEMEs, but the leap from the First to the Second Tier of human thinking systems.

This time the *limbo* (from the Latin for 'on the edge') is especially precarious since we are experiencing simultaneous action, reaction, counter-action, and conflict within and among several 'MEMEs. When their expressions are both volatile and creative, the entire Spiral comes under threat as many 'MEMEs begin to compete for global niches. These conditions lead to Change of the 7th Variation. If we are to avoid Humpty Dumpty's fate *in limbo*, new leadership alloys must be forged in the social and technological crucibles that result in business, religion, education, and politics. The people who possess the minds and personalities to deal with these levels of complexity, never before encountered in our long history, will be shaped from these new alloys by the energy of the **YELLOW** and **TURQUOISE** 'MEMEs. They are the Spiral Wizards.

Wizard 1. (archaic): a wise man, a sage; 2. one skilled in magic, a sorcerer; 3. a very clever or skillful person. *Webster's Ninth New Collegiate Dictionary*

Every epoch, generation, culture, and ethnicity has produced its own wizards, those very special people who have insight, powers, and skills that transcend more common folk. These 'wise ones' typically arise in times of crisis and rapid change when old patterns and forms are being replaced by the new. They inhabit the shadows and in-between places – edges, cusps, verges, caves, brinks, rims, fringes, and divides – those misty realms that are no longer one thing but not yet another. Anything can happen in these haunts, the borderline spaces and times. Chaos could be loosed at any moment upon a defenseless world, or order upon one in quest of an anchor.

Ancient wizards possessed great knowledge that sprang from the very nature of their beings. Though men and women in form, they were thought to encapsulate something of the nature of animals, plants, winds, thunder, lightning, moon and stars – all the things in heaven and Earth and even from below. Some were malevolent and ruthless, but the best had greatness of heart to match their spectacular wizardry. They served as guides and guardians for the lesser folk around them. Some appeared to see into the future, as did Nostradamus. Others seemingly possessed magical powers to transform and influence, as did Merlin.

They examined the world emerging around them, naming and reordering its base elements into golden new shapes and patterns. Most worked quietly offstage, king makers and breakers behind the scenes. Their deeds come down in fragments of song, in tattered scraps of history and legend. Like Melchizedek, the ancient priest-king of Jerusalem, their origins are swathed in mystery and intrigue.

There are still wizards among us, today. They are the alchemists of ᵛMEMEs, seeking to transmute stale, leaden systems into shining opportunities. Some function best on the psycho-social landscape of a single ᵛMEME. They specialize in the nurturance of its unique force field as ᵛMEME Wizards. Others are adept at bridging transition zones between one ᵛMEME and another. These Change Wizards are masters of the dynamics of the cusp. Now, a new species of Wizard is appearing for the first time on planet Earth, here in this Age of Limbo. They are the Spiral Wizards. More about them shortly.

ᵛMEME Wizards

Each of the ᵛMEMEs on the Spiral of human emergence has awakened its own characteristic expression of wizardry. These ᵛMEME Wizards know how to function as modern day 'guides and guardians' for those who share their world views; hence, they come dressed in each of the Spiral's colors. While ᵛMEME Wizards may be one-trick ponies, they perform that trick so brilliantly that everybody wants to see and the whole human circus thrives because of it. We will summarize ᵛMEME Wizardry briefly here, then present the detailed ᵛMEME Wizard's Field Manual in Section 3.

The **PURPLE** ᵛMEME continues to produce its mystics, soothsayers, diviners of the spirit, and witch doctors. Sometimes they write epic poetry or sing songs. Other times they exude charisma at just the moment we crave such cocooning leadership. From the **RED** ᵛMEME come modern-day versions of Zeus and Venus, god-like epic heroes and heroines. Some are dominant political figures; a few are quasi-religious despots; and many appear as mythic role-models like Superman, the Power Rangers, and even Teenage Mutant Ninja Turtles.

The **BLUE** ᵛMEME's Wizards draw lines between good and evil, the right and the wrong. They offer meaning and purpose to a life that looks for social stability and civility. Billy Graham has long been a most respected Wizard in **BLUE**. He is regularly called upon by whoever is in the White House to provide advice, a moral compass, and comfort during national crises. South African President Nelson Mandela emerged from prison as a universally honored quasi-saint, speaking the **BLUE** ᵛMEME's language of righteousness, sacred duty, and patriotic nationhood. Mother Teresa teaches **BLUE** charity and Christian love.

Motivator Zig Ziglar is among the best Wizards of the steady in-between, those whose expertise lies in a transition zone between two core ᵛMEMEs. Ziglar's contribution is in awakening the healthy **ORANGE** 'enterprising self' in conjunction with a solid base of responsible **BLUE**. Our friend Dr Lair Ribeiro in Brasil is doing an amazing job preparing literally millions of people in South America for a similar transition up the Spiral to individual empowerment.

Lee Iacocca, Bill Gates, Rupert Murdoch, and even Donald Trump are Wizards in **ORANGE** because of their capacities to fix things, facilitate developments, renew images, and disseminate technological savvy. Carl Rogers and other **GREEN** ᵛMEME giants in the field of transformational psychology have awakened many to the 'mystical' realm of deep human feelings and interpersonal bondings. Names like Cavoson, Cousteau, and Lovelock reflect wizardry in eco-consciousness. We will visit more ᵛMEME Wizards in Section 3.

Wizards of Change

Change Wizards understand the cusps between ᵛMEMEs. President Ronald Reagan resonated with both **BLUE** Patriotic/Doctrinaire and **ORANGE** Individual/Elite world views. While he made little sense to the **GREEN** Egalitarian community and frustrated **YELLOW** with over-simplifications, he reigned successful over the end of the **BLUE-ORANGE** Cold War era.

Malcolm X has been a model change Wizard for many African American youth because he moved from **RED** (the pimp), into **RED/blue** (the convert), into **BLUE/red** (the zealot) and then into peak **BLUE** (the believer after the

Haj experience). He – a Change Wizard – rather than Rev. Martin Luther King, Jr. – more of a **BLUE/orange** Systems Wizard – has been the hero for youngsters going through similar passages. Change Wizards provide developmental stepping stones and model the way. Unfortunately, like Fidel Castro or Mikhail Gorbachev, they may not keep up with the parade as it moves up the Spiral beyond their range.

Change Wizards have significant impact because they intuitively understand that effective leadership usually combines elements of both Individual/Elite (warm color) and Communal/Collective (cool color) 'MEMEs. **RED** PowerGods need **PURPLE** subservience. **ORANGE** game players require **BLUE** followers of the rules. **BLUE** TruthForce imposes order on **RED**'s anarchy. If both the followers and the leaders change at about the same rate, an active relationship can last a long time. However, Change Wizards tend to be zone specialists. When simultaneous handling of a number of 'MEME junctions is required, something even more powerful is needed. The ability to consider broad spectrum views and many systems at once is the essence of the third form of wizardry, the Spiral Wizard.

Spiral Wizards

Spiral Wizards instinctively roam over vast mindscapes seeing patterns and connections others do not notice because the First Tier's filters do not allow them to. They can move through the spine of the Spiral awakening, unblocking, empowering, or repairing each of the 'MEMEs in an organization. This Wizard appreciates chaos and thinks more like a creative designer than even a reengineer. The process links functions, people, and ideas into new, more natural flows that add precision, flexibility, rapid response, humanity, and fun to getting the work done. That is the power of Second Tier thinking: constantly survey the whole while tinkering expertly with the parts. Monitoring the full Spiral is especially vital during periods of large-scale turbulence and change; like right now.

Leadership from the Second Tier

The Second Tier's leadership is built with the core intelligences of **YELLOW** and **TURQUOISE**. **YELLOW** provides an inner-directed, individualistic viewing point that connects particles and sub-systems into natural sequences. The focus is on the integration of previously separate entities and their functions into linear or, more likely, systemic flows. This might mean something as simple as connecting past-present-future along a time line or as complicated as a value chain that interlinks suppliers, customers, in-house producers, and investors throughout a business. Lest we forget, the

YELLOW ᵛMEME acts in self-interest by impacting those things that threaten its quality of being. This Individual/Elite component of Spiral Wizardry has a decidedly technical, practical, action-oriented, and 'left-brain with feelings' bent.

Once it is awakened, the newer **TURQUOISE** ᵛMEME adds a Communal/Collective perspective that shapes and maintains ordered relationships for the well-being of the Spiral (rather than just the members of **GREEN**'s closed loop). Various living systems, fuzzy concepts, power centers, and force fields blend together in balanced relationships. By returning orderliness to the Spiral, this ᵛMEME maco-manages its energies and parts in a holistic manner, much like an orchestra's conductor shapes its sound or a biologist works to understand an ocean vent's ecosystem. Since **TURQUOISE** acts for the greater good, it is concerned with the *overall life* of a company, a school, a community, a nation, or of Gaia, the living planet. This adds a sacrifice self-interest understanding and the 'right brain with data' sensitivities that give Spiral Wizardry its whole brain balance and integrity.

Today's Spiral Wizards represent a new perspective on leadership and social influence, rising from the unique *Life Conditions* that now confront us in the 1990s. This new breed of leaders distinguishes itself from others who have come before by *how* they think about things as well as what they are capable and willing to do. They naturally reflect the principles of Second Tier thinking in their personal lives and intuitively apply those insights professionally. You may detect the awakening of one or more of these dimensions in yourself if you are experiencing transformational change. You probably recognize the emergence of these features in individuals you know and in the mind syndicates of the finest organizations.

Some specifics of how Spiral Wizards actually work in applying their thinking and problem resolution skills from a Second Tier perspective will be spelled out in the next three chapters. Chapter 6 explores leadership components in 'Spiral Wizardry.' Chapter 7 places the variables in sequence through 'Spiral Alignment.' And Chapter 8 connects everything to everything else with 'Spiral Integration.' The following are identifying marks of the Spiral Wizard.

The Seven Marks of the Spiral Wizard

1. Spiral Wizards Think in OPEN Systems rather than CLOSED Final States

Spiral Wizards recognize that human life forms are continually passing from one plateau to the next. Each stage only represents a transitory resting place before the next is mounted, then the next, and the next. We are still in the foothills of human development as practically every scientific and social discipline is revisiting the whole scope of evolutionary – 'to roll out' – thinking.

Spiral Wizards recognize that new conceptions of *self and other – I and thou –* emerge in people, thus adding levels of complexity to personalities. Organizations are in constant search for new structures to match changes in their internal and external environments. Societies ebb and flow, wax and wane, progress and regress along an evolutionary pathway.

These Wizards pose a threat to people who believe that any particular 'MEME is the final destination for all, particularly when those same people are selling tickets. Spiral-conscious futurists acknowledge there are different futures, different next steps, for different 'MEMEs in time. Accordingly, Spiral Wizards need not jettison older, traditional structures and life-forms in favor of some 'new-and-improved' version. Rather, they incorporate what has come already into the overall scheme of change because they sense time's swirl among past, present, and future.

Enlightened organizations seek out their Spiral Wizards and protect them from dress codes, ego infringements, political games, or bureaucratic constraints. You should put them in the think-tank, nerve center, or decision loop and allow them to scan for patterns, relationships, and messages from the future. Let them generate and test scenarios. They will tell you what kinds of leaders are needed now and what the followers will be like tomorrow. If you are clever, you can find them throughout the ranks and at all levels.

2. Spiral Wizards Live and Work within Natural Flows and Rhythms

Spiral Wizards accept the inherent flows within both chaos-driven and order-shaped time tables. These dynamics generate seasons of stability and periods of change and transformation. Understanding this, the Spiral Wizard exhibits a sense of patience, a reality that people cannot be until they are, and a willingness to walk away from situations when the timing is wrong or they are not the right person to make a difference. They know when to let nature take its course and when to stir things up. They are sensitive to the downstream effects from upstream interventions and have an uncanny ability to spot the first trace of a new trend coming because they are able to learn a lot from a little. In the process, they detect the underlying attractors that impact connections and memetic alignments at the surface.

3. The Ultimate Goal of Spiral Wizards is to Keep the Spiral Healthy

Spiral Wizards are, essentially, engineers who tend to the flow of energy, resources, and defense mechanisms along the entire Spiral. These Wizards have a Vertical awareness of multiple 'MEMEs that allows them to recognize stratified layers and sense the needs of various levels besides their own zones of comfort.

- They can 'see' through surface level distortions, smoke and mirrors, into the ᵛMEME stacks of individual, organizational, and societal Spirals.
- They are the midwives who preside at the birth of new ᵛMEMEs or the rebirth of an older one that has atrophied and needs rejuvenation for the good of the Spiral.
- They often mediate between two conflicting ᵛMEMEs by focusing on Win:Win:Win outcomes – the Power of the Third Win – namely, the health of the Spiral.
- They scan for ᵛMEME malignancies that endanger the rest of the Spiral. This includes forces like predatory incursions from ruthless **RED**, virulent zealotry out of the **BLUE** ᵛMEME, or the excesses of materialist pragmatism that spew out of **ORANGE**.

In doing this scan, Spiral Wizards rely on two guiding principles. First, they seek to *assist each ᵛMEME to develop* Horizontally and remain in a healthy condition so that it can add to the life of the Spiral. Second, they strive to *keep the Spiral Open* Vertically so new ᵛMEMEs can awaken and Obliquely so the existing ones can adjust as *Life Conditions* dictate.

This sort of ᵛMEME splicing, intervention, and alignment occurs at a level that only Spiral Wizards can detect; yet its impacts are obvious to anyone. Just as a chiropractor manipulates the junctures of bones, Spiral Wizards are adept at sorting out and adjusting the ᵛMEMEs on the spine of the Dynamic Spiral. When the ᵛMEMEs are set right and the Spiral is Open, individuals 'get it together,' companies are suddenly effective, and communities are healthy again.

4. Spiral Wizards Interact Comfortably with Many Conceptual Worlds

Spiral Wizards respect the integrity and importance of each of the ᵛMEMEs. Like mythical wizards of old, they can change form and appearance. Self-control allows them to subdue their own priorities and prejudices so as to get on the psychological frequencies of various ᵛMEMEs. They will wear a three-piece suit or blue jeans, whichever is appropriate. They can celebrate different cultures and share the experience without passing judgment. Good Spiral Wizards can speak multiple ᵛMEME languages – fluent **BLUE**, snappy **ORANGE**, or **RED** – like a native.

Spiral Wizards are free to enlist the assistance of ᵛMEME Wizards and Change Wizards when they are more in sync for a given situation. They derive satisfaction from solving a difficult problem or aligning systems in a natural way, not necessarily from high profile influence and recognized control.

5. Spiral Wizards Possess a Full Complement of Resources, Strategies, and Skills

Spiral Wizards wear many different hats and can play a myriad of roles. Just as they can fit in many worlds, they can adjust styles, being sensitive when appropriate and ruthless when necessary, even walking away when their own interests and needs take them elsewhere. They have very few boundaries, off-limits, or narrow, confining ruts to restrict their thinking. Nor are they impeded by the artificial separations imposed by disciplines, fields of knowledge, sacred territories, restrictive traditions, or separate divisional titles in a company. They are resourceful enough to experiment with the novel or make do with the ordinary. Historic differences in terms of church vs. state, public vs. private, one level of government vs. another, or one category of person vs. another have little significance.

'Who is right?' is not as important as 'what does the Spiral need?' Competency is more valued than seniority; knowledge is more useful than status. The mind is free to learn anything from anybody in any manner necessary. Nothing from the past is thrown away and nothing from the future is rejected out of hand. In practical terms, the Spiral Wizard's tool kit is filled with all sorts of systems, structures, and gadgets since they must be equipped to provide the appropriate technology or leadership package for each ^{V}MEME.

They draw from a full bag of decision-making techniques. Spiral Wizards carefully select from them to resolve issues in diverse settings, using compromise sometimes, negotiated settlements where relevant; authoritarian conduits when necessary; and other complex problem resolution formats as the ^{V}MEMEs demand. (See pp. 282–4 for additional competencies.)

They are also equipped to navigate through the stages of change and facilitate the passage for others. They are prepared to hold the hands of those who need supportive reinforcement or kick the butts of those who need encouragement. Their responses will be tailored to the unique needs of each person, each ^{V}MEME, and the health of the Spiral. They resist putting everybody through the same training and development 'car wash' since ^{V}MEMEs exist in their own self-contained worlds requiring their own instructional packages. Overall, they act on behalf of the entire organism (person, company, or society) for both the greater good *and* individual gain.

6. Spiral Wizards are Systemic Thinkers and Integrative Problem Solvers

The minds of Spiral Wizards are configured in ways which often make them appear a bit strange, especially to those blocked in First Tier ^{V}MEMEs. As systemic thinkers, they combine an awareness of natural processes and flowing interconnections to create a holistic understanding of a complex problem, event, or situation. They reject simple cause-and-effect links, cosmetic quick-fix solutions, and reliance on artificial interventions. They search, instead, for the one or two critical logs that lock up the entire log jam. They scan for the critical pressure points and release valves that regulate the life blood of the organism. They detect major mismatches and misfitness which, unless corrected, will create situations that no amount of training, incentivation, or discipline can resolve.

For example, Spiral Wizards quickly see why quality programs, reengineering ventures, and global marketing initiatives tend to fail if they have been designed by too many linear, 'left brain,' systematized, or even strategic thinkers. It takes the insights of Spiral Wizards to factor the full range of human emotions, needs, and ᵛMEME relationships into holistic packages that are both 'high tech' and 'in touch.'

As integrative problem solvers, they serve like networking software to link many functions together. They are able to mesh and mobilize a vast array of resources and intelligences, then focus them like a laser beam on specific targets. For example, many local communities are wrestling with crime, gangs, and inadequate education. While expressing deep concerns, churches, schools, the business sector, political entities, civic clubs, helping agencies, and private citizens continue to act in an ad hoc, piecemeal, and fragmented fashion. They are plagued by turf battles, territorial demands, proprietary budgetary constraints, and strong egos. By working on basic ᵛMEME conflicts and misalignments, Spiral Wizards provide the perspective and mechanisms to get all of the stakeholders on the same page and working in the same direction. They have the tools to *integrate, align,* and *synergize* all elements into a cooperative effort. The Spiral forms the unifying principle, connective glue-like tissue, and a common pathway that the divergent and diverse parties can pursue together. Everybody can then contribute to the greater good once the change processes (described in Chapter 4) are being accommodated.

7. Spiral Wizards Possess a Unique Blend of Personal Beliefs and Values

Spiral Wizards mesh 'left' and 'right brain' capacities since they are both **YELLOW** ᵛMEME engineers and **TURQUOISE** ᵛMEME mystics. They sense both particles and waves. They dream like poets and plan like computer programmers. They revel in paradoxes, enabling them to resolve the impasses between such forces as individual rights and communal concerns or growth-and-development versus quality of life priorities. Their minds' eyes see global and local needs simultaneously.

You will find Spiral Wizards in all walks of life, at any educational level, and throughout the ranks in companies. They tend to be resourceful, fearless, creative, tough, yet playful people who are often invisible as they move in and out of situations. These are not better people. They are not necessarily even more 'intelligent' in the usual sense; they are simply different kinds of minds. Sometimes they are prophets crying out loudly in the wildnerness. Sometimes they are quiet, calm, voices whispering words of encouragement and gently pointing out alternative pathways and solutions. Like old-time wizards, they are not always recognized in their time. Acknowledgement may only come in a later day, or from a different generation.

An Illustration: The U.S. Military as a Macro Model of Leadership

Military operations are large in scale and the issues are truly life-or-death. That is why people are intrigued by the likes of Sun Tzu, Hannibal, Shaka Zulu, Alexander the Great, Sitting Bull, Field Marshal Montgomery, Erwin Rommel, George Patton, Moshe Ahrens, Alexander Haig, and Norman Schwartzkopf, to name but a few. Ross Perot, the American corporate maverick and 1992 Presidential candidate, was enthralled with Attila the Hun's leadership style and advocated it widely. Business discussions are full of references to warfare and metaphors of battle. What does the U.S. military teach us about the Spiral?

Following the stalemate in Korea and the disastrous lessons of Vietnam, American military think-tanks began reevaluating our approach to waging war and peace. It took the 'loss' to challenge the system (a national BETA and some GAMMA) and spawn a DELTA-search for new models for extending power.

In Vietnam, many field grade officers acted more like IBM or GM executives than leaders of troops. The Agent Orange that poisoned vegetation and personnel also colored the leadership model. Inter-service rivalry was rampant as tickets got punched and empires were built; command structures were top-heavy, status-bound, and bureaucratic. The elegant strengths in the **BLUE, RED**, and especially the **PURPLE** ᵛMEMEs were overlooked by the 'sophisticated' Americans while being cultivated by the tenacious and more Spiral-wise North Vietnamese.

The trauma of that experience and the soul-searching which followed forged a new approach. These changes were not triggered by lectures at the War College, goal-setting sessions at the Pentagon, or case studies at West Point. They came about because the *Life Conditions* on a high-tech, highly mobile, rapid-response, ideologically ambiguous battlefield present new memes and demand new ᵛMEMEs to match. The test came in the war called Operation Desert Storm.

Enter some candidates for Spiral Wizard: General 'Stormin' Norman' Schwartzkopf, the co-architect and commander of Desert Storm; General Colin Powell; Admiral William Crowe; and other post-graduates of the Vietnam era. Let us disregard the politics and justifications of the 1991 Gulf

War and just look at the differences in leadership/management between Vietnam and Desert Storm. The difference between traditional First Tier **BLUE-ORANGE** and the new **ORANGE-GREEN-YELLOW** ranges include:

- The military experts ran the war, not the politicians.
- The various military branches were woven seamlessly together in the Order of Battle, constantly informed by complex technology, and deployed by a singularly integrated and unified command staff.
- Power and authority were dispersed in the intelligence-rich smaller fighting units operating with considerable autonomy close to and within the battle zones. Yet, tight, unified, open-systems command and control structure was apparent at the macro-level.
- Rank, privilege, the accouterments of power, and other status differentiations were suppressed, as modeled in Schwartzkopf's personal style, dress, and manner. Imperious leaders would be ineffectual or openly rejected by followers in a volunteer force at more complex levels on the Spiral. The stars-and-bars of rank dropped in impact while functionality, knowledge, and competence were on the rise. Powell and the Joint Chiefs had no needs to upstage their field commander(s).

Clearly, a new approach to the battlefield had emerged, along with congruent management systems and personnel who both expected it and could handle the greater complexity. These forces were deployed against Saddam Hussein's Iraq, an adversary which, in spite of relatively sophisticated technology, was operating through an earlier pardigm more suited to World War II than the late twentieth century battlefield. A sophisticated, integrated military model appeared to overwhelm a feudal, punitively authoritarian adversary in the field and sustained few direct casualties in the process. Of course, who will actually be the 'winner' in the long run is yet to be determined. That battle came to an end but the war of big ᵛMEMEs in North Africa and the middle East has only begun.

6

Spiral Wizardry

Now it is time for Spiral Wizardry. The simplicity beyond complexity is the connection of ideas, structures, and programs on the Spiral. You will need to call up the entire spectrum of ᵛMEMEs in your mind. Your task is to lay out the options, make choices, and then implement a precise and focused process of morphing leadership to match the thinking systems. ('Morphing' is the special-effects process that causes one image to change into another before your eyes. The technology was used in the films such as *Star Trek VI* and *Terminator 2*, and is now available in graphics packages for your laptop computer!)

Spiral Wizards employ the following five principles to the process of reconstituting leadership and managerial packages to blend with individuals and organizations:

- Recognize the ᵛMEMEs in people, companies, communities
- Incorporate the universal 'P-O-A' leadership style
- Exercise the appropriate intervention option(s) in the situation
- Follow the six 'Rules of Thumb' for Spiral leadership
- Activate Second Tier thinking to focus leadership and managerial packages

Recognize the Spiral – in People, Companies, and Entire Societies

In Section I we described the Spiral and introduced the ᵛMEMEs that form it. Now comes the question: 'How do I determine which ᵛMEMEs exist in a person or situation and how can I sketch in the profile I am to manage?'

For a moment, think like a guitarist. Your challenge is to manage notes and build chords. A chord is a blend of tones which, when played together, produce a sound all their own. ᵛMEME profiles are similar mixtures. Johnny

One-Note is a rarity; virtually nobody lives a pure tone of a single ᵛMEME. To some extent, we are all blends, admixtures, and combinations in flux. Most are harmonious and fairly 'normal,' but some are discordant, troubled, and harsh.

In stable entities, the **50% Rule** often applies: one strongly dominant ᵛMEME is accompanied by two or three softer background tones which account for the other half of the energy. For entities in transition, look for an Individual/Collective Pair: a strong warm-colored, Expressive, internally controlled ᵛMEME will bond with a complimentary cool-colored, Sacrificial, externally focused ᵛMEME as energy oscillates between them.

In a business you may well hear chords of different ᵛMEMEs playing in production, sales, research and development, human resources, or elsewhere. Even within those functions there will be harmonic variations in work teams, locations, and functional areas as the notes vary among players.

Often, the job of leadership is tuning the Spiral so the parts resonate with positive synergy instead of interfering to cancel each other out. Like a conductor who takes the podium, the Spiral Wizard who can coordinate multiple ᵛMEMEs cuts through defenses and pushes disguises away from the systems so all play better than ever before. Begin by getting each ᵛMEME to display itself. Send in experimental probes – ᵛMEME-laden questions ('What is an ideal supervisor like?'), tasks to perform (rearrange the workplace, for example), people to deal with (bring in an outsider), and situations to confront (introduce a new mission element). Watch how individuals and groups respond. With that information you can begin to balance the ᵛMEMEs, tune the Spiral, and eliminate non-productive noise.

ᵛMEME Detection: A Check-List of Recognition Principles

The following Recognition Principles can be of use to interviewers who are assessing job candidates; salesmen who are sizing up a potential customer; negotiators who are searching for patterns in an adversary across the table; nurses evaluating a patient; employees picking a new team leader; or, simply, somebody who seeks to understand somebody else.

1. *Step outside your own ᵛMEME profile.* Take off your colored glasses and turn down your own internal boom-box before you try listening to someone else's tune.

2. *Identify the prevailing Life Conditions.* The *Life Conditions* a person or group defines as their 'real world' usually determine the active ᵛMEMEs and their priority.

3. *Ask the 'why?' question.* Look and listen for the differences between the *schema* (how the system thinks – its ᵛMEME structure) and *thema* (what the system thinks – its attitude, belief, and value contents).

4. *Different ᵛMEMEs may brighten in different situations.* Since people are not 'at' single levels on the Spiral, particular kinds of ideas may be attracted to different ᵛMEMEs in our stacks. We can think about different things in different ways.

5. *Realize that an organization is also a mixture of ᵛMEMEs, not a simple type.* Groups contain elements of receding and awakening ᵛMEMEs in their members and collective culture. Like musical chords, there are many variations on how we create them.

6. *Remember that ᵛMEMEs ebb and flow as conditions get better or worse.* Expect a person, organization or even a society to be fluid, not consistent. We slide along the Spiral in response to the world we perceive around us.

Let us illustrate the complexity of the recognition issue. Suppose a person says she believes in mandatory testing for the HIV virus. That is the 'what,' the *thema*. As a Spiral Wizard, do not respond to the content until you ask: 'Why do you believe so?' Her first answers will be restatements of her position or superficial arguments in its defense. If you concur, you merely become an agreeable ally. If you disagree, you will be arguing in circles all day because you still do not know the real reasons for that person's point-of-view.

Spiral Wizards get through the confusion of content and speak directly to the big ᵛMEMEs of the Spiral. Put aside whether you agree with the ideas or not; just keep probing. If you are persistent, you will uncover the thinking behind the attitude, the underlying ᵛMEME-based *schema*. In this example, it might be:

- 'I believe we should keep the blood line as pure as God made it since AIDS is a punishment from Him.' The Punitive arm of the **BLUE** ᵛMEME.
- 'I just bought into a medical testing lab and this will enhance my own investment.' The side of **ORANGE** unconstrained by principles.
- 'My gymnastics coach said everybody should be tested and whatever she says is what I think.' The aspect of **PURPLE** that follows the leader.
- 'The cost to treat AIDS will overwhelm the world's medical and economic systems while depriving the Spiral of many great souls, so we must be aggressive in isolating the virus without taking people's dignity.' The **YELLOW** mix of ideas.

By probing for 'why' instead of stopping with 'what,' you have done your research and are beginning to understand the Spiral you are facing. Your next response can be directed to whichever ᵛMEME-based *schema*(s) you hear because that is closer to the core thinking system. Through that process you really begin communicating.

Take a look within yourself by completing two questions. Simply rank order the letters beside each completion to match your liking, 1 most like you to 7 the least.

1. **IN A GOOD ORGANIZATION . . .**
a   loyalty earns job security now and guarantees future rewards ☐
b   they stay off my back so I can do what I've got to like I want to ☐
c   the primary concern is with our role in the 'living system' ☐
d   my people feel safe and our folk ways and rituals are honored ☐
e   an opportunity exists for people to excel and become winners ☐
f   the people and our feelings come first as we join in community ☐
g   natural differences, inevitable conflict, and constant change energize
    me ☐

2. **A MATURE PERSON SEEKS TO BE . . .**
a   safe, like a member of an extended family that looks after its own ☐
b   successful, independent, innovative, and competitive winners ☐
c   functional and flexible within my own personal principles ☐
d   responsible beings, aware of community and Earth ☐
e   macho and powerful because strength and respect matter most ☐
f   warm and supportive so that all can grow and be fulfilled ☐
g   purposeful and disciplined as directed by rightful higher authority ☐

If you have not figured out the process already, here is a key to match the letters with the likely ᵛMEMEs.

1. IN OUR CULTURE . . .	2. WE SEEK TO BE . . .
a – BLUE	a – PURPLE
b – RED	b – ORANGE
c – TURQUOISE	c – YELLOW
d – PURPLE	d – TURQUOISE
e – ORANGE	e – RED
f – GREEN	f – GREEN
g – YELLOW	g – BLUE

Apply the Universal "P-O-A" to Build Positive Relationships

What is it about certain people you meet that draws you to them? Why do you get the feeling one person is truly interested in what you have to say while another really could not care less? Magnetic personalities often show genuine interest in you; make it easy for you to express yourself; and have the personal power and presence to act on their convictions. It is nothing so mystical as charisma. Effective people have simply mastered the 'universals' that all Spiral leaders should exhibit, especially when engaging a new person or group. Clare Graves' exhaustive research identified three essential factors in healthy transactions – Politeness (P), Openness (O), and Autocracy (A). They are the basis for skillful mangement and effective leadership.

Like a three-legged stool, the **P-O-A** triad represents the base skills every Spiral manager, coach, teacher, or counselor can stand on when working with anyone. If one of the three legs is weak or missing, the enterprise may topple. Once solidly in place, though, **P-O-A** provides a foundation for building specific training programs, tailoring O.D. interventions, restructuring organizations, and preparing for change.

P-O-A sets a constructive tone when first engaging large audiences, potential client groups, or individual employees, particularly in times of uncertainty. It is the entry phase research tool to use when you do not know for sure which ᵛMEMEs are in charge. Later, when you have a better reading of the Spiral, these protocols continue to wear well over the life of a leader/ follower relationship since they keep things 'clean' and above-board. They are 'universal' because **P-O-A** generates positive (at the least non-toxically neutral) responses from all bands of the Spiral. They are not 'traits' of leaders alone because everyone should apply them.

P – The Politeness Factor

Politeness is defined quite simply as being civil, friendly, cordial, considerate, genuine, empathetic, firm but fair, civilized, and sensitive. (Words describing its absence include: crude, harsh, cynical, arrogant, disrespectful, critical, brusque, punitive, negative, judgmental, and condescending.) During a conference we once heard a senior executive say, 'I don't have to be polite; I'm the boss.' That outfit is no longer in business.

When was the last time you heard of 'Politeness training' for executives? While the derogatory term 'charm school' is applied to everything from diversity to media relations programs, at what point do today's managers get a refresher in being decent human beings? In an era when the 'me' ᵛMEMEs are so strong, it may be time to rethink good manners and offer some help to those with a civility gap. This is not to advocate fuzzy **GREEN** love-fests and neo-Sensitivity Training, but a very straightforward approach to decency, humanity, and respect for others and self.

Here are some dynamics of Politeness:

- Shows genuine interest in persons. The Spiral leader respects them as human beings with the potential to develop beyond where they are but grants them the right to be who they are.
- Adheres to the established social norms and niceties in doing what is proper in terms of honors, condolences, and other personal or professional recognitions. While these may be irrelevant to the leader, they matter to the other person(s). Politeness is a response to others' needs on their terms, not one's own. The Polite leader respects cultural differences.
- Strikes a good balance between interest in the lives of others and their right to personal autonomy, privacy, and freedom. The leader is

concerned without being nosy or intrusive. Involvement is appropriate in degree, authentic, and genuine, not phony or contrived.

- Listens without becoming distracted or ego-speaking, yet can express personal time constraints honestly and directly such that the other person does not feel high-handedly 'dismissed.'

As a result of Politeness, **PURPLE** feels safe and included; **RED** has less reason to feel alienated and senses respect; **BLUE** recognizes the presence of 'basic goodness and decency'; **ORANGE** does not feel threatened or challenged; **GREEN** feels the presence of compassionate human beings, not titles; **YELLOW** appreciates a non-intrusive, pleasant climate where curiosity and wonder are the norms; and **TURQUOISE** is free to explore without ridicule.

While the behavioral details of Politeness will differ between a National Football League locker room and a tea party, the principle is universal. Effective leaders can show genuine (not painted on) warmth and interest in others. The particulars relate to both the leader's personal Spiral and those things that matter to the follower.

O – The Openness Factor

Openness is expressed in two ways. First, it is the extent to which the leader is authentic, transparent, sharing, available, and emotionally above-board. (In contrast to devious, closed, shady, two-faced, deceitful, biased, gamy, withholding, and secretive.) Openness runs together with the degree to which people in an entity trust each other. If trust is weak, Openness will be, as well.

Second, Openness fosters a climate that gives permission for others, as individuals or groups, to be communicative and straightforward. For example, the early interest in diversity centered around the Politeness leg. The current emphasis on business ethics, values, and more expansive diversity includes Openness, both within organizations and in their roles as involved corporate citizens. 'Do as we do, not just as we say.' Few psychological games are played when authenticity is the norm. What is said is what is meant, good news or bad. Critical information is accessible and flows freely without the need for rumors or reinterpretation. That does not mean everything is an open book; but when confidentiality and security are important, the need is explained up-front. Appropriate privacy is as much a part of an Open arrangement as disclosure.

When both Politeness and Openness are healthy, interpersonal communication improves and relationships cannot help but strengthen. This does not mean lots of chatter and hugs, but clear, concise, accurate exchanges of both content and feelings without fear of reprisals or exploitation. People can say what is going on with them, as well as what is off limits, without repercussions. Conflict management and resolution extend from the workplace into the community, families, schools, churches – everywhere. These daily interactions keep tension and misunderstandings from building up and resulting in emotional confrontation or miscalculations.

When Openness is strong, **PURPLE** feels safe to express fears and attachments; **RED** can speak its mind without being judged, punished, or put down; **BLUE** can take moral stands and discuss grievances through channels; **ORANGE** can argue a case and disagree without being disagreeable; **GREEN** is reassured as everyone is legitimized and their feelings acknowledged; **YELLOW** can say what needs to be said, when it needs to be said, but knows that chit-chat is not mandatory; and **TURQUOISE** can connect with the full range of insight sources without asking permission. Of course, this also depends on a solid Politeness leg; otherwise, Openness is high-risk behavior.

A – The Autocracy Factor

The third leg of the **P-O-A** stool is Autocracy. Are you surprised? In recent years there has been an emphasis on softer tones, participative management, decision-sharing, and workplace democratization. Spiral Dynamics supports the trend, especially in the communal 'MEME ranges where self-managed work teams and similar group structures are most appropriate. However, that does not eliminate the requirements for accountability and a contact point. Someone in charge is still essential when the **PURPLE** through **BLUE** 'MEMEs are active and quite important to **ORANGE**.

The word 'autocrat' has a negative ring. To some it reeks of the cigar-smoking executive like Mr Dithers, Dagwood Bumstead's boss in *Blondie*, the tyrannical supervisors in films like *9 to 5*, *Working Girl*, or *Norma Rae*, or even the archetype, Ebeneezer Scrooge. To others it suggests an elitist idea that some are destined to lead while others must resign themselves to follow the likes of Captain Bligh through a hierarchical **BLUE** world.

Yet in Gravesian terms, Autocracy simply means taking charge, accepting responsibility, knowing where 'the buck stops,' and being willing to put one's self on the line. Even if Politeness and Openness are solid, when the decisive A leg in weak mangement is called wimpy and the 'hey, that's not my job' syndrome prevails. When the Spiral is in control, managers are paid to 'manage' and leaders to lead through **P**, **O**, and **A**.

The leader with healthy Autocracy does not become a tyrant. Rather, he, she, or even they (Autocracy can be collective as well as individual) act like Spiral Wizards to determine the appropriate decision system for the situation, people, and expected outcomes, then implement it quickly. When accompanied by Politeness and Openness, the tug of authority and control sends more positive than negative messages and fear leaves the equation. Some firm Autocracy actually feels good because there is a baseline, things are happening, and there is clear direction.

This is how Autocracy is expressed as the Spiral manager either exhibits it or causes it to be exhibited through a range of decisive styles. **PURPLE** relishes a strong 'chieftain' from within the clan and a council of 'elders;' **RED** only respects assertive toughness (as long as she or he can be tough, too); **BLUE** wants to hear the voice of righteous higher authority; **ORANGE** thrives on fast-track action and individual initiative; **GREEN** accepts Autocracy when all benefit and share in it; **YELLOW** is most comfortable with functional flexibility and competency-driven systems; **TURQUOISE** is beginning to explore the need for unified controls on a very large scale.

Even traditional organizations like Eastman Kodak are collapsing their rigid hierarchies into lean, quick reacting integrated networks with more assertive and autonomous work units. They must now survive and prosper in a fast paced, highly competitive, and technologically sophisticated global environment. If a large part of the Autocracy skill bundle is out-placed in down-sizing, the new self-managed teams will not know how to self manage. Spiral Wizards must shift leadership quickly between intense group processes and decisive executive actions to make certain all three competencies of the **P-O-A** trio remain intact. This shift to Second Tier thinking is important for governmental entities contemplating privatization and the military, in particular. First Tier technologies will not get the job done any more.

To summarize, Politeness, Openness, and Autocracy establish the base and levels the field. By doing so, it enables leadership to get a better lock on the 'MEMEs which must be addressed both short and long-term, then to shape the messages, methods, and media for the specific 'MEME profile. By adjusting each of the **P-O-A** elements up or down as needed, the entity stays in balance with its *milieu*. Besides the bottom-line advantages of efficiency and functionality, healthy **P-O-A** just creates a far more pleasant place to be for all concerned.

The Spiral Wizard's Options for Situational Intervention

How does a Spiral Wizard decide whether to get involved in a particular situation? Consider the following options:

Option 1: *Just Walk Away*
First, as you read the situation *the best option may be to walk away* – 'just back off,' to use Graves' pet phrase. It may even be prudent to run in haste if . . .

- The cards are stacked against what you want to do.
- You are fighting entrenched interests at City Hall.
- the die is cast and it would be futile to continue.
- The 'MEMEs you need are inaccessible as things are.
- The systems where you had hoped to operate are irrevocably Closed.
- You have neither power nor support to implement change.

Option 2: *Reframe the Conditions*
Even though things may not appear to be in your favor at first, there may be ways to rearrange them. You may be able to gently realign some of the priorities before proceeding any further. While you get new ideas ready for people, you need to work simultaneously in the other direction and get the people ready for the ideas. You can prod issues to intensify certain 'MEMEs, shake things up to reawaken others, and resolve current problems to dim others down.

Propagandists use martial music, colorful flags and banners, enemy-baiting, and a host of other devices to raise **BLUE** in an audience. Pep-rallies, sales meetings, contests, and competitions brighten **ORANGE**. Sharing feelings and mutually supportive group projects turn **GREEN** on.

Skillful communicators have long recognized the power in manipulating the way a candidate, idea, or product is initially defined. What they do, of course, is speak the languages of the Spiral as (a) they paint the subject with 'MEME colors and (b) activate particular filters in the audience. The ethics of the speaker determines how true the imagery is and whether the strategy is for good or bad. Here are some possibilities for Spiral-based communication:

- If a company is beset by fear because of impending downsizing, expect **PURPLE**, **RED**, and **BLUE** 'MEMEs to brighten while the more complex processing systems – **ORANGE, GREEN**, and **YELLOW** – will dim. The colors that are pulsating must be dealt with by addressing the problems they sense.

- When in dangerous, war-like conditions, the systems of some people will down-shift into **PURPLE** and **RED** basic survival impulses. These will be highly visible and active. In the extreme, prepare for an increase in cases of cruelty, sexual harassment, and even violent acting out. The 'MEMEs that understand and accept the rules and constraints (**BLUE** and above) may be on HOLD until peacetime conditions return. Responsible leaders must anticipate this human regression or be held to account for war-crimes. The majority of people will go on with their lives, disturbed but fundamentally unmoved on the Spiral.

- Attempts to privatize an activity (brighten **ORANGE**) are often sabotaged by bureaucratic **BLUE**. Several options are available to those wishing to shift or transform a public organization into a private enterprise. Among these are:

(a) You may utilize a jump-start technique to determine where more **ORANGE** potential shows up. Simulations are useful in this regard. Another tool is to set up competition with an outside entity and see who takes charge. The capacity may be latent but ill-defined in some, absent in others. (Indeed, the public-to-private transition is **BLUE** to **ORANGE**, though **GREEN** may initiate (and fund) the action and **YELLOW** ultimately has to clean up the mess).

(b)   Additional **ORANGE** thinking people may have to be inserted into the organizations to create a more favorable critical mass, one that understands and can accept the challenge of moving from a rigid pyramid to a strategic enterprise. Effective recruitment, selection, and placement do wonders compared to remedial training or managerial fixer-upers.

Option 3: *Connect Ideas with* ᵛ*MEMEs*
If the necessary ᵛMEMEs are in place and at the desired intensity, the task becomes confirming the connection between new ideas and those internal systems. Leaders must translate from their own language to well-crafted Spiral-ese. To check the translation, send in your probe to see how the people respond. This may take the form of trial balloons and customized versions of the same message in different wrappings.

In the film, *Close Encounters of the Third Kind*, the Earthlings sought to connect with the extraterrestrials by broadcasting a pattern of lights and musical sounds. Both entities sought for a common pattern. The climax of the movie occurs when the Earth station and visitors found synchrony in the key tones of John Williams' riff for tuba, clarinet, and flute – *re me do* $_{DO}$ *so*.

The same thing happens in leadership. Leader and follower discover a common language and pattern. Each system has its own radar scope on which a particular image must appear for it to feel connected. ᵛMEME systems constantly scan the world looking for similarities. Effective managers build those links among people, organizations, and tasks.

Once the link-up is achieved, though, the management system best not stay at the same place as the followers. The effective leader's thinking is always a bit more complex than those being led, though the leader's behaviors are not so far ahead that a good fit is lost. If people are OPEN (Change Condition 1) and in the First Tier (**PURPLE** through **GREEN**), the ideal leader is about a half step ahead. If the group is centered at **BLUE**, the **BLUE/orange** is fine and **ORANGE/blue** might work, though more skill would be required. The style of Peak **ORANGE** is too far away to be effective and **GREEN** may actually set up adversarial relationships instead of cooperative leader/follower linkages.

Change often follows frustration. If leaders learn behavioral skills and traits but do not alter their thinking, followers can outstrip them quickly. When the workers' insight outgrows the managers', you have problems with morale, turnover, productivity, and costs. Leadership systems must move before the process of change process is finished in the followers or leaders will quickly become irrelevant or, even worse, perceived as barriers to be stepped around or blown up.

Rules of Thumb for Spiral Leaders

1. If the critical mass of thinking within followers is more complex on the Spiral than proposed leadership, that leadership can only take control through

intimidation or force. Once it grasps power, the more complex thinkers will go into hiding, exile, or premature graves. Revolutions will certainly be on the horizon. (One of Somalia's warlords ordered the massacre of 3–400 of the more complex thinkers – professionals, teachers, business people – the night before the U.S. Marines landed. With several hundred thousand up-Spiral Somalis already in exile in Kenya, the remaining 'leaders' eliminated the very people necessary to build a more democratic society, thus preserving their own empires but risking that barely developing nation.)

2. If the followers are in Closed or Arrested conditions (Change Condition 1) at a specific level on the Spiral, the leadership approach needs to be calibrated for that identical level – **BLUE** for **BLUE**, **GREEN/orange** for **GREEN/orange**, and **red/BLUE** for **red/BLUE**. The leader may be Arrested but must not be Closed or the enterprise will inevitably collapse when *Life Conditions* change. If the leaders are in the Open condition, the entity can last a long, long time.

- A dedicated and highly disciplined monastery might best be under the control of a stronger, experienced **BLUE** True Believer who has the best grasp of Truth (and the recipe for cognac!).
- The best leader of a highly competitive sales staff might be the super-salesperson who knows all the tricks, ploys, and risks. If all the followers want in life is to make more money and to be more successful, that relationship can also be congruent. If their success awakens them to the damage they have done to the family, or to what they have missed while living 'the good life,' they will need leadership that also understands **BLUE**, **GREEN**, or both.

3. If the followers are in the Open condition, the optimum management is about half a step beyond their position on the Spiral. Leadership will occupy the range that many are just now entering, and can literally show them the way. Gurus come and go because the followers eventually pass them and their theories by being en route to more complex modes of living.

- A gang leader will share some of the same **PURPLE** and **RED** thinking with gang members but must have something more, either structured discipline from emerging **BLUE** or better strategic planning from concurrently rising **ORANGE**. You may impact that leader with devout **BLUE** or **ORANGE** economic incentives.
- For a minister or church leaders to be effective in managing a congregation, they must (1) identify with the core beliefs but (2) stay about half a step ahead of the members to answer the questions they are now beginning to ask, and new ones they are about to raise in the next awakening. Yet church leaders cannot appear to be too far out of sync or they will be declared heretics and/or driven away by the righteously Closed.

4. If the group is highly diversified, leadership must come from the most complex system available in the group. YELLOW in the Open condition, though has the built-in flexibility to shift into congruence with lower systems on the Spiral when appropriate. It is also the best way to manage Second Tier systems until **TURQUOISE** and beyond awaken further. Open persons in the **YELLOW–TURQUOISE** range can work in First Tier systems so long as they are also in the Open condition and meet at least some Second Tier needs. Keep in mind that if you manage Open people successfully, you may well fulfill the other Six Conditions for Change and release the next ᵛMEME on the Spiral, thus mandating a change in your leadership.

5. If the leadership model is too far ahead on the Spiral, it will destabilize and overwhelm the group or leave them asking 'Where's this idiot coming from? What a flake. Does anybody know what he's talking about?' Many leaders have been drummed out of the corps, burned at the stake, or banished into oblivion when their thinking became too complex for the followers to understand.

This has been the experience of many prominent African Americans who have moved into **ORANGE, GREEN,** and **YELLOW**. They are quickly labeled 'Uncle Toms' or accused of 'not being Black enough' by self-styled revolutionaries still in the **RED** to **BLUE** range. Today, Black vs. White tension is often evidence of an internal power struggle for control of a Black community between **red/BLUE** and **blue/ORANGE** ᵛMEMEs within it. Those tensions raise antibodies in whites who then start acting out, **RED/ blue** looking for a fight and **red/BLUE** anxious to put everyone in their place. The resulting conflict is attributed to racial problems when, in fact, they are Spiral problems. Similar conflicting ᵛMEME patterns held in the last century for Irish-Americans and occur in Hispanic and Asian-American communities today. In the past, 'White Flight' was credited with weakening of inner city areas. Civic leaders are now recognizing it as abandonment by those possessed with the **ORANGE** ᵛMEME from across racial lines. Reinvestment and community renewal must be run through the Spiral, not a stereotyped focus on race or ethnicity.

Each of the Spiral's ᵛMEMEs grows the political and organizational forms which fit its world view, perform the functions it deems necessary, and meet its specific bottom lines. Debates about which leadership form is 'the best,' whether in the General Assembly of the United Nations or in a university management seminar, miss the point. The argument shoud turn on what are the prevailing *Life Conditions* and which ᵛMEMEs will awaken. Once the color(s) are identified, the appropriate leadership follows naturally.

More complex ᵛMEME systems overwhelm less complex ones by injecting psychological viruses into their cultures. Global television broadcasts programs from **ORANGE** and **GREEN** societies onto the screens in **PURPLE, RED,** and just Entering **BLUE** households. Without the immunity of progressive development through the Spiral's layers, the less elaborated

An Example: U.S. Presidents on the Spiral

If you apply Spiral Leadership principles to recent Presidential politics in the U.S., you see why President Nixon's ORANGE/blue (with some RED on tape!) was ideal for both the Soviet Union and China of his day. They still do not understand why he resigned. But he lost sync with his constituencies at home, just as he would later become an anachronism to the Chinese who once embraced him.

Jimmy Carter's orange/GREEN leadership style was Arrested at a position one to one-and-a-third of a step beyond where the American people were centered. Ronald Reagan's blue/ORANGE image was just barely ahead of 'the electorate' – a third of a step or so – and fit the leadership requirements just right. Thus, his 'Teflon' coating and ability to remain an effective leader whether or not he dozed off at cabinet meetings. Thus, also Jimmy Carter's coninued global presence as peace negotiator in a world steadily more in line with his ᵛMEMEs.

In his day, former President Bush was in sync with the voters' ORANGE Peak and became the custodian of the 'me' era's ᵛMEMEs. However, he did not take the next one-third step in complexity to lead (as opposed to being liked and respected). Arrested at ORANGE, Bush did not seem to 'get it' when compared to the Clinton campaign's stretch into ORANGE/green messages that were now beginning to resonate with voters. Reagan's success with supply-side economics had introduced a new set of problems which Bush's advisors failed to detect. He accepted the notion that the *Life Conditions* were stable and it was still 'Morning in America,' one of Reagan's highly effective marketing themes. 'Why transform what ain't broke?' Bush probably thought. Yet, to the Republican new-right wing, even Bush's blue/ORANGE pragmatism represented a sell-out of resurging BLUE/orange ideology since even the orange was fading.

Thence came Ross Perot to carry the BLUE banner of Truth (in spite of his history of ORANGE wheeling and dealing and excess of Autocracy at the expense of Politeness and Openness). Once he had slipped into incautious RED a few times, though, the Perot phenomenon faded like his charts.

President Clinton defeated them both because his team understood that the country's *Life Conditions* were unstable and there was turbulence in the Spiral. The electorate sensed it, too, and wanted change, any kind of change. Clinton presented a leadership style one-third to half a step ahead of the voters' present center of gravity. His use of organizational clusters, 'People First' slogans, and inclusion politics were consistent with the ORANGE/green and orange/GREEN range many activists were embracing.

Whatever one thinks of his ideas, Mr Clinton's actual thinking may be as much as a full step or more ahead of the population mass. The First Lady has exhibited GREEN/orange rather consistently and must beware of the appearance of arrogance. The same holds for the ORANGE/green pop culture consultants and staffers that continue to surround the First Family. That a serious gap has existed between the President's ᵛMEMEs (and those of the Democratic Party) and the active voters was made all too evident in the results of the 8 November 1994 mid-term election as the political center snapped back toward the BLUE zone. Given the pace of change, we can expect other snaps to occur very rapidly.

systems are highly vulnerable to the 'too much, too soon' illness. False expectations of the 'good life just around the corner' are raised prematurely. Many Third Worlders actually believe everybody in Dallas lives like a millionaire.

The Spiral Wizardry Package

What are Second Tier approaches like? For one thing, we know they will incorporate Individual/Elite themes from **YELLOW** and Communal/Collective themes from **TURQUOISE**. Though they do not know it, the **YELLOW** ᵛMEME is currently the 'hot topic' of many stump-speaking managerial gurus churning out books around the world. A few are even coming to recognize that the spiritual balance **TURQUOISE** provides is also a crucial ingredient for successful Second Tier transitions. Spiral Dynamics will give you a leg up so you can place what they are suggesting on the overall Spiral framework, flesh it out, and then see how it fits ths specific zones which concern you most directly.

YELLOW

TURQUOISE

Systemic Flow

Holistic Organism

Characteristics of the Second Tier Leadership Package

- Each person is free to choose whether to put up with, try to change, or even to walk away, but he or she will take individual responsibility for the consequences.
- Managers act as go-fers (not *super*visors or *over*seers) for the worker, getting necessary information and materials to the right place as needed. They may also empower, enable, facilitate, and inspire when required to do so.

- Contracts are made with employees such that a very specific 'what' should be done, and by 'when.' However, there are great degrees of freedom regarding 'how' and no pretense that the job can only be done in one way.
- People are focused on an agreed, joint purpose that supersedes the person or group itself, yet serves to make each life healthier and enhances the overall life of the Spiral.
- At first, 'less is more' since the most effective use of resources makes possible the pursuit of other equally valuable and simultaneous projects. Then more can be more.
- Second Tier thinking uses human diversity constructively by neither worshipping it nor advocating sameness. In this view, people have unequal competencies and unequal needs since differentiated intelligences are spread among us all, but not in accordance with economic class, gender, or race-based distinctions.
- People are naturally productive if the organization is designed and aligned to match individuals with functions they find stimulating. The Spiral Wizard helps diverse mindsets target specific outputs in a functional flow and move around as needed.
- People, technology, nature, and procedures are interwoven and integrated into the stream of work.
- Conflict is inevitable in any living system but the Spiral Wizard actively manages it to promote the health of the interactive Spiral, not to favor any isolated faction or personal agenda.

Characteristics of Organizations in the Second Tier

The whole range of ᵛMEMEs may show up in a Spiral Wizard-designed organization – a **RED** Empire, a **BLUE** Pyramid, and an **ORANGE** goal-centered hierarchy, for example. Whatever the mix, the forms will be designed and aligned to accomplish specific functions in an Open condition video-tape, not an Arrested or even Closed photo album.

In Second Tier organizations:

- Functions are holographic. Sales, accounting, training, safety, and quality exist everywhere, in the minds of all people, instead of being located in a single niche on the pyramid. You look throughout the entity to find its ᵛMEMEs, yet its discrete chunks are fractals with Autocracy enough to stand up for the whole.
- Because Openness is present, information flows through a minimum of filters, gate keepers, functional boundaries, or territorial hoards. Knowledge is effectiveness, not power.
- External and internal worlds are constantly scanned to detect subtle changes, potential flash points, messages from the future, or early warnings of turbulence.
- Change is a fact of life. It is programmed into the organization 'DNA.' *Life*

Conditions are monitored in a command and control center. People are seen in terms of growth and evolution, a process which is fully supported.

- Morphing (changing shapes) occurs on an ongoing basis. The organism can adjust its style to match the needs of clients, customers, and others yet retain the integrity of its core ᵛMEMEs. Those who need **ORANGE** can find it. Those who seek **GREEN** will perceive that component. The whole is interconnected like the atmospheric highs and lows swirling around the equator.

The style adjustment is expedited by Second Tier intelligences which can detect what the customer expects and can put together the personnel and programs that radiate back, as in *Close Encounters* . . . , the key values code. Salespeople are assigned to specific customers. Marketers appeal specifically to values-delineated account segments. Even receptionists who greet visitors or first answer the telephone listen for the operating system(s) of a client and then direct that person to the congruent zone within the company. Distinctions between 'inside' and 'outside' are blurry since parts can spin off to connect in strategic alliances and outsourcing partnerships, then blend back in when the tasks are completed.

- Ethical codes are taken seriously and enforced universally. Standards, regulations, and prescriptions are designed to maintain the life, health, and vitality of the Spiral. This ethical perspective is quite unlike **BLUE**'s narrowly rule-bounded definition of 'morality' or even the **ORANGE** doing 'what's prudent' on its terms. It has little of the relativism of **GREEN** since there are absolutes in the Second Tier and even humanistic concerns yield as broad principles take charge.

- Since Second Tier entities see themselves as groups of competent people who could move into a number of different industries or operations, any repetitive cycles of success and failure are easily accommodated. With 'have-to' compulsiveness and 'what if?' fear diminished, they can exhibit high degrees of freedom.

- The culture is celebratory. A broad range of life choices and beliefs can be expressed and exercised right along with responsibilities of being a good worker, neighbor, citizen, and even Earthling. People in Second Tier organizations are either having fun with their lives or they move on.

Spiral Managing the Whole Spectrum

Human beings are actually collections of interdependent entities – free-thinking blood cells swimming around, organs held loosely together by slimy plumbing, eggs and sperm anxious to get it on, bacterial subcontractors handling waste management, and a brain that maintains a semblance of order for the 70 or 80 years before our infrastructure gives out.

Second Tier organizations are much the same. They are organic gathering places for intelligences and ᵛMEMEs. To serve in the brain syndicate of such an enterprise, the Spiral Wizard must first understand the anatomy of each component's leadership, then dissect the structures to learn the care and feeding of each part. Think of this as Spiral biology 101, the organizational forms. You will experience 102, the ᵛMEMEs themselves, later in Section 3.

Leadership Assumptions of the Core ᵛMEMEs: An Anatomy

SECOND TIER

TURQUOISE

- Spiritual bonds will pull people and organizations together across space/time
- Work must be meaningful to the overall health of all life
- Organizations are responsible for the impacts of their activities
- The universe is a single entity of elegantly balanced, interlocking forces
- Experiencing feelings and information together enhances both

YELLOW

- People enjoy doing that work which fits who they are naturally
- Workers need free access to information, tools, and materials
- Organizations are only transitory states because change happens
- Learning and understanding motivate people, not payoffs or punishment
- People have different competencies and capacities, and most are OK

FIRST TIER

GREEN

- People want to get along and be accepted by their peers as friends
- Sharing and participating lead to better results than competing
- Emotions need attention, but hard feelings should be avoided
- All members of an organization should have their say and be included
- The organization is responsible for its community's well-being

ORANGE

- People are motivated by opportunity to achieve and acquire material rewards
- Competition improves productivity and fosters growth through opposition
- The tried-and-true is best, though it can always be improved upon
- Workers want to get ahead and have more influence over others
- Here-and-now success is evidence of rewards to come in the future

BLUE

- It is mankind's lot to work for the glory of the one True Way and keep a job
- People must be shown their duty and learn by being punished for failures
- Workers are cogs in a system, fulfilling roles they are destined to
- Higher authority rules by rightful compliance, not by might or fear
- Workers owe the organization loyalty as it provides their well-being

RED

- People must be dominated by stronger force to keep their lusts in check
- Workers will put up with a lot so long as their basic needs are met
- The haves are owed their status and perks just because of who they are
- Have-nots probably deserve their status and have no right to complain
- Payoffs get results, nobody can be trusted, and everyone has their price

PURPLE

- People are 'married' to the group and nepotism is a way to take care of our own
- Workers owe their very lives and souls to the paternalistic organization
- People follow their leaders willingly to honor their ancestors and the spirits
- Anyone will sacrifice self without question if the group needs it to survive
- Adhere to traditional ways and customs without change or disrespect

Dissecting First Tier Organizations on the Spiral

The GREEN ᵛMEME's Leadership Package
Social/Communitarian

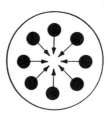

Social Network

- People work in order to have more human contact, learn about others and come to know their inner being more fully.
- People feel that being liked and accepted is more important than economic rewards, competitive advantage, material gain, or supporting rules from outside the group.
- People value peer approval and consensus in a climate of openness, trust, and sharing, but fear rejection and disapproval

Within the GREEN ʸMEME's Aura: GREEN organizations are proactive on behalf of human rights, community enrichment, and full opportunities for all to develop and grow. It is not altruism; the entity takes care of itself and does things that make it feel good. Barriers and restrictions are eliminated without excuses, be they physical or social. Hierarchies, competitive career ladders, and executive privilege blur in favor of frequent, open communication and accessibility. Everybody is on a first name basis and management helps them come to know each other.

Most large entities are just awakening their GREEN ʸMEMEs. They've talked 'caring' talk, but it has been out of BLUE obligation or ORANGE manipulation for productivity and positioning at the Chamber of Commerce banquet. Authentic GREEN puts people first, and most of today's executives still do not know how to do that very well. Self-disclosure and openness scare them to death. The three-piece 'suits' of industry have much to fear with the move into more GREEN.

People Under the Power of the GREEN ʸMEME: Involvement and participation are keys to satisfaction. The person's identity is closely allied with the group. The role of 'leaders' is not so much to direct as to facilitate by joining with the people to help them like each other and get along while they are getting a job done. Everybody gets a share in benefits, often of their choosing. All 'belong' in a pleasant work environment with people-friendly gathering spots and politically correct, eco-conscious recreation facilities. The group listens to gripes and complaints; everybody has the right to be heard. Interpersonal competencies are stressed in addition to technical skills. The entity's profile is usually quite flat in terms of both salary and management layers.

Leadership for the GREEN ʸMEME: Leaders strive to achieve organizational goals by providing satisfaction of affiliative needs if people perform as the group desires, but withholding love and attention if someone does not. Management does not deny the satisfaction of basic economic (ORANGE) or security needs (BLUE) if organizational behavior is not as the group desires; but it does isolate the nonconformist from what the group can provide. If the misbehavior continues, the source of disharmony may be asked to leave. In this view, people are productive when they receive positive affect and acceptance for it. They will work hard to avoid rejection by those whom they value. The manager is more of a colleague and friend than boss since reciprocal participation is inherent in the GREEN structure where all 'are in it together.'

The GREEN ʸMEME's Vision: Socially responsible, environmentally accountable goals which benefit all members of the organization and the overall community with which it identifies are typical of GREEN. It need not be non-profit, but the economic bottom line is not the ultimate objective. The purpose is more to render meaningful service and find pleasure doing it than to make huge profits.

GREEN has emerged in some self-managed team environments where the need for consensual problem resolution techniques outweighs the individual needs of those involved. Likewise, the necessity of equal access to information, made necessary by flattened organizations and easy by computer networks and E-mail, reflects the circle-of-equals notion of GREEN. As the Army discovered many years ago, a keyboard has no button for 'Salute!' Information inputs from a corporal or a colonel look the same on screen.

There is a catch with intense GREEN – sometimes productivity goes to pot. The entity will be notoriously productive in crisis situations since all have cause to pull together, but the surge is difficult to maintain over the long haul. When all is well, complacency sets in. The frequent response is to cut demands and let people get by doing less to avoid hurt feelings. This permissiveness produces expensive GREEN give-aways and soft touches that forgive too much. Since organizations are prone to regression when under pressure and can down-shift surprisingly fast, prepare for abandonment of 'we, the people' in favor of the heretofore buried ORANGE economic drives and even the use of BLUE dogma as a weapon when GREEN starts to swamp.

The ORANGE ᵛMEME's Leadership Package
Rational/Economic

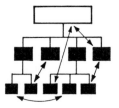

Strategic Enterprise

- Each person calculates the actions that will maximize his or her own advantages and leverage competitive opportunities.
- People are driven by economic motives, and will do almost anything if you only know the rules for their proper manipulation.
- The individual, beyond being an economic being, is a passive organism meant to be maneuvered by external forces.
- Human beings are like replaceable parts in a machine that can always be improved. The economy is driven by market forces which, under the control of the 'invisible hand,' has a life of its own.

Within the ORANGE ᵛMEME's Force Field: The entity buys service to meet its objectives from people who can be molded to suit its needs. The organization reserves its greatest rewards for those who do what it says most successfully. However, that obedience (**BLUE**) eventually builds up hostility to the organization and loyalty is replaced by self-interest. The **ORANGE** ᵛMEME prefers to be coldly logical and in control. It becomes irrational if it gains too much since it can then quit working and declare a holiday, all expenses paid. Loyalty is a commodity, not a commandment.

ORANGE is viable so long as there are plenty of opportunities for many people to get a piece of the pie. For its influence to endure, there must be a hope-filled dream. Work is characterized by specialization of function, objective qualifications for positions, and constant evaluation of performance. Administration is pragmatic, according to 'scientifically' established standard operating procedures and a stream of statistical measures. The system runs through a politicized hierarchy with economic and status rewards as the means to the end. Outcomes are usually material, rather than spiritual, although just winning 'the game' can become the greatest payoff of all.

People Under the Power of the ORANGE ᵛMEME: In this zone an effective person is like a well-oiled machine that works as expected. Money, perks, and opportunities to advance are the lubricants for productivity. The person wants to succeed and advance toward ultimate independence. Design of the work is critical to success, since power ratios, titles, and the physical appearance of facilities influence performance. The person needs clear goals, objectives, targets, and reference points just beyond their reach. They want 'a piece of the action,' not lock-step promotion or salary grades. Closed personalities caught up in **ORANGE** never have enough or finish the game, even when they have no opponents left. The proverbial carrot is always just out of reach.

Leadership for the ORANGE ᵛMEME: Management and leadership are based on the assumption that the world and the people in it are but vast mechanisms that can eventually be perfected. Objective data – 'The facts, ma'am; nothing but the facts' – provide the tools for control and managed information keeps the entity well lubricated. Management's role is to plan, organize, motivate, control, and evaluate work. The executive's first responsibility and primary concern is the viability of the organization and its competitive posture; its people are necessarily secondary. The leadership role includes determining: Who reports to whom? Who does what job? How are jobs best designed? How to develop and manipulate necessary incentives? How to measure success? How can we gather more information to use against the competition?

The bored **ORANGE** leader may begin to 'play' with parts of the organization – job descriptions, technological experiments, organization charts and forms, etc. – in a quest for a new and improved structure. People are puppets with strings to pull and buttons to push, so necessary things get done in ways that please the manager. Carrots and sticks motivate personnel, and both are used very calculatingly. Unkind **ORANGE** discards people like worn out machine tools and replaces them with newer ones in the name of progress and necessity. Kinder **ORANGE** helps them become serviceable again, just at a lower cost or somewhere else.

The ORANGE ᵛMEME's Objective: The **ORANGE** purpose is simple: To be the best, most successful competitor in the field, whatever it is right now. The measure of that success often takes the form of making greater profits for 'ourselves and our stakeholders,' since the 'money is life's report card.' The goal is to grow, expand, and extend influence to either dominate a market niche or be a major 'player' in many domains at once.

The pitfall of **ORANGE** is that the efforts to maximize individual gains often consume so much material and energy that the source of the work itself is destroyed. Mega-dollar sports stars and greedy owners are putting the games at risk when they begin to ignore their client fans and concentrate, instead, on comparing their own egos. The collapse of the U.S. Savings & Loan Industry also illustrates the point that a few elites with excessive **ORANGE** can demand so much cream it kills the cow. Japan is also feeling its pinch. In politics, the energy invested in bringing down an adversary just because it can be done may, in fact, destroy a whole governmental structure.

The BLUE ᵛMEMEs Leadership Package
Moralistic/Prescriptive

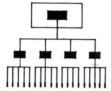

Authority Structure

- Humans are born into many classes of unequal rank at birth.
- The Higher Authority has laid down a design for living and assigned positions, duties, and standards for all to obey.
- The individual will be subject to eventual judgment based on the principles of living in the class to which rightful Authority has assigned that person.
- For everything there is a purpose, a reason, and a season within the master plan, though mere mortals may not understand.
- There is generally some form of hereafter, and one's worthiness for it is tested during this life.

The BLUE 'MEME's Membership: BLUE organizations are hierarchical and rigidly structured. There are sharp lines between ranks – no fraternization – and people are sorted and separated by 'worthiness.' There is often a classification scheme that is reflected in a social chain-of-command, residential patterns, and socioeconomics. Power is in the position, not the personality. The entity does not open up the world to all people, but expects all to be the best they can in their right and proper places. Race, age, gender, national origin, religion, and many other factors have determined rank in BLUE where diversity means categories.

BLUE time is linear and sequential – one thing at a time along Newton's 'straight arrow.' Discipline is strict – nuns-with-rulers – and punishment is public – flogging in Singapore, for example. A code of honor, concern with reputation, pride in craftsmanship, and a sense of guilt are built into the entity. Good works serve the Higher Power or the Just Cause, then the organization, and finally the individual. As the U.S. shifts away from BLUE industries, it also surrenders BLUE jobs to Mexico, Korea, Taiwan, Malaysia, and the Philippines where this 'MEME is now beginning to flourish. After a while, Africa will take the BLUE work away from them.

People Under the Power of the BLUE 'MEME: BLUE is natural for skilled, semi-technical jobs requiring from some to quite a lot of specific learning. The person feels a duty to work and 'hold down a job' – Puritan or Confucian work ethics. Laboring diligently is rewarding both in terms of immediate satisfaction and the belief that greater reward will come in the afterlife and/or accrue to the valued establishment. Innovation and risk-taking are at low-ebb, so the person wants and needs clear direction with certain outcomes on a regular schedule.

German trains are run by BLUE. Fine Swiss watches are manufactured by BLUE craftsmen (and then marketed by ORANGE). The post-World War II miracle in Japan was administered through BLUE 'MEMEs and resonated with Japanese PURPLE, as well, to set the standards for mass-produced quality, reliability, and attention to detail. In an enterprise rooted in healthy BLUE, the traditional worker would expect life-long employment, live quite happily in company housing, shop at the company store, and name a first-born son after the CEO.

Leadership for the BLUE 'MEME: Moralistic-prescriptive BLUE management encodes the Truths from the dominant ideology and rewards believers, faithful servants, and those who work 'long hours in the vineyard but faint not.' The manager is judge and representative of even higher authority, usually with reference to The Book. Length of service awards, elaborate retirement ceremonies, somber funerals, patriotic displays, and a sometimes rule-bounded but orderly workplace are the result of BLUE labors. However, punishment is used quickly on the unfaithful, the undisciplined, and the rebellious so be not late. It can be stringent, since suffering is for one's own eventual good and redemption – 'to beat the Hell out of . . . '

Management is based on the assumption that we are born into classes of unequal rank. The 'betters' have the responsibility – *noblesse oblige* – to take care of their lesser's through charitable acts which also serve the higher authority. Leaders oversee the needs of followers and regulate their conduct *in loco parentis*. This applies both within the organization and to life in general, since the reputation of the entity is always on the line.

The BLUE ᵛMEME's Purpose: BLUE seeks to do what is right and what is ordained to serve the greater good. It believes that the grand plan has laid down a class-ordered life in which all should live according to the traditional rules of proper behavior. The greater purpose of an organization is to maintain order, provide security, meet basic needs, and guide all to future reward if they live and work as prescribed. It is necessary in hierarchies where ordered discipline is critical to doing the work.

The **BLUE** ᵛMEME need not be loaded with deep guilt, imperatives to bow to authority, or willingness to sacrifice self compliantly while others prosper. Fairness, equity, and consistency are the more common themes. Doing what is 'right and proper' is the concern. Continually check for a functional understanding of the work to be done and where it fits into the entire flow since **BLUE** often counts trees instead of surveying forests.

Heavy **BLUE** is common in fundamentalist doctrines which structure every aspect of living. Some are religious, many are secular. Either way, life is devoted to service of the authority, obeisance to its directives, and self-sacrifice in the mission. The organization, not its members, is paramount and will endure.

The RED ᵛMEME's Leadership Package
Exploitive/Egocentric

Empire

- The human is inherently lazy and must be intimidated, coerced, or enticed by promises of rewards to do very much of anything.
- People's natural goals run counter to the organization's. Most people are incapable of self-discipline or self-control and cannot be trusted.
- Leaders must suppress natural human tendencies. Through force, fear, or bribery their job is to get the individual to do what he or she does not want to do. Since a few are self-motivated, they should assume control of all others. These dominant ones accomplish organizational goals by selecting from the masses a similar number who are desirous for more and teach them how to get the rest to do the work.

The Dominion of the RED 'MEME: RED assumes that those of demonstrated superiority have the right, because they are the 'chosen,' to organize the efforts of lesser people through force toward whatever ends the superior conceives as good for him or herself.

The structure involves a Big Boss at the top of the pecking order, a few Work Bosses who see that the work is done, and a largely unskilled mass doing the labor. This produces the classic have/have-not and can/cannot disparities common in so many developing nations and seemingly intensifying in the U.S. In the extreme, RED resorts to slavery. More moderated forms include indentured servitude and piece-work, as well as sweat shop operations remotely subsidized by ORANGE corporations and their customers.

People Under the Power of the RED 'MEME: The RED 'MEME shakes out the world as follows:

a)   A few people's ideas work quickly; they get rewarded; they learn to do it again. These chosen ones have something special and they become the *elites*.
b)   Many others' ideas don't work, don't bring rewards, and they become the *masses* to be exploited. They must struggle just to meet subsistence needs and have no surplus energy to awaken alternative ways of thinking.
c)   Some get rewarded now and then; and they become the *desirous* of niches nearer the elites above the masses. Since they have some surplus energy, they vie for position unmercifully and have some motivation to awaken alternatives.

RED learns by operant conditioning – reinforcements given or withheld steer the person's development. The recurring question is 'What do I get out of it – what's in it for me?' Payoffs may be in cash or drugs, but can include excitement, power to wield over others, and sensual pleasures. When this 'MEME is dominant things tend to be physical, emotion-laden, and gut-level.

Leadership for the RED 'MEME: Management is based on the assumption that most people inherently dislike work, have little ambition, wish to avoid responsibility and have to be forced, threatened, or coerced to do a job. The Boss believes that the world, all its people and all its things are there to use as his or her means to exert remorseless power. Further, RED believes that only superior strength can challenge – sometimes in actual combat – his or her management decisions and procedures.

RED exploits the masses to accomplish the desires of the few. Since the human is seen to be inherently lazy and unmotivated, leaders must do whatever it takes to get people to do what they are not naturally inclined to. Both sugar and the whip are legitimate incentives when this 'MEME prevails.

This is the pattern. A Big Boss (BB) selects a few Work Boss lieutenants (WB) from those most desirous of having more. The BB dictates what, how, and when to do his or her will. The WB gets it done or else. BB asks no questions, accepts no excuses, cares only about results. WB is selected because of having the best ideas among the desirous or winning the fight before the selection interview. However, he or she must avoid direct threats to BB who will be ruthless in maintaining ultimate power, as portrayed in *The Godfather* model. WB pays tribute to BB, but can also take a cut from exploitation of the masses as long as the BB approves and does not feel it. If WB skims too much or is 'caught with a hand in the cookie jar,' then it is, per the Queen of Hearts, 'Off with her head!' The next among the desirous gets a promotion.

WBs have free rein so long as the BBs goals are attained. When times are good, WB can afford to be kind and considerate in maintaining a level of opulence for the workers. When times are bad, however, WB will use force, fear, and intimidation to exact all he or she can from the masses while still satisfying BBs demands for tribute. In terms of human energy and environmental resources, **RED** organizations will use as much or more than necessary to get work done since waste is no problem, consequences do not matter, and the prime directive is that the BB should never suffer.

Such exploitative leadership, whether benevolent or cruel, works well when the masses are uneducated, uninspired, and their warm bodies are plentiful. The work must be simple and supervision has to be constant in this oppressive environment. The view from management is that people can be easily replaced, even on a daily basis, so long as the basic needs of the remaining have-nots are met steadily.

The RED ᵛMEME's Drives: The central objective is to extend power and control; that pleases the Big Boss. The **RED** entity exploits the masses to fulfill the wishes of a few. If the BB has grand designs, the system will need a large number of workers. Monuments and 'wonders of the world' have been built through the **RED** ᵛMEME. Since a surplus of unskilled, uneducated labor is conducive to **RED** approaches, controlling its spread presents one of the great problems for Spiral Wizards in Third-World settings.

In its heavy form, **RED** responds to toughness, a bigger stick, instant gratification, 'do it or else' commands, and risky challenges. It views softness and hesitation as signs of weakness. Above all, it demands respect for self and can only respond to leadership that has earned that respect.

A degree of **RED** is a normal sub-theme in organizational functions where tough empires are appropriate. In such cases, instant piecework pay is better than a monthly salary. Free-wheeling work environments are better than time clocks and dress codes. Rules and regulations are there to be tested or ignored. **RED** surges in times of uncertainty or crisis when strong, charismatic, high Autocracy leadership is appropriate.

RED works if—

- there is an uneducated, uninspired, numerous mass of workers
- benevolent exploitation has been the norm
- scarcity leads to fear of deprivation
- there can be constant oversight
- there is a 6–13 person span of control
- things need doing quickly
- there is a surplus of labor to replace losses

RED fails when—

- the population becomes educated and/or aware of alternatives
- Big Boss is too openly greedy or needlessly cruel
- Work Boss(es) take too big a rake-off and basic needs are not met
- The mass shifts away from **PURPLE** and **purple/RED** to **red/BLUE**

The PURPLE ᵛMEME's Leadership Package
Communal/Tribal

Tribe/Clan

- The world is under the control of magical, animistic spirits which must be placated to keep the forces of nature in check.
- People are connected by kinship bonds and historic customs that supersede organizational needs or political interest.
- People must adhere to complex rituals that reckon time, form relation- ships, and define passages in 'growing up.'
- Leaders should come from within the indigenous tribe or clan. If not, they must act with the support of the shaman, elders, or chieftain.
- Work is rhythmic, close to the earth, and does not violate traditional gender, age, and social roles.

The Homeland of the PURPLE ᵛMEME: Living and work structures are circular and communal, though a core of semi-elites – the elders, the shaman, the chieftain – have greater influence than average others. Reciprocity is the dominant rule – 'If I find food I will share it with you, today, because, tomorrow, you may be the one who finds food and I will be in need.'

People Under the Power of the PURPLE ᵛMEME: To understand the PURPLE worker, learn about the customs of the clan or tribe. The person is an extension of the group and owes first allegiance back to it. Traditional ways of doing things, showing due respect to ancestors and their ways, and attention to the spirit realm are necessary to organizational health.

Decisions are made in circles where everybody has a say but the accepted 'leader' announces the consensus. Much energy will focus on meeting daily needs and those of their extended families. Fluid PURPLE 'trible-time' that relies on seasons, places, and events rather than digitized ORANGE or BLUE clock-ticks regulates activities, much to the distress of work schedulers and punctuality fanatics.

Dealing with fear, omens, and threats to the group are constant issues. The focus will be rather narrow and immediate, though memories of past events – grudges, slights, feuds, debts – may contaminate present operations until resolved. Maintaining harmony among the people and with nature is often a central theme.

The PURPLE ᵛMEMEs Ritual: The objective is to perpetuate the family, clan, or tribe by preserving its place in the animistic world meeting its subsistence needs. Most work is tied to the mystical spirit world, whether openly stated or not. Continuing to provide for the daily needs of food, housing, water, social interction, and protection from enemies occupy the attention of this ᵛMEME. Others may reach out to it, but it will not actively extend its influence very far.

Leadership for the PURPLE ᵛMEME: For PURPLE the leader must concentrate on the whole group rather than picking out individuals in compensation schemes, discipline, and communication. Rewarding someone too visibly may break the group bond and isolate that person disastrously. Indigenous leaders have to be respected and honored appropriately. Effective managers do not violate the internal social dynamics of PURPLE groups; instead, they learn about and utilize them as the whole entity observes seasonal festivals, rites of passage, and other celebrations.

The organization must be sensitive to the in-group vs. out-group polarizing tendencies when the PURPLE ᵛMEME is strong. Most Westernized executives (and diplomats) have never experienced true inter-tribal conflict and are unprepared for the intensity of feelings blood-bonds generate. At the same time, leaders should be aware of the potential for very sudden ᵛMEME shifts once PURPLE safety and security needs have been met, alternatives are introduced by TV or travel, and other ᵛMEMEs begin to awaken.

The next two chapters return to Second Tier principles and technologies.

7

Spiral Alignment:
*Stream*ing Visions into Reality

Management's Gospel of the 1990s proclaims quality as 'job 1.' What was 'job 1' before the quality revolution? Think about it. Profits? Production quotas? Executive perks? Time or motion efficiencies? Employee satisfaction? Beating the competition? Social responsibilities? Get real.

In spite of its popularity in executive suites and consumer groups, not everybody has joined the quality revolution. 'The Total Quality movement, one of the biggest fads in corporate management, is floundering.' So reported *The Wall Street Journal* (May 14, 1992). The article cited results of a comprehensive review of quality-management programs by Ernst & Young and the American Quality Foundation. Based on a survey of 585 companies in the U.S., Canada, Germany and Japan, the study details failings across a range of quality-improvement activities in the auto, computer, banking and health-care industries. Most professionals in the quality industry report mixed results from their clients and customers. Something is missing. What is it?

Companies that rush into quality-based initiatives without careful thought and preparation create a mess. Pronouncements from the 'suits' fall flat. Skeptical workers pay little heed. Mid-level managers resist, caught up in deadlines and turf battles, knowing that 'right-sizing' may mean their jobs. Sponsors of quality processes grow weary when the going gets tough and the newly-converted lose their enthusiasm and return to their old ways. Highly publicized programs fizzle out early, cold shower casualties of 'how it really is.' The initiative bogs down as **BLUE** turns it into a doctrinaire quasi-religion and **ORANGE** demands instant results or else heads will roll.

The 'quality circles' (QC) movement, ignited in the early 1980s with great fanfare, flamed out at the end of that decade. Many began to see these efforts as cosmetic quick fixes. Employees were encouraged to problem solve in teams. Yet, they were expected to stay in their respective places, at the bottom of the organizational pyramid. Involvement in the QC program was on a volunteer basis and nobody on the line would benefit financially from working 'harder and smarter.' But shareholders, stockholders, and executives would. No wonder enthusiasm waned.

Now reengineering projects are being questioned for similar reasons. Most applications largely ignored the humanity factor in their slash-and-burn activities. Downsizing efforts are being revisited, too. While the proud visionaries at the top and worker-bees on the production floor remain, the people who linked them in the mundane middle are gone. The resulting 'self-managed teams' do not know how to self-manage, plan, or connect.

What is wrong? Attempts to overlay innovative, new generation programs on preexisting structures, alien cultures and smug ᵛMEMEs backfire. Naive change agents roll out these programs from the corporate core, only to encounter booby traps and saboteurs out in the field. We shudder when told of plans to 'drive change' down an organization, as if it must be shoved down the throats of people and groups against their will.

If you are serious about change, be prepared to move beyond manipulation, authoritarian mandates, and even consensus-driven group process. The Spiral's framework lets you construct designs that fit who people are and the work they do. The 'run 'em thru the carwash' mode is out; detailing is in. Even the best approaches to comprehensive strategic planning miss the core mechanisms that link everything together. To uncover them, add the customizing features of Spiral Dynamics to the process. Then put your energy into the careful alignment of people with jobs, functions with outcomes, and styles with systems. Get down to the ᵛMEMEs of the matter.

The Design and Alignment of 'Natural' Systems with Power and Precision

Cutting-edge managerial thinking is far beyond (1) attacking what was wrong with the old ways and (2) alerting everybody that it is time for change. Bright people recognize that already. Instead, those at the cutting-edge are looking to design, align, and implement systems through forms that will actually work in the fast-paced, complex, and multifaceted world of the late 1990s and beyond, like nature would have done it. They need the power to effect Vertical change and the precision to do it right the first time by thinking as chemists, biologists, ecologists, systems engineers, sleuths, anti-terrorists, and anthropologists – all at once.

In Chapter 6 we added a range of organization ᵛMEMEs profiles, motivation menus, and leadership patterns framed through Spiral Dynamics to your Wizard's tool kit. The next section will introduce two more tools for organizational alignment, Graves' elegantly simple **Design Formula** and a **Plumb Line Process** to keep it straight. As the old proverb says: 'No more prizes for forecasting rain; only prizes for building an ark.' To become an organization shipwright you will need to master a pair of related skills – Spiral Alignment (*Streams*) and Spiral Integration (*Templates*).

SPIRAL ALIGNMENT (*Streams*) . . . is a comprehensive, 10-element design process that forces the organization to sequence its future visioning, strategic thinking, long- and short-term planning within a connected, river-like flow. You look upstream, downstream, and midstream, all at once. For the first time, leaders can fine-tune their organizations Spirals by aligning all aspects of *Life Conditions* with the ᵛMEMEs at work so as to *get the system right* before trying to force a new managerial *style* to fit.

SPIRAL INTEGRATION (*Templates*) . . . meshes your thinking on three levels into one organism. They are: (1) the specifics of the *job to be done*. (2) the *support systems* for the people who do the job, and (3) the overarching *executive intelligences* necessary for the macro-management of everything and everybody while it is being done.

With all of that done, you can start reconstruction.

The Design Formula: Framing the Right Questions (before giving premature answers!)

The Spiral Wizard asks the right questions – about people, motivation, communication, and learning. We generally ask the wrong question – 'How do you manage people?' Instead, we ought to be asking 'What is the nature of these people to be managed? What makes their *Life Conditions* unique? What system(s) of managing, training, or motivating will be most congruent with them and the work to be done at this time?'

'Right' questions show we recognize the flow of differences in people, understand the nature of change, and are prepared to deal with the continual movement of ᵛMEMEs along the Spiral. When speaking with business groups, Clare Graves often used the following question as a quick-check. To answer it well, look at your entity as a mathematical calculus:

HOW *should* . . . **WHO** *manage* . . . **WHOM** . . . *to do* **WHAT?**

By **HOW** he meant the management procedures, motivational techniques, teaching styles, public health-care practices, law enforcement methodologies, development schemes, or other systems appropriate to diverse ᵛMEMEs profiles on the Spiral.

By **WHO** he meant the specific person, agent, or group which does the influencing. Optimally, the 'who' should be chosen for congruence with the Spiral and fluency in the psychological ᵛMEME language of the group.

By **WHOM** he meant the follower, employee, helpee, or client organizaton taken as is. Graves had another favorite saying that always stuck with us:

> 'Damn it all, a person has a right to be. A person has a right to be what he is. He shouldn't have to change to get your work done. Be flexible enough to manage him in the way HE needs to be managed for him to perform the work, not you.'

For things to work well, Who and Whom must have a special relationship, a mutual bonding, a strategic alliance. Think of leaders and followers, coaches and players, teachers and students, or any helpers and helpees. This Who–Whom relationship is issue-specific; it is not necessarily fixed. The roles may reverse.

Either way, influence flows from Who to Whom. But it is the Whom that assigns power, status, and intent characteristics to Who. Leadership connections exist more in the mind of the follower than any personality traits of the leader. A serious misalignment between Who and Whom may well undermine anything else you do in the Design Formula.

Now, consider **WHAT** – the knowledge to be gained, the task to be accomplished, the goal to be achieved, or the outputs to be produced. Beware of taking this as 'a given.' Organizations frequently do not know what business they are really in, why personnel continue to put up with what they do, or what the true priorities need to be.

Think of **HOW, WHO, WHOM,** and **WHAT** as seamless whorls of a spiraling sea creature, critical nodes in a living, interactive network. When one is altered, the others feel the impact. In First Tier organizations, they are dealt with in isolation and allowed to run separately. Second Tier outfits think in terms of integrated systems on an interactive Spiral.

The Plumb Line Process

Perhaps you have watched a bricklayer construct a wall. If so, you may have noticed a plumb bob – a pointed metal thing hanging on a string. The cord is tied to something solid directly above a critical spot on the foundation. The straight line the plumb bob establishes is a vertical reference to which all the courses of bricks can be aligned.

A Spiral plumb bob is useful to align the elements in the Design Formula and keep them connected. With the plumb hovering over the reason the entity exists – the job to be done, the mission, and/or the desired output(s) – everything in the organization, like bricks in the wall, line up. The Plumb Line is not permanently attached. You may need to

... hangs from a
solid hook in
corporate ethics,
individual principles,
or universal standards

... aligns ...
Job Requirements
People Profiles
Recruitment
Selection
Placement
Training
Management
Organization Form

Points to the
job to be done

rehang it because of changes in vision, alterations in the market, or other significant events in the *Life Conditions.* Each time something moves, check the alignment against what has come before and the future you have now laid out. Some bricks for your structure might include:

- Job Requirements (the work to be done)
- People Profiles (those people who perform that work naturally)
- Recruitment and Selection (identifying those same people)
- Placement (placing congruent people into job functions)
- Training & Development (enhancing competencies and capacities)
- Management (managing people in ways that fit them and the work)
- Form (designing the organizational structure to fit people)

1. Job Requirements   Know what business you are really in. Hang the Plumb Bob directly over the critical point – the task to be performed and the thinking necessary to perform it. The job might be narrow-gauged, linear, and sequential or broad-gauged, expansive, and fluid. Sketch in the parameters of the work – a job model, a portfolio, a node, a set of rhythmic movements – virtually any kind of human activity. Think like an engineer as you survey and chart the movement of knowledge along the input-throughput-output flow.

Refine the job model by using people who actually perform those functions as consultants to design two bench marks. The first benchmark describes the minimum characteristics required to qualify for the job. The second benchmark describes the people who exceed the base – the best, highest level functioning, most mature and experienced. You have now built in an expansion joint for growth and a track for continuous improvement through training and development.

Suppose you work in airline flight attendant supervision. You can create a benchmark job model. The first point is the essential base requirements that a new supervisor has to meet just to get the job. Now, find your best supervisors, those generally recognized to be at the top in performance. Ask them to help you chart how they differ from the novices – more savvy, more experience, better supervisory skills, specific knowledge sets, insightfulness? Nail that down. You now have the raw material to construct an expansive job module – a competency ladder. It gives you criteria that everyone can understand for merit increases, meaningful performance appraisals, training needs assessment, career progression, and documentably non-discriminatory promotions.

2. People Profiles   Now, identify the ᵛMEME profiles of people who do jobs naturally, the **WHOM** from the Design Formula. Going to work need not be as much work as it is for many people. Getting the right person into the right job at the right time is not difficult if you can align the requirements of the task with the ᵛMEME profiles of people who can think in ways to do the job, be it individual workers or executive brain syndicates.

How often have you known of a situation where the very best technician was promoted to be the supervisor, only to be among the worst in that job? Even after being sent to the **ORANGE/green** human resources department to get fixed and learn how to deal with people (in a two-week course taught by an **ORANGE** consultant), it does not take. The once terrific worker in a **BLUE/orange** role now feels like a failure in one requiring **ORANGE/blue** thinking. The poor soul's victims feel done in. Everybody loses.

Many organizations assume the core competency 'to get the job done' is identical to the core competency 'to manage the getting of the job done and those who do it.' These are actually very different tasks. Each should have its own competency ladder. While some people will be good at both, others will not. It does not mean one is the better or worse human, only that they have different ᵛMEME profiles which produce different competencies.

3. Recruitment and Selection   At this point in the Plumb Line Process you have both job and person models lined up. The next challenge is to recruit and select the people who can perform those jobs naturally. Too much time and energy is wasted trying to reshape people to do jobs for which they were unsuited from the start. Since you have a ᵛMEME profile in mind, you can recruit people accordingly:

- what ᵛMEMEs must be active to do the job – able to think How?
- where you can most likely find people with those capacities?
- what recruitment ads and images will those people most likely detect and respond to?

But recruitment is not enough. You must then select the best candidates. Be certain your selectors have the eyes to see, the ears to hear, and the minds to understand the full Spiral. Not all do. Many human resource departments have rather narrow ᵛMEME profiles, themselves. More than a few 'personnelists' operate from ARRESTED, even CLOSED First Tier states. Be sure your interviewers can recognize the people who are best aligned to do the work.

As you explain the job (and the company) to the candidate, you both must keep reality in mind. When applicants know what the 'exciting, romantic' job they fantasized is really going to be like, they often de-select themselves, saving both parties the grief of wasted training and feelings of failure.

After the nature of the job has been defined, align and then bond a human being (or group of people) to that job model. Merge the often-overlooked human factors with appropriate technology and the requirements of the job itself. For example, if the job requires the integration of complex information under considerable stress in a rapidly changing environment, competencies in **ORANGE** and **YELLOW** would certainly be necessary ingredients. This would be no world for dominant **PURPLE** or **BLUE**.

However, if the job to be done is highly repetitive with little external stimulation without much opportunity for advancement but demands for consistency, think twice before putting a fast track, ambitious heavy **ORANGE** go-getter into that function. It would be better to find someone looking for a secure nest where things do not change around all the time (strong **BLUE** and even **PURPLE**). There are plenty of fine, intelligent folks with these 'MEMEs active, too.

4. Placement At this point, job requirements, people profiles, recruitment and selection components have been aligned. Place the people into the jobs they do naturally, but stay open to reassignment if they change. Most people will. Placement can be approached in two ways. Historically, we have shaped the person to fit the job niche. One was expected to conform to the requirements of the job or seek employment elsewhere. However, if the Plumb Line process has been used carefully, there will be very little shaping to do and things work out just fine. The well-selected person will like what he/she does because it lines up with who he or she is.

Another approach is actually to build the job around the person, to create a virtual job portfolio to match what he/she does best. Say you find a highly competent human being. Rather than asking the person to conform, you find appropriate things for that person to do. This permits a great deal of mobility within the organization, breaks up the traditional hierarchy, unlinks the rigid chain-of-command, and uncovers new functional slots. Such an idea is disturbing to First Tier entities, quite natural in Second Tier structures.

5. Training and Development (T&D) Education programs and developmental initiatives should be crafted to fit the ways people naturally learn. Different minds explore their worlds in different ways. Different jobs, tasks, activities, or functions carry with them built-in accessing systems, codes and protocols. Read the 'MEME profiles and then offer packages of information, insights, and skills that fit in. Human brains are curious and want to learn, but on their terms. You can always employ the insights of gurus and prophets; just be a Spiral Wizard in the application.

Spiral Wizards know many ways to teach, learn, and develop. **BEIGE** survival oriented learning is *INSTINCTUAL*, accomplished by varying the intensity of stimulation of the senses. **PURPLE** learning is stimulated *CLASSICALLY* through modeling, repetition, rhythm and storytelling. **RED** learning is *CONDITIONED* by hands-on activities accompanied by immediate, external reinforcement. **BLUE** familiar *AVOIDANT* 'book learning' is oriented towards content and facts, rather than towards process and ideas, and is reinforced by standardized testing, by obedience, and by punishment for mistakes. **ORANGE** *EXPECTANCY* learning is geared towards real life experience, trial-and-error experimentation, competitive games, case studies, and simulations. **GREEN** *OBSERVATIONAL* learning is stimulated by reflection, interaction, involvement, and attention to feelings as opposed to merely dry content and hard facts or anticipated rewards.

Moving onto the Second Tier, we find that **YELLOW** *INFORMATIONAL* learning is self-paced and tailored towards the needs and interests of the particular individual. Rewards are intrinsic rather than extrinsic, and discovery-based learning overtakes programmed, scripted knowledge. **TURQUOISE** *EXPERIENTIAL* learning takes place in communal networks – both social and electronic – involving a deeply felt sharing of consciousness and insight. The Spiral Wizard, in the final analysis, is able to create a learning environment that befits a wide variety of styles, not just his or her own preferences.

6. Management   The nuts and bolts of management – systems, styles, procedures, and persons – should be arranged along the Plumb Line to fit the way particular workers, doing particular tasks, are most naturally managed. Horror stories abound of workers promised one thing in the job only to find themselves managed through a toxic, contrary approach – 'do as we say, not as we do.'

7. Form   The form – command and control points, culture, even physical spaces – of the organization should be tailored to its unique functions and to the kinds of people who naturally perform those functions. We have traditionally built organizations from the top down, reflecting the whims of executives or the authoritarianism implicit within the **BLUE** and **ORANGE** ᵛMEMEs that have driven both public and private sector thinking to date. When a new managing director is brought onboard, the tendency has been to adapt to that M.D.'s personal philosophy and style, whether properly aligned or not. Sometimes things get better; often they get worse. This is certainly not to indict all top-down systems; there are places on the Spiral where they are best. At other times – especially when **GREEN** is awakening or the entity is moving toward Second Tier conditions – they are bureaucratic catastrophes.

Building everything from the bottom up is just as bad as top-down. In its egalitarian, power-to-the-people enthusiasm, **GREEN** sometimes puts too much of its energy into the lowest echelons. Everybody gets a say, whether competent or not. Nobody's opinion carries more weight than anyone else's. When misapplied, this noble philosophy only leads to a pooling of ignorance and wasted time. The one or two people with real expertise are shouted down by know-nothings getting their share of consensus. The **ORANGE** 'MEMEs which play the game of entrepreneur so well are driven away to less **GREEN** pastures or start a business on the side. **BLUE** blows its whistle and calls for an investigation by higher authority. **YELLOW** loses patience and simply disappears.

Form should follow function, and function follows the Spiral. Second Tier organizations have room for many sub-Spirals inside. All the secondary plumb bobs point to the same common spot, but the strings are flexible enough to permit specialization, customization, and fine-tuning throughout the organization according to the Plumb Line Process.

Spiral Alignment through *Streams*

Overview

Now, think about the Mighty Mississippi. Like all rivers, she has her headwaters, watersheds region, tributaries, and outlet. Streams flow through channels, some parts deeper than others, some broader, as they cascade downstream with variations in volume, speed, and turbulence.

The Mississippi has a life of her own, moving inexorably toward the Gulf. From the air, you see a smooth brown ribbon meandering across the land. Yet experienced river pilots will tell you of the many currents, sand bars, and treacherous undertows that shift with the seasons and the terrain. And sociologists will tell you about life along the shore and how the Mississippi impacts human existence in mysterious, surprising ways.

Once you grasp *Streams*, you will begin to have a Mark Twain-like comprehension of the dynamic forces that impact flowing organizations. Think of your group as a tow-boat crew pushing a string of barges from New Orleans up to St Louis. The engine is the people, management system, technologies, and fiscal resources. The barges are the products, services, and outputs of your enterprise. You, the Spiral Wizard, are at the helm. During the voyage you will look upstream to see what new things are coming at you, midstream to scan where you are now, and downstream so you do not forget lessons of the past or leave important cargo behind.

PHASE 1

1. Decide what business you
   are really in

2. Chart big picture flows and
   patterns in the milieu

3. Take inventory of resources,
   capacities-within, and life-cycle stages

4. Establish values set-points,
   and identify cultural flywheels...."DNA"

PHASE 2

5. Develop and propagate a strategic vision

6. Connect everything to everything else

7. Design an ideal hypothetical
   TO BE model

PHASE 3

8. Realign and reshape current AS IS systems
   fitting the structures and functions

9. Place the right person into the right job at the
   right time with the right tools and support

10. Build in realignment process for
    constant change and updates

Choosing the *Streams* Team

The kinds of eyes, ears, and minds that are assigned to monitor *Streams* projects will determine what is seen, heard, and understood. Included in this group are your organization's lookouts. If you are searching for detail, be certain to include some good left-brain digital processors. If your soundings must include an intuitive picture of the shifting sands, send along flow-state, right-brain conceptual minds. If you intend to understand the deepest currents, include another whole-brain Spiral Wizard or two who can fathom the complex behavior of the entire system.

During the early days of deregulation, an American communications giant formed an elite group of planners and sent them to a retreat for a month with the mandate to design a new 'deregulated' telephone company. As utilities are inclined to do, they had appointed 'MEME Wizards, not Spiral Wizards. When the report arrived, it was clear the planners had simply 'reinvented' the old model, only smaller. No doubt many in the group had strong ORANGE/blue 'MEMEs and so were dedicated to creating an entity that would do more of the same, but do it better. Because it was only looking at part of the stream that company experienced many false starts and much agony in dealing with deregulation. Some Spiral Wizards could have saved their fiber-optic bacon from start-up competitors roaring down the Infobahn.

In 1991, our friend Loraine Laubscher, a South African consultant who works with migrant mine workers, formed a group to design the new living and social facilities at a deep gold mine. The participants were from five or six different tribal groupings which were mixed in the work force. When the miners completed the project and submitted their designs, Laubscher exclaimed: 'Look what you guys have done. You have just reinvented *apartheid*! You totally separated each tribe into its own space, with its own culture, food service, and life style. Is that what the new South Africa will look like?'

PURPLE and RED would have prevailed had not Laubscher helped the workers to see the fuller Spiral and activate more complex thinking. She led the workers in writing a non-racial, not-tribal BLUE constitution which established the elective office of senator. She then trained the representative senators in how to manage in a BLUE manner, laying the groundwork for the ORANGE to come. The fully integrated mine still works well as the rest of South Africa catches up with the Spiral.

When to *Stream* the Spiral

*Stream*ing is a situational activity designed to introduce Second Tier systemic thinking whenever, wherever needed. Some people do it naturally, but most need a course in navigation since steering among the Second Tier (YELLOW and TURQUOISE) 'MEMEs is new to them. *Streams* can be used in a number of situations:

- In the design of a new business or start-up company
- In the creation of a new division or marketing initiative
- When new technology is introduced requiring a major over-haul in how the organization operates
- During the acquisition or merger process when something new needs to be blended across several entities
- Under BETA conditions when a company is experiencing turbulence and needs significant realignment and tuning
- During GAMMA conditions when the entity is literally fighting for survival, as in Chapter 11 bankruptcy or labor–management rifts

- In the throes of down-sizing or reductions in force, when the entity must be recast to fit the model necessary to survive and compete when an upturn occurs

You can also use *Streams* to fill the information/insight gaps experienced by top level executives and think-tank participants. As genuine empowerment schemes emerge and begin to have an impact, the ideas derived from *Streams* should flow throughout the organization.

How to Align the Spiral: The 10 Elements in the *Streams* Sequence

There are ten elements in the *Streams* process. They logically roll out in a time and priority sequence. The first time through, each needs to be underway before the next begins. During that initial sequence, feedback loops will form. From then on, the activity is self-sustaining. You can home in on element(s) to get specific answers, or use *Streams* as a generic survey tool. To handle this kind of open-endedness, you need Second Tier thinking.

At the launching, the *Streams* Team must first get its own house in order and jettison any baggage which can interfere. Interpersonal squabbles or unresolved power issues must be ceremonially dumped overboard so they will not distort the process. Team members, individually and collectively, should clarify their intents by putting what motivates them to participate in the process right on top of the table. That done, you are ready to set out.

Element 1 – Decide What Business You Really Are In: You may be in for a surprise. While they may have assumed general agreement, decision-makers frequently discover they are actually pursuing multiple goals, some of which are downright contradictory. If the players are not in the same game, that diversity will shape their ability to agree on strategy and tactics. If there are hidden agendas, they will sabotage the process and erode necessary levels of genuineness and trust.

Frequently, the perception of 'the business we are in' changes as it is opened to more in-depth analysis and questioning. This review of why the entity really exists can expose new avenues of thinking, revitalize research and development efforts, polish marketing strategies, and point out necessary adjustments in the ᵛ*MEME* stack. For example:

- Black and Decker, an American company that long thought it made drills and saws, finally recognized it actually made holes and cuts, broadening its industry from laser technologies to vacuum cleaners to pick up the dust and coffee makers to celebrate the end of work.
- Halliburton, an international oil field service company founded on the **BLUE** ᵛMEME of Oklahoma, explored becoming a diversified **ORANGE** conglomerate as the working rig count fluctuated in the late

1980s. If the corporation can reframe its specialty to constructive management of Earth's crust on principled **YELLOW** terms, it will open vast new markets without abandoning its expertise or rich 'MEME heritage and prosper again.

• Avon, a direct sales cosmetics company, realized early that it was also very much in the communications (some might dare say 'gossip') business in rural areas since its representatives would convey information about what was happening socially, thereby linking distant customers and participating in communities.

Once you have a good idea of the business(es) you are in, declare an initial Grand Vision of the future that clarifies your deepest purpose, states a central mission, and encompasses your broadest objectives. During this assessment of purpose and direction, ask questions like: 'Why does this enterprise exist? What do we do? What can it become?' (The output will become a working statement you will polish in Element 4.)

Toyota is famous for its 'Global-10' and 'Gobal-12' visions, indicating what percentage of the world's automobile market the company planned to control. Others seek to be recognized as 'the best' in their niches or to earn the 'finest service' ranking in a field. Several companies have been quite devoted to the business of winning the Baldridge Award.

A new football coach may lay out a five-year program when hired, first with visions of instilling pride and then winning the conference championship. A young couple may target building their 'dream home' and then focus career plans around doing just that.

These are familiar **ORANGE**-tinged aims. As you assess your own and other's visions, look for expressions of **BLUE, GREEN, YELLOW**, and even **TURQUOISE** intentions. In a few you will find **RED** and **PURPLE**. In some you may even discover the whole Spiral. For example:

We, the extended family of Acme Corp.,
the scrappiest, hardest-working SOB's around,
cherish our tradition of service and honesty,
since it keeps us No. 1 and growing all the time,
as a responsible corporate community member,
making an environmentally sound high-quality product,
for the good of human-kind and future generations,
in our new virtual factory in cyberspace.

Sometimes, the critical step is just opening up to the bigger picture of the business we are in. In retail, employees who are not managed on the Spiral often fall into adversarial relationships with each other or customers. They misperceive their roles as enforcing rules and defensively protecting company assets in each little sale. They concentrate on the First Tier and that often leads to miserable service and poor customer relations.

Home Depot, the highly successful building materials retailer, has defined a major part of its business as developing customer satisfaction and loyalty by taking a broader, service-oriented view. There is a very practical reason. Over the life of a thirty-year mortgage, the average homeowner will spend $50,000 on fix-up items. Home Depot is in the business of having it spent right there, part of their expansive Second Tier vision.

Element 2 – Chart Big Picture Patterns and Flows in the Milieu: Now the organization must power-up its capacities for serious environmental scanning. First, explore up-stream. Search for future scenarios by sending your visionary scouts ahead of the flow so you have a sense of what is heading your way. Let them write stories about the future, hypothetical plots, movie scripts, what-ifs, if-thens, and risk analyses. Peter Schwartz, in *The Art of the Long View*, suggests a series of early signs, trend indicators, and critical events that sketch in messages from the future.

Second, look straight down. Probe for the deepest currents. Track the undertows. Monitor the shifting sands. Search for the well-springs of ᵛMEMEtic change in the marketplace, the industry, the representative technologies, the value systems of employees, the financial conditions, and movements of competitors. Look within your company. Still waters often run deep.

Third, look downstream. Survey where you have been and what got you where you are. Acknowledge the strengths of the past so you do not sacrifice them in the name of progress. Companies in transition often 'throw out the baby with the bath water,' then struggle to reconstruct what they already had if they had only recognized its value. The **BLUE** ᵛMEME is particularly vulnerable when **ORANGE** takes over because it often tries to get rid of the old-timers and traditions, the very foundation on which the future must be built.

Fourth, look everywhere at once. The Spiral Wizard's thinking process is systemic **YELLOW** and holistic **TURQUOISE**. Such a big picture view examines how all of these currents are interrelated. Force yourself to step away and look at the overall Spiral system, not just the waves rolling by. This search for flow-state patterns, although tentative and often fuzzy, is critical to the process. Far too many decision teams launch into strategy and even tactics before they have fathomed the currents and charted the obstacles in the fluid environments where they will function. That locks them into First Tier answers, even if Second Tier questions raised the issue.

Contemporary Chaos Theory has made a rich contribution to systemic thinking and understanding flows. In place of mechanistic and deterministic views of how nature works, chaos theorists have described the erratic nature of change itself. For one thing, the camel's-back model has been validated. If the 'final straw' is put on the stack, suddenly and without warning the poor camel collapses. Dramatic awakenings begin precipitously, often when we least expect them.

Or, consider the butterfly effect. If a butterfly flaps its wings in Paris, might the undetected flutter begin the chain of events that results in a hurricane in Miami? Clearly, we can never identify or control all of the elements that shape *Life Conditions*. But nonlinear dynamics helps explain why the best laid plans of mice and men and senior executives are rudely upset by events that appear to be irrational and unpredictable. Yet, an eerie order may well exist beneath the most confounding chaos. Look for it, too.

Element 3 – Take Inventory of Resources, Functional Capacities, and Life-Cycle Stages: When designing a new entity, be certain you have an accurate inventory of available financial, human, technological, and knowledge resources. If you do not have access to a work force with Information Age competencies, chances are you do not want to open a software support facility, especially if public school math scores are low in your city. If you lack enough capital or breadth of managerial talent to operate in a number of different locations, keep your **ORANGE** urges in check.

Start-up entrepreneurs in the airline industry all seem to have been infected with the 'growth virus' carried in the **ORANGE** ᵛMEME. Once they successfully find a niche and begin to show a profit, they become overly ambitious, eyeing expansion like hungry buzzards. They are bedeviled by the self-assured **ORANGE** and egotistical **RED** demons always lurking just beneath the runway. They want to see themselves and their brainchild, Upstart Airways, on the cover of *Business Week* or *Fortune*, so they decide to take on such big boys as American, Delta, Southwest, United, British Airways, and Lufthansa.

That is when they move beyond their niche. They lease more airplanes, hire more people, open more bases, and expand their clever advertising. The big boys match their fares and start playing hard-ball. Because of bigger war chests, the majors can lose money longer. Then comes crunch time when reality hits the fan. Shiny planes are returned to creditors, resold and repainted for someone else. Only unwanted cabin utensils, now for sale at a surplus store, fly the corporate colors and briefly-proud Upstart Airways logo.

The point is, you must know what your assets are. They are not just goods and services, but those things plus their life-cycles. Leadership must identify the evolutionary stages of products, equipment facilities, and of managerial maturity. Ichak Adizes, in *Corporate Lifecycles: How and Why Corporations Grow and Die* (Prentice Hall, 1988) identifies ten of them: Courtship, Infancy, Go-Go, Adolescence, Prime, Stable, Aristocracy, Early Bureaucracy, Bureaucracy, and Death. According to Adizes, by understanding the inevitable lazy-S curve, decision-makers can continually renew the organization by bringing it back to peak and 'prime.'

When realigning an existing system, you must audit its flexibility and change potential. Look around you and downstream. How many of the Six Conditions for Change does the structure meet? Do the people have capacities to absorb new and more advanced technologies? Do you have time to deal with the barriers? Some organizations are as difficult to turn as a supertanker; others agile as a tug boat. You must know what you are steering before deciding which Variation(s) of Change are appropriate.

To quickly assess capacities, try drawing three parallel Spirals for essential aspects of the organization: (1) Technology – Material Resources and Equipment, (2) Business Systems and Management, and (3) Human Resource Staffing and Competencies. Compare them with the overall Spiral of your organization. Is one of the three behind the others? Is another far ahead? Are two in sync with your purpose while the third is a ᵛMEME or two away?

This simple exercise will give you a quick scan of what needs must be addressed and where you may have untapped assets. It can also direct you to realignment as you proceed with *Streams* so the business you are in and the tools you have for doing it match. Only when that is accomplished do you meet Change Condition 2 – current problems of existence being solved. Until then, your efforts to implement movement may be for naught. Even if you build it, they may not come.

Here is the essential question: 'Where can this thing go and how fast can it turn?' Some entities simply cannot be transformed or realigned in spite of attempts to jump-start change. There may be too much psychological luggage in the organization's ᵛMEMEs. The entity may be too tied up in an older First Tier paradigm or caught up by the momentum of a single, Closed way of doing business. A union agreement may be too restrictive and binding (BETA and Barriers). Anger and deep grudges from unresolved past issues may be too intense (potential GAMMA Traps). Having taken inventory if it appears that the system can be changed, *Stream* on.

Element 4 – Develop and Propagate a Strategic Vision: The future should play a more powerful role than the past in shaping the present. 'Strategic' means determining how to get from Point A in 'the present' to a future condition defined as Point B. It is useful to set up a sequential measurement process to determine how well you are doing at each stage along the way. Otherwise, business-as-usual tends to win out.

This A-to-B 'strategic vision' is a step toward the grand vision you created in Element 2 by defining the business you are in and what you intend for it to become. Point B may not be that ultimate aim, but it represents the next realistic step en route to it and it determines some concrete means for getting there.

By 'propagate' we suggest the importance of sharing this vision with everybody in the organization in terms that are meaningful to them. All the stakeholders should have a sense of what is going on and what lies ahead. Better yet, they should be actively involved in developing the strategy, based on their relative competencies and access to information and know-how.

Do more than print nice posters and offer glib pronouncements. Show people you are serious and it is more than pie-in-the-sky. Use imagery for effect. The strategy should be translated into powerful, practical metaphors like the over-used 'phoenix rising from the ashes' to enable more people to understand and embrace the essence of the vision. These 'right-brain' images and symbols help give people a much deeper sense of commitment.

Beware of buzz-words and jargon in fancy packages, though. Many media experts hear their professional balloons pop after convincing the client CEO to take an extravagant dog-and-pony-show to the troops, only to hear it snickered at, lampooned, and resented. They forget that the workers may not share the 'MEME stack of the **ORANGE** corporate board or **ORANGE/ green** head office clique back in the screening room. They are nonplussed when challenged with questions like: 'Why did you waste money on all this B.S.? Why didn't you just pay us more?' Anyone who tells you, 'It's going to be a piece of cake,' is probably First Tier.

When you communicate, speak through the Spiral in its 'MEME languages, not just to yourself. Most executives formulate company visions, missions, and goals for themselves. What begins as rich, powerful, flowing ideas is often reduced to a stagnant pond of clichés tacked up in little black frames on walls and bulletin boards. Because the entire *Streams* process has not been implemented, the exercise becomes just that, a workout for appearances more than substance. Good strategy formulation is not a single planning event that occurs in isolation from the real world. Rather, it is a continuing process requiring the skill to scan and monitor the internal and external environments, as well as the built-in capacity to make midstream adjustments as the currents shift.

Element 5 – Establish Set-Points, Locate Flywheels, and Map the Organization's Psychological 'DNA':   Every culture – corporate or social – has set-points that define its character. These are self-sustaining principles, norms, assumptions, and beliefs that most people in the entity would consider 'self-evident.' Flywheels spin around these set-points with a momentum all their own. Once put in motion, it is very hard to make flywheels change direction, much less stop. Their energy is transferred to everything they touch. It may crop up in print, be loudly proclaimed in staff meetings, or passed around informally in break-room chatter. In any case, flywheels turn around the memorable events and core beliefs that bond people into clans, clubs, and corporate families.

The Momentum of Flywheels: Each 'MEME creates organizational life forms according to its assumptions. In compact, stable entities they may sound relatively pure tones; more often, the cultures are admixtures. Here are some examples:

BEIGE	The Bush	'Just making it through the day and night'
PURPLE	Enchanted Forest	' . . . ghosties and ghoulies and long-leggedy beasties and things that go bump in the night . . . '
RED	Jungle	'Make my day!'
BLUE	Cathedral	'Theirs not to reason why, theirs but to do and die. Into the valley of death rode the Six Hundred'
ORANGE	Marketplace	'Better things for better living through technology.'
GREEN	Commune	'Everything (and everyone) is beautiful, in (his, her, or its) own way.'
YELLOW	Natural Habitat	'So much to learn and explore, so little time.'
TURQUOISE	Global Village	'Fine-tuning the music of the spheres.'

The driving forces that get the Flywheels turning and keep them well-oiled may be expressed in a strong personality (**RED**), policy manual (**BLUE**), or a series of (**GREEN**) 'this we all agree' statements reached through group consensus. They embrace the operating philosophy, ethical standards, and general beliefs about people, their rights and responsibilities.

Each core ᵛMEME establishes its set-points differently. When the task at hand is to change, alter, or transform an entity's culture, you need to know which ᵛMEMEs are dominant. If only one or two are bright, you can focus directly on them. However, to move a complex enterprise from First Tier to Second Tier functioning, a broad spectrum effort that addresses multiple ᵛMEMEs simultaneously is called for. Every change strategy in a broad spectrum entity must include actions for all of the colors in its vertical stack.

- **PURPLE** set points are wrapped in myth and mystery. They are inherited from ancestors (or the company's semi-sainted founder), emerge from spirits (the good fortune that protects the company and its people), and permeate every area of life. Circumstances, places, objectives, or relationships assume a magical aura. Workers wear identical clothing (T-shirts, caps, ties, patches, rings, and jackets) and sing, chant, or clap to rhythmic beats. Curses, blessings, and hexes are commonplace, regulating social affairs and access to jobs. A company with heavy **PURPLE** will be full of ritual, traditions, and symbolic if not literal shrines. Keepers of the magic conduct rites of passage and ceremonies like dedicating the corner stone, transferring pictures of the founding principals to the new place, and placating the old spirits while enlisting the assistance from the new ones.

- **RED** set points lie wherever power resides – raw, ego-serving, and impatient. The driving forces rest in powerful persons who deserve R-E-S-P-E-C-T more than in beliefs. These god-kings can just order change. Colonial management was full of them. The **RED** legends are rife with feats of conquest when powerful ones prevailed against gigantic odds. Social memories and story-tellers perpetuate the mythology. Change agents must exploit the perceived power symbols and 'fight it through.'

- **BLUE** set points are carved in stone. They are absolute Truths, sanctioned by the Higher Authority, and 'written on the hearts' of all righteous people. The sacred foundation blocks are planted deep; anchors tied to them hold fast. They are the ultimate purpose for the very existence of a company. Typically, mission statements are as revered as the Ten Commandments. Change must come from on high down the chain of rightful authority and fit with tradition.

- **ORANGE** set points are chalk marks that act as reference points for individual decisions and boundaries for the corporate 'game' that all are expected to play. Without fixed limits, the **ORANGE** flywheel articulates ways to engage in win-lose competition, search for pragmatic solutions and spin up status rankings. Change is based on demonstrable personal advantages to be gained and new opportunities for growth.

- **GREEN** set points exist within the hearts and minds of the people. They are situational instead of absolute, often echoing more of symbol than substance. They define goals and objectives in human terms, and spell out the nature of interpersonal relations in the core community. The group(s) must meet, share, and discuss change so it becomes an agreeable norm. Continuing to belong and be accepted extends from within the organization throughout its communities and social interventions.

- **YELLOW**'s controlling and instructional set points are respected because they serve to keep the total entity healthy, aligned, and generating useful outputs. **YELLOW** flywheels spin around functional outcomes and enhance the overall quality of systems. They revolve to keep the whole Spiral healthy, aligned, and generating useful outputs. They are the result of broad gauged, inclusive, practical thinking which represents the best information from all sources and leads to outcomes which enhance outputs while reducing harms. If these flywheels represent something quite different to other 'MEMEs, that is OK, too. Any change, however, must deal with the realities inherent in the shifts from the old paradigm to the new. The explanations can be multi-valued.

While you can recognize the prominent flywheels in a company fairly easily, do not be surprised to find smaller ones turning in slightly different directions in sales, human resources, production, and customer service. Consider these possibilities:

- The Sales flywheel spins from an **ORANGE** center of gravity focused on commissions, risk-taking, fast-track advancement, and competitive energy. Running loose, it becomes make-a-buck, whatever it takes.
- The Research and Development flywheel spins around **YELLOW** abstract ideas and distant future payoffs, rewarding imaginative theory building and off-the-wall creative dabbling. Unchecked, it ignores costs or practical application but relishes learning glorious new things.
- Human Resources' flywheel may spin around a **GREEN** social center of gravity with a constant focus on monitoring the needs of people. The set point may be taking care of people within the extended work family. But Personnel Departments often include a **BLUE** flywheel, as well. It spins around generating reports, getting forms filled-out punctually, and filing everything away.
- Accounting is also known for its cautious **BLUE** set point and its respect for patience, order, and accuracy. When it is too rigid, the flywheel revolves around bean counting. More 'creative' accounting adds **ORANGE**. Skillful auditing of entire systems includes **ORANGE**, **GREEN**, and **YELLOW** ᵛMEMEs, as well.

To impose sameness over these diverse ᵛMEMEs introduces friction against their flywheels. At best they slow down. At worst, the resulting turbulence sets up vibrations which destroy the natural sub-systems, ultimately destabilizing the whole. While you cannot realign ᵛMEMEs without imbalancing their flywheels somewhat, the process can be regulated and greased by a healthy *Streams* team.

Mergers often fail because (a) the joined entities have very different set points, (b) nobody identifies them or bothers to balance the flywheels, and (c) the resulting ᵛMEME mixtures are in conflict instead of synergy. If one entity will dominate as the surviving company, leadership should involve both groups in forming a distinctly new culture that has a new hook for the Plumb Lines and synchronized set points. A Streamed culture ought to emerge with one dominant flywheel which drives various others in a very creative and market-sensitive entity. Most of all, the ᵛMEMEs must be tuned through P-O-A while the set points are relocated and everybody learns where they are.

Element 6 – Connect Everything to Everything Else: Traditional hierarchies freeze position power and pecking orders. They define organizations as assemblages of particles, not rolling waves. The vast majority of organization charts fail to recognize the natural patterns in which real people interact, often bypassing the formal chain of command. Bureaucracies take care of themselves, not the flow of work.

To break out of First Tier hierarchical thinking, *Stream* the critical elements that link input, throughput, and output together. The Second Tier form that emerges will trace the business to be done, the services to be delivered, the products to be made and marketed, or the information to be disseminated. The structures that arise naturally from such an activity may take one or a combination of several forms: networks, clusters, clover leaves, capsules, organisms, or even pyramids. The key notion is integrative structures.

Remember poor Upstart Airways? In addition to the **ORANGE** growth virus infecting its corporate officers, poor Upstart was structured traditionally through **BLUE**. That meant separating various functional lines of authority – pilots, flight attendants, reservations, mechanics, and marketing – into isolated branches with their own unions and management structures. The only linking occurred at the very top, and the top was greedy. If you wanted to turn Upstart Airways into Seamless Airlines, Inc., you would *Stream* everybody together in a natural flow – support teams, launch teams, and flight teams. The action of the airplane in transporting people would provide the metaphor for managing the process.

Streams, unencumbered by authoritartian boxes and territorial empires, offers the flexibility necessary to compete in the global, high-tech, and rapidly changing work environment of the twenty-first century. This is essential to 'agile manufacturing' and the need to organize around the flow of market information rather than the materials becomes more prevalent.

For example, the moment a 7-Eleven shopper in Japan purchases a soft drink, that information goes directly to the bottler. Distributors are also in the real-time loop and know the specific hour when the new supply must be delivered and to which of 4,300 stores.

Just as 'Army Surplus' is almost a thing of the past because of better planning, purchasing, and just-in-time inventory control by the military, the whole marketplace is becoming immediate feedback-oriented. Warehouses have become 'switching yards' instead of 'holding pens.' Wal-Mart's remarkable success and ability to undersell local competitors is due in part to the fact that the costs associated with keeping inventory stacked in warehouses are largely eliminated. Whenever a customer buys anything in a Wal-Mart store, that information goes in 'real-time' to the manufacturer's plant. Manufacturers unwilling to integrate with the system in a strategic alliance are replaced by others who will.

There is some risk in mixing Second Tier methods with First Tier forms. Without much inventory, a strike in a General Motors parts plant can domino and shut down many other facilities. Until the human factors Spiral catches up with the manufacturing technologies and business systems, GM's data-dependent model is vulnerable. (Peter F. Drucker capsulized this trend in *The Wall Street Journal*, September 24, 1992):

> 'But the biggest implication is that the economy is changing structure. From being organized around the flow of things or the flow of money, it is becoming organized around the flow of information.'

You will see how to organize the work around the flow of information under the X Template in the next chapter.

Element 7 – Design an Ideal Hypothetical Model Fitting Structures to Functions: At this point in *Streams* you create a hypothetical model, an idealized, tailored organization that fits with the design constructed in Elements 1–5 and fleshes out the connections made in Element 6. Create a supporting structure that manages, surrounds, and nourishes the natural flow of work according to your vision. (We will explore this further during Spiral Integration on the Y Template.)

The structure you build must be congruent with the flow of work itself. In *Power Shift*, Alvin Toffler describes what he calls the 'flex-firm:'

> 'We actually have an immense repertoire of organizational forms to draw on – from jazz combos to espionage networks, from tribes and clans and councils of elders to monasteries and soccer teams. Each is good at some things and bad at others. Each has its own unique ways of collecting and distributing information, and ways of allocating power.' (p. 186)

Heed the words of Barbara Jordan once again. You must have firmly in mind what it is you are changing to and what it is you are changing from. If you do not you will just go in circles. Also, remember that this is a fluid, hypothetical model at this point. You must have it in mind, not set in concrete.

Element 8 – Liberate, Realign and Reshape Current Systems to Fit New Model: So we continue to answer the question, 'how do you change a company?' If you are starting a new enterprise, you simply need to find the people and the systems that can fit the model you have in mind. On the other hand, if you are repairing or updating a pre-existing entity, the task is to transform the culture, personnel, and systems from the old in the direction of the new.

Altering Company Cultures: Many consultancies are offering programs on managing change in the workplace. The various strategies fall into two theoretical groupings. One school of thought is heavily laced with **ORANGE** manipulative assumptions about change. In this view, people will change if they are motivated to do so, especially through rational arguments and attractive perks. They are driven essentially by economic motives and can be 'bought off.' Change can be inserted from the top down.

Pacific Bell wasted millions of dollars in a manipulative training program that forced all employees to participate in a contrived, sensitivity-type group experience. The 'bell-shaped' **BLUE** phone company 'MEME rebelled. **RED** ignored it as another rip-off. **ORANGE** was not about to bare itself in front of potential competitors for limited slots. The San Francisco company was sued by a number of employees because of the program. Telephone customers were enraged.

A second approach relies heavily on participative, consensus-driven processes, usually from the bottom up. It assumes that people will freely change once everybody has had an equal say and a chance to reach agreement through dialogue and mutual understanding. You should now recognize this as a **GREEN** initiative.

When **ORANGE** is dominant, the first approach is tenable (just not in the form tried by Pacific Bell). In communities of heavy **GREEN** thinking, the second is appropriate. What both techniques lack, however, is an understanding of the roles **PURPLE, RED, BLUE, YELLOW,** and **TURQUOISE** 'MEMEs play in the dynamics of culture change. This is the missing link that explains why some corporate change strategies work but the others fail so miserably.

If you want change to occur, do it through the Spiral. For example, here are three more ways to cut the **PURPLE, RED,** and **BLUE** anchors which are so very change-resistant:

1. **PURPLE**: With the aid of 'chiefs,' 'the elders,' or those fully accepted within the **PURPLE** circle, the bonding to one company, its icons and symbols can be replaced by a bonding to a new entity. The change rituals may consist of elaborate ceremonies of 'saying good-bye' and the celebrations associated with entering a new relationship. It should be emotional and full of symbols. These processes are not to be taken lightly since the **PURPLE** 'MEME exists deep within each of us and is often brought tearfully closer to the surface during times of uncertainty.

2. **RED**: For a **RED** system to 'change' it needs to hear firm change mandates from the powerful ones in straight, tough talk. No fancy language, far-fetched promises, or high levels of sensitivity; these will not be trusted, raising suspicions of a con job. Never forget that the **RED** 'MEME can be active in those of high intelligence. It helps to offer instant, tangible rewards at each step or stage of the change activity. Show 'what's in it for **RED**.'

3. **BLUE**: The **BLUE** 'MEME demands a new system to embrace, a new cause to espouse, and a refreshed purpose. Change must be orderly, consistent with principles, and sanctioned by those 'in authority.' Attacks on the older order will not work; they will only trigger resistance. The new system needs to be explained using **BLUE** terminology and honoring the past.

Too many change programs start out with the claim that 'everything is going to change' in an attempt to start the bandwagon effect. Spiral Dynamics suggest that a softer, more low-key approach which places transition within the normal, natural flow of events is more compelling. There is no value in raising the antibodies of the **BLUE, RED,** and **PURPLE** systems unnecessarily. In fact, these 'all or nothing' and 'now or never' demands often make things worse, not better.

Options for Alignment: In forming a new organization, decisions regarding staffing, facilities design, compensation packages, appropriate technologies, and information networks should be made with the ideal model firmly in mind. If the option is to shape and revitalize a pre-existing system and structure (as described in Element 3), several alternative steps should be considered:

- A match may already exist between the current and projected systems. If so, avoid stirring things up just to be trendy or because someone else in the industry is.
- In case of a moderate mismatch, it will be necessary to reassign people to new jobs, arrange for a considerable amount of retraining, or even encourage early retirements to open up space for fresh thinking. An investment in human decency during this phase is not only right, it will bring returns later.
- If major gaps exist between the 'as is' company and the 'to be' version, it might be possible to create a totally different business to accommodate the people who are unable to work effectively within the new model but have useful skills. Eventually, the new entity can achieve its own autonomy.

If there must be major movement on the part of a large number of people to produce the new congruence, here are some guidelines. (You may wish to refer again to Chapter 4 on the general topic of awakenings and change.)

1. Introduce some **dissonance** into the organization culture to see how the systems define the situation and respond. These problems or trial balloons can give you a good sense of what to expect when real change comes down the pike. These perturbations, as they are called, may be enough to give the wake-up-call to ALPHA complacency and denial, triggering the BETA condition and start a Reform Option. If people are already trapped behind GAMMA, however, they will be severely threatened by the trial change stimuli. You will need to remove the prod quickly or it may spark a Revolutionary onslaught. If that is what you want, of course, just keep poking.

2. In some cases you can move a system out of danger and into the cooperative range through **satiation** by meeting Change Condition 2 'to the max.' Fill it up until it can take no more. When there is fear, satiate with safety. When there is chaos, introduce order. If there is competitiveness,

bring on the games. Solving the problems at a level frees the entity to consider new options as the other five Conditions are met.

3. In some cases you may have to **replace or release** a large number of people who simply cannot respond to the new work challenges and responsibilities. Be kind, be swift, be thorough. Certainly, outplacement counseling and other transition programs should be made available to assist employees in finding suitable employment under this last resort scenario. Avoid the **ORANGE** throw-away mentality – 'Surprise! Here's a cardboard box – be out in 30 minutes' – and be humane. Look for alternatives where human beings' competencies may fit. Too often, downsizing becomes an excuse for cruelty.

On the other hand, there are alternatives. The leaders of ESCOM, the largest electricity supplier in southern Africa, were having difficulty getting more **ORANGE** from the managers of the company's power generating stations. They had concluded that progressive alternative thinking was needed both to support the expanding grid and the interests of employees in blossoming communities. Attempts at unfreezing through experiential training and the imposition of small business unit (SBU) structures did not bear fruit. So the company tried something more radical, although still a First Tier approach.

a) All the jobs were eliminated, but the incumbents were requested to stay in their functions in an acting capacity.

b) A new job model was cast, putting more **ORANGE** strategic thinking and competitive elements into running power plants.

c) All the incumbents were then asked to reapply, if they wished, for the new jobs. Many did not, realizing they no longer fit the profile. They did not lose face by 'resigning' – their old positions no longer existed. Those that did not measure up were simply not selected for the redefined slots.

d) The rest rejoined the company in other capacities. There are plenty of **BLUE**-oriented jobs in the utility business and these were made available to the employees who did not fit the new more **ORANGE** requirements, yet had experience and knowledge which were still useful. Thus, very few people were actually put out of a job.

The organization was indeed changed by altering the ^{V}MEME profiles of these management positions, but not necessarily into a better fit with the enormously complex *Life Conditions* ESCOM faces. While the total impact of this strategy is still unclear at the time of writing, the question of why more competitive, individualistic, entrepreneurial **ORANGE** thinking is needed inside power generating plants remains. Were corporate leaders trying to clone themselves? Spiral Dynamics suggests taking a whole-Spiral, Second Tier approach to issues as multifaceted as energy production and delivery in developing lands where many ^{V}MEMEs are simultaneously needed. First-Tier stop-gaps at **ORANGE** (or even sensitive, generous **GREEN**) will not suffice. The same cautionary advice applies to U.S. utilities trying the same thing and especially governmental functions in the throes of privatization: beware the romantic lure of **ORANGE** sirens who sing glibly of simplicity that is not there and profit centers which may put you on the rocks.

Element 9 – Place the Right Person into the Right Job with the Right Tools and Support: The term 'right' translates as a proper fit, congruent, in sync, appropriate to, in harmony with, and tailored for. In other words, doing what comes naturally. Over the past few years, the emphasis in human resources has shifted from attempts to 'fix' or 'change' people who were indiscriminately assigned to jobs as 'warm bodies' to a focus on careful selection and placement up front with respect for people as they are.

Many variables need to be considered in creating the job match. Education, experiences, task-related knowledge, personality characteristics, and other work-specific traits should be factored into the equation. In particular, consider ᵛMEME **stacks** and **patterns of thinking** in people.

ᵛMEME Stacks: ᵛMEME stacks refer to the mixture of ᵛMEMEs a person or organization exhibits. Jobs can be color-coded in terms of the active ᵛMEMEs necessary to perform them naturally. There is no excuse for 'work' being so much 'work.' People have a right to enjoy their lives and merging their ᵛMEME profiles naturally with jobs helps them to. How and why we do something contributes much more to job satisfaction than the nuts-and-bolts of what we are doing.

- If the job requires high levels of risk-taking, goal-setting abilities, and crisp wheeling-and-dealing, you had better look for people with a healthy dose of **ORANGE** in their profiles. For heaven's sake, do not select Closed **BLUE**; every day will be a struggle. Choose too much **RED** and you will end up in court.
- If you need to find a top level executive who can manage broad diversity in the decade ahead, you might want to find a candidate who expresses some **YELLOW** and even **TURQUOISE**. (Be certain those ᵛMEMEs are awake in the selection interviewers so they will discern authentic Second Tier thinking in the candidates.)
- If you have a job that requires a tough-minded person, one who can make hard decisions in times of crisis, beware of heavy **GREEN** egalitarianism – too soft – or excessive **RED** – too hard. Find someone with warm colors dominant, but enough cool to be human – just right. Solid Autocracy, at least moderate Politeness and healthy Openness complete the package.
- If the job calls for someone who can meet-and-deal in a personable manner, massage groups, and listen to what is going on with people empathetically, look for a healthy dose of **GREEN** backed up by enough warm **ORANGE** to insure that assertive negotiation skills are available – strong Politeness, moderate Openness, with some Autocracy.

Patterns of Thinking: Patterns of thinking reflect the differences in how people's minds handle inputs, including their *multiple intelligences* (not just 'intelligence') and what is commonly called *brain dominance* and often discussed in right-brain, left-brain terms. (We generally prefer 'analog/ digital' and 'chaos/order' language to distinguish Spiral Dynamics' applications from the mechanics of neurology.)

There are many useful ways to view these patterns, including temperament models, complexity theories, and myriad personality assessments. Whichever you include in your tool kit, it is critical to factor this component into the job model and selection technology. Three *Patterns of Thinking* models are particularly relevant to the Spiral.

The first is Howard Gardner's perspective introduced in *Frames of Mind: The Theory of Multiple Intelligences* (Basic Books, New York, 1983). In this view, there are several important human skill bundles that can all be called 'intelligence.' Most evaluations, ranging from the SAT to Civil Service exams, have relied on only one or two – Linguistic Intelligence or Logical-Mathematical Intellgence. Yet Gardner makes a case for Musical Intelligence, Spatial Intelligence, Bodily-Kinesthetic Intelligence, and two Personal Intelligences (Intra- and Interpersonal), as well. In Element 9, ask *which intelligences* are relevant to the job to be done and how will they be expressed through the different ᵛMEMEs.

A second perspective that is useful in conjunction with the Spiral is represented by the popular Myers-Briggs temperament model based in the work of C. G. Jung. The resulting quadrants profile people among 'Sensors–Intuitors,' 'Thinkers–Feelers,' 'Judges–Perceivers,' and 'Extroverts–Introverts.' The Jungian approach adds a useful set of behavioral characteristics which paint a more complete picture of the person and the job.

Finally, consider Elliott Jacques' Complexity of Work Model. It defines seven levels of complex thinking required by different jobs. These begin with Level 1 work which involves short time-frames, dealing with one concrete task at a time, and maintaining a constant work flow. At the other extreme are Level 7 jobs which involve executive leadership of multinational corporations, governments, and large-scale systems. These most complex jobs require judgments about sociopolitical trends in time-frames up to 50 years with many interlinked variables. Clearly, this is not work for someone Closed in First Tier ᵛMEMEs.

Element 10 – Build in Ongoing Realignment Processes for Continuous Shifts and Changes: Stability and permanence are comforting illusions. Change is a constant. Every blinking nanosecond marks small steps or bold leaps in some Variation, somewhere. The concept of time has changed remarkably from the gentle seasons of hunter-gatherers to the tick-tock-tech of atomic clocks, instantaneous CNN coverage, and real-time globalization.

QUANTUM MIND

DIGITAL, PARTICLIZED
PROCESSING
MODULES

ORDER & CHAOS

ANALOG, WAVE-LIKE
PROCESSING
MODULES

ORDERED DETAIL

Characteristics

Penchant for detail, precision, accuracy
Regulated by clock-tick time and technology
Names, lists, pigeon holes, defines, classifies
Lines up, measures, calculates, regulates

Blind Spots

Enslaved to numbers; emotionally flat
World reduced to bits and details
Measures, nitpicks to the Nth degree
Stereotypes: Mr Spock (Star Trek)
            E Scrooge (A Christmas Carol)
            Joe Friday (Dragnet)

Seen in number crunching jobs; accounting, finance,
technology and computing; reflected in numerous
collecting hobbies

CHAOTIC CONCEPTUAL

Characteristics

Synthesizes the kaleidoscopic whole
Zigzags through complexity and chaos
Explores new visions; experiences imaginative leaps
Early warning scanning detects changing conditions

Blind Spots

Details fall between the cracks as ideas soar
Lives in dreams and visions but gets little done
Roams the terrain but neglects to water the trees
Stereotypes: Carl Sagan (Cosmos)
            John Denver (Rocky Mountain High)
            Buckminster Fuller (The Futurist)

Displayed in visionaries, creative marketing strategies," big
picture" thinkers, and rich imaginations, ect.

ORDERED SYSTEMS

Characteristics

Maintains consistent, structured, tight systems
Linear, logical problem-solving skills
Preserves the order; follows the procedures
" Lines up the ducks" in a reliable fashion

Blind Spots

Imposes inappropriate, stifling rigidity
Tends towards being judgmental/moralistic
Often displays a boxed view of reality
Stereotypes: Hilga (Hagar the Horrible's Wife)
            John Phillips Sousa (Stars & Stripes
            Forever)
            Archie Bunke (All in the Family)

Seen in systems engineers, bureaucrats, educators, law
enforcement, etc.

CHAOTIC EXPRESSIVE

Characteristics

Rides the waves with gusto and grace
Heightened sense of drama and emotions
Challenges boundaries: spontaneous and colorful
Impulsive, gut-level and interpersonal

Blind Spots

Lives on emotional roller coasters, moody/erratic
Trapped in a world of impulses and fantasies
Chaotic lifestyle; lives for the moment
Stereotypes: Mohammed Ali (The Champ)
            Madonna (The Entertainer)
            Hagar the Horrible (The Viking)

Expressed in" people" people, the arts, risky jobs," on the
edge" life styles, frisky fun, etc.

In such a context, these monitoring and feedback functions should be built into each node, network, and process of the Second Tier organization:

- *Environmental scanning* (both internal and external) should occur throughout the organism, especially in front-line eyes and ears which see and hear so much but are so rarely asked for their observations.
- *Freedom to report negative news* should not be impeded by the fear the messenger will be killed. Second Tier companies demonstrate Openness.
- *Monitor trust levels* and keep them high. Validate ethical stands; support proactive inclinations; foster interactive communication as needed in every direction; learn from any source; and recognize anyone for going the extra mile, whatever the job.
- *Downplay status* distinctions, political games, turf protection, and 'hey, that ain't my job' mentalities which keep organizations blocked on the First Tier. Keep Politeness part of the mutual contract in which everyone is significant.

With these lookouts in place, the capacity for minor readjustments and major realignment can be built into organizations themselves, into their conscious operating systems and unconscious assumptions, and into the mainstream of how they do business. Once this is accomplished, impending BETA conditions are quickly recognized, GAMMA Traps are avoided, and repairs can be made either to restore the ALPHA or ease the Reform passage to a new one.

8

Spiral Integration: Power and Precision in Organization Design and Transformation

---

The word 'template,' from the French *templet* (Latin *templum*), refers to a set of instructions, a gauge, a pattern, or a mold used to guide the form of a piece yet to be made. Templates can be used over and over again. In chaos theory, a 'strange attractor' formed by a pattern repeating from larger to smaller qualifies as a sort of template.

We use 'Template' metaphorically to describe an adjustable overlay, an expanding and contracting map, and a graphic image for the flow of organizational energy, relationships among processes, decision time-lines, and work-streams. Templates are designed and shaped by the ᵛMEMEs in our psychological 'DNA' and sketch in the parameters of our real-worlds.

Organizations are constructions of the mind. Words printed on wall charts, symbols of rank worn around the neck, and spaces occupied as manifestations of power are but artifacts and icons. The real connections are within ᵛMEME profiles of people, those invisible webs that order society and snare relationships. We carry them with us in our heads every waking moment. Each location along the Spiral has its own mental configuration like a radar scope on which the contours of its ideal life form are painted. Which blips are most important varies depending on which ᵛMEMEs are active. The screen appears to . . .

PURPLE...as a magic circle that makes all inside feel safe.

RED...as a self-centered empire where one feels powerful and in control or weak and submissive.

BLUE...as a fixed pyramid that gives stability, permanence, and assigns one's place.

ORANGE...as a game-board matrix that promotes opportunity and rewards skill.

GREEN...as a warm, supportive community of equals that cares for its own.

YELLOW...as flowing networks that shift functions up, down and across natural layers.

TURQUOISE...as a living organism that brings order from within chaos.

The Wonderful World of Virtual Reality

'Red Right, Double Post, Left Cross 10, Swing Right – on TWO' barks the quarterback of the Dallas Cowboys in the huddle of a National Football League game against the Washington Redskins. That coded message sends precise instructions to each of the eleven players as to what he should do. The play, which has been designed to exploit the weakness of the Redskins' defensive formation and specific personnel, was diagrammed on paper and 'run through' many times in practice.

Good football plays have alternative scenarios built into their designs. The quarterback and pass receivers will have worked out a series of flexible options to be exercised based on the initial moves of the defensive backs. The Redskins might suddenly change formation, causing the Cowboy's quarterback to call an audible in response. Sometimes he will even ask for a 'time out' to think when the *Life Conditions* are too confusing and seek assistance from his consultants on the sideline. These are called strategic retreats in contemporary corporate lingo; saving your ass in football.

As the players approach the line of scrimmage, they have been taught to visualize exactly what they plan to do when the quarterback yells 'hut – HUT.' The team executes the play mentally before it runs the play physically. This model in their minds connects them in a sequence of well thought out, well coordinated movements in what we will call a 'Template.' This ability of the team to pre-create the play, to feel themselves moving across that mental screen, and then to adapt the visualization to the reality confronting them, is a form of virtual reality.

There are more technical ways. Meld a brain with a good computer and Virtual Reality (VR) is the best connection between human and machine yet devised. By attaching fingers, ears, eyes, voice, and brain waves directly with the microprocessors, one can move around in simulated 3-D space and do things in an electronic domain that seem quite 'real' but only exist in the cyberspace between mind and chip. Soon, football players will conduct drills wearing VR helmets, gloves, and suits designed to let them feel the action as various scenarios are played out. There may even be silicon-based cheer-leaders to go with the binary socks and jocks.

Many 'virtual corporations' will be formed and sustained in a similar joint electronic–human domain. As Second Tier thinking takes off and post-Information Age work becomes even more cerebral and less muscular, members of the virtual company will work at home or in a shared neighborhood facility. Already cellular phones and multifunction computers have become so portable that many people carry their offices in a brief case. Pocket-sized world-wide electronic access is only a couple of years away.

Fancy atrium headquarters to entertain clients, elaborate power desks to show workers their places, and even face-to-face meetings to compare shoes and executive cologne become unimportant in managing the virtual corporation. Buildings exist to hold useful and necessary things, not as temples to the manipulation of others. Offices, if they exist at all, are functional gathering points or quiet places to reflect, not status-rich turf to protect. Second Tier clients are impressed by excellence of function, not superfluous forms they ultimately pay for. The organization exists in the individual and collective minds of stakeholders and in the information systems that connect them. In the past we saw 'the company' as the mill, the office suite, on the organization chart, or at a conventioneers' display of products or services. For a Spiral company such as we are describing, you might have to log onto a network to 'see' the staff. Its headquarters, if one is even needed, will resemble a healthy small town more than a monument. Once again, people will not so much go to work as simply begin to work at their cottages in the information village or the factory downstairs. Drive-time radio will be scrounging for listeners again and airlines' computer nets will be far greater assets than their aluminium cans stuffed with *revenue passenger miles* nibbling peanuts.

The Need for Templates: An Illustration in the Air

By the twenty-first Century the U.S. Federal Aviation Administration had hoped a $32 billion plan to reform air travel, dubbed A.E.R.A. (Automated En-Route Air Traffic Control), would be up and running. Optimal spacing of airplanes, voice recognition computers that understand spoken commands, navigation via GPS (global-positioning satellites) and direct links between ground and cockpit computers were to be commonplace. This would be a far cry from the FAA that the now-forgiven PATCO air traffic controllers struck during the first Reagan administration, or even the upgraded but still very much the First Tier FAA of today. For the system to work, the FAA will have to put this new, high-tech wine into fresh Second Tier wineskins instead of just rinsing out the old, musty organizational forms of the past. Frankly, the odds are not good.

The FAA's World War II era, First Tier model – Washington's National

Airport still depends on vacuum tubes – links together a series of Civil Servants ranks in boxes, separated in geographic regions, through a vast **BLUE** governmental pyramid with a few **ORANGE** perks. The twenty-first Century FAA must shift into a flow-state design that can facilitate the movement of many kinds of traffic – both air and ground – through information-rich conduits where territoriality does not fit. Its thinking has to become global instead of regional or even national. The FAA must cut some new Templates. If it is unable to adapt, the functions will simply be privatized into the hands of some new kind of entity which can.

The FAA is not at-risk alone. IBM, Digital Equipment Company, and other high-tech monoliths have almost met their Waterloos because they were structured around a nineteenth century machine-age template. Engineers decided what could, should, and would be done. The customer had to take what the engineer-priests decided to give them. IBM held onto its proprietary control, trying to make the mainframe customer dependent on Big Blue's whims and peculiarities. Even as the computer business grew by shrinking, supposedly user-friendly Apple would be guilty of this archaic view.

Technical advances are shaking out the thinking machine industry. Restructured IBM and Apple are holding hands with Motorola while Big Blue reassesses the lucrative mainframe niche. The PC has become a commodity that practically anyone can turn out. Young and successful entrepreneurs, intimately connected to the needs of the user and peripheral developer, now construct interactive template formulas that bring suppliers and the market-place into their rapid-response decision streams. The same can be said for Southwest Airlines, Federal Express, Wal-Mart, United Parcel Service and others who were awakened by alarms years before their **BLUE** brothers sensed the danger. As cited above, even Eastman Kodak, 'the great yellow father' of chemical photography, has begun to realign its templates for the digital age.

How Templates Work on the Spiral

Templates outline the most natural designs for people, technology, and work flow to accomplish specific outcomes. Each Template must be cut to a specific circumstance, the indigenous *Life Conditions* and ᵛMEME systems. Such issues as rank, ideology, territory, interpersonal relations, and tradition are initially set aside. This is Second Tier work. The rigid, pre-cut First Tier shapes of **PURPLE** through **GREEN** are temporarily shelved, too. For now, they are contaminants. Awaken, instead, the **YELLOW** and **TORQUOISE** ᵛMEMEs, rouse Second Tier models and follow closely.

Visualize the motherboard of a PC with its synergistic blend of modules, components, channels, and processors all connected in a grand design. The ten-element sequence of *Streams* is the leader's diagnostic that identifies which ᵛMEMEs to plug where in the organizational circuits because they are congruent with the work and *Life Conditions* in that space. The three Templates give Spiral managers the tool to customize, tweak, integrate, and upgrade the corporate machine's operation by applying principles of Second Tier thinking.

Instead of being rigid, permanent cutouts, Spiral Templates are alive, like the interdependent layers that fuse together, stretch, and adjust in our skin. For now we will artificially separate the three Templates to explain their different functions, though they actually mesh together so that what happens in one instantly impacts the others. In fact, a person's job may well include functions on all three Spiral Templates.

Spiral Integration: Power and Precision in Organization Design and Transformation

Spiral Templates can be designed under two conditions. First, they may be drawn from scratch for a start-up company using the *Streams* process (especially Element 5 – *Establish Set-Points* and Element 6 – *Connect Everything to Everything Else*). Or second, they can be created in the midst of reengineering an entity fluctuating in the throes of chaos and change. Under those circumstances, you may want to design two organizational models. One will be the standard First Tier form that shows traditional reporting bases and budgetary responsibilities to satisfy here-and-now needs of anxious directors and financial backers. The other, your Second Tier approach, will be Templates-based and oriented toward the specific Strategic Vision you develop in **Streams'** Element 4 and the encompassing Grand Vision you outlined in Element 1. Both designs will be useful in the uncertainty of transformation from the present toward the future entity.

Back at the turn of the century, merchants and military men envisioned a short-cut for shipping through the Americas. France attempted to build this Panama Canal by just digging a huge ditch, a First Tier approach which was a malarial disaster. Learning from the French mistakes, the Americans took it on. Their strategy was to drain the swamps and build housing and long term support facilities that fit the *Life Conditions* of construction in a Central American jungle. The job was still terribly difficult, but it was successfully accomplished and marked an early step toward Second Tier thinking.

Today, far too many quality programs and O.D. interventions try to dig right through mosquito-infested swamps without building the necessary support systems of **P-O-A**, congruent leadership packages, or appropriate forms of compensation for the 'MEMEs doing the digging. They assault mountains 'full speed ahead' rather than following natural contours. The efforts fail because the planners do not first align their **Templates**.

In the previous chapter we added three tools for engineering flow of work: (1) the **Plumb Line Process** which establishes the highest priority of the entity then aligns everything else with it, (2) Graves' elegantly simple **Design Formula** which asks How Who should manage Whom in doing What, and then (3) the ten-elements of *Streams* which sequence future visioning, strategic thinking, long and short-term planning along a single strand. Now for the next tools in your Second Tier Wizard's Kit, the **X, Y** and **Z Templates**.

The X Template: The Most Natural Forms and Flows for the Critical Functions

Scripting and Charting the Job-to-be-Done 'from Alpha to Omega'

On the X Template every variable that influences the job to be done is included in the work flow. It extends far beyond the shop floor and traditional company limits to include initial suppliers of information and raw materials at one end, the ultimate satisfaction of customers at task completion the other. The X Template has no fixed boundaries, either inside the company or between the company and its environment.

The **Streams** process lays out the specifications for constructing the X

Template. When finished, X traces the optimal shape that has been chosen for the entity and then locates the specific pieces needed to get the work done under the circumstances. Like the computer-guided fabric cutters in a clothing factory, it seeks to minimize waste, maximize utility, and custom tailor to meet the needs of the particular customer.

To be successful, every piece of the organization must be involved at the beginning. Traditionally, layout decisions of this nature have either been made by 'the authorities' or 'those experts' and handed off for implementation. Maybe others, at lower echelons, were invited to fine-tune, make adjustments, or look for ways to reduce costs; but they were not involved in pattern making at the start. One of the revelations in the participatory management upsurge has been that those who plan the party have the best time.

In Second Tier Spiral thinking, everybody involved in the process must have direct input into the design of the X Template at the front end. Engineers, production people, salespeople, personnel specialists, even custodians join in the process. This certainly extends to 'outsiders' – suppliers, regulators, and end users – since they are also integral to the job to be done. This value engineering technique takes a scalpel to cut away waste at the design stage instead of relying on shears downstream when major errors may not be correctable or, if they are, cost a fortune or a career. A good illustration of this kind of approach is the designing of Boeing's 777 aircraft, the first plane to fly directly from ideas in global networks to machine tools.

Such terms as Value Analysis, Value Chain, Simultaneous Distributed Work, Work Mechanics, Enterprise Networking, Concurrent Engineering, and Horizontal Management have been used to describe this aspect of the process. Here are some other transport illustrations:

- When Toyota designed the Lexus motor car, the company first began with the cost to the consumer, and then worked backward. They centered the Plumb Bob over the price point. Then every stage and function in the traditional design and production stream was involved at the front end. The journey covered five years; involved 2,300 technicians, 1,400 engineers, 450 prototypes, millions of test kilometers and 300 patent applications. It produced a fine new family of autos.
- Ford's Team Taurus project used a similar value chain. Purchasing, design, quality assurance, marketing, sales, distribution, repair, personnel, environmental relations, legal and even insurance company inputs were integrated in the simultaneous design process. The project was brought in for $250 million less than budget. Not only was the quality good enough for the model to be exported to Japan and Germany, but the design cycle has been reduced from 5–6 to 2–3 years. The venture deserves credit for helping turn Detroit's fortunes around.
- The United Auto Workers joined with General Motors management in a

'Committee of 99' (40 per cent management, 60 per cent union) to design the new Saturn Division from the ground up. The joint venture created the product, located the plant, and produces a world-class car at a highly competitive price. A uniquely involved and service-oriented dealer net completes the package. Though **RED, BLUE,** and **ORANGE** contamination from both GM and the UAW keep Saturn chasing after **GREEN**er Japanese-managed competitors, it continues to be a remarkable case study.

- When British Airways decided to do a major overhaul of its entire customer service and marketing function, it relied on a number of problem solving groups to redesign the system. Michele Heyworth of their Market Research team discovered a company that specializes in bringing passengers and providers together to talk about the key needs and services that would make a vital difference.

  Forty managers from Sales, Cabin Services, Brands and Brands Development, Overseas Marketing and Sales, and Catering and Design got together with ninety frequent fliers from all over the world. David Charlton, Group Brands Manager, noted: 'The idea was to find out where our products and services fit into their lives, rather than the other way round.' Very sensibly, the Plumb Line was centered over the air traveler. British Airways makes extensive use of project teams that engage all elements impacted by a decision in its making and full implementation.

- In 1992, New York Telephone commissioned an eight-person commando team and charged them with rethinking how the telephone company goes about 'provisioning' customers with one of its most advanced products. They were then to restructure how the work gets down. The commando team was staffed jointly by 'craft' (union) workers and first-line managers and told to get on with it. They sought after input from a Science and Technology expert, a systems laboratory, and an anthropologist. They consulted customers and users.

  By looking at the process 'from A to Z', reported 22-year veteran and union member Leroy Gilchrist, 'it was the first time that anybody had an idea of what the whole process looked like.' Filling an order, the group discovered, involved 126 work steps and more than 40 people. No wonder customers were frustrated; the process was costly; and things continued to fall between the cracks.

- Motorola, Federal Express, American Express, Glaxo, Merck, Nike, Apple Computer, Honda, Boeing Aircraft and Intel have intuitively made extensive use of **X** Template technology. Advanced information systems make possible the tracking, continuous monitoring and improvement, and fine-tuning of work flows. These natural structures and scripts are replacing traditional organizational charts and their inevitable bottlenecks.

The visualized **X** Template may resemble a network, a cluster, a clover leaf, a neuronet, interlocking Olympic rings, a starburst, a constellation, a game board, a story line, a time sequence, the passage of people through stages, or any other pattern that accurately describes the flow of work. The form will be dictated by the function. You may or may not be able to find this Template if you visit the company to observe its activity since the **X** Template can exist quite well only in the minds of people and their computer links.

Earlier in this section we cited evidence that the quality movement has lost some of its luster because it appears not to be producing the results that were either expected or promised. Much of what is done in the name of the Total Product Quality (TPQ) initiative has elements of the **X** Template. Among these are flowcharts, statistical measures, decision-trees, and time-lines. However, many TPQ projects have caused more problems than they have solved because the client company cultures were simply not ready for the technology, and the implementation was incomplete. The supportive ᵛMEMEs were not yet awakened and the other two essential Templates were not committed to the process.

Managers bought promises of increased productivity and cost efficiencies without understanding how and why the entire culture had to be altered first. They could not bring themselves to embrace all of the philosophical assumptions that Deming's way requires, especially the need to remove fear and eliminate appraisal-type ratings of people.

There is a great deal of the Second Tier in Deming's point of view, but it is rarely carried through to implementation. Arrested **BLUE** is put off because it breaks set. Overly **ORANGE** executives want to pick-and-choose from Deming's points while overlooking the essential human factors. Closed **GREEN** sometimes thinks 'competitive advantage' is a dirty word and 'progress' is a threat to harmony. Deep-seated ᵛMEMEs permeate every aspect of corporate life. Unless you recognize the Spiral and align it properly, expensive and time consuming TPQ and TQM (Total Quality Management) initiatives, as well as noble reengineering efforts, sink in the bog of tradition, blame, and excuses.

Linking of Customers, Clients, Stakeholders, and Functions in Strategic Alliances on the X Template

The term 'strategic alliance' has entered the mainstream of managerial thought. It describes mutually beneficial relationships among a company and its customers, regulators, suppliers, competitors, and other stakeholders. If you belong to American Airlines' frequent flier program, you can also qualify for award mileage by flying British Airways, TWA, Singapore Airlines, staying in Sheraton hotels, renting your car from Avis, and charging it all up on a special Master Card that reconnects with American.

We have already said that involved outsiders may be asked to supply their input on matters of common interest when laying out the X Template. In a strategic alliance, those entities play an even more vital role in the success of the enterprise. This is not to say the alliance is always sweetness and light. Often it is as troublesome as a shotgun wedding and produces strange bedfellows, indeed. The partners may be in need, not in love. If the 'MEMEs never mesh, the alliance will surely break up.

Another form of alliance is outsourcing. In this case, a specific internal function is actually turned over, lock, stock, and personnel, to an external entity. EDS (Electronic Data Systems) was built on the premise that it would take over the entire information processing function in a client company and do the job better, even for one as fine as Xerox. EDS must be able to morph itself to client 'MEMEs or it will trigger antibodies and the relationship will become toxic. Today, everything from management training to custodial services to running national parks is handled on an 'outsourcing' basis. You really have to trust outsource partners because you may literally give them the keys to your building.

Value is potentially added through an alliance by sharing competencies. Personal relationships, always including Openness and Politeness, may be enhanced. Information is distributed throughout, based on the functional need to know and carefully regulated by healthy Autocracy. More can be done with greater efficiency.

But good things generally have an opposite. In such cases a naive alliance partner becomes vulnerable to rip-off's, industrial espionage, and spin-off competition because of the very Openness that gives the venture strength. Again, for outsourcing it is critical that you pay close attention to the dominant 'MEMEs and ethical systems of a potential partner. Be especially wary of the guiltless side of RED and the deceptive, 'whatever you want to hear,' angle of ORANGE.

Assign people whose 'MEME profiles are complementary to each entity but who also recognize the common Set-Points to complete the link. To close the deal you must identify what each potentially needs from you to connect psychologically, as well as economically. Some strategic partners need to sense RED power before they can link comfortably; others are more drawn by an ORANGE high-tech, high-potential display; yet others would like to feel an expression of sensitive and socially-conscious GREEN. Think of the initial connections as a FAX-like handshake between 'MEMEs. The secret is to think like networking software to hook up diverse individual profiles, organization flywheels, and cultural 'MEMEs because these are the real bonds that ultimately make or break the arrangement.

Design of Job Models and Work Modules within the X Template

Competency models and the careful matching of people with jobs are replacing 'warm body' hiring practices. In the Design Formula we discussed how you constitute effective matches. An expansion joint should be built into every job model so a person can grow either in the function or by changing roles. That is the simplest way to build a continuous improvement feature into an organization.

Some entities may choose to define jobs more generically. They prefer to assemble teams who are virtually interchangeable in doing several tasks. Members can rotate through the jobs to avoid boredom. They might both operate machines and fix them, reducing the amount of time any particular unit is off-line. In many cases, the team actually can self-manage, thus sharing the pay that once would have gone to a non-producing supervisor. A good **X** Template will delineate the selection of people who have that kind of flexibility.

Whether narrow or broad based, job models require a sensitivity to the unique characteristics of persons. An understanding of ᵛMEME profiles and Patterns of Thinking (from Chapter 7) becomes essential from two perspectives. First, the total culture or 'capability based environment' (CBE) must be fully understood before attempting to 'dig the Panama Canal.' Second, understanding human differences assists in the alignment of people with technology and work flows. This critical matching of job functions with minds and ᵛMEMEs has been long in coming in organizational life. Crenier and Metes say it clearly in *Enterprise Networking*:

> 'Besides the obvious language differences, personal likes and dislikes, ideologies, prejudices, and traditions that separate people, certain emotional as well as cognitive traits are particularly inhibiting to produce information sharing in distributed environments. Suspicion, protection of territory (conceptual and physical ownership), conventional beliefs in the supremacy of one's own creativity, vision, methods, and tools create key psychological and social barriers.' (p. 55)

Their terms 'emotional as well as cognitive traits' match our ᵛMEME profiles and Patterns of Thinking. Organizations have been reluctant to fully acknowledge these differences in the recent past because of **BLUE** and **GREEN** blinders. Good intentions did not allow us to recognize individual uniqueness or differentiate competencies. Now, better intentions expect no less.

ᵛMEME Profiles and Levels of Complexity

Because they reflect layers of complexity, ᵛMEME profiles impact the way individuals filter, interpret, and respond to the entire *gestalt* of issues. The particular *Life Conditions* of a job require that certain ᵛMEMEs be active and that others be turned down. A description of the essential thinking, whether in ᵛMEME colors or some other language, should be included in the job profile to match people with various areas of the **X** Template. Then, job applicants from either side or outside can be evaluated fairly in terms of their access to these processing patterns.

For example, when selecting a high performance team, its overall composition of ᵛMEMEs should be crafted and stacked in the direction of the essential outputs. If the team is to be involved in a critical strategic issue, it should have a heavy **ORANGE** cast to enable it to find the 'best solution,' and then deploy assets in a quick and efficient manner. You would also need some **YELLOW** thinking to inject long-term implications and someone leaning toward **BLUE** to determine what is proper and in line with standards.

Applying Patterns of Thinking and Natural Intelligences

Our thinking about people in general, their nature and potentials, has shifted from 'empty brains' and 'anybody can do anything' to an acceptance of unique and innate differences and capacities. Mind/brain research, gene mapping, and even analysis of identical twins who were reared separately have heightened our awareness of both differences and similarities. The nature vs. nurture dial is shifting from 'mostly nurture' to synergy between the two. In Spiral language, we are slowly draining the **GREEN**, egalitarian swamp and revealing natural differences in complexity of thinking. We are uncovering **YELLOW** and awaiting what **TURQUOISE** will bring.

For example, what kinds of minds were needed to work as air traffic controllers in high density airports in the days before powerful computers? The ability to visualize airspace three-dimensionally was crucial to sorting out and aligning blips on a flat radar screen. Quick decisiveness was also important since each green dot represented a different kind of aircraft, at a different altitude, speed, and trajectory. The controller was called upon to sequence airplanes for landing by integrating a large amount of data. Even though they were highly 'intelligent' up to 90% of applicants washed out during training because the X Template was ill-defined and it was not until several weeks into the course that the 3-D thinking capacity was tested.

Job models, however, do change. Now the FAA must select different kinds of people who are more adept with information management tools than sorting out airplanes in their minds. Some current employees will make the transition easily; others will not. Certainly, the X Template must be re-cut if the agency intends to implement A.E.R.A., much less a Second Tier initiative.

Thinking back to the last chapter, you want to look at similar patterns of thinking in selecting visionary thinkers and good scouts for your *Streams* team. The best candidates are most often Chaotic–Conceptual in focus. They perform well in open, free-wheeling, and highly creative activities. Abstractions play to their strength. Their weakness is that strength pushed to excess. Do not expect them necessarily to be good with details, precise lineups, or repetitive pages. You will need to select other minds, with different kinds of thinking, to do those things.

In summary, the X Template is designed to link together all of the variables that impinge upon the job to be done so that they are handled in a sequential and logical manner. The three sub-Spirals of technology, human factors, and business systems are in sync. The payoff is that the ultimate output will be clean, focused, strategic, and lean.

The Y Template: People Factors and Management Systems

While we wrap the Y Template around the X Template, that does not imply 'better than,' or 'superior to,' only 'different from.' Those performing X Template functions are focused on getting the job done. People and resources operating on behalf of the Y Template support, facilitate, assist, enhance, and improve the X Template's performance and procedures. In Second Tier entities they are not bosses *per se*; they do not pull rank; they do not play games. Their primary purpose is to add value, make repairs, and fine-tune while the work is being done. Many people function on both X and Y Templates at once.

As we have pointed out, many TPQ, TQM, and reengineering intiatives run aground because they have been unable to reshape the total culture and specific leadership behaviors of the Y Template to match X Template's needs. For example, in the past, mid- and top-level executives have had perks and bonuses at the obvious expense of 'the line' or 'first level' employees. They have been riding the backs of the X Template. That must change for the Templates process to work. The X Template, where the jobs are actually performed, must be enriched before any cream is skimmed at the top.

The X Template must be laid out first since it is where the Plumb Line points. Once those decisions are made, you are ready to do Y Template things like the design of management systems, motivation packages, dispatch of human and other resources, and engineering maintenance. As the Y Template goes into place you can begin to think more broadly and start putting together the kinds of Command Intelligences (Z Template) necessary to deal with your specific X and Y Templates.

The tasks, people, and technology mix of each particular X Template function will dictate what needs to happen when and by whom on Y and even Z Templates. By hanging the Plumb Bob so it points to a given job (or assemblage of people) on the X Template, one can then determine what needs to happen at Y level to support that job to be done and foster synergy among that group. If a **RED** empire is necessary to get the job done, the capability to manage and motivate **RED** Empires must exist on Y. It will be legitimized and kept healthy from the Z Template for the good of the organization's whole Spiral as well.

Templates end the debate as to the 'right' or 'best' way to manage people. The issue, rather, is how to manage or facilitate those people doing those jobs in those *Life Conditions*. Looking through the Y Template, you assess the ᵛMEMEs and Patterns of Thinking of those people who naturally perform the work laid out on the X Template. Then you align Y accordingly. Repeat the Design Formula – 'how should who manage whom to do what, and when?' Arguments over contrasting managerial theories, competing gurus, or trendy training packages are fruitless. You simply lower the Plumb Bob and then lay the packages and protocols that will both serve the immediate needs of the people at that place on the X Template and the interests of the entire company as well.

There is no standard form for Templates, period. Companies, particularly those who are global in scope, must be sure that in shaping the X Template they do not force a single prescription over their many diverse sub-cultures. Rather, each version of the X Template must be indigenous to its *milieu* and to the kinds of ᵛMEMEs and Patterns that *milieu* presents. Beware of simply importing the latest managerial fad into your company until you have sorted out your own Design Formula, Plumb Line Process, and *Streams* sequence for your X and Y Templates. You may have the best solutions already in hand.

Using the Y Template for Selection, Alignment, and Integration of People and Processes

The function of the Y Template is managing, facilitating, leading, and expediting the human factors within the X flow. This Second Tier process should be operationalized through Spiral Wizardry since there must be heavy involvement and consultation with the X Template people directly involved in production because it is they who are the most knowing about the job(s) being done, but they are also the most likely to represent widely diverse ᵛMEME profiles.

Grenier and Metes (p. 119) list the following competencies which fit the Y Template:

- Network fault analysis and resolution management [finding faults and fixing them]
- Configuration management [arranging people, technology, and facilities in functional streams]
- Performance management [effective supervision of people and systems]
- Security management [keeping things and people safe]
- Accounting management [taking care of the books and fiduciary obligations]
- Applications management [dispensing new ideas through the template]

Let us add knowing how to support and coordinate multiple ᵛMEME systems since the Y Template is concerned with the health of the entire work stream – individuals, the organization, and the community at large. You create this healthy climate by a multi-colored strategy of embellishing, strengthening, and enhancing all of the ᵛMEMEs that exist within the entity. Think of this as preventive maintenance for human beings. To illustrate . . .

- **PURPLE** is nutured through observing seasonal rituals, honoring individual's rites of passage (weddings, graduations, funerals) and expressing a sense of enchantment and magic in life's mystery. Let the groups have their special time together.
- **RED** is nurtured by preserving the stories of company heroes, or by celebrating the great feats of conquest when the company, figuratively at least, 'slayed the dragon.' Provide positive outlets for energy, like sports and constructive activities that get out and build something keep it fit.
- **BLUE** is reinforced through appeals to traditions, by respecting the past, by honouring length of service and loyalty. Various forms of patriotic appeals and charitable sacrifice should accompany observances of national, religious, or secular holidays and commemorative events.
- **ORANGE** is exercised by displaying symbols of progress, success, growth, and accomplishment. Individuals or groups who excel should be recognized for their achievements. They like a piece-of-the-action but also enjoy getting good things done.
- **GREEN** is enhanced by stressing the importance of human beings and the warmth that exudes from a feeling of a caring community. Socially responsible activities should become tastefully visible as everyone in the group contributes.
- **YELLOW** is enhanced by conveying a sense of personal freedom with emphasis on getting an important job done without specifying how it must be done. Here, especially, flex-time, alternative working hours, remote working, and job interchange are ways to avoid over-managing.

While every set of Templates will be different, one basic Second Tier principle runs throughout: Decisions are made by the people most competent to make them and as close to the X Template as possible, not by some large class of 'managers' or 'executives.' The nature of the problem to be solved, decision to be reached, or issue to be resolved will determine who is involved and where the buck stops. Furthermore, compensation for all kinds should be calibrated with levels of competency, implications of ideas, consequences of contributions, and the extent to which people add to the life of the organization's Spiral throughout the Variations of Change.

Y Template Management of Technology, Resources, and Facilities

These functions involve hardware, maintenance, house-keeping, up-keeps and up-dates, and other tasks often assigned to engineering, facilities and personnel departments. If you are using Templates there is a difference since the corporate Plumb Line now hovers over X outputs, not titles on office doors or pay grades. Support functions now become integrated across the input-throughput-output flow as the Y Template shifts them to where they are most needed rather than to where they fall on charts. Training and selection functions become so closely integrated with X Template requirements that the so-called 'line' vs. 'staff' conflict cannot happen because everyone is now in the same business.

The healthy Y Template is lean, flexible, apolitical, and demands P-O-A. It morphs, changes, and reconstitutes itself as new needs arise from X. Interpersonal squabbles and 'Us' vs. 'Them' conflicts are nipped in the bud. Enhanced information systems provide the same knowledge base to all three Templates so rumors and allegations of injustice or mismanagement can be quickly resolved.

After his stint on the General Motors Board, computer magnate Ross Perot contrasted the way his former company, EDS, operated as opposed to GM's culture. He said that if EDS people saw a snake, they would kill it. Whereas traditional GM management, after going through the time-honored committee investigation, would dance around while trying to find the proper person somewhere in their vast hierarchy who was the authorized 'snake killer.' They might even hire a search firm to do the looking. In the meantime, the snake would probably get away, especially if it was Japanese. (Perot has never been charged with political, much less 'animal rights,' correctness.)

Day-by-day Monitoring of Events, Issues, and Performance from the Y Template

The functional differences between the X and Y Template are more of degree and scope than type. People in the Y Template need to exercise a broader perspective than X operatives who concentrate on getting the work out. They should be able to call up more resources to sort-out problems and bring more knowledge to bear on the situation. They may be expert workers who also can act as facilitators, supervisors, or managers as needed. Y Template personnel have to see the value chain from start to finish, from supplier to customer. In Second Tier entities they operate more in *ad hoc* decision teams than permanent structures. The lines of authority between X and Y layers are kept deliberately fuzzy, making it difficult to start territorial battles and keeping good outputs part of everybody's job.

Unlike traditional 'up the organization' models, a pro-motion does not mean having to move from the X Template to Y responsibilities in Second Tier entities; that is only one option. Each job in the company will have its own benchmarks and a built-in advancement track. A healthy Y Template makes it possible for a satisfied X Template person to climb a horizontal competency ladder by learning more, doing more things, accessing more knowledge about the entire value-chain, or acquiring new skill bundles for future use. Through

Change of the 1st or 2nd Variation the person has become more valuable to the X Template and thereby has enhanced the Spiral. An entire, satisfying career might be spent on the X Template. If Change of a higher Variation is underway, then the Templates can make room for that option as more complex thinking appears.

In summary, the Y Template is responsible for fine-tuning the flow of work, monitoring all of the vital signs, enhancing the competencies of people doing the work, and providing the integration necessary to produce a seamless company. The Y layer is not the filter or intermediary beween Z and X. Its role is to unburden the X Template from ancillary tasks and extraneous duties that divert it from the job to be done. If you want a graphic of Y, turn a typical organization chart up-side-down like SAS (Scandinavian Airlines) did. Now, the mechanics and customer contact people – 'where the rubber meets the road' – have priority. The executive level supports, rather than 'lords over,' the people performing the critical jobs of the airline. This form comes naturally to Spiral Wizards because it involves integrating ᵛMEME Profiles and diverse Thinking Patterns in complex systems, not mastering a few Traits of a Leader or demonstrating the habits of success.

Z Template: Command Intelligences

Many organizations are trying to become thin, lean and efficient. Some simply lay off middle managers. Others crack the whip harder at the lowest echelons while the top layer prospers. In entities managed by Spiral Wizards, more power, responsibility, and resources flow into production/service streams while executive trappings and expensive perks go away. Be not mistaken; this does not mean the company is being given away to the employees, or that quick **ORANGE** minds are now surplus property, or that **GREEN** relativistic impulses are replacing **BLUE** heritage. Something else, something more profound, something downright **YELLOW** is happening. People on both X and Y Templates have more power because of access to information and fundamental shifts in the human ᵛMEME stack.

The role and scope of the executive function is shifting. Fewer entities are relying on quasi-military chain-of-command structures where power is vested in single persons or elitist groups up and down a power pyramid. Rather, they are now forming task-specific brain syndicates, a new decision-team approach that relies on competency, trust, cooperation, independence, and consensus combined.

Business issues are more complex and multidimensional today. The environment in which critical decisions are now being made is more chaotic, faster paced, and less forgiving. More CEOs and senior level managers are aware of the incompleteness of their own knowledge and insight base, particularly where human dynamics are concerned. What they learned in

MBA programs or executive seminars is no longer sufficient or even particularly relevant. New priorities far beyond bottom-line performance such as social and environmental citizenship are being imposed. In response, many executives, through interactive planning and visioning activities, are broadening the base of participation in decision making. Companies, today, are more high-tech, information rich, global in scope, and integrated in operation. Diversity is appreciated and flexibility is essential.

Fewer and fewer stakeholders are willing to put up with the extravagant, flamboyant egos that have existed at the top of corporate and governmental ORANGE. When President George Bush escorted American CEOs to Japan with hats in hand in 1992, it dramatized the differences between executives in two societies, framing America's version as over-paid, over-egoed, and out-foxed. No wonder the President got ill.

The Z Template is not home to red carpet VIP's but to Command Intelligences. By this we mean the collective wisdom, knowledge, and judgment that is focused on specific problems and issues, both long and short term. In the traditional pyramid, the only opinions that count are housed at the top; in spite of their intelligences, everyone else is essentially 'along for the ride.' In a Second Tier organization, all knowledge is important. The unique insight and wisdom of the Z Template comes in two forms – the Executive Core and Focused Intelligences.

First, Z houses the Executive Core (EC) which monitors the whole process like the CPU in a computer. The EC will be small, consisting of the CEO and others who have been chosen because of their scope of vision, necessary experiences, maturity of judgment, abilities with P-O-A, and competency. It is accountable for the whole entity – fiduciary, legal, ethical, productivity, and financial. This Core represents the microcosm of thinking required to (a) coordinate X and Y Template functions and (b) maintain a lookout to enable the organization to thrive in the *milieu* at large.

The **Executive Core** looks and behaves more like a creative and inclusive 'skunk works' than a top-level, exclusive club. It functions as a complex, high-order *Streams* team for the whole entity (as opposed to issue-specific teams taken from X and Y Templates). A natural tendency of any organism is to explore outside, then change inside. The EC constantly reshapes the company to fit the *Life Conditions*. Of course that disturbs the ᵛMEME stack. The EC, having worked on the outside, then has to fix the inside. Once the inside has been rearranged, it must again focus on the outside. The EC is a busy place requiring persons of high energy, interest, scruples, and abilities. Organizationally, the Executive Core floats in the midst of the three Templates. If the Templates are a three-ring circus, then the EC is ring-master.

The second function of the Z Template is to bring **Focused Intelligences** to specific problems. Under the direction of the EC, intelligences from throughout the three templates are assigned to a given task. The Value

Engineering discipline or similar collaborative models are used to tap the talents and insights of everybody involved in an objective, clean, non-political, and non-territorial fashion. Persons from the Executive Core participate directly with those from the X and Y Templates. Knowledge, know-how, and informed perspectives transcend position and rank in making decisions. The Executive Core sees to it that the best decisions are being made. 'What is right' is always more important than 'who is right.'

Continuous Scanning of Present and Future from the Z Template

Just as the Y Template monitors all aspects of operations, the organization's Z Template tunes in to the kinds of exotic messages from the future such as those needed for *Streams* Element 10. Visit an organizational grave yard and look at all the tombstones of airlines, steel companies, and banks. Most died because they failed to keep their eyes open to what was coming at them from upstream, got blind-sided while looking at the bottom-line, or lost touch with their moral anchors and went adrift. Many were weakened by the diseases of greed and arrogance, final state blindness, Quick Fixitis, and Do-or-Die quarterly reports.

The Command Intelligences, coordinated from Z but dispersed through-out all three Templates, should include an early warning device that identifies potential flash points like these before they ignite and sensors that constantly sweep both the internal and external environments for what is coming 'round the bend. These include forces of the marketplace, emerging technologies, shifting population trends, 'strange' behaviour from competitors, and the first signs of political turbulence. Usually, 'Bad' news is more valuable than good.

The Z Template: Macro-Managing the Total Organism

Every organization has vital signs, indicators of its health. Some of these are seen in the usual spreadsheet numbers – from productivity measurements and quality statistics to Return on Investment. Most of the cultural life signs are more intangible, illusive, and harder to figure.

Everybody's eyes and ears are needed to recognize signs of distress or sighs of satisfaction. This is also Command Intelligences at work. Every company will, at some time or another, encounter the stresses of BETA conditions. The sooner those are recognized the better lest a GAMMA Trap be sprung. Denial, political gamesmanship, or self-serving gatekeepers often isolate executives from knowing what is going on until it is too late to avoid the jaws of disaster.

As former Southwest and Braniff Airlines CEO Howard Putnam points out, 'you should get mad at situations, not people.' If workers fear for their professional lives every time they make a mistake, two things will happen, both bad. (1) They will not risk, take a chance, or venture into the unknown. (2) They will hide their mistakes or pass them off to others, perhaps causing a more serious foul-up in the future. Under such terms, several Change Conditions are unattainable and anything beyond the 1st or 2nd Variation is out.

The Templates approach gives people more freedom and more safety. It allows for the design and deployment of a wide range of unique cubbyholes, niches, and microsystems which function independently of the traditional lines of authority or bottom-line accountability. Thus, key people from all over the organization can be brought together in an emergency or assigned on a temporary basis – Focused Intelligences where it counts, when it counts.

Some clusters drawn from all the Templates might include . . .

- **Wild Duck Pond:** a place where bright, nonconformist individuals can 'swim alone' to explore off-the-wall ideas without getting punished or threatening more traditional structures.
- **Nursery:** a developmental track where neophytes can be nurtured through a series of training experiences and simulations before they are exposed to mainline functions in any of the three templates. They can 'learn the ropes' without imposing on people engaged in serious X Template activities or mess up Y Template operations during their learning curves. All too often secretaries have to train their new bosses who are simply paying dues en route to the top of the organization while the much lower pay grade 'executive assistant' actually holds down the fort.
- **War Room:** either a physical space or an information network that displays the vital signs of the company, models of the environment, profiles of competitors, and other antagonists. The War Room can simulate alternative responses to particular scenarios before they are implemented in the 'real' world.
- **Play Pen:** a loose and creative environment where teams can attack very serious problems through playful brainstorming, model building, and scenario construction, forcibly liberating their 'right brain' capacities and scanning potentials.
- **Crisis Team:** a rapid response 'A-Team' of experts from the X, Y, and Z Templates that can be deployed quickly anywhere in the environment to fend off danger, stabilize functions, and repair damage to keep the organization functioning.
- **Rescue Squad:** a source of nurturance and support that dispenses 'chicken soup' to ailing parts of the organism after a crisis is over. It could mobilize in case of work-related accidents – either physical or emotional – to get things stabilized, personal problems dealt with, and the entity back to a new state of normal. All major air carriers have what American Airlines calls 'the care team,' a group of experts that rallies to action in case of disasters.

- **Wizard's Tree House:** a periodic convocation of Spiral Wizards who scan far out into the future searching for new trends, new opportunities, and new dangers. It feeds ideas to both the Z Command Intelligences, and *ad hoc* Streams Teams.

Shaping Large Scale Change and Strategic Interventions

The X and Y Templates monitor and support the day-to-day operations of the entity. Compared to Z their view is more linear and focused on the nature of the job to be done. The Z Template's Command Intelligences really take hold when the organization goes into BETA because it needs a major overhaul, a significant change in direction, or to be reconstituted following a merger or acquisition. The Intelligences to do these things permeate all three templates; everyone in the organization is potentially a Z agent. The Executive Core which coordinates this is also headquartered in Z and functions as the unified command and control center for the enterprise, mobilizing the Command Intelligences as needed. It behaves very much in the fashion of General Schwartzkopf and his staff during Desert Storm.

Since a Template company has a built-in change capacity dispersed throughout its operating units, it automatically morphs itself, adjusts quickly to new shapes, forms, networks, and tasks, and fuses itself with new entities as need be. Empowerment is disseminated throughout the organism. That appropriate Autocracy – remember, it is vital – connects with competency to allow quick decisions to be made and judgments to be exercised without having to ask permission or look to one's backside.

Jobs are defined differently in a Template arrangement. Instead of the traditional one-person-assigned-to-one-job-in-one-place mentality, each contributor may have pieces of a number of functions all along the value-chain. If you look in anyone's locker, you may find a cap with a 'Z' on it. Traditional models encourage competition between engineering and production, line and staff, and regions and home office. The Spiral Wizard's Templates weave a seamless process, one that focuses on systemic outputs, not narrow functions. Cooperation and synergy among separate components are stitched into the design. Everybody is rewarded for pulling together, but also for excelling alone. This instills a unique flexibility in the culture; namely, the ability for individuals to adjust quickly to new assignments and responsibilities. Nobody needs a course in managing change; it is already part of the process. Barriers and boundaries never become permanent in virtual reality.

To summarize the Z Template and end this chapter, consider six intelligences. We identified these in development research for the Brain-SCAN Assessment, now part of the Quantum Mind research package. These capacities are:

- **World sensing:** Like an absorbent sponge, sweeping radar, and early warning detector. It is high in non-quantitative market research and public relations professionals and others who rely on 'sensing' information and guided intuitions.

- **Sequential plan construction:** The capacity to locate entities in space, in sequence, and in order. Often high in planning departments, layout functions, and orderly bureaucratic jobs. NASA's planners who have the patience to specify the essential activities at every second of a projected space flight must be high in this competence. It is crucial for logistics operations.
- **Complex plan execution:** Ability to suppress competing stimuli, block out distracting events, and integrate complex ideas and flows. High in good emergency room physicians and nurses, sales professionals who must negotiate deals under pressure, and others who must select among options, orchestrate plans of attack, and mesh a number of tributaries while on the go. This capacity is imperative for successful military leaders and event managers.

Included in our studies were chief executive officers and managing directors from around the world. They demonstrated these three distinct 'Executive Intelligence' patterns:

- **Entrepreneurial intelligence:** The impulse to start something new, to peer into the future, a fierce determination to succeed, a penchant for high risk, unconventional freedom, a creative resourcefulness, integrates complexity, focused to obtain a pragmatic outcome, the ego strength to stand alone, a demand for total control, and a practical visionary. High in CEOs who built their own companies or in innovative leaders who cut their own pathways. Excels at managing start-ups, either within or outside of larger companies. This intelligence could be utilized in new product sponsorship; sent to inaugurate a new outpost; or assigned to head up new ventures.
- **Translational intelligence:** Essential in the maintenance of systems, continual monitoring and fine-tuning, and the guarantee of consistent standards and quality. Shows patience and tolerance of sameness and regimentation, satisfied with small victories or incremental improvements, and able to reduce uncertainty, tension, and internal conflict. Excels at looking after large systems, adapting and implementing new ideas into a steady state. Adept at taking over as Chief Operating Officer after start-up entrepreneurs have reached their levels of incompetence.
- **Transformational intelligence:** Essential in navigating through changing chaotic environments while using sketchy blue-prints to literally transform a system, company, or society from one world to the next. Excels during periods of profound and rapid change. Transformational Intelligence is high in Change Wizards who rescue a company from failure, or

merge several entities into a new organization. This element is necessary in managing a company through its inevitable life cycles on the S-curve.

The Intelligence Core of an organization should have all six of these Patterns at its disposal, along with representatives who speak for all the ᵛMEMEs. Otherwise, there will be serious gaps in both perspective and action. Put them all together, though, and add them to the Wizard's Tool Kit and Spiral Dynamics is yours.

It is not all that difficult to do. The twenty-first century company, like the twenty-first century country, is still a work in progress; but its outlines are beginning to jell. Leaders everywhere are attempting to design and manage revolutions of huge magnitudes of scale – geopolitical, technological, and human – all at the same time. New markets, extraordinary advances in communications, and global sources of brain power and skilled labor will herald an explosion in business opportunities.

The Spiral Company, one that can function and thrive in such a rapidly evolving environment, will require new leadership, no matter how the old approaches have been repackaged or reengineered. This emerging executive intelligence will stand in striking contrast to the gray flannel 'organization man' of the 1950s or even the smartly-suited Harvard MBAer from the 1980s.

Such leaders must mesh global markets with local operations and vice versa. They must be open to new ideas, tactics, and technologies. Leaders of the Spiral Company must encourage information-sharing and innovation throughout organizations which are continually in process of being aligned and integrated. Perhaps above all, they must value ethical behavior, integrity, and fair play. At the same time, they must be irreverent about hierarchy and office politics, tolerating, even enjoying, some unruliness. They must reward those who work smartly, produce high-quality goods and services, and thrive on the challenges of the times with personalized recognition, continuous training, and a good living.

But even this will not be enough. Spiral Company leaders must also be responsible human beings who enrich families, neighborhoods, communities, nations, and life itself. They will hear the faint beat of ancient drums while they also sense the electronic pulses of worlds yet to be. Human society's crucibles are beginning to forge beings of just such intelligences in significant numbers. As they take on the tasks that await them, they will do well to summon a Spiral Wizard to their sides.

SECTION 3

The Spiral Wizard's Field Manual

This section describes each of the 'MEMEs in detail. It will give you a sense for how they impact behavior, how they grow and decline. We have tried to give you a useful 'feel' for the 'MEMEs rather than a theoretical discussion so you can begin to use Spiral Dynamics every day.

In Chapter 2 we took you on a flying carpet ride and whisked you to meet unique people under the power of different 'MEMEs. We revisited them ten years later and observed myriad 'MEME adaptations. Chapter 4 explored why the diverse change forms occurred. Now you are going on a real 'MEME hunt.

This time you will be armed with your understanding of the 'MEMEs' core intelligences, Change Conditions and Variations, and Recognition Principles. With those firmly in mind, this 'Field Manual' will help you in your quest to chase down the elusive 'MEMEs in your world.

Each of the eight chapters in this section is sequenced according to the three phases in the 'MEMEs' natural life cycle.

- **Entering** as the vestiges of the previous system hang on
- **Peak** as the thinking is centralized in the 'MEME
- **Exiting** as the next *Life Conditions* ($LC^{1, 2, 3, 4, 5, 6, 7, 8, etc.}$) appear

You may find it useful to think of the *Life Conditions* ($LC^{1-8, etc.}$) attached
to each 'MEME as levels of increasing complexity in a constantly changing 'World to the Power of 1, 2, 3, 4, 5, 6, 7, or 8'.

We will assist you in your field exploration by identifying some of the essential characteristics of each of the 'MEMEs. Be on the look out for them. These will include the following:

- The **BEIGE** Survivalistic 'MEME – 'Tracks'

- The **PURPLE** Animistic ᵛMEME – 'Signs'
- The **RED** Impulsive ᵛMEME – 'Flags'
- The **BLUE** Purposeful ᵛMEME – 'Mottos'
- The **ORANGE** Achievist ᵛMEME – 'Flashes'
- The **GREEN** Communitarian ᵛMEME – 'Fuzzies'
- The **YELLOW** Integrative ᵛMEME – 'Flows'
- The **TURQUOISE** Holistic ᵛMEME – 'Holons'

A map of the phases is shown below.

Control Inside   Control Outside

The Sequence of the FIRST TIER ᵛMEMEs

BEIGE & (LC[1])*

    BEIGE/purple

      beige/PURPLE

        PURPLE/red   PURPLE & (LC[2])

    purple/RED

RED & (LC[3])

     RED/blue

       red/BLUE

        BLUE/orange

ORANGE & (LC[5]) blue/ORANGE   BLUE & (LC[4])

      ORANGE/green

    orange/GREEN

              GREEN & (LC[6])

       GREEN/yellow

    green/YELLOW

The Sequence of the SECOND TIER ᵛMEMEs

YELLOW & (LC[7])

    YELLOW/turquoise

      yellow/TURQUOISE

    TURQUOISE/coral?   TURQUOISE & (LC[8])

9

BEIGE   *Survival/Sense*
The Instinctive ᵛMEME

- Automatic, autistic, reflexive
- Centers around satisfaction of human biological needs
- Driven by deep brain programs, instincts, and genetics
- Little awareness of self as a distinct being (undifferentiated)
- Lives 'off the land' much as other animals
- Minimal impact on or control over environment

At the Core of BEIGE – *Life Conditions*[1]:

'My existence centers on survival. Energy is devoted to staying alive and meeting the needs of my physical being so I am not hungry or thirsty. I must reproduce my kind so I respond to sexual urges as they occur. I do not know what you mean by 'future,' laying plans, saving for a rainy day, or 'self.' My body tells me what to do and I am driven by senses talking to my brain, not so much a conscious mind.'

Awakening of the BEIGE ᵛMEME

Most people believe we were created by God, the goddess, or embrace some other myth of origin. Some maintain it is the Promethean genes in our cells, whatever their source, that are our tickets to travel the Spiral. Yet others propose cosmic forces, natural selection, and the cold-blooded Darwinian odds have brought us here. Whatever beginning works for you, human nature was not – is not – fixed.

While no one can pinpoint the threshold that transformed us, it is clear from both the archaeological record and DNA analysis that a significant change occurred. Our kind parted from our hominid ancestors (and closer Neanderthal relatives) to become what we are today. It takes less than 1% difference between our DNA and that of chimps to explain why humanity develops new 'MEMEs while the apes, whales, and dolphins do not. In any case – divine direction, evolutionary process, a comet's fall, or something else – that difference is the impetus which sets human dynamics in motion.

At the Core of BEIGE

- Survive at the most basic level
- Satisfy physiological needs
- Form protective/supportive bands
- Entities exist as biological units
- Simply make it through the night/day

BEIGE is a virtually automatic state of existence. It is driven by the imperative physiological needs which dominate in LC^1 and trigger the very basic survival equipment with which we are born. With only this 'MEME active, one is clearly a human being but barely recognizable as a personality. If higher order brain functions have never been activated, this is but a step beyond a vegetative condition. If more complex thinking once did exist, physical illness, accident, or psychological trauma may diminish access to it, thus causing BEIGE to take over. The regressive state may be transitory or permanent.

Tens of thousands of years ago BEIGE was the cutting-edge 'MEME. It was our ancestors' advantage over gorillas and woolly mammoths. Now, in Graves' words, it is . . . 'the world of the physical infant, possibly the world of the simplest of food gathering cultures, the world of the severe senile deteriorate, the world of he who has regressed severely under the stress of war, the world of he who has been kept alive by the compassion or guilt of his fellow man.' Clearly, no longer state-of-the-art thinking.

TRACKS: The Most Basic Human Needs

BEIGE is concerned with satisfying basic biological needs – food (not to feel hunger), water (not to feel thirst), temperature control (not to feel too hot or too cold), sex (to procreate), and, to a limited extent, safety (not to be eaten by a lion or trampled by buffalo). In this zone, 'normal' behavior comes from deep-brain instincts which require very little higher-brain reasoning. Most actions are by reflexes rather than volitional, logical choices. Thus, parents must keep poisons out of little children's reach ('Me feel thirst' = I drink whatever is wet; 'Me have hunger' = I eat anything I can reach). We need not discuss the realm of diapers.

BEIGE thinking dominates infancy. If this 'MEME resurges late in life due, for example, to Alzheimer's disease, nutrition and personal hygiene must again be provided for the infirm elderly since even the basics of LC^1 may have become too complex to manage. It reactivates with some mental illnesses and can arise situationally. The 'Animal House' drunk may down-shift toward BEIGE, overlook social niceties, and invade the neighbors' garden when his bladder demands relief and the porcelain convenience is occupied by a fraternity brother's tipsy date.

In the BEIGE zone emotions are few. There is no surplus energy to mobilize into anger or fear, hate or jealousy; practically all resources go to just staying alive day-to-day. The ᵛMEME is essentially amoral: '. . . behavior resembles more the imprinted duckling than an independent human being,' according to Graves. The individual has no real sense of a distinct self because 'I' and 'thou' and even 'it' are indistinguishable. There is little comprehension of time or territory beyond right here, right now.

In *Up from Eden* (Anchor Press, New York, 1981) Ken Wilber identifies BEIGE as the first link in what he calls 'The Chain of Being.' He notes:

> 'Dawn Man, in other words, began his career immersed in the subconscious realms of nature and body, of vegetable and animal, and initially "experienced" himself as indistinguishable from the world that had already evolved to that point.'

Let us emphasize that BEIGE does not necessarily mean a stupid or deficient human being, only one for whom LCᴵ problems are intense. It is the beginning point for all of us, and many exit through BEIGE at the end of life's journey. Tragically, a lack of stimulation or malnutrition can leave BEIGE disproportionately strong and may well limit access to more complex thinking for millions of youngsters. This entrapment may haunt the twenty-first century as much as global war influenced the twentieth.

TRACKS: Survival Skills and BEIGE Intelligences

BEIGE intelligences emerged for survival on the savanna, in a rain forest, wandering the bush, and the tundra. Even today, pockets of semi-'Stone Age' humans who depend heavily (by twentieth-century standards) on BEIGE intelligences are encountered now and then by adventurers and merchants in South America, the African bush, and the Pacific Islands.

Upon discovering such BEIGE groups (although just who 'discovers' whom, and to what advantage, is always open to discussion), the First World has erred in two directions. Either we have arrogantly dismissed BEIGE as primitive, backward, and needful of enlightenment or we have romanticized indigenous people's ancestors as having been more noble than people today. Both views have served the ᵛMEMEs of explorers far more than the explored, propping up the ethnocentric assumptions of colonial administrators and relegating whole civilizations to the status of museum curiosities.

However, in slight support of the myth of the noble savage, it does seem that a healthy BEIGE system intertwines with nature and can access senses that most of us have lost and will not rediscover unless (a) we again confront LC^1 and (b) have the flexibility in our Spirals to down-shift to congruence. Although 'modern' science does not understand it, the **BEIGE** ^{V}MEME seems to have intuitions about impending events (better access to the Time dimension, perhaps) and to possess a unique spatial awareness. After near-death experiences some patients report having watched the surgical team perform. Might a remote viewing, out-of-body capacity be part of our deep brain repertoire of survival skills covered over by several thousand years of 'rational' thought?

After a couple of weeks in 'the bush,' experienced adventurers (and combat veterans) report their senses of hearing and smell heighten markedly. Perhaps this is a latent capacity of the **BEIGE** mind system that allows humans to compete with animals on their terms under LC^1. Someday we may find genetic memories and other senses readily accessible by removing the 'clutter' of such higher brain functions as self-conscious shame, rationality, guilt, and strategic planning. Students of yoga and meditation claim abilities to control the distractions of inter-^{V}MEME noise right now.

If you access your **BEIGE**, you can think like a trout, see like a deer, and live off the land. This layer may be where Jung's archetypes reside (pity the serpent and the spider!), along and some of the urges that crop up from deep inside us – disgust at the smell of rotting flesh or sexual arousal when certain $100 an ounce pheromones are present; 'eyes in the back of your head' so you know you are being watched by that weird guy beside you in the pickup truck; and the little voices that get us out of danger if we heed them.

When **BEIGE** is in control, people forms bands (not yet organizations), just a step above the herd. The objectives, though unstated, are survival and procreation. Band members seem to have a holographic sense of place and each other, much like a herd of elephants, a flock of geese, or a pod of whales, and may well communicate on frequencies with which 'civilized' people tuned out many moons ago. The endorphin release that so often eases the final hours of the terminally ill may be a residual **BEIGE** adaptation to grant the wounded individual peace and thereby release the group to move on, often a necessity under harsh LC^1.

Today, one can always find examples of **BEIGE** in cradles and kinder-gartens, among mentally ill street people, or in hospitals. Sometimes **BEIGE** surges when a person is psychologically overloaded. Extremes of stress – the nervous breakdown, profound grief, a catastrophe like Rwanda, or even trying to live in Sarajevo under attack – will trigger regression toward **BEIGE** for some people.

With the exception of newborn infants who pass quickly through the **BEIGE** zone or those with brain damage who may be blocked there, the **BEIGE** we find today is more often a backwater, regressive ^{V}MEME. In fact, many of the seeming **BEIGE** manifestations – dysfunctional street people, victims of famine or warfare, extremes of poverty and deprivation – are fallout from more complex 'MEMEs at work in society as they draw energy and resources into their spheres, leaving others without.

While Graves was critical of both exploitive **RED** and self-righteous **BLUE** motivations in perpetuating large clusters of **BEIGE** in populations, he believed 'the arch criminal' in fostering negative, unhealthy **BEIGE** is the **ORANGE** 'MEME:

> 'From his lofty position of relative worldly success and occupational superiority,' Graves said, 'he looks down in sneering condemnation on man at the first level [**BEIGE**]. "If he had any gumption he'd take himself in hand and get out of his condition," says materialistic [**ORANGE**] man in haughty condescension. "I did it. Look at me. I made it up here on my own. If he had anything on the ball he would do it too." '

Only when there is a profit – economic, political, or pseudo-spiritual – does **ORANGE** intercede with **BEIGE** dilemmas. In general, First World (**ORANGE**) and Second World (**BLUE/orange**) societies prefer to sweep **BEIGE** under the rug, out of sight, and, hopefully, out of mind rather than to confront its difficulties and limitations. Until the TV crews begin live coverage and activists begin acting up, relatively little is done by the 'movers-and-shakers' because **BEIGE** is almost off their radar scopes, thus easily ignored. Thus, help arrived in Rwanda a tad late for thousands of children.

TRACKS: Dealing with the BEIGE 'MEME

Whether temporary or permanent, **BEIGE** is best managed through nurturance and tender loving care. Often, people in this zone cannot even ask for help; it must be delivered. When a tragedy occurs and there is a large loss of life, some of the survivors and loved ones regress, temporarily at least, into a **BEIGE** state of being. Their basic needs must first be met hands-on by a group – like American Airlines' Care Team – to stabilize their condition. Then a stair step process can be constructed to lift them out of the traumatized condition, through the stages of grief, and back toward functionality.

If heavy **BEIGE** is relatively fixed, a caretaker system should be employed. Medications and meals must be administered, not just offered. Since **BEIGE** includes no conception of health or wellness, only pain or comfort, monitoring is essential if the surrounding world is complex beyond **LC'**. Do not expect time-competence or for the person to save for the future or step far outside the present. Written directions are useless and even oral instructions must be simple and repeated frequently because symbol-handling capacity is slim.

As the technology for keeping people alive improves, and the cost of treatment increases exponentially, we will encounter more pressing ethical issues regarding **BEIGE**. As we periodically watch horrible scenes of starving children, be they in Africa or the Balkans, we see the descent into a **BEIGE** hell. Why do we 'advanced' beings let it happen? The answer lies in central questions such as: How much of our mainstream resources are we willing to spend on people who exist in the backwaters? What value do contemporary humans put upon the **BEIGE** 'MEME intelligences? And who decides when to interfere with the cold-blooded side of the Spiral?

BEIGE/purple: Exiting Phase

- Informal band-type human existence is seriously challenged by competition over food resources, mates, and territory.
- As LC^1 basic survival needs are met, new brain connections form which create a distinct awareness of 'me, myself, and I' as different from other people, vegetation, or animals.
- With time to think about why things happen, direct observations begin to link cause with effect. (Everything else is attributed to 'magic.')

As we leave the core **BEIGE** world of infancy and illness, LC^2 appear. With them comes the recognition of danger (threats from nature and other people) as the self begins to differentiate and one senses the power in the imposing, scary, outside world. Since there is strength in numbers, it fosters attention to ongoing relationships, kinship, and emotional ties. The deep-brain genetic programs and instincts join neocortical processing as the brain elaborates and complexifies. Memories begin connecting now with then, actions with outcomes. New-found feelings bring attachment to persons and objects. Tangible relics of this second great awakening are found in bone totems and stone fertility charms left by early man, much as we more 'advanced' people may store our once-beloved toys and teddy bears in the attic or keep a pressed corsage from a long-ago prom. LC^2 take us into a new world where magic, togetherness, and the mysteries of **PURPLE** love take hold.

10

PURPLE *Kin Spirits*
The Clannish ᵛMEME

- Obey desires of the mystical spirit beings
- Show allegiance to elders, custom, clan
- Preserve sacred places, objects, rituals
- Bond together to endure and find safety
- Live in an enchanted, magical village
- Seek harmony with nature's power

At the core of PURPLE – *Life Conditions*[2]:

'We seek safety and security for our kind through trust in blood relationships, extended family bonds, and magical powers which reach into the spirit world. We honor our ancestors' ways as sacred for they are even with us. Our path is full of seasonal rituals, rites of passage, traditional music and dance. We seek to live in harmony with nature and her ways through our ceremonies.'

From Instincts and Biology to a Conscious Mind

Human nature alternates through spurts of growth and periods of consolidation. Each transition is a state of dynamic tension between a more complex ᵛMEME which is brightening and the preceding one which is fading to less influence. At the end of the stressful passage, if it ends, there is stabilization into a new ᵛMEME arrangement suited to the now altered *Life Conditions*.

The **PURPLE** ᵛMEME was first awakened when successful **BEIGE** living permitted curiosity about the larger world 'out there' and awareness of all the threats to safety and security it holds. While herd-like **BEIGE** existence meets biological requirements, it does not address social needs that rise under **LC**[2] as other people enter the scene.

PURPLE is the mother of Communal/Collective 'MEMEs and the first to deal with forces outside the individual. It makes way for the family (necessary to organize close relationships), then fosters clans and tribes to regulate families. Kinship and proximity are the binding elements. Failure to cement these bonds into the person's repertoire during early childhood may leave a void to be filled later in life by gangs, cults, and fragile marriages.

When the PURPLE intelligence asks why things happen, it finds answers in unseeable natural forces and actions of powerful spirit beings. While BEIGE does not comprehend causes, that capacity activates with PURPLE. In the overall historic context, perhaps:

- loose bands of gatherers began to over-use local resources, found the need to move to greener pastures, and became more organized as they traveled; or
- Migrating groups would encounter 'others,' creating the need for interpersonal rules and social structure to maintain harmony. (Ten to twelve members seems to be about the right number for PURPLE span of control.)

The success of families, clan, and tribes in organizing people and improving the chances for survival liberated energy for matters of the mind – mythology, art, oral history, sport, ceremony, and ritual. Emerging culture put more demands on neurological capacities to analyze, understand, retain collective memories, and even plan for the future. A set of dynamic, if still relatively simple, world views emerged to produce the first cosmic pictures and models of reality. The rich imagination of PURPLE saw creatures in the stars, animals on cave walls, and pixies in the many enchanted forests.

beige/PURPLE: Entering Phase

LC^2 call upon the internal equipment designed to connect events into cause and effect sequences. For example, a cow dies when the moon is full. Thenceforth, the fullness of the moon contributes to the death of cows. Such experiences become superstitions, travel in sagas, and even get set down as laws. The origins of many truths are lost in the mists of history.

The early roots of animism are planted as beige/PURPLE concern with natural phenomena: rivers, mountains, sun, sky, and fire. With a bit of adaptation, these forces became portable as fertility symbols, totems, amulets, relics, lucky charms, and medicine bags. In this zone there is no sense of being able to control nature, only to placate the indwelling spirits in hopes of avoiding harm and achieving harmony.

The '. . . ghoulies, and ghosties, and long-leggedy beasties . . .' that populated the ancient world crawled forth long before Greek mythology and slithered through Shakespeare to nip at Stephen King. The Brothers Grimm and Mother Goose addressed the fears as **BEIGE** yields to **PURPLE** and beyond. Today, Sesame Street and Barney do the job. They also reflect the child-like wonderment the ᵛMEME carries in our often blasé world.

The rise of **beige/PURPLE** marks the end of infancy and the beginning of childhood. The baby begins to recognize that some behaviors get food and hugs. Symbolic thinking begins and words like 'mama,' 'dada,' and 'nanna' soon follow. The body and its functions are intriguing because **beige/PURPLE** thinking is still immediate and organic. When adults' *Life Conditions* regress to this zone through illness, the ᵛMEMEs brighten accordingly – the bathroom and chicken soup take precedence over business, politics, and the gaping hospital gown.

Children developing through the **beige/PURPLE** zone become reliant on objects in their sphere: a security 'blankie,' rubber ducky, potty, or Pooh Bear (who will later be taught **RED** submissiveness and learn right-from-wrong as **BLUE** emerges.) Around the middle of the first year, children begin to understand that people (and animals) are sentient beings rather than mere objects. It is a developmental step that many young criminals (and serial killers!) seem, unfortunately, to have missed.

PURPLE: Peak Phase

While we experience **PURPLE** thinking daily in various forms, it is difficult to imagine what its initial expressions tens of thousands of years ago might have been like. Edward Harrison describes this magical world in these terms:

> 'It was a vibrant universe awakened each day by the Sun spirit and mourned each night by the Moon spirit. A universe of starlike campfires across the night sky; of chromatic sky spirits manifesting as rainbows, sunsets, and northern lights; of mighty earth spirits rumbling beneath the ground and spewing forth from volcanoes; of flittering little folk dwelling in secret places and stealing lost children. A magic universe haunted by the unborn and dead forever calling. Words cannot recall nor the mind recapture the extreme vividity of its imagery.'
> (*Masks of the Universe*, Collier Books, 1985, pp. 22–23).

SIGN: The mind of PURPLE is animistic, shamanistic, and mystical

The **PURPLE** ᵛMEME is heavily laden with such so-called 'right brain' tendencies as heightened intuition; emotional attachments to places and things; and a mystified sense of cause and effect. The mind's eye is occupied with mana, totemism, fetishes, charms, shamanism, sorcery, hexes, fertility, superstitions, and myths of origin. Individuals move about, often fearfully, in a cauldron of omens and spells. A vivid collection of myths, legends, and parables flourishes in **PURPLE**, so much so that the line between what is real and what is fantasy often becomes blurred. Just as children often have trouble differentiating the truth from imagination, organizations in the **PURPLE** zone confuse fables with 'scientific' facts.

The ᵛMEME glorifies ability to divine the spirits, skills at hunting or finding water, and gathering medicines. Likewise, those who have special abilities to read emotional nuances in people and fine-tune relationships are honored since they play so major a role in maintaining the harmonious existence that is critical to group's survival.

By itself, **PURPLE** is pre-literate. Writing requires the linear, structured thinking found more toward the **BLUE** range. However, it is often rich in folk stories, songs, drawings, dances, artworks, and elaborate customs passed from one generation to the next. Sir James Fraser's *The Golden Bough* is a compendium of **PURPLE** beliefs, myths, and activities compiled through English eyes back in the nineteeth century when the world was so much larger. Philosopher Joseph Campbell brought **PURPLE** alive more recently. The Disney Corporation depends on it in 'Imagineering' theme parks, as do stuffed-animal manufacturers and air-port gift shops around the world.

PURPLE thinking is dichotomous. People are here or not here, of *us* or of *the others*. In death one may change state to join the ancestors in the spirit realm, or perhaps just not be. Time is more circular (even spherical) than the straight line most of us understand, meaning that degrees of past, present, and future are often indistinguishable to the **PURPLE** mind. A report of *when* something happened will relate more about a place and who was there than a clock. This link to context and the experience instead of GMT (Greenwich Mean Time) often baffles 'sophisticated' Westerners who take offense at missed appointments or fluid work habits in 'primitive' places where healthy social interactions take precedence over production schedules.

SIGN: The collective memory carries the little memes for PURPLE

The **PURPLE** collective memory holds vast wisdom which is often ampl-ified, mystified, and extended through the folk ways of a people. Fables, sagas, and legends likely trace back to actual events. Many religions share similar **PURPLE** roots. A great flood (which geologic evidence supports) is common to many of them. Some have kept relics and icons from their more **PURPLE** days intact for centuries. Numerous church holidays coincide with pagan moon and sun cycles because the impetus simply transferred from **PURPLE** to **BLUE**.

SIGN: The group is concerned with its survival and well-being of its own kind

The group, whether small like the Hopi Indians or large like dynastic China, sees itself as 'The People.' The 'others' are outsiders, curiosities, non-persons, or threatening foreign devils, a term still used in New York's Chinatown. This intense in-group/out-grouping is both strength and weakness for **PURPLE**. The inwardly focused energy addresses the safety/security problems, but it also isolates the **PURPLE** group so that the tighter it becomes, the farther it separates from others and their discoveries. Sometimes this leads to inter-clan or intra-tribal warfare in the name of 'ethnic cleansing' or 'racial violence,' as in Bosnia or the New Guinea highlands.

The traditional ways are inherent to the very nature of things, not arbitrarily chosen. **PURPLE** cannot imagine other ways to be and there is tumult if alternatives are imposed. The inability to adapt to suddenly-changed *Life Conditions* has led to the demise of many **PURPLE** peoples and the total absorption of others into societies operating elsewhere on the Spiral, usually in the colonial **BLUE** or industrialized **ORANGE** zones.

Today, Native and African-Americans, Aboriginal Australians, and even Mongolians are trying to grab hold of what remains of their **PURPLE** pasts before yet another generation of dilution occurs. The Japanese subsidize 'living national treasures,' recognizing that **PURPLE** story-telling, arts, and history rest in persons who cannot be converted to videotape. The subtleties tend to die out once the industrious but impatient **ORANGE** ᵛMEME takes hold. The deep significance of ancient customs is lost in textbooks; sacred **PURPLE** pots become collectibles; and once-private rituals become tourist kitsch as **PURPLE** fades. The spirits do not look favorably on exploitation and abandon places that charge admission or where the ceremonial dancers expect tips.

Though fragile, this is a very powerful and ancient ᵛMEME that attracts both good and bad. During World War II, mystical symbols and rituals drawn from the **PURPLE** layer rallied followers of the 'Heil Hitler' cult. Creating the Aryan mythology and centering it around a dominant personality hooked deeply into Germany's LC² fears and feudal heritage, in addition to the power, dogma, and expansionist urges from farther along the Spiral. The lesson is that if leaders can reach the **PURPLE** layer, they have a strong hold on people that 'the facts' and even human decency may not break.

SIGN: One for all, all for one

Reciprocity is part of the **PURPLE** compact and is a key organizing principle for virtually every tribal society. Property is (for the most part) communal because of the uncertainty in the world: 'If today I find food, I will gladly share it with you because tomorrow you may be lucky while I'm not.' This cooperative interdependence forms the basis for the African socialism/

humanism that is generally referred to as *Ubuntu*.

When distribution of goods is necessary, it is often controlled by a particular clan (the Antelope Clan reassigns the few available homesites at New Mexico's mountain-top Acoma Pueblo) or established custom (primogenitor or the house to the youngest daughter) to minimize strife. Competitive individualists put the group in jeopardy.

In this sacrifice-self view, one's life belongs to the tribe. Like World War II Japan's Kamikaze or the parents found lying protectively on top of their children at Pompeii, individuals willingly give themselves up for the safety of others and the survival of the whole. Since in-group and out-group lives have such different worth, it is no wonder human sacrifice occurred in those societies where **PURPLE** communal spirit dominated.

At a more commercial level, strong **PURPLE** makes pay and benefits programs somewhat difficult, since rewarding individual accomplishments also separates the good performer from the group. On the other hand, something taken from one member of the team is taken from all, and all must share in the emotions of loss. If one is caused to lose face, all are diminished. An entire family may be obligated to restore honor by carrying on the feud. The full membership of a labor union may strike in favor of a lockstep pay increase rather than make the ᵛMEME shift to individual incentives.

Social events in **PURPLE** groups are ceremonial and ritualized to provide assurance that time is continuous and emphasize the link with ancestors. Chants and repetitive percussion bring comfort to **PURPLE** and order to the collective mind. The clicking prayer wheels of Tibet, the traditional rhythms that surge in the arts of native peoples, and even the pulsing beats of Rap and Country-Western reverberate on the **PURPLE** band. Contemporary churches are well advised not to abandon all the rich aspects of ritual and ceremony this ᵛMEME attracts since it ministers to the Spiral in ways doctrine and prosperity messages do not.

SIGN: Shaman, Elders, and Chieftain

To deal with the awesome and inexplicable ways of nature, **PURPLE** groups seek out people whose view is a bit more elaborated than the rest. Such ones appear closer to the spirit realm and more in touch with the forces of the Great Mother. Whether called shaman, medicine man/woman, oracle, conjurer, or even witch, this person becomes the contact between the tribe/clan and the other world, the interpreter of messages from beyond, and the oracle of what is to be.

The shaman's role likely includes healer and medicine-person. While interpreting omens, dreams, and signs, **PURPLE**-based healers compound potions to ward off evil spirits or gain advantage over enemies (recall the songoma in Chapter 2). They often influence the political leadership and may have parallel or greater power than the 'chief.'

Among the Zulus, one's *muti* – medicine and magic – is absolutely crucial to life. There is much more *muti* in modern medicine than we in the West have been prepared to admit. The placebo effect seems to be the activation of the **PURPLE** band to invigorate the body's systems against disease. The mythical power of garlic to keep vampires away is matched by its demonstrable ability to control cholesterol.

While **BLUE** prays for healing grace and **ORANGE** works on machines that replicate human organs and employs genetically engineered chemicals that simulate nature, **PURPLE** aligns forces in the body with touch and natural herbal remedies. Chinese traditional medicine and acupuncture recognize the **PURPLE** zone. To a lesser extent, osteopathy and modern holistic treatments attempt to reconnect with the power of **PURPLE** to effect positive change. One of the many reasons for concern about loss of the great forests of the Earth is the concurrent loss of **PURPLE** resources as the indigenous healers are eliminated and their pharmacopoeias are ground into pulpwood or burned over for farmland.

PURPLE relies on taboos and the people's customs for direction. Some of these beliefs are deep within the Spirit – the abhorrence of incest, for example. The **PURPLE**-based avoidance of pork, codified by Jewish and Islamic **BLUE**, is really quite sensible for peoples without refrigeration or a treatment for trichinosis. For centuries, mental illness (lunacy) has triggered **PURPLE** fears, much as AIDS and the word 'Cancer' frighten people today.

The intelligences that **BEIGE** instinctively draws on become more deliberate as **PURPLE** grows. Dream walking, visits with the spirit realm, and out-of-body travels are attached to this 'MEME. Various forms of meditation and religious studies focus on this aspect as a door to altered consciousness. Legitimate parapsychology is trying to understand these aspects of mind, and high-priced telephone 'Psychic Hotlines' exploit the gullible with them.

In addition to the shaman, elders are highly respected for their stored wisdom and experience. They embody connections with the past and will some day join the revered ancestors. The council of elders is often the clan's decision-making body with the chieftain as the 'chair' or voice for decisions. That role often follows lineage with duties and privilege determined by kinship arrangements, although selection as most worthy by consensus of the tribe, and even tests by the spirits are possible criteria. However chosen, his or her role is to consult with the ancestors and elders, seek advice from the possessor of magic, and interpret the will of the people. In the **PURPLE** world the position is not one of absolute ruler, but opinion coordinator, facilitator, and monitor of the group's well-being. The chieftain's life belongs to and must serve the clan, not vice versa.

SIGN: Spirits, spirits everywhere

In animistic, nature-based **PURPLE** there are spirits and souls everywhere.

Beneficent and malignant forces must be kept in balance and harmony. Demonology, exorcisms, and vampires ride the **PURPLE** ᵛMEME. Witchcraft is both feared and respected, and those with wide **PURPLE** bands are reluctant even to talk of such things with 'outsiders' or 'newcomers.' Magical places and individuals with powers – the 'evil-eye' or the healing touch – are commonplace when the **PURPLE** is on top.

PURPLE assigns life force and intentionality to nature and objects (animism). The old oak tree is not just potential timber or an aesthetic comfort; it is the home of spirits and living witness to countless events. The heavier the **PURPLE**, the more relics and sacred grounds. Mountains are inhabited, rivers are sacred, the stars watch over us. The old midwestern family farmstead is often washed with **PURPLE** memories of births, marriages, and deaths. The land is rich with the ancestors' dreams, calamities, and gravesites. No wonder selling it to an agribusiness conglomerate is so painful.

Family heirlooms – grandmother's dishes or grandfather's shaving mug – attach to **PURPLE**. Chinese junks still have eyes, Davy Crocket named his rifle 'Old Betsy,' pro football players wear 'lucky' shoes, and Taiwanese executives dine on endangered tigers to impress their friends and bring good *joss* to billion dollar deals. Golfers have mystical beliefs about putters, harried executives talk to their autos, and both aircraft and ships are called 'she' since fragile lives depend on them.

We mentioned Winnie the Pooh earlier. Who could tear the arms off a Teddy bear? Unconscionable. Even the suggestion of such an horrendous act grates on our **PURPLE**. Broken dolls go to the doll hospital. The death of a pet can be as emotionally stressful as the loss of a parent if the animal has acquired **PURPLE** character. In fact, many people who are centralized much farther up the Spiral shift back toward the **PURPLE** zone when talking to 'Kitty,' or 'Spot,' or 'Budgie.'

Religious medals, wedding rings, and lucky charms often carry **PURPLE** with them, and their loss can be traumatic and frightening. While extending their faith into predominantly **PURPLE** regions, Catholic missionaries traveled with statues, crosses, chalices, and other tangible signs of the faith; the souvenir business at Lourdes still thrives. The old family Bible often conveys as much **PURPLE** as **BLUE**.

The plastic Jesus on the dash, regal costumes of Mardi Gras, rabbit's foots, knocking wood, and salt over the shoulder reflect the mysticism of **PURPLE**. The Liberty Bell, the English Crown, and the city of Jerusalem all have strong **PURPLE** aspects. Halloween and the Day of the Dead invigorate this ᵛMEME annually.

The photo of a child worn in a locket near the heart, pictures of grand children in one's billfold, and the mementos that decorate so many office desks are elements of the **PURPLE** reliquary. Firefighters are well advised to salvage family albums before worrying about stereos or color TVs. Insurance can never replace lost **PURPLE** objects and the memories they symbolize.

It is present in the many superstitions we easily dismiss – thinking twice about black cats in the path or the courteous *gesundheidt* to keep one's soul intact and the demons at bay after a sneeze. Even *Sports Illustrated* talks about jinxs now and then; hex signs sell well in Pennsylvania. Potions abound in Port au Prince and New Orleans. The volcano gods are still active in Mt Pinatubo; Pele consumes **ORANGE** real estate regularly in Hawaii; and Fuji's spirits are tended by Shinto priests and seismologists alike.

SIGNS: Calling on mother when times are tough

Since these systems are in people, a sort of **PURPLE** haze may appear over many of our thoughts and behaviors. While many First-Worlders presume they are only slightly impacted by this ᵛMEME, it quickly reactivates in them when the *Life Conditions* become unpleasantly **PURPLE** – profound fear, stress, threat of illness, children in trouble – or positively **PURPLE** – children celebrating life passages, falling in love (again), or just hearing 'our song.'

Some of the deepest **PURPLE** aspects relate to parental bonding and the nuclear family. It is an essential ingredient of the healthy personality and one which busy, go-getter lifestyles sometimes overlook. If children skip through this passage too quickly the Spiral that grows on top is on shaky ground. Love has many forms, but one of the most enduring, intense, and unconditional is within the **PURPLE** ᵛMEME's field. It is also the hardest to put into language.

SIGN: The map is the territory

The word is the thing; the map becomes the territory. Some words can be so sacred they may not be spoken except in certain places – by the men in the *kiva*, for example. Acts can be 'unspeakable' because of the power in them and describing them invokes forces of evil or good. 'Don't say it or it might come true. Knock wood. Abracadabra.'

The US is surprisingly **PURPLE** with regards to the American flag. Many patriots are ready to die for the fabric as well as the fact, and the desecration of flags is far more significant than it is in most other places in the world. Perhaps the relative youth of the European-dominated culture makes the symbol of democracy especially important.

PURPLE art leans to two-dimensionality and symbolic distortion. There is frequently emphasis on enlarged genitalia, breasts, and fertility. Many pieces are representations of gods or offerings to the spirits. Contemporary 'lawn art,' be it a statue of Quan Lin or a garden gnome, has **PURPLE** overtones. Patrons frequently pat the Buddha's belly after a Chinese dinner and their fortune cookie.

When **PURPLE** is strong, people leave signs of territory or danger for others of their kind. Hobos subtly labeled the homes of those likely to provide a handout – a 'mark.' Gypsy signs, gang graffiti, and grandparents' bumper stickers are evidence the ᵛMEME is active. These communiqués are easily overlooked by outsiders whose ignorance of the **PURPLE** codes leaves them vulnerable to the in-group and at risk of unintentional results. The unique, unwritten languages of the Irish Travelers still protect those shrinking bands of gypsy-like tin-smiths and merchants from unwanted intrusion by outsiders. The 'Old School Tie,' 'Kappa Key, or a street gang's choice of shoe lace 'colors' are tangible if subtle signs of belonging in a **PURPLE** structure.

SIGN: Gender, Sex, and Kinship

Social life is shaped by small cohesive groups with tight kinship bonds. Tasks are specified by age or gender and assigned to particular sub-groups – manly work and woman's place. When **PURPLE** is active children have separate clubhouses for little girls and boys. Grown-ups have their secret handshakes, symbolic colors and costumes, rites of passage, and mating ceremonies. When conflict occurs with other tribes, it is more ritualized show according to protocol and 'counting coup' than the bloody mayhem of modern mechanized warfare.

Woman's 'moon time' (which became the **BLUE** 'curse') and the deep **PURPLE** urge to protect the procreating mother for the survival of the tribe still subtly influence decisions about women's role in combat. Whether the society is patriarchal or matriarchal, there tends to be gender-based division of labor and social roles. **PURPLE** undercurrents still slow gender equality in many businesses where good-ol'-boy and/or -girl networks endure.

PURPLE sex is neither **RED** conquest nor dutiful (or guilt-ridden) **BLUE**, so it is a very easy part of living. While the transfer of genetic material is an instinctive drive from **BEIGE**, in **PURPLE** it takes on the aspect of perpetuation of the folk and family and tribe – spreading the seed. The **PURPLE** LC²s mandate high birth rates since death rates are also high and manual labor is essential to survival. (Thus the frequent preference for males.) Children are **PURPLE** social security and protection in old age. (In parts of India only sons can perform funeral duties, so the family grows until enough boys are born.) Offspring can also occupy lands for the tribe and may be used to build liaisons with other clans, a role often fulfilled by bartering daughters – even selling them – and arranging marriages.

Nepotism is natural to **PURPLE** with its extended kinship structure. The family takes care of its own first. 'Blood is thicker than water,' 'blood oaths,' and 'blood brothers' are the heart of **PURPLE**. In much of Africa, custom obligates the surviving brother to care for the wife and family of his deceased brother, taking the woman as one of his own wives. (Because the practice increases the working population, **PURPLE** is often polygamous, as well as polytheistic.) If the brother died of AIDS, however, a viral wild-card of major proportions enters the equation. Generally, the **PURPLE** tradition (along with **RED** impulsivity) wins out since **ORANGE** and **BLUE** health care are still not prevalent. Thus, AIDS is rampant across the center of Africa and in regions of southern Asia where similar ᵛMEME stacks are in control.

SIGN: Impact on the environment

PURPLE living is very organic and, so long as populations are small, has little impact on the environment. However, when factors from up the Spiral intervene to alter the delicate balance, as **ORANGE** has in Amazonas, southeast Asia, the Pacific islands, and much of Africa, **PURPLE** living can be extremely destructive. When **PURPLE** systems are contaminated by impulsive **RED** and short-sighted **ORANGE**, forests are eliminated in slash-and-burn subsistence agriculture or just for firewood, as in Rwandan refugees' camps in Zaire. Delicate soils are sacrificed for a few minerals and wildlife populations are decimated for food or the money to buy what can no longer grow. Biologic diversity and nature's genetic storehouses are sacrificed for 'cash' crops since those abstract ideas count little for hungry people or those aspiring to a bigger TV for the village. Generations of delicate, ancient wisdom go silent virtually overnight, cut down by disinterest and chain saws, the few lamentations drowned out by rock-and-roll.

PURPLE/red: Exiting Phase

- Greater exposure to the world reveals how baseless many of the superstitions actually are, challenging the credibility of the **PURPLE** leaders.
- Meeting the safety and security needs of people releases energy and resources, thus putting the system in a state of readiness for change.
- To keep **PURPLE** under control, leadership pours on more tradition and ritual, stifling those yearning to break free. The need for personal autonomy creates anarchy (renegades and misfits) in the well-wrought tribal order.
- The natural competition for richer niches ultimately pits **PURPLE** groupings against each other, rewarding those who assert themselves (like Shaka Zulu) and take charge. There can be only one bull in the kraal.

Andrew Bard Schmookler's *The Parable of the Tribes* (University of California Press, Berkeley, 1984) describes the inevitability of a shift from **PURPLE** to **RED**. It seems impossible for relatively equal groups to maintain a shared territory for very long. For one reason or another, one group will move to dominate the other(s) and push the Spiral on.

At the Exiting **PURPLE/red** range, the person starts dreaming of taking direct action as the ego pops up. The individual begins to find weaknesses in the 'leaders' (mommy and daddy are not infallible!) and comes to the conclusion that the spirits are not all-powerful and can even be maneuvered. At first, one challenges in little ways, talking back or ignoring minor omens. The audacious person dares retribution, pushing the limits of myth and taboo to see if the spirits come down hard or not .

As **RED** looms up, there is a growing sense that a powerful individual can actually influence the world. Placating the spirits does not always work – they are unreliable, unpredictable, and sometimes whimsical. The Exiting **PURPLE/red** gods – Zeus, Thor and Co., Wotan, even Yahweh – all have anthropomorphic personality defects – vengefulness, arrogance, and quick tempers. As **red** starts to intensify toward **RED**, less-than-mystical spirits like these can be used to empower the self since they are susceptible to payoffs, flattery, and manipulation. It was quite Wagnerian.

Yet the intimidating **red/PURPLE** tribal warrior who looks and sounds so powerful turns out to be weak and indecisive without the supportive group nearby. The contagious enthusiasm of collective action makes elite heroes for the moment only. The uncertain gang-banger is toughest with the pack around, weaker when separated and left alone. In this zone, bravado still works best when the audience cheers the daring deed.

Recall that at Peak **PURPLE** the chieftain is a coordinator of the group's activity and spokesperson. The Exiting phase means more personal clout. There is as much reliance on strong persons as the spirits, and the Chief takes on new authority – the leader of the pack with charisma.

This is the beginning point for personality cults. In its healthy form **red/PURPLE** is the emergence of the assertive ego and self-confidence in child development. A profoundly unhealthy version evolved among the followers of Jim Jones in Guyana and within the Charles Manson Family. Whether positive or negative in form, **RED** marks the great upsurge of raw, individual power and is the pedestal from which to shout, 'I exist!'

RED *PowerGods*
The Egocentric ᵛMEME

- **In a world of haves and have-nots, it's good to be a have**
- **Avoid shame, defend reputation, be respected**
- **Gratify impulses and senses immediately**
- **Fight remorselessly and without guilt to break constraints**
- **Don't worry about consequences that may not come**

At the Core of RED – *Life Conditions*[3]:

'Life is a jungle. It's survival of the fittest. I'm tough and expect those around me to be tough or else. I take charge of people and can win over nature, bending her to my will. Respect and reputation matter more than life itself, so you do what it takes to avoid being shamed or put down. You don't take anything off anybody, not if you're worth anything. You always get them back. Whatever you need to do, you do without guilt. Nothing and nobody can stand in your way. Right now is all there is, so I'll do what makes me feel good. You can't worry about what hasn't happened yet. I'm all I've got, and I'll make it or die trying.'

purple/RED: ENTERING

The communal, clannish ways of **PURPLE** offer safety and relative security for the group in its niche. Those problems resolved, the ᵛMEME loses some of its magical, fear-based control and frees individual energies. The **RED** world awakens Promethean myths and a new breed of warrior bent on predatory expansion. With the blaring of trumpets and the adoration of lesser beings (even if it is just the family dog!), the PowerGod strides on the scene.

RED is the first clearly express-self, 'I'-oriented ᵛMEME. At first blush, it seems raw, impulsive, and wild; yet it is also liberating and creative. For children, the thinking begins to awaken at the end of the first year and flares in 'the terrible twos,' then again around middle school time. For humanity at large, **RED**-dominated periods are marked by warlords, exploration, exploitation, empires, and the idea that nature is there to be conquered.

RED stubbornly resists power exercised over it. When thwarted, the ᵛMEME produces a cauldron of negative emotions such as rage, vengefulness, hatred, and furious anger. When properly handled, this raw self-assertive power contributes to a positive sense of control, lets the group break from constraining pro forma traditions, and energizes a society to reach for the very ends of the Earth.

RED FLAG: From Magic to Machismo

As the spirits, magic, and myths of **PURPLE** fade into **RED**, spirits turn god-like. Reverence for the Earth mother turns to contests with her – to beat the rapids, climb the mountain, master the sea, or survive the desert. Magic becomes a weapon for control of people and events. The harmonizing traditions of the ancestors become inspiring legends about heroic deeds, vanquished enemies, and doing the undoable. The **PURPLE** 'other world' becomes better organized like a Valhalla or atop Mt Olympus. The gods acquire human foibles; they are spiteful, demanding, jealous, and whimsically beneficent. **RED** deities populate Hinduism, were served by the Aztecs, and hide as *takalashes* beneath African beds or monsters in American children's closets.

FLAG: From Consensus to Dominance

PURPLE's leaders announce consensus and serve to balance the group. As **RED** intensifies, strong individuals take unilateral control. Because the Individual/Elite ᵛMEMEs prefer vertical distributions, the chieftain rises to be THE CHIEF at the apex of a power pyramid – 'L'état, c'est moi'. The shaman is Merlinized as magic becomes quite useful for the intrigue rampant within a court of rivals.

When **RED** is the dominant express-self ᵛMEME and **purple** the sacrifice-self back-up, certain assumptions pertain:

- **RED**'s desires are met by the powerless since their reverence was got by being strong, breaking bonds, standing free, and being courageous. The ᵛMEME system incorporates both the powerful (haves) and the powerless (have-nots) into the compact.
- **RED** uses intimidation, charisma, and physical force to impose his/her will without guilt or compunction – the kiss of death.

- **RED** guiltlessly exploits **PURPLE**'s superstitions through spells, witch-craft, and curses to control the people and eliminate competitors or enemies.
- **RED** spawned the absolute rights of monarchs, reciprocal feudalism where knights protected serfs who fed them, a Chief's claim to first night with brides (à la David Koresh), the right of the hustler to hustle, and repressive colonialism.

This ᵛMEME likes the **BEIGE** biological urges which expand the **PURPLE** clan. Body parts and sex are integral to routine discourse, and the four-letter old English grunts are a weapon **RED** uses to get control of offended **BLUE**. The 'locker-room' emphasis on genitalia is related to dominance, power, and pecking order far more than procreation. Witty repartee gains little favor in this gut-level world. (Recall the Street Kid in Chapter 2.)

When **purple/RED** is active during warfare, massacres, rape, and pillage are common because warriors shift to fit the brutal *Life Conditions* – survival of the strongest, quickest, and most potent – while also insuring at an even deeper ᵛMEME level that 'our kind' will prevail genetically.

Survivors of violent **RED** conflict may be taken as slaves or prizes. Heads, scalps, and ears are carried off as proof of victory and mutilation of sexual organs after a killing is the final *coup d'*dis-*grace*, depriving the victim of reproduction or pleasures, even in an afterlife. Victorious Zulu's in the 1879 battle of Isandlwana in Natal (South Africa) opened the bellies of the British dead to release the **PURPLE** spirits. A few American troops collected body parts in Vietnam. In the 1990s, the Serbians are said to have used rape to increase their tribe and dilute the 'seed' of their Bosnian adversaries in the former Yugoslavia. The Tutsi and Hutu of Rwanda strove to decimate their niche rivals in the 1994 uprisings as the **RED** and **PURPLE** ᵛMEME ruled the day again.

FLAG: It's in Every One of Us

RED is not an aberration, but a normal part of the human ᵛMEME repertoire. The healthy fleshing out of **PURPLE** is essential to child development as the young acquire the skills to navitate through the **RED**'s dragons, pitfalls, mean little kids, and 'bad' people. The **PURPLE** to **purple/RED** transition continues in youngsters between 3 and 5 years. Since acceptable means for expressing the ᵛMEME are just developing, inappropriate acting out and nightmares are frequent vents. Heavier **RED** will also surge during the hormonal confusion of puberty, a state which many do not outgrow.

If authoritarian parents squash the child's first expressions of rebellion and independence, they may well freeze in anger for life. The fully functionng person must learn to deal with obstacles, manage personal power, and confront life's monsters. Overly protective parents compromise their children's abilities to deal with the real world outside the nest.

The person in this **purple** to **RED** transition zone is becoming unwilling or unable to tolerate constraints. Yet while **purple/RED** is screaming 'leave me alone,' the shouts are directed against the watching family, neighbors, teacher, or peers to get a reaction. While quick to register an insult or a put down, it is also free about giving them. Non-verbal displays include the glare, sneer, and other disrespecting 'I dare you' poses or unidigital gestures that send a clear dominance message (often in sexual terms). Verbal taunting and 'trash talk' follow, then physical confrontation if the sequence goes unchecked.

American youngsters used to play at 'war' and 'cowboys and Indians.' Now the **RED** (and **PURPLE**) 'MEMEs act out more realistically and violently. To gain membership in street gangs, youths hijack autos or shoot a random victim as part of initiation rites. (There were 10 such attempted shootings in one evening in Ft Worth, Texas, during 1994.) If the innocent target is hit and dies, so much the better. When a mystical **PURPLE** belief in reincarnation is added to the fatalistic street existence, there is truly nothing to lose by high-risk behavior. Romanticized in Bernstein's classic, *West Side Story*, or discussed more recently in films like *Boyz 'n the Hood* and *Mi Vida Loca* (My Crazy Life), we see powerful individuals competing to the death under these transitional $LC^{2/3}$. (Always look for the **PURPLE** fear and small-group bonds that usually underpin what may seem like purely **RED** behaviors. 'MEMEs rarely live alone, and the failure to resolve the most basic **PURPLE** problems – 'A positive somebody cares about me and I have a safe place to be' – contributes to the escalation of **RED** on the streets of major cities around the world.)

RED: Peak Phase

In U.S. history, the fabled Mountain Men like Jim Bridger had wide **RED** bands which drove them to Go West, away from the restraints of 'civilization.' Fortunately, there was the frontier where they could be free and explore. One of the greatest challenges facing the developed nations today is finding new horizons where **RED** energy can be released constructively. This is difficult because bottling it up in urban squalor only builds anger, yet colonial exploitation of the Third World is not acceptable as it once was. Where can **RED** go for fun and adventure? The streets and video games.

Strong positive **RED** examples abound in cartoons, legends and myths – Paul Bunyan, John Henry (the Steel Driving Man), Big Bad John, Rambo, and Arnold Schwartzenneger's *Terminator*. Note the maleness. Only recently has U.S. society acknowledged that while testosterone may play a part in **RED** behavior, the 'MEME is equally accessible to women. 'MEME liberator

Tanya Harding indelicately disclosed that **RED** is present in figure skating as well as ice hockey.

FLAG: It Ain't My Fault

Clare Graves first isolated this ᵛMEME in his data in 1958. Like all of us, he had encountered **RED**, but could not get people in the system to respond to his interview questions, much less fill out pencil-and-paper tests. (He was generally told all sorts of places where he might put his research instruments, none of which struck him as attractive.) The theme he finally uncovered was 'thou shalt express self at all costs rather than suffer the unbearable shame of loss of face and in order to be praised, one who will live forever in the mouths of men.'

He found that people thinking this way tend to locate the cause of difficulties and failures outside self. You may have heard these statements before: 'They are out to get me. It's a conspiracy against us to keep us down. I would be somebody if it weren't for her. He asked for it.' In other cases the credit of fault lies with 'the Man upstairs' or to a super-spirit that determines luck.

Unable to exercise restraint or plan very well, **RED** fails to save for a rainy day, engage in preventative maintenance, or keep daily commitments. The boom-box is thrown against a wall if the batteries quit (bad Bunny), the out-of-gas car is abandoned in the Arabian desert (bad Benz), the errant golf club is tossed into the water hazard (bad Bertha), or the spouse is kicked out of the house in a fit of rage (bad Bubba).

In the early 1980s Graves flew with us to New Orleans where Bourbon Street is a Mecca for **RED**, especially during Mardi Gras. The purpose was to meet with several members of the staff of the Saints football organization, including then head coach O. A. 'Bum' Phillips who had always been one of his favorites because of straight talk and genuine style. (Both Professor Graves and Coach Phillips had more than a little **RED** in their personal ᵛMEME repertoires.)

The cocaine problem was just surfacing in the National Football League. Graves made the point that the molecular structure of cocaine fit perfectly with the **RED** ᵛMEME since its chemistry seems to link the needs for instant gratification and feelings of omnipotence. Because the **RED** ᵛMEME has neither guilt nor remorse, the player caught in the act would openly deny any involvement with drugs. The crack form has proven to be even more insidious because it slices into the brain far more efficiently.

FLAG: Grandiosity

As in childhood fantasies of being the hero in charge, **RED** wants to be bigger than life – awesome. Arch-villains such as those that challenged James Bond abound. The **RED** needs include breaking loose from the clan, exerting independent control, and testing the self against others to establish dominion. Ultimately, the objective is to challenge death and win. One must have 'the right stuff' since breaking with the pack and pushing the envelope are givens. It takes overwhelming outside force to slow **RED** down, and even then one may not give up without a fight.

RED thinking is egocentric and unabashed. Strong self-assertiveness, claims of power, and assumed prerogative are the norm since there is neither guilt nor concern for others. These are the people who dare stand up to the **PURPLE** spirits and seek to conquer the world or die trying. Disgrace and loss of face are to be feared, but not a glorious death. At some level, it gives release from the pain of **RED** existence and builds up all-important reputation so one is revered in hearts and minds forever. Or so **RED** imagines.

President George Bush defined Saddam Hussein in **RED** terms, just as the U.S. is viewed as 'the great Satan' by many theocratic Iranians. The compelling evil of gangland in the *Godfather* series and most martial arts films draw on **RED**. Richard III, Ghengis Khan, the Vikings, and Caligula have **RED** reputations. The guillotine lopped many aristocratic **RED** heads during the French Revolution while equally **RED** members of the bourgeoisie cheered the 'painless' mechanism on.

FLAG: When RED First Appears

In addition to **PURPLE** magic, children's literature abounds with **RED** wolves, wicked witches, and monsters. Both television and video games cater to it because **RED** themes are so important when the sense of self is being consolidated and first checked out. The 'MEME awakens in us all during childhood. Becoming 'mature and responsible' entails keeping it in check except at appropriate times when revelry and 'hell-raising' are socially approved. **RED**'s party side is loosed on the Greek Island of Eros, in sections of Bangkok, honky-tonks in West Texas, during Carnival in Rio, and through a tequila fog on a Tijuana Saturday.

RED's Dark Side, to cite the *Star Wars* reference, contributed much to the disastrous Rodney King incident which led to the Los Angeles riots of 1992. The police concluded that Mr King was dangerously **RED** which justified force. Several of the officers apparently had their own **RED** buttons pushed, as well. Later, truck driver Reginald Denny was pummeled by citizens as the 'MEME spread destructive energy throughout the neighborhood. (Fortunately, cooler **BLUE** heads regained control, but **ORANGE** had already begun pulling its investments away.)

Inflated **RED** ego often puts a person in harm's way because of the belief that 'I am special . . . I'll live forever . . . I'm immortal, not like other humans.' Like 18-year-old drivers of 'muscle cars,' they are invincible. The pain threshold may actually be higher when **RED** is active. Recognizing that

ᵛMEMEs and neurotransmitters are directly linked (researchers are just beginning to discover how), there seems to be an increase in endorphins which modify the sensory chemistry of the brain. When this surge is joined by a rush of adrenaline, it helps explain why soldiers continue to perform their duties after receiving grave injuries, why some people relish barroom brawls while others find fisticuffs disgusting, and why anger runs hand-in-hand with foolhardiness. The person operating out of strong **RED** may deny injury and, like the young Evel Knievel, walk away from crashes that would immobilize the rest of us. (The aging daredevil, having added more **BLUE** and **ORANGE** to his repertoire, recently advertised a drug-free pain management device on a TV infomercial.)

In the age of AIDS, sexually active people regret their lapses into **RED** and the subsequent unprotected dropping of restraints (and trousers). **RED** thinking is non-consequential, particularly for hormone-rich, denial-laden teenagers needing to prove fertility and make quick conquests or drug users for whom 'the high' is what life centers around. The concentration on immediate gratification and refusal to think about negative outcomes escalates both unwed pregnancies and disease. As we pointed out regarding central Africa in the previous **PURPLE** section, the rapid growth of AIDS in Asia is largely attributable to the prevalence of the **PURPLE** and **RED** ᵛMEMEs (and **ORANGE** truck transportation). This is one of several diseases that are opportunistic in attacking through the Spiral's ᵛMEMEs and which prosper anywhere they enter communities of that at-risk profile.

FLAG: LC³ are the REAL WORLD for Millions of People

Tragically, the milieu of the urban poor is often dominated by negative **RED**. Neighborhood streets, housing, and schools are risky. Under LC³, mugging tourists or dealing crack may be effective adjustive behavior for someone who sees the world in **RED**, whose **PURPLE** anchors are in a gang because there is no family left, and who sees insurmountable barriers – whether real or imagined – to moving elsewhere on the Spiral. Being the best drug dealer on the block may define success. A short life expectancy and constant danger come with the territory. (The justifications for the prostitute–pimp relationship or toleration of domestic violence and spousal abuse also lie in this range, though outward appearances may be of affluent **ORANGE** or virtuous, pillar of the community **BLUE**.)

When **PURPLE** families break down and no other communal, sacrifice-self system is available to take their place, a surge of **RED** follows. Nuclear families in America and elsewhere are in disrepair, so **RED** is still on the upsurge and the Spiral is tipping sharply to the 'me' and 'my' side.

Contrary to what many politicians and commentators believe, neither more jails nor simplistic, self-righteous preaching will fix the problems. Alternative **PURPLE** nests – sports teams, surrogate families, effective child care, and good nutrition begin the process. Then, carefully managed programs converting unhealthy to healthy **RED** can be introduced – the discipline of martial arts, Outward Bound-type adventures, and cleaning up trashed neighborhoods to make them safe.

Lessons in finding **BLUE** moral anchors and learning **ORANGE** business skills can only take root if the ground is prepared through healthy **PURPLE** and **RED** base-building. Such steps are needed desperately, but rarely offered. Trying to force **BLUE** prematurely over **RED** only proves that life is unfair and fighting back in the best course. Instead, meet **PURPLE** belonging needs and work on turning unhealthy **RED** into positive forms. Then the questions will probably arise that only **BLUE** can answer.

Instead of moving out of **RED**, many teenagers, even pre-teens, speak with pride of the length of the 'rap sheets' – the list of the criminal offenses. In an LC³ world, it is good to be 'bad' and feared. Arrests are evidence that one is a fighter, not a wimp. No wonder guns are showing up in elementary schools and bullet proof vests are more important than apples for the teacher. The old 'crimes' of tardiness, gum chewing, talking in the hall, and even playing hooky are replaced by assault and attempted murder.

FLAG: A Life's Not Worth Very Much

Peak **RED** does not learn through punishment since actions do not connect to deferred consequences, guilt is absent, and problems are always someone else's fault. The question is: 'What's in it for me, now?' If there is no payoff, no learning occurs. Skinnerian-style conditioning works for **RED** and offers some hope for altering inappropriate patterns if the person is reinforced quickly for appropriate behavior and controlled to prevent inappropriate actions. Never make threats, only promises since backing down is a sign of weakness. 'No' means 'hell, no!' not 'maybe.' Metaphysical certitude is required in these boot camps for the mind. Never promise more than you can deliver. Outcomes must be realistic and appropriate.

For people truly blocked in negative forms of **RED**, confinement, and some argue, elimination may be the only treatments. The 'three strikes and you're out' life imprisonment fad is a **BLUE** answer for unmanageable **RED**. **ORANGE** has managed to turn this prison-building boom into a multi-billion dollar growth industry. Unfortunately, most prisons are only government-subsidized reproductions of LC³.

Even **red/BLUE**'s death penalty has little if any preventive effect on heavy **RED** because the ᵛMEME acts on impulse (not premeditation) and does not see distant consequences. For the saddest cases, there is nothing left to lose since life has no value. If swiftly implemented, executions do save prison space, let **BLUE** witness just retribution, and give **GREEN** something to protest. However, they also model the brutality of which **RED** is judged guilty and validate the **RED** world view in tooth and claw.

RED: Life is a Jungle

Simply put, living in the **RED** zone is like survival in the jungle. The weak will lose and they deserve to because they are weak. Each person is an island, though they can draw together for strength when it is mutually useful. When no longer convenient, **RED** groups fragment and relationships are cast aside; loyalty is transitory. It is a world of victims and predators, eaters and the eaten.

Sometimes apparent **RED** is just posturing, bravado, and ego-defensive cover-up. Puncture the balloon with greater strength and there may be a regression down the Spiral to **PURPLE** or even belly-up **BEIGE**. But do not bank on it. What you see and hear may not be for show, but a genuine display of to-hell-with-the-consequences confidence. The feral youth in the alley may 'just as soon shoot you as look at you,' so take no chances and back off unless the confrontation is unavoidable. Remember that **RED**-dominated warriors are oblivious to others as sentient beings with rights and personal worth. Innocent victims of a drive-by shooting are '. . . just mushrooms that pop up and get in the way of what's gotta' be done. She shouldn't have been on that porch, anyway.' If you must engage, do it quickly and with overwhelming force (like a SWAT team on a drug raid) to minimize the urge to fight back. Be respectful, but act with absolute, unquestionable authority. The gentlemanly rules of the Marquis of Queensbury do not apply in **RED**.

This lack of concern for others is taken as a demonstration of toughness and self-control – 'I don't need nobody. Nothing gets to me.' (The old term 'sociopath' may apply to Closed **RED** at an unhealthy extreme, but other ᵛMEMEs are equally eligible to insanity; they just act out differently.)

Unfortunately, some people try to put a racial face on these deep and destructive trends. That is wrong. They have far more to do with *Life Conditions* and the ᵛMEMEs they awaken than any skin color or blood line. One's race, gender, measured intelligence, or ethnicity can certainly influence opportunities for employment, housing possibilities, education, and treatment under the law. The number of minorities in American jails and prisons speaks volumes about the *Life Conditions* that have existed, and also about the value systems that are active and absent in many communities.

Instead of asking 'Why are disproportionately more Black males in prison than whites?' it might be useful to consider these questions: What has caused the elevation of the **RED** system in so many of our communities? Why has an ethic emerged that praises 'doing hard time' in jail as a positive accomplishment? What people and forces keep the healthier alternatives blocked off? What can Spiral Wizards do about it?

Another **RED** upsurge appears in the 13th generation of Americans, the children of the Baby Boom. Many feel that Boomers failed as parents on two counts. First, they withheld critical discipline (too little **BLUE**) from their children because of trendy humanism and permissive child rearing practices (perhaps over-reacting to their own parents very **BLUE** Depression-Era cautions). Second, they gorged on material splendor at the expense of future generations. Now the aging Boomers are about to start drinking from the social services trough at the same time that the non-burger-based job market is shrinking for their progeny.

Unless today's economy makes a turn and there is a surge in niches that can use brain-power, the 13ers will not have as much as their parents did and so must redefine their values or face doing with less. The perceived inequity between generations has elevated a sense of anger and egocentric **RED** thinking in the ten- and twenty-something group. The scarcity of niches will, for many, only sharpen **PURPLE**-based fear lines based on race and ethnicity and **RED**-based anger derived from widening have, have-not gaps. We must face these schisms straight up and 'tell it like it is' since this ᵛMEME has a superb bullshit detector which sees through false promises and does not tolerate deception.

FLAG: A Society of Unequals – HAVES and HAVE-NOTS

A **RED** society consists of a few dominant haves and many have-nots. The aggressive haves flaunt their victories, knowing they can get away with it. They contrive to keep the have-nots subservient and needy, tossing out enough crumbs to keep them hopeful but weak. Making examples of those who fail to serve well motivates those desiring to move from have-not to have-a-little status. No one dares look behind the drapes to see the Wizard of Oz or criticize the emperor's new clothes.

The behavior of **RED** have-nots is often clandestine and devious. They flaunt what little they do have when even weaker ones around and the have-a-lots are not watching. This produces the school bully syndrome and the straw-boss shop manager who exploits underlings mercilessly. Organizations (and cultures) built on **RED** see bribes and kick-backs as natural ways of doing business. There are requisite payoffs (*mordida*, baksheesh) for everything. What some might call corruption and violence is taken as normal practice when the **RED** ᵛMEME is growing.

There is no altruism at this level, but there is manipulation of indebtedness and exchange of favors. 'You scratch my back, I'll scratch yours.' The debts can be called in at any time – 'You owe me.' Likewise, grudges and vendettas can extend for years without forgiveness or compromise. **RED** has a long memory for perceived slights and waits bitterly to 'get even.' Mixed with **PURPLE** bloodlines, these debts are passed across generations as ongoing feuds (the Hatfields and McCoys) and ethnic conflicts (the former Yugoslavia) since, like the snapping turtle, no one centered in the **RED** zone is willing to let go and may rather enjoy the fight. The 'troubles' in Northern Ireland were exacerbated by **RED** cheering sections on both sides of the Atlantic and the Channel.

The world of **RED** is tactile, concrete, and specific. A roll of cash in the pocket or gold chains around the neck are far better than 'worthless' scraps of paper (bonds and even checks). Banks are not to be trusted. If **RED** owns a truck, car, ranch, or 'date' you had best stay clear. Do not 'dis-'(respect) unless ready to do battle. Look for a bumper sticker like 'This Vehicle Protected by Smith & Wesson' or a sign at the pasture saying 'Trespassers will be shot on sight.' And beware of Winchester Barbie; she is just as dangerous as Gang Banger Ken.

RED is a component of the blood-sport mentality. Bear-baiting, cock- and dog-fighting, and even the highly ritualized (**PURPLE**) bull fight glorify 'gameness' and put a 'noble' death above routine life. Professional wrestling, rugby, and full-contact kick-boxing appeal to the **RED** layer in fans, male and female alike, and foster a **PURPLE/red** heroic mythology which is sometimes hard for stars to uphold. Tennis has added some **RED** thanks to Messrs McEnroe and Nastase to widen its appeal. Liverpool soccer fans are renowned for **RED**, basketball is now a contact sport, and even cerebral baseball has found that dugout-emptying brawls are good for the TV ratings.

FLAG: Who's AT-RISK, Anyway?

Although you probably recognize its 'for-worse' results more readily than its 'for-better' aspects, the **RED** ᵛMEME is a vital part of human nature, neither inherently good nor bad. The proud, lusty, assertive way of being can be energizing and imaginative. Healthy **RED** is fun loving, creative, and free enough to explore and enjoy life to its fullest. In breaking with 'the system,' it produces innovations that would be impossible within the bonds of **PURPLE** customs or **BLUE** mandates. It energizes the Spiral like a catalyst whose presence triggers actions and reactions.

People centered here constantly prove themselves through 'heroic' deeds – leaning out the window, balancing on the ledge, and brazenly stepping on the grass. (One man's hero is another's childish fool.) Living is a series of tests, dares, and challenges to defeat the dragon. In organizations these often take the form of power contests with supervisors or management. Winners move on to the next thrill until they, too, lose or other ᵛMEMEs take control.

At the peak, **RED** cannot look at itself objectively. Ego involvement is very high; there is instant defensiveness when ideas are challenged. Since the person is unable to step away and appraise objectively, practically everything is taken personally. When this ᵛMEME is in control, calm rational discourse is unlikely.

RED/blue: Exiting Phase

This is the rigidifying position for **RED** where guilt begins sneaking in and the ᵛMEME is desperately hanging on to dominance. There are now inklings of problems in the world that a tough individual cannot manage alone. Yet listen for loud denial of guilt, responsibility, and accountability. Look out for deliberate acts to disprove caring about others. An anti-achievement ethic may set in as 'bad' starts looking 'good.'

In the **RED/blue** zone one doth protest too much, for the calculated bad deeds are the proof of awareness that **BLUE** is watching. Doubts about unbridled desires and impulsive acts are creeping in. Brazen courage is maladaptive in a more orderly world that seeks meaning and purpose in life.

Both the haves and have-nots die, sharing in mortality if little else. The haves rejoice in learning that their good fortune is also God's will. The have-nots justify their long suffering with the hope that everything will be set right sometime 'in the great by and by.' Both groups begin to feel an overarching power may be intervening in spite of their best laid plans and intentions. Slave and master are both sinners in the hands of an angry God.

The elite haves begin to forcefully impose their version of morality and order to confront the emerging **BLUE** Problems. The system is shoved down the throats of the mass by the ruling few 'for their own good.' (Inquisitors tend to enjoy their work.) Formal rules (not personal whims) appear and prescriptions for righteous living like the Ten Commandments (not arbitrary demands by the elites) transcend classes of people. A militant deny-self theme is imposed with an iron fist.

The God of Abraham spoke to **RED/blue** in terms the people understood – much righteous smiting of disbelievers and Divine barkings of orders. No more **PURPLE** polytheism or **RED** idolatry. The *Law* must be obeyed; it is neither suggestions nor guidelines. There is little room for debate and no tolerance of back-talk. Retribution is swift, but under the Law instead of the liege.

In both Judeo-Christian and Islamic history, the **PURPLE** and **RED** tribes required a vengeful, wrathful God to bring them out of chaos toward authoritarian order. Those who speak for this God talk of fire and brimstone, physical punishment or banishment, and the eternal sulfurous pits of Hell. **RED** can get with that and even preach it from a soap-box like our zealously reformed New York Street Kid + 10 back in Chapter 2.

King Arthur (Coeur de Leon) endeavored to introduce **BLUE** around his feudal table. Magna Carta clarified the ᵛMEME's secular role. Captain Bligh's British Navy was built on the assumption that sailors were predominantly **RED/blue** and had to be managed through intimidation and a ration of grog. The 'drunken sailor' was a **RED/blue** ruffian, handled by flogging and the stringent discipline of his gentlemanly (**BLUE/orange**) betters. Because the sea presents unforgiving **PURPLE** and **RED** Problems to those who dare to go down to her in ships, it makes sense that **RED** means and **PURPLE** myths were long the mariners' way.

Those centered at **RED/blue** show concern over self-serving impulses since awareness of others is creeping in. They think about consequences, but put more energy into rationalizing their actions than worrying with redemption. Such persons believe they are superior and take on the mission of getting the rest in line. This may be with the stick or the carrot, but it is clear who is in control and speaking for whatever other power there may be. Obedience to that ultimate authority is the essence of **BLUE**.

An Illustration of ᵛMEMEs at WORK
New Black Panther and White Aryan Nation Summit in Dallas:
Not Black and White but **RED/blue** and **RED/blue**

On May 29, 1993, a strange and unexpected summit-like meeting occurred in Dallas, Texas. The 'New Black Panther Party' rally drew nearly 200 people. They wore stern faces, black shirts, military style pants, and black berets. The fiery speeches were laced with calls for violence, revolution, 'urban guerrilla warfare,' and attempts to overthrow the federal government. The people were angry **RED** but also articulating a **BLUE** mission. They were purposeful, willingness to sacrifice (even die) for a cause, and accept authoritarian management.

What made the meeting interesting was that Tom Metzger, head of the White Aryan Resistance group, was warmly received by the all-black audience (*Dallas Morning News*, May 30, 1993, p. 32A.) That such a meeting occurred must have been astonishing to Flatlanders locked into the bipolarity of white vs. black stereotypes. In Spiral terms, however, both Metzger and Black Panther leader and former Milwaukee alderman Michael McGee were saying the same thing. They want a revolution. They agree on separate 'states.' There was concurrence on achieving their goals by 'whatever means necessary.' While their races were 'Aryan' and 'Black,' their minds were **RED/blue**. They were psychological twins and therefore could 'respect' each other.

In a Spiral complex, the **RED** ᵛMEME is like the first stage of a rocket. It makes a loud noise, pushes off mightily, but fizzles and falls back to Earth after that surge of power. In organizations, projects are launched with great fanfare but soon fail for lack of follow-up. The capacity for concerted action, trusting relationships, and long term planning initiatives have not emerged. There will be too many Chiefs and not enough Indians. The PowerGods continue to demand honor, respect, and special privilege as the enterprise crumbles. The compromises necessary for a turn-around are impossible under such conditions since the egos cannot yield and may not understand a higher purpose.

When **BLUE** first begins to slip in, the alliance with **RED** creates a volatile force field, one that has historically spawned both brilliance and cruelty. The **BLUE** component legitimizes the **RED** actions; the **RED** enforces the **BLUE** standards. Bloody revolutions and insurrections, purges, 'rogue' cops, headwaters. But so did the astronomical and mathematical insights of the Maya, the construction skills of ancient Egypt, the impetus behind great religious traditions, and any number of military and sports heroes of any nation you can name.

BLUE *TruthForce*
The Purposeful ᵛMEME

- Find meaning and purpose in living
- Sacrifice self to the Way for deferred reward
- Bring order and stability to all things
- Control impulsivity and respond to guilt
- Enforce principles of righteous living
- Divine plan assigns people to their places

At the Core of BLUE – *Life Conditions*[4]:

'A single guiding force controls the world and determines our destiny. Its abiding Truth provides structure and order for all aspects of living here on Earth and rules the heavens, as well. My life has meaning because the fires of redemption burn in my heart. I follow the appointed Pathway which ties me with something much greater than myself [a cause, belief, tradition, organization, or movement]. I stand fast for what is right, proper, and good, always subjecting myself to the directives of proper authority. I willingly sacrifice my desires in the present in the sure knowledge that I look forward to something wonderful in the future.'

red/BLUE: Entering Phase

In the **red/BLUE** zone we find the little bit of guilt of **RED/blue** has become centralized. Attention to consequences and deferred gratification are clearly replacing the **RED** ᵛMEME's egocentric impulsiveness. Other people become increasingly relevant as beings with rights and worth; the world looks 'civilized.' But there are stipulations. We are not all equals. **red/BLUE** thinking produces the self-righteous fault-finder and condemnatory judge who tends to sort 'the good' from 'the bad' and make others feel shame for being who they are. The **red** side wants to vanquish impure, unrighteous thoughts while **BLUE** imposes justice and order.

The ᵛMEME awakens to stabilize the tumultuous rivalries of **RED**. Individual egos must be quelled by a Higher Authority stronger than any of them or their lesser gods. In the Old Testament, Moses' delivery of the Ten Commandments from Mt Sinai signaled **BLUE**'s arrival. Such absolute 'thou shalts' and 'thou shalt nots' are necessary to introduce order, discipline, meaning, and purpose into the human evolutionary stream. How better could the runaway barbarians, warlords, and soldiers-of-fortune from blood-drenched fiefdoms be bridled than through fear of a wrathful God with absolute power to dispatch them into a Dantesque Hell or grant life everlasting among angels?

This ᵛMEME binds impulses within rather than wildly expressing them outward. One finds virtue in stiff-upper-lip restraint and has a disposition to self-sacrifice – willingness to die for a just cause or to subject one's body to punishment, deprivation, or the strictest of dietary habits and/or lifestyles. As **BLUE** awakens, penance feels good and a bit of physical suffering at the knees or back is inspirational. There is abiding satisfaction in doing duty, standing proud, 'taking licks,' and surrendering worldly pleasures to a higher calling.

As a stage in 'growing up' the first blush of maturing **BLUE** is marked by a child's tentative experimentation with right–wrong, fair–unfair, sharing equally, and resolving problems with the aid of authority – 'ask the teacher.' It solidifies as the pre-teen emotionally embraces a cause like recycling and the frustrated teenager hiding in headphones wrestles with the question: 'What is it all about?'

The ᵛMEME really stirs when LC⁴ start closing in and mortality is at hand. Only the foolish overlook the tough **red** streak in this transitional zone, though. If the **BLUE** is not yet solid or during a stressful regression one may slip back to stronger **RED**. The protesting activist might injure a lab worker in the name of animal rights or the abortion protester kill a physician in the name of the fetus. When confessing to a crime recently in Ft Worth, the murdering neighbor said to the police: 'I am not a bad person. But he stole my property and so I shot him. Now I'm turning myself in to take what's coming to me.' Classic.

A driving force in **red/BLUE** is the purging of impure thoughts and the conversion (or elimination) of those who think wrongly. It is often the home of militancy because awakening **BLUE** needs purpose and the **red** craves action. The battle lines are drawn sharply – defending the faith, enforcing the right – and almost always in lieu of short-term selfish gain. The ᵛMEMEs are strong among both radical Zionists and old-guard Palestinians, with militant separatists in the Ku Klux Klan and Black Muslim community, Marxist insurgents, democratic revolutionaries, or neo-Nazi skinheads.

BLUE: Peak Phase

When the **BLUE** ᵛMEME takes firm hold, one feels the joy of purpose, reason, and direction in life. The 'right brain' capacity to recognize and bond with abstract ideas (instead of **PURPLE** clans or **RED** payoffs) increases. There is now an identifiable Higher Power watching over and regulating human existence. The 'born again' religious conversion, for example, has all of the marks of **BLUE** at work. When it surges, this ᵛMEME clears the decks by allowing a fresh, 'forgiven' start. One must purge the old ways and find new significance in a mission, role, relationship, or -ism. 'Though I was lost, I am now found,' one thinks, 'because I have become a Christian [or Muslim, Frenchman, African, pro-choice activist, Harvard alumnus, feminist, or certified Citizen of the World].' **BLUE** turns lives around.

While it is liberating the spirit, the ᵛMEME is conserving a status quo which may be politically left- or right-wing, even entrenched in moderation. When you are looking into **BLUE**, it is particularly important to differentiate the container and its contents – how one thinks (the nature of the big ᵛMEME intelligence) versus what one thinks about (the particular constructs it attracts). For example, there are **BLUE** fundamentalist Christians and rabid Atheists who believe quite different things but who go about their believing in the same dedicated way.

BLUE MOTTO: Bringing order to the chaos and structure instead of anarchy

BLUE movements, whether religious, cultural, or nationalistic, are forged from conditions of chaos, deprivation, and suffering (usually extensions up-Spiral from **RED** or regressions down-Spiral from ill-timed **ORANGE**). LC⁴ cause people to seek order instead of anarchy, meaning in the malaise, and a rationale for suffering. **BLUE** thinking is required to sort the social mess out. When the ᵛMEME arrives, people gladly accept authoritarianism to clean things up and get the trains running on time again. New sources of wisdom and Truth are revealed (often reverberating with **PURPLE** mysticism and symbols, as well).

Any One True Way that latches onto the ᵛMEME assumes a life of its own. Obeisance to its authority (rather than the assertion of now-demonized individuality) becomes a driving influence. It puts everyone into right-and-proper social roles, castes, grades, races, classes, seniority levels, or military ranks. This provides the well-ordered stability the LC⁴ crave. One is expected to know one's place and keep to it, not to fraternise with one's betters, make the most of what has been allotted, and be thankful for that.

When **RED** was dominant, immediate personal desires were what counted. At **BLUE** the expectations of 'the system' define what is right and good. Individual and social priorities shift from express-self to sacrifice-self for the common good. Because the thinking is also polarized, non-system approaches are implicitly wrong, possibly sinful, and may have been introduced as tests of faith and commitment to the True Way. Again, overt self-interest is wicked and proves one is not worthy of fellowship with the believers.

The categorical world **BLUE** creates is also hierarchical. The Absolute Authority (the word of God, teachings of the Master, the Commander-in-Chief, or 'the manual') sits at the pinnacle and speaks to secular authority who speaks down the chain-of-command. What **RED** got away with through cunning and clout must now be earned through patience, righteous living, doing duty, and paying dues. Spontaneity yields to compliance, binding **RED** impulses firmly in check by obeying orders. Even the prodigal has hope for redemption if he or she but confess transgressions and reform.

MOTTO: The mood of BLUE

Temperamentally, **BLUE** often comes across as rigid, dogmatic, and redundant. That is fine so long as you are in agreement. The person keeps repeating the same thing again and again to prove it must be so. To the question, 'Haven't we heard this before?' comes the response, 'Yes, but it will be good for you to hear it again.' 'What does this passage mean?' . . . draws the response . . . 'It means just exactly what it says.' The book is to be taken literally, verbatim. Its depth can never be fathomed. There is no room for variance in interpretation. Many fundamentalists aand orthodoxies reside comfortably and unwaveringly inside their **BLUE** walls, studying the sacred texts and trying to live up to the standards therein.

Guilt peaks in **BLUE** (it surges in a different form in **GREEN**) and is integrated as a routine part of living. The ᵛMEME is satirized in many a stand-up comic's 'Jewish mother' [or Italian, Russian, etc.] stories based on the caring but judgmental parent who injects the emotion for control – comedian Richard Lewis cites his parents' home in New Jersey, 'the house that guilt built.' Parochial education – nuns with rulers wrapping naughty knuckles – used to rely on **BLUE**. Although from a different theological base, the Nation of Islam provides **BLUE** educational models, also complete with neat uniforms, to reduce **RED** jealousies and fights over physical possessions.

MOTTO: The rightful exercise of just authority

In further overcoming **RED**'s extremes, **BLUE** assumes a stern demeanor, but not a joyless or unloving one. The pleasure in life comes from serving the Way and obedience. The Amish culture around Lancaster County, Pennsylvania, endeavors to maintain life as it was a hundred years ago, as their God intends it to be. Hassidic Judaism shares a similar ᵛMEME profile, as did the celibate (thus departed!) Shakers movement. Indeed, most people need a

BLUE rock, be it Christian, Confucian, Hare Krishna, or secular onto which to tie their lives and anchor morality, ethics, and civility.

Far too many young people today have not found a sacrifice-self moral compass and so must rely on self-interest and their own desires – certainly no way to run a railroad. The backlash to that often becomes heavy handed BLUE authority – punitive, stern, Puritanical, wrathful, and non-demonstrative. The 'generation gap' of the 1960s pales in comparison to the ᵛMEME chasm in many families right now.

MOTTO: Right and Wrong

In this range, Good opposes Evil in an ongoing battle for dominion. The outcomes may include enlightenment, eternal life, oblivion, or unimaginable torment (intended to keep RED in check). There is no room for compromise or gray areas among the devout True Believers for whom wishy-washy moderation is worse than declaring with the enemy. Algeria is presently moving through this RED to BLUE range along with southern Mexico and parts of Detroit.

In its extreme forms, BLUE must call down evil-doers – *j'accuse!* The transgressor (guilty until proven innocent) faces punishment after doing wrong. At the same time, they must speak out against the failings of others and the errors in their ways, as in China's Cultural Revolution or 1980s Iran. In its more stringent forms, BLUE leads one to quiver in fear lest improper actions lead to condemnation, shunning, or excommunication. The person is always worried about messing up and violating some arcane rule; behavioral freedom is tightly restricted by guilt and the fear of punishment. (Such persons may ricochet back into red/BLUE when the bonds finally break. This is the 'wild and crazy' time after a divorce for some and 'middle-age crazy' for others. Walls and statues topple as the old guard is vanquished.)

After a fire in a chicken processing plant where several workers died because exits were chained shut (by ORANGE), ostensibly to keep out flies and 'cut down on pilferage,' the BLUE ᵛMEME spoke through a victim's relative and said of the negligent executives, 'They will be punished in the name of Jesus.' Invoking the sacred name of Authority is part of BLUE, whether the Lord, the Prophet, Chairman Mao, or 'in the name of the Law.' The word symbols become icons themselves as they resonate with PURPLE's deep emotions.

MOTTO: A reason and a purpose

Everything in BLUE has a purpose, a place, and a reason. The world is neatly bordered with tidy picket fences and well-trimmed hedges. Time is sequenced along a single track (monochronic), one thing following another.

('Do it right, then go on to the next item.') Ultimate judgment awaits us all at the end.

There is a grand design behind existence and purpose to everything, though mere mortals may not comprehend it. The Higher Authority is always watching, 'making a list and checking it twice.' Ultimate reward awaits those who queue up and do what is right. Woe unto the rest, for they shall get no gold watch.

Because of this eternal reward/punishment component, the 'MEME has time on its side and so can be more patient, less Quixotic than antsy **RED**. Nikita Kruschev said 'We will bury you' to the Capitalists, naively believing in his **BLUE** that the Communist plan would endure and that rival forms would not win out as the world moved along the Spiral. Ideologues have faith in their beliefs and the inevitable victory of their version of Truth; its collapse invariably astonishes them.

Those **BLUE** doctrines are generally documented in 'the book' since written language is part of this 'MEME's intelligence. From the library at Thebes to the county records office, knowledge is set down in enduring form, overcoming both the loss of detail and the mortality of **PURPLE** oral traditions. Holy books, tracts, and manifestos are catalogued and filed neatly, usually in triplicate and without typographical errors. The hand-scribed Torah scroll so precious to the congregation of a synagogue (a single mistake means starting over) is an example. Many Christians believe their Bible is the inerrant, literal word of God transcribed by men without omission. The inexperienced young Army Ranger lieutenant is well advised to consult the manual (as well as the top sergeant) before barking too many orders.

When the **RED** 'MEME chooses to attack **BLUE** systems, it sacks the libraries, burns the books, and smashes the museums in the belief that destroying the contents can also defeat the 'MEME container. When ideologies do battle in a predominantly **BLUE** world, they sack selectively, purging ideas for correctness, censoring the libraries, sorting 'facts,' charging heresy, and reading history to fit their renditions of the Truth. (When **ORANGE** appears, we begin to 'make up' some truth and revise history to fit our agendas.)

The **BLUE** 'MEME is quite busy in the late 1990s. Virtue and morality are major political themes. Immigration laws and nationalistic identities are debated all over. In the U.S. many elections have become one-issue races where a candidate's position on something like abortion or gun control is all that matters; other strengths or weaknesses are irrelevant. Whether in the States, Germany, or Japan, attempts to go 'back to basics' or restore those solid values, morals, and traditions that made 'us' great should be carefully scrutinized for their positive and negative influences.

The *Fort Worth Star-Telegram*'s lead editorial for December 12, 1993, called for 'A revival of traditional values' and insisted we all '. . . reconstruct the moral order . . . Americans might find it to be strange, in this final decade of the twentieth Century, that the pendulum is swinging from a focus on self and what self demands to a recognition of the need for basic, fundamental values.'

Note the words 'revival' and 'reconstruct.' Both indicate something that was is now missing and must be replaced. It is often expressed as a breakdown in family values or a lack of personal character. Obviously, LC[4] have resurfaced as the **ORANGE** 'me decade' is giving way to another 'us' epoch.

Writing about William Bennett's 831-page *Book of Virtues* in the March 7, 1994, issue of *Time* magazine, Lance Morrow warns: 'In a sense, nostalgic moralists are almost always right. The problem is that nostalgic moralism may turn itself into a political program which produces jackboot simplism, the fascism that feels the breath of fresh air as it approaches, and like an apocalypse in its aftermath.' The danger lies in the promise that greatest reward-to-come is reserved for heroes, martyrs, and soldiers in the cause.

Mandatory national service is popular when **BLUE** is strong since it can indoctrinate with responsibility, discipline, and attentiveness to others. Everyone sacrifices for the common good. (The 'MEME fought both World Wars.) Roosevelt-era service programs in the U.S., like the Civilian Conservation Corps (CCC), Works Progress Administration (WPA), and even more sophisticated Boot Camps for the Mind, should be established to meet needs of Exiting **RED** and Entering **BLUE** if **ORANGE** is looking to cut prison costs and develop capable citizens while getting necessary work done.

The wave of nostalgia on the fiftieth anniversary of VE day, which heralded the end of World War II in Europe, resonated with the **BLUE** 'MEME. Many people in the First-World West seem really to miss the idea of sacrificing for some unquestionably just cause, a theme which now echoes strongly in the Muslim lands and Second-World regions across the planet where **PURPLE** and **RED** are fading.

MOTTO: Who goes there? Friend or foe?

People respond judgmentally, not compassionately, when their **BLUE** is engaged; understanding and tolerance are limited. We will eventually get just what we deserve under the master plan. In its more negative forms, this means fault-finding and assigning blame to some guilty party will take precedence over recognizing good performance. Indeed, the stern task-master may never be satisfied with less than perfection. He or she may have to find something wrong during a 'white glove inspection' as a matter of principle since no mere mortal deserves a perfect score. Children are never allowed to be good enough, for sparing the rod might spoil them.

In **BLUE** people are selective in their choices of friends. Close associates tend to share the same beliefs, even the same religion and politics. For business, **BLUE** liaisons through church or the masonic Lodge insure both a client base and a dependable network of suppliers. The diamond trade has a lot of **BLUE** along with its **ORANGE**; and a handshake still closes many oil deals in West Texas. One tends to have only a few intimates, but they will have proven trustworthiness. These inner circles are the keepers of the faith, the accounts, and children's future. When conflicts break out within **BLUE**, however, they are vicious because both sides know too much about how to hurt the other most deeply. The brothers may never speak again and Civil Wars are the least civil of all.

MOTTO: Order and regimentation, everything in its proper place

When in their **BLUE**, people prefer tight structure, certain schedules, and clear consequences. The 'MEME lives on absolutes – a lifetime guarantee and metaphysical certitude. Oaths and promises are inviolable, so honour codes are most effective when people are in the **BLUE** zone. Today's military academy cadets promise not to lie, cheat or steal, nor to tolerate among them those who do. (Scandals arise when **RED** or **ORANGE** 'MEMEs take over.)

Like old-time factory work rules, the standards for proper behavior are detailed and strictly enforced. Adherence to authority's regulations is part of the **BLUE** *raison d'être* and guilt for violations assumed. Signs are obeyed and speed limits mean something even when the traffic officer is not watching.

One's sense of personal worth largely comes from evaluations by outside authority. Benefits perceived as unearned or undeserved produce guilt and are likely to be demotivating. Too much freedom and the lack of clear direction is stressful. Dress and hair regulations, language standards, and good manners are sharply defined. *Robert's Rules of Order* provide decorum in meetings, just as gentlemanly rules of engagement applied on **BLUE** Bosworth Field or through the Geneva Convention.

This 'MEME produces an orderly life, a neat toolbox, and a strong need to stabilize turbulence. When the 'MEME is healthy we find some of the most comfortable, assured, and tranquil humans on Earth. They *know* why they are here and what is to come. Only contradictory messages from equally respected authorities disturb LC^4. So long as 'the word' is consistent, the Spiral is balanced and lives are at peace.   .

Patient workers in the **BLUE** range perform tasks out of duty and obligation to the State, the Church, or The Company, People are meant to 'work' and hold down 'a steady job,' not to be idle. Diligence avoids guilt and service brings satisfaction. (The warm-'MEME family's elation at individual achievement does not reawaken until **ORANGE**.) **BLUE** used to run American railroads and still operates many European trains. **BLUE** also populates 'smokestack industry,' and many individuals' Spirals begin to topple as the mills shut down or **ORANGE** robotics (and Koreans) take over from skilled Japanese hands who thought they had a job for life.

Traditional pomp-and-circumstance is comforting and restorative for
BLUE. 'The old time religion' and familiar anthems keep things stable. One's
heritage is an extension of the time line which is to be passed right on to future
generations. In the U.S., the Tomb of the Unknown Soldier at Arlington
National Cemetery is the only monument with a 24-hour military guard,
insuring the inviolability of BLUE. (Lenin was not so fortunate as BLUE
faded in the Kremlin.)

The guard also changes at Buckingham Palace, whether the Royals are
getting on well or not. However, if family troubles or budgetary problems
increase, the British Monarchy's publicly BLUE Spiral may collapse in
dysfunction since there is little space for crass RED or too-overt (read
'common') ORANGE in the Pageantry Industry.

There tends to be little room for levity in a stringently BLUE organization;
there are many solemn occasions – 'These are not laughing matters.' Sobriety
is requisite for the heir(s) to a throne or chairmancy of the board. Ebeneezer
Scrooge would have said as much before retiring for the night before
Christmas. The ʹMEME is not uncharitable, though. In fact, many BLUE
beliefs mandate sharing, charity, hospitality, and taking care of one's fellows in
trouble. After the Ghost of Christmas Future took him for a journey,
Mr Scrooge dropped his harsh red side in favor of Peak BLUE obligation to
serve others. Tiny Tim was saved by the Spiral!

Programs like Alcoholics Anonymous and similar 12-step models are more
accessible than Christmas ghosts but also lead to positive BLUE while helping
people manage addictions. Enhancing the ʹMEME offers authority of the
Higher Power outside the self and support of a strong Communal/Collective
with some PURPLE to counter the immediate (RED) rewards of drugs,
drink, and denial. Abusive behavior and other disorders can be managed by
turning one's life over to a healthy BLUE structure so long as the ʹMEME is
accessible on the person's Spiral and there is adequate support to keep it in
control.

There is the catch. Some people have a very faint BLUE band which, even
if awakened, is not strong enough to balance the RED chemistry, the tug of
LC^3, or smug ORANGE arrogance. Treatment modalities must be congruent with Spiral's accessible thinking systems. Trendy generic therapies
that do not take this into account are assured a high rate of failure, though they
can be just as profitable for the entrepreneurial clinician treating 'at-risk'
youth or over-stressed executives.

In summary, the orderly Newtonian world of the BLUE ʹMEME offers
great satisfaction to those discovering their rightful places and staying with
them. People with a well-nourished BLUE system find peace-of-mind, have a
clear hope for the future, and an abiding faith that there is meaning and
purpose in living. Civilization owes much to this 'thrifty, brave, clean, and
reverent' ʹMEME, whose exponents are often eulogized as 'the salt of the
Earth.'

BLUE/orange: Exiting Phase

The obedient straight-arrow good Scout reflects a 'MEME, not a type, though. Once **BLUE** stabilizes the world and brings reliable order, 'me' has the luxury to begin stirring again. At this Exiting phase of **BLUE/orange** we find a cautious, inoffensive, controlled move back toward independent thinking. Peak **BLUE** was compliant and obeisant to authority. Here there is a shift from passive acceptance to modest license and control, even doubts whether the authority is all it is cracked up to be. A nostalgic reverence for the past endures as the need to exercise carefully monitored autonomy crops up. Fundamentalists start writing in their diaries about reforms they want to implement and True Believers dare to voice quiet uncertainty among their peers at coffee shops.

The truth for **BLUE/orange** is what one hears from one's own respected, proper authority. There is still no latitude for deviation from this interpretation; but note that this 'proper authority' is no longer the universal standard. Instead, it is now the particular authority within the '-ism' the individual has selected. This bit of **ORANGE** leads to profound disagreements within the congregation of believers, since those in Exiting **BLUE/orange** have begun to distinguish among versions of the Truth and turn them into personal property. They have an air of easy condemnation for those who disagree and dismiss any contrary views out of hand, disturbing Peak **BLUE** no end. Even though the arguments are often punctilious and focus on semantics, not broad principles, religious denominations split apart and political parties factionalize over just such 'small' matters as these.

Problems hit in business when **BLUE/orange** enters contract negotiations. The parties' representatives listen to all sides trying to figure how to out-argue the opposition and win the point, not to find common ground and stop the game. Frequently, discussions decay into definitional squabbles to mask ego battles among the players instead of addressing substantive issues.

These intra-'ism' arguments can become quite emotionally loaded if others from elsewhere on the Spiral join the debate. That is not easy, since **BLUE/orange** expends considerable energy protecting its little world from challenges and threats. They prefer compatible allies, 'our kind of people,' who are obedient to the interpretation of Truth and somewhat respectful of the self-defined authority within. However, people with this 'MEME profile are susceptible to becoming surrogates and proxies for **ORANGE/blue** since it is their preferred leadership style. Introduce a bit of feisty **RED** or some liberal **GREEN** and there will be quite a show as Presbyterians, Freudians, or Republicans 'duke it out' in committees and platform hearings.

In this zone there is still a greater need to submit than to express one's own point of view, but the scales are tipping toward autonomy. The person does what authority wants, but begins to think about doing it in his/her own way, particularly when authority is not watching. This calls for careful self-control and marks the beginnings of calculatedness. The lack of freedom under the **BLUE** umbrella causes bitterness which stirs the **ORANGE** issues of independence, personal competence, and self-control inside the guidelines.

While at Peak **BLUE** one strives to do things absolutely right but knows only God can make a tree. In the Exiting phase, perfectability seems almost possible through independent thinking and just a little less constraint from The Establishment. With individuality creeping back in Authority is about to be challenged. Doubts about its infallibility allow for reinterpretation of the Truth to fit more 'real-world' issues. This constrained freedom produces a self-righteous way of life that in its more unpleasant forms becomes pompous, glib, and self-satisfied but does not resort to the harsh judgmentalism that **red/BLUE** favors. Instead, there is a bit of *Brideshead Revisited* criticism of almost everything and a hauteur that says 'I am the best, most deserving, of the believers.' Noel Coward made the Victorian **BLUE** to **ORANGE** transition amusing, if uncomfortable. Many small 'Our Towns' are still dominated by this thinking.

When service to the cause is viewed as one's purpose for being, compassion for human weakness and failings is hard to come by. While **BLUE/orange** may assist others out of a sense of duty, obligation, and sympathy, true empathy is rare. Kindness extends to those outside the Way – *noblesse oblige* – but more in the mode of the paternalistic overseer than warm, accepting friendship. That produces a broad circle of respectable associates, but few ever become very close. Most people have difficulty meeting the **BLUE/orange** standards of proper family values, moral behavior, and uprightness. Those in the **PURPLE** and **RED** zones are quite out of luck.

BLUE/orange flaunts its self-righteous discipline and condemns weakness in others while working to exceed standards themselves. Such persons sometimes become compulsive about getting the most done within the existing parameters. They are driven to get it just so and reach closure, only to get right on with whatever is next on the schedule. Perfection is the objective. The need to achieve (David McLellan's 'N-ach') is high in this zone, but it is still heavily group-bounded. There is as yet no intense pressure to go it completely alone.

MOTTO: Work!

Work is still supposed to be work at **BLUE/orange**. There is no room for **RED** horse-play and no time for just enjoying one's self in this highly compartmentalized thinking; even the prayer–breakfast camaraderie of **BLUE** is diminished. Getting things done is reward enough. The Puritan work ethic is heavily **BLUE/orange**. One feels a moral commitment to produce neat, precise, and successful outputs. Joy and relaxation come in the afterlife, not now.

RED is prone to 'push the envelope,' daring the impossible and risking it all in the hope of glory – a barnstormer doing the outside loop. **BLUE**, on the other hand, is good at preventive maintenance, inventory control, and monitoring the specifications – the maintenance test pilot. As **BLUE/orange** takes over, the trains do not just run on time, they become faster and more reliable while adding restricted first class 'Orient Express' accommodations. The emphasis in on quality over quantity, very much the Rolls Royce or Lamborghini manufacturing mentality. Things are custom fabricated, hand finished and gently fitted with 'old world craftsmanship.' The **BLUE/orange** objective is not to make the expensive or showy, but to do it right, as well as possible.

Apprenticeship and the guild system fall in this range of the Spiral. Licensure, tests, and permits are assurances of meeting **BLUE/orange** specifications. The thinking is prevalent in the fire service of most nations, many police agencies, career military, and the Ivory Towers of compartmentalized academia.

This is still a tight, narrowly confined area of the **BLUE** zone, though. Rules are rigidified and sometimes used as punitive sticks to beat uppity people into submission or lazy ones into production. Often, employees feel assaulted and restrained by excessive authority that demands more productivity.

The individual functioning here is deferential and cordial to superiors, but can be high-handed and cruel with subordinates. **BLUE/orange** feels ridden by authority, and therefore may ride anyone below like a mini-tyrant. They carry a monkey of obedience on their backs, resent its presence, but are too fearful to cast it off. The monkey, though heavy, represents the stability they still need. The excesses of **BLUE/orange** are a common problem in the fast-food business where teenagers still consolidating their own Spirals are employed trying to manage others also in transition.

Such leaders profess concern for their fellows, but are constantly evaluating both their performance and who they are as persons. **BLUE/orange** managers tend to drive workers, becoming beneficent dictators who continue to push for more and faster results. While protesting otherwise, this person loses sight of employees as human beings and is inclined to the 'hired hands' approach, readily discarding personnel who fail the tests of acceptable behavior or break under pressure. (Unlike **RED**, there may be counseling and even out-placement assistance rather than just 'hit the door and don't come back.')

Still, such systems are just asking for unionization. Often, they have no idea why the discontents arise. The manager says, 'They should be grateful to me for a job and fair pay. What more do they expect?' Employees reply, 'Why should you get so much for what you do while we get so little in comparison? You expect gratitude for giving us less than our due.' This problem rooted in the **BLUE/orange** band is the American labor-management dilemma.

The **BLUE/orange** range was perfect for Frederick Taylor's scientific management – time-motion studies and the like. The thinking often makes for a compulsive laborer, but perhaps a satisfied one. Companies used to love these workalcoholics with green eye-shades as long as they were not in slots that require creativity and adaptability. Stereotypes of clockmakers and the tool-and-die trades fit this 'MEME, as well as many old-time insurance agents and bankers who got the gold watch at retirement. If one accepts toil as one's purpose in being, then hard work and sweat are profoundly rewarding; mandatory retirement may be fatal.

Entities blocked in **BLUE/orange** thinking reach an impasse. They achieve a level of competence and cannot move on to greater complexity. Managers entrench and build authoritarian fiefdoms that perform adequately, but often with high turnover, low morale, and much grousing from those under their control. The archetypal low-level Civil Service *petite-bureaucrat* is often **BLUE/orange**. Even large corporations (like the U.S. auto industry) struggle to escape this zone and its narrow, adversarial view. It is right at this level that many 'reengineering' and 'total quality' programs have been directed with limited success. Until they shift along the Spiral, the Humpty Dumpty Effect will prevail.

Just like managers, parents Closed at **BLUE/orange** often engender simmering hatred in children. Many old-time military families (as in *The Great Santini*) were susceptible to **BLUE/orange** problems. In this view, it is not wrong for righteous dictatorship to exist. While it promotes self-confident assertiveness through duty, penance, and discipline, it simultaneously leaves deep doubts about love and acceptance. Those in authority may become the arrogant voice of derision, setting standards guaranteed to be unattainable. For some, that challenge promotes movement up the Spiral, but others hunker down, become embittered, and pass the emotional scars right on.

On a more positive side, **BLUE/orange** thinking often excels at organizing things and taking charge according to authority's directives (thereby avoiding censure, blame, and criticism). Such persons find worthiness regulating themselves and their environments, but always within the parameters of right-and-proper behavior. One aspires to be known as good-and-true, dependable, and always prepared – Semper Fi (et paratus, too). This zone of the Spiral has been a major resouce of philanthropy, volunteer labor, and middle-class stability for several generations. The Red Cross and United Way depend on **BLUE/orange** to gather their 'fair share.'

When **BLUE/orange** is working with others, the focus is always on accomplishing the mission. The task is more important than social needs or feelings and will be completed or else. That strength is also a weakness for managers when they fail to recognize that other people will have priorities from elsewhere along the Spiral (such as their families or control of time). It is particularly difficult for **BLUE/orange** when dealing with **GREEN** and **YELLOW**, two 'MEMEs that simply do not respond to the leadership style that fits this range so well.

MOTTO: Authority on the Move

When centered near the middle of **BLUE**, the authoritative opinions of those with seniority or recognized position power weigh most strongly. Toward the Exiting phase **BLUE/orange** it becomes possible to deviate from the certified Truth so long as one remains proximate to authority. The emerging independence still does not allow much latitude for experimentation, so one tends to avoid the extremes, the singularly novel, or the risks of innovation. Color right up to the lines, but not beyond (until **ORANGE** is brighter).

While the basic **BLUE** view is 'sacrifice now to obtain later at the behest of proper authority,' the Exiting range becomes openly disdainful of any authority which does not act like good authority should. At first, **BLUE/orange** begins to gently assert the self against the deficiencies and errors. In the classroom, for example: 'But, sir, wait just a moment, please . . . according to . . . you seem to be mistaken.' [wink, wink; nudge, nudge]

The assessment of proper authority is moving from the outside locus back within one's own right-thinking mind, a mind, as Graves said, '. . . that knows that it knows that it knows . . .' Quietly, **BLUE/orange** comes to believe that 'I am a better authority than you.' (Whether deservedly or not, the Clinton Presidency has been victimized by it.)

If the perceived misdeeds continue, political scandals and visits from the *60 Minutes* crew are the frequent outcome of **BLUE/orange** 'whistle-blowing.' Woe unto authority with feet of clay. Misdeeds will be investigated and gleefully reported to yet higher authority for appropriate (punitive) action, a dressing-down, and the correction of faults. Often, that is exactly what is needed.

The **BLUE/orange** zone is also the home of self-made martyrs. To gain credibility, such leaders need to be punished by 'the system' so they can be reborn even stronger. By reacting, 'the establishment' legitimizes the **BLUE/orange** thinker as a relevant force. One then becomes more convinced of being right because 'they' had to attack. If ignored, the person will contrive to be arrested, jailed, or somehow made a victim.

This is a stock ploy of the demagogue and propagandist. Hitler understood that assaults by 'the enemy' are enlivening, stimulating, and useful for recruitment; **RED/blue** followers eat it up and make good Brown Shirts. If thwarted still, **BLUE/orange** first becomes righteously indignant at a press conference denouncing the oppressor. If that does not work, they drop the facade of equanimity and go on the offensive in the name of the just Cause.

This **BLUE/orange** world view favors a no-nonsense approach since there is important work to be done. The Singapore model is a case in point. Strict discipline, clear expectations, and an ethic of obligation to the common good keep potentially volatile **PURPLE** factions in check. The 'caning' of the American teenager charged with vandalism (with the compromise of fewer licks) was this 'MEME in action.

Yet this Exiting phase can be turbulent and strife-ridden. On the one hand the person tries to hang onto absolute Truth to maintain stability, yet on the other authority is also teaching independence of thought. Contradictions between anchor points – within and without – stimulate confused guilt. It sometimes takes the form of negativism and a zealous drive to fix-up evil and make things right. Questions about where Truth lives, who is authorized to interpret it, and how to enforce it are constant issues.

A great many aspiring entrepreneurs, restless souls about to try out some alternatives in their church, and budding politicians move about in this range of the Spiral. It is both painful and invigorating. While the old certainties are in jeopardy, the pendulum swing toward independence is also exciting. The world has new complications, as well as possibilities. The infectious enthusiasm of **ORANGE** is catching on.

ORANGE *StriveDrive*
The Strategic ^VMEME

- Strive for autonomy and independence
- Seek out 'the good life' and material abundance
- Progress through searching out the best solutions
- Enhance living for many through science and technology
- Play to win and enjoy competition
- Learn through tried-and-true experience

At the core of ORANGE – *Life Conditions*[5]:

'I want to achieve, and win, and get somewhere in my life. The world is full of opportunities for those who'll seize the day and take some calculated risks. Nothing is certain, but if you're good, you play the odds and find the best choices among many. You've got to believe in yourself first, then everything else falls into place. You can't get bogged down in structure or rules if they hold back progress. Instead, by practical applications of tried-and-true experience, you can make things better and better for yourself. I'm confident in my own abilities and intend to make a difference in this world. Gather the data, build a strategic plan, then go for excellence.'

blue/ORANGE: Entering Phase

In the context of European history, the **ORANGE** ^VMEME sprang to life with The Enlightenment after the Middle Ages. The old (**BLUE**) world had been resplendent with sacraments, formalities, and rigid social structures. Its success, however, planted the seeds that were to threaten the underpinnings of that established order. Five forces set into motion five or six centuries ago are still resonant in the 'modern' age:

- market economy (as described initially by Adam Smith in *The Wealth of Nations* in 1776)
- utilitarian political philosophy (as reflected in the rise of the nation state)
- narrowing of science (as conceptualized in the objective, positivist scientific method that supplanted myths, superstition, and 'blind' faith)
- popularization of technology (as played out in the Industrial Revolution and the rapid spread of machines to replace human labor)
- rise of the individual (as expressed in various guarantees of freedom, liberty, rights, and personal autonomy)

The 'MEME awakens a middle class between haves and have-nots with the recognition – and exaltation – of bootstraps by which almost anyone can supposedly pull themselves up in this world. The pre-**ORANGE** existence was often one of considerable poverty, disease, feudal empires, and stagnation. With its addition there is a new kind of hope for individual achievement.

Emergent **ORANGE** carries with it a sense of personal power derived from the **RED** intelligences and purposeful existence derived from the **BLUE**. From **RED** it also gains a desire to do as the self desires. That is now tempered by **BLUE**'s recognition of the rules and a compulsion to strive for the completion of a cause that gives life meaning. With this mixture to energize it, the **ORANGE** 'MEME has insinuated itself into practically every nook and cranny of the planet via television and MTV. Once upon a time it even propelled us into space with dreams of 'a better life' just ahead.

Individually, the theme song for Entering **blue/ORANGE** might be Frank Sinatra singing '. . . I did it my way.' The 'MEME instills caution not to arouse undue ire in others, so the person (discreetly) screams to be free and liberate the repressed self, and (subtly) longs to tear the barricades down. Then he apologizes for all the noise.

In this Entering **blue/ORANGE** transition zone, one shows respect when authority is present (as in **BLUE/orange**), but becomes downright derogatory when it is not. Soon, these confrontations between an empowered 'me' within and residual authority outside turn into 'pissing contests' and psychological games about who gets in the last word. The person begins showing overt rejection of authority instead of the grudging obeisance of **BLUE/orange**. It is the stock relationship for loud parent/teenager transactions and the heart of much civil litigation.

Autonomy layered over a belief in absolute truth leads to a sense of one's own total rightness. With stability and security guaranteed by **BLUE** and an afterlife (either in heaven or on Earth) assured through successful works, questions arise about the price of glory. The saintly, rigid, and sacrificial lifestyle which has dominated begins to wear thin as the Individual/Elite form begins to rule.

Freedom from constraints imposed by relations with other people or the limitations that accompany faith in doctrine are central to this 'MEME's happiness. When it is strong, the person feels – sometimes shows – great anger when external boundaries constrain the complete independence that **ORANGE** craves. Attention goes to breaking shackles, whether real or imagined, and empowerment and entitlement are recurring themes. Mix in some **RED**, and they become demands.

In fact, much behavior of this ᵛMEME mix is reminiscent of the extreme self-confidence of **RED**. But the trip through **BLUE** rounds raw edges from aggression into assertiveness and turns shrewd cunning into artful calculation. Since the time concept lengthens with added **BLUE**, impulsivity (**RED**'s 'now or never') smoothes into self-absorbed urgency.

These adjustments are why a **BLUE** passage is essential in helping **RED**-dominated youth to move along the Spiral. If that **BLUE** ᵛMEME is bypassed altogether in the rush from toughness to prosperity, patience, responsibility, and attention to consequences will be overlooked as well. That is a formula for failure when the person is called on to fit into organizations and demonstrate a reliable work ethic.

Whereas the Exiting **BLUE/orange** may adopt a negative, judgmental tone, the character at Entering **blue/ORANGE** can be aggressively hostile, volatile and explosive. Those emotions are usually tempered because the person at this level understands that flagrant rejection of authority costs support of those who still believe in it. The attacks take the form of sarcasm, selective interpretation, and manipulation of the facts. 'Always tell the truth, but the whole truth need not always be told.'

In business, **blue/ORANGE** is known for playing 'hard ball.' It introduces the notion of calculated risk and the 'nothing ventured, nothing gained' thinking which is essential to further elaboration of the Spiral. The ᵛMEME mix ran the flowering of the Industrial Age when it was determined that God wanted mankind to succeed, not just obey. This is the world of the clever entrepreneur, professional baseball, the cold-blooded (but responsible) task-master, and the pin-striped capitalist who is reverent to **BLUE** on Saturday or Sunday but can do 'whatever it takes' to attain objectives during the week. These ᵛMEMEs that built Big Oil in the early 1900s are breeding fast in Russia, eastern Europe, and South Africa now that the solid **BLUE** walls are coming down.

The **BLUE** to **ORANGE** transition opens the Truth to the masses, not just the priestly class at the top of the hierarchy. Volume production and distribution put the content of the holy texts into the hands of anyone. The people begin to read and become hungry for information. Not surprisingly, there is a huge literary market in **blue/ORANGE** selling the wisdom of experts. Whole racks of books, magazines, audio- and videotapes are devoted to self-help, how-to-succeed, how to empower the giant within you, being your own best friend, tightening your buns, and becoming all that you can be. The consumers carry enough residual **BLUE** to need permission from wise authority before they are comfortable with autonomous action, but now they can buy the authority themselves and listen on their own terms. It is the staple 'MEME mix of talk radio and television public affairs programs.

People breaking free as 'independent' thinkers also shatter the fatalistic know-your-place-ism of **BLUE** society. A few will regress down-Spiral into **RED** anger, but most move up toward **ORANGE** aspirations for affluence and influence. Doing it too fast leads to charges of being 'uppity' and a 'bounder' since Entering **blue/ORANGE** often triggers antibodies in rivals who perceive themselves having prior claim on the same niches. The strident, demanding tone of Entering **blue/ORANGE** causes negative reactions by attacking barriers rather than adroitly removing them through skillful alliances. The requisite 'manners' of **BLUE** have faded so the nouveau-empowered are often irritatingly clumsy with their autonomy, using it more as a club than a lever. Organizations must have tolerance for this brash thinking since it is a necessary component in the Spiral, understanding that subtle *savoire faire* does not appear until more **ORANGE** develops.

While the overall tone in this range is of driven autonomy, **blue/ORANGE** needs someone else around to blame for failures since (as in **RED**) the fault is surely not one's own. Learning how to delegate problems up to authority or pass the buck down subordinates relieves much troubling accountability. Often **BLUE** will go ahead and assume the responsibility since obligation comes so easily and carrying the burden alleviates guilt. (You will soon see that **GREEN** will also cast on blame, particularly for social ills and inequities.)

In management, **blue/ORANGE** grants unimportant power to underlings, since they are often viewed as incompetent, unmotivated, or stupid from this lofty perch. The real leverage it keeps for itself. In such systems, executive elites invariably give each other hefty bonuses, even when the company is in a general decline. Of course the very same phenomenon occurs when unhealthy **blue/ORANGE** runs the union. Adversarial war-games put workers on the streets and close factories while their ostensible leaders continue to sip *cappuccino* with the negotiators and the MBAs.

The elitism creates interpersonal distance. Individuals in this zone are too critical and discriminating to build many trusting relationships, though they may be surrounded by yes-persons. Anyone who risks getting close will be vulnerable to attacks of emotional dumping and efforts to displace faults while absorbing credit. Always evaluative, one usually comes across snobbish, disgusted, and distant instead of comforting or supportive when others are troubled. The implication is 'Can't you take care of yourself? Grow up.' Divorce lawyers thrive because of this segment on the Spiral.

It is also abundantly clear when someone in this zone is bored. They rarely listen without evaluations (voiced or not) and become quickly distracted, fidgety, or dismissively '. . . have to make a call.' Surging self-centeredness precludes a genuine, altruistic focus on someone else so the **blue/ORANGE** span of attention is strictly limited by one's own curiosity. You will often sense it in the contrived warmth of a gladhanding salesperson or the individual who shifts into a 'counseling' mode until he tires of it and abruptly closes the conversation. In the family setting, parents grant young children an audience; later the pattern reverses.

A useful trait of **blue/ORANGE** is the ability to excel at start-up's and initiating action. However, this 'ideas person' may begin time and again instead of carrying anything through to completion. The joy comes from the chase, not the capture. (**BLUE** will finish, regardless, whereas **GREEN** has trouble deciding what to start.) There will be many enthusiastic and often ingenious initiatives, but they will only move forward if associates with complementary (not more **ORANGE**) 'MEMEs pick up the ball. The person understands what is desirable and what would be best, but cannot hold focus long enough to achieve it. Thus, **blue/ORANGE** desperately needs others, yet the picky, demanding temperament often makes it very difficult for them to stay close. Many a 'genius' in Hollywood and the arts becomes lost in unfulfilled dreams, fading to oblivion at a little theatre in Kansas.

When individuals in this range are better with ideas and objects than with people, their managerial vulnerability is interpersonal skills. The fine technician whose genius is manipulating data rather than relationships may be promoted to become a rotten supervisor. The once-terrific salesman becomes manic and disorganized as a desk-bound administrator of the sales department.

To force team-work' onto this argumentative system is a waste of energy, though Team Building is exactly the remedy Human Resources departments often implement for **blue/ORANGE** problems. While people in this range may use teams and appreciate productive outputs from group activities, they never join them. Such characters are reluctant to contribute to group efforts in which they have to yield control or risk being shown up. It is also difficult to give a group its due when one is convinced all good thoughts come from within the self.

Those centered at the Entering **blue/ORANGE** zone hunger for opportunities to express themselves and excel. The competitive zeal of **ORANGE** along with a belief in **blue** standards to be exceeded drive it. Motivational seminars, self-help cassette programs, plaques, and 'rah! rah!' sales meetings give them the necessary boost. Even computer games that keep a running score are invigorating. Such ego-building can have very positive, constructive outcomes on productivity, especially when the cause is worth while and the energy well-focused.

Yet the intense, achieving behavior of **blue/ORANGE** can lead to premature burn-out. Cardiovascular disease and gastrointestinal problems are physical manifestations of the stresses this way of thinking/living can engender. So long as one is driven to accomplish, still feels a little guilt, and fails to monitor internal strains, explosions are likely. This is a major risk for Japan and the Asian 'little' giants where large groups of managers are moving rapidly, narrowly, and compulsively into this part of the Spiral.

blue/ORANGE is becoming unbound by what others say or do. It is not the contrarian, to-hell-with-the-consequences of **RED**, but a sense that one's own good mind is superior. Advertisers play on this theme trying to sell everything from cars (using names like Achieva, Excel, Intrepid, and Impreza) to designer fragrances. The tobacco industry has been particularly adept with it in target marketing to women into this zone and to the Second- Third-Worlds in general.

One is told to strike out to new territory by pushing the accepted limits without quite exceeding them. In **blue/ORANGE** there is not yet enough individuality to disregard what others think while there is a strong desire to lead the pack. The hyper-designedness of Barcelona for its Olympics illustrates the ᵛMEME at work. It is also the mindset of many aspirants to the lifestyle of elite suburbs and self-contained, walled-in communities.

This ᵛMEME transition is underway for millions of people leaving **BLUE**'s rigid classifications on their way up the Spiral. For example, the near-resolution of food and population problems in China have stored excess energy and resources, thus creating the LC^5 necessary for a massive activation of consumer-based, expansive, and elite-driven **ORANGE** ᵛMEME. From its breeding grounds nearby – 'How're you gonna' keep 'em down on the (collective) farms after they've seen Hong Kong?' – the thinking is strong in China's southern provinces and will grow across the mainland in a very few years.

India, by contrast, still lives much more through her ancient sacrificial ᵛMEME family – **PURPLE** clans and spirits, **BLUE** castes and many paths to God, and **GREEN** unity in diversity. Britain's brief two-hundred year **blue/ORANGE** colonial rule did little to bend the sacred river of Indian history and the pluralistic spirit endures. Individualistic **ORANGE** stands aside.

While this awakening of **ORANGE** lessens **BLUE**-based guilt, it does not eliminate awareness of it since other people are still factors in life's equation. One must find ways to manage whatever residual guilt there is, to convince oneself not to be constrained by it, and to redefine negatives so they become positives. 'I am meant to prosper and achieve abundance.' The person at **blue/ORANGE** needs to justify actions, but is beginning to learn how easily such good excuses can be found once the Ten Commandments become suggestions and 'The Little Brown Church in the Vale' gets an 800 number. (In more extreme **ORANGE** it becomes a 900 number!) You can already *fax* your prayers to Jerusalem where a service is available to slip them into the Wailing Wall for you. Cellular confessionals are probably next.

When this thinking is active, many diverse ideas are worth considering but most will be judged of low quality and deserving to be dropped. Whereas polarized **BLUE** sees dissenting ideas as diabolical, **blue/ORANGE** dismisses them as merely dumb. Other people need to come into compliance with the best and proper way to do things – one's own. Obviously, if the **blue/ORANGE** person is intelligent and incisive, his or her ideas may well be the best. However, those from elsewhere on the Spiral often rebel against the self-important assurance of **blue/ORANGE**, if not the substance of its thoughts. When several such people bump together, the competition in the board room or the bedroom can be fierce.

ORANGE: Peak Phase

ORANGE FLASH: Change, not permanence, is how nature works

Evidence from physics, astronomy, and biology proves that systems are active and in constant flux. Eventually, humans can manipulate nature (a) to learn its secrets and (b) to create a better life here on Earth since science and technology equip us to do virtually anything so long as we do not bog down in metaphysical ramblings or pointless debates. Individual humans can grow, improve, and progress toward being the best if they but choose to act. 'Modern' life results from labor saving devices that free the spirit for better things, superior health care and medicines, improved animals and plants, and a belief that we hold dominion over all things.

Whereas **BLUE** thinking is absolutistic (only one right way), **ORANGE** takes a multiplistic view – many possible ways but one is best. There is also a shift from linear, step-by-step straight-arrow time to polychronic time as **BLUE** weakens. Now, many important things can happen at once and the person may quickly shift attention among them. The more intense the **ORANGE**, the more irons in the fire and the greater skill at maneuvering to keep them all hot. This thinking is essential on Wall Street and the complicated marketplaces of the world. At the Entering phase, there was still a residue of rule-boundedness, adherence to tradition, and obligation to authority, characteristics which now dissolve into a pragmatic results orientation.

FLASH: Authority lies with experience, experiments, and one's own right-thinking mind

Demonstrated opposition to authority becomes less important as one moves toward the center of **ORANGE**. The person concludes that with skill authority is easily placated or simply ignored. Faith in dogma is gone, replaced by experimental data, 'the scientific method,' and ongoing appraisals to determine what works best for now. Successful actions establish what is right, not the directives of a Higher Power or orders from authoritarian figures. In Europe, medieval **BLUE** was written over in **ORANGE** on the Wittenberg door and THE TRUTH became subject to debate.

Possibility thinking, here we come. Opportunity abounds and autonomy rules the middle of the competitive **ORANGE** band. Above all else, the person is determined to be independent and in control. This is a being standing apart in the universe who must rely on innate abilities and competencies. To succeed in the **ORANGE** life there is no room for guilt, and no time or energy to be wasted. As in the Entering phase, there may be occasional sympathy (a very judgmental emotion) but no empathy (a non-evaluative 'walk-a-mile-in-your-shoes' phenomenon). Self-confidence intensifies as **ORANGE** becomes convinced of its correctness. This is 'a take-charge kind of guy' and 'a woman who knows what she wants and how to get it.' Both want it all and want it *now*.

People in this zone appear materialistic and acquisitive, but that is because money is life's report card and 'nice goods' are tangible evidence of successful **ORANGE** functioning. The thrill of victory and achievement are the real rewards for **ORANGE**; life is a game in which second place is the first among the losers. In most of the world, **ORANGE** is beginning to bloom, while in the U.S., the Reagan/Bush years with their Yuppies, S&Ls, conspicuous consumption, and growing deficits may prove to have been the peak of the **ORANGE** curve.

FLASH: People are meant to succeed and become winners

The 'MEME arises in the person or group seeking to exploit opportunities to create 'the good life'; navigate among failures to successes; manipulate events and persons who contribute to the bottom line; employ a vast array of analytical problem-resolution skills for optimized solutions; and orchestrate complex decisions. In addition, **ORANGE** embraces values and beliefs that stress materialism over spiritualism, pragmatism over principle, and short- range victories over longer term guarantees. There is a desire to get on with life and not bog down in quandaries of absolutism or picky, picky, picky theology.

Multiplistic thinking is comparative; life is competitive. The absolute, ideological standards of **BLUE** are replaced by situationalism and prudent pragmatism – doing what works while saying what they want to hear. Flexibility and rapid responses to a changing marketplace are 'the name of the game.' However, when naive **ORANGE** managers take charge of organizations they try to drive out the **BLUE** past through layoffs and forced retirements, producing houses of cards without loyalty to the mission and a pack of competitive underlings out for themselves. Little is sacred except growth and expansion. Principles are gelatinous and ethics tend to be overlooked in the rush toward quick prosperity.

FLASH: 'If 'twere done, 'tis best 'twere done quickly (while I can get the recognition)'

ORANGE wants to be directly involved in (and credited for) progress. That often limits the time-line to 'on my watch' and during one's tenure in office.

Long-range planning, if it does not make **ORANGE** look good now, is bypassed in favour of short-range, results-oriented projects that do. Hidden infrastructure is neglected in favor of polish for showier monuments. Strategic planning, goal-setting, and visioning are recurring themes, their *bon mots* adorning the corridors of power. Because of their Spiral's history and even the sacrificial remains of the Code of Bushido, Japanese corporations have thus far been much better at stretching **ORANGE** plans across **BLUE** and **PURPLE** than their more impatient, shorter-sighted American competitors.

The middle of **ORANGE** has its own popular journals like *Forbes* and *Fortune, Savvy, Self, GQ, noir, Cosmopolitan, Architectural Digest, Southern Living, Money, Essence, Connoisseur, Vogue*, the Nieman's Christmas Catalogue, etc. (The more 'upscale' and 'A-list,' the more appealing something is for **ORANGE**, particularly the Entering nouveau-riche.) One strives to keep current, to hone one's edge, and to stay one up on the competition. Although not necessarily well read, **ORANGE** knows what it needs to know and concentrates on becoming expert in that field. Life is a series of executive summaries, sound bites, and quick takes.

FLASH: Conformity to the image of success and fashion

Much of Peak **ORANGE**'s self-concept is reflective, in spite of the protestations of individuality and personal freedom. One is free to conform to the ways of the elites and success really depends on their reviews. The primo lifestyle to which **ORANGE** aspires features psychoanalyzed minds and high dollar suits, trophy spouses for display at Cannes (a new-and-improved bouncy or studly one to replace the frumpy, flabby, 'out-grown' **BLUE** that helped work one's way through school), and recognition at fashionable eateries and upscale shops. The ᵛMEME is found cruising the Mediterranean aboard a yacht, has a 'little place' in Palm Beach or Springs, and knows the Concorde intimately.

When **ORANGE** is active, image often counts more than substance. When not counted among 'the beautiful people' at least **ORANGE** can drive a status auto and appear eligible – 'you are what you drive.' The brains behind the wheels of these trendy cars become self-ordained VIPs and courtesy gives way to competition – zip, zip, zoom, zoom. There is usually not the crass tire-squealing of **RED**; instead, **ORANGE** simply presumes that other drivers know to get out of their way. Twenty-two-year-old women adjusting their make-up while 'networking' on cellular phones, like the blow-dried gents out 'to close a deal' and 'make a killing,' are convinced they have leased the driving skills of Mario Andretti along with the Corvette.

Since facades work, one need not actually own the tangible goods to appreciate 'the good life' in **ORANGE**. Although a knock-off is not as good as a designer original, the right look is better than 'dweeb' or 'nerd' status (unless those looks are 'in'). A confident bearing and appearance of prosperity can work wonders on the **ORANGE** band. **RED** relies on unethical but aspiring **ORANGE** to buy merchandise of doubtful provenance – 'such a deal I have for you on a genuine Rolex, Mac. Want some studio speakers, cheap?' So long as one is in fashion and 'with it,' the possibility of becoming a 'player' is always right at hand, a fact well understood by Las Vegas casino managers, Aspen hoteliers, and theatrical producers with casting couches.

FLASH: Growing up with the ORANGE world

One would think that the children of affluent parents and circumstances would automatically acquire their values and aspirations by osmosis. Some do, but most do not. Learning to handle LC^5 requires more than having possessions. Even in an economically impoverished home, child rearing experiences that reward industrious behaviors, independent action, and self-reliance can awaken **ORANGE** competencies. A youth's paper route, exposure to the Puritan or Confucian work ethic in school, or even participation in a Rap group will help young minds cope with **ORANGE**. Then the questions arise. Which beliefs and ideas will it attract? Is the **BLUE** foundation solid enough to discern right from wrong? What form will this **ORANGE** take?

ORANGE-centered parents see baby (and themselves) as the center of the universe. When they are courteous, the attentive parenting is charming to behold. Alas, some **ORANGE** parents become so infantocentric that they are genuinely astonished that everyone else does not find baby's squalling and biologic offerings fascinating (**RED** tends to yell even louder and ignore the latter, which is worse!) On airplanes, the progeny of **ORANGE** parading the aisles make for long, long flights – not to mention the post-landing ritual of getting the titanium-framed, Gore-Tex lined, monogrammed stroller and Gucci diaper bag from the overhead bin.

Residents of affluent suburbs world-wide expect **ORANGE**. The up-and-comers want their very own piece of the action, whether a McMansion with mini-pool and micro-lawn or whatever else represents competitive success in their milieu. Be it leaving Soweto for a town house in Johannesburg, or Liverpool for a flat in London, **ORANGE** and mobility run together. Keeping ahead of the Joneses is part of the game.

The 'MEME produces personalities which are calculating, accepting of responsibliity, and anxious to dominate. They command out of a sense of greater capabilities and maintain this self-image in spite of criticism, rarely changing their minds as a result of feedback. Yet **ORANGE** is constantly asking for feedback – 'tell me what you think about me' – but then rejects the critique if it does not match preconceptions. They believe their way is obviously the best and must be convinced otherwise.

FLASH: Life is a series of challenges, tests, and opportunities to do better

ORANGE enjoys argumentation and debate as much as sport. They are self-assured about ideas, but always proving themselves with little victories. Truth for ORANGE depends on self-discovery and their own keen observations. Sometimes they deny the validity of contrary information or turn and attack the source. Often, though, greatest credit goes to adversaries who give as good as they get and anyone unable to join the game is discounted. Probing questions should be expected; if you fail to 'do your homework' before meeting ORANGE, you are doomed.

FLASH: 'Run it up the flag pole and see who salutes'

ORANGE business and politics are full of military and sports metaphors. Life is a series of maneuvers with espionage, liaisons, and allies. One attacks the competition and out-flanks their marketing with an end-run. The trap, of course, is that while focused in the skirmishes they take so seriously, a third, larger force overwhelms both sides of the ORANGE game. (You might review the Strategic Alliances discussion in Chapter 8.) Ineffectual, unhealthy ORANGE drops the ball, puts too many irons in the fire, and gets caught playing both ends against the middle. When their operations are revealed, the strategy is to intimidate, unbalance, and shift blame with elaborate cover stories while maintaining 'plausible deniability.' Be cautious around these characters. While they slickly convince themselves of their own virtue and the foibles of their incompetent associates, careers are built on the corpses of unwary colleagues who play a lousy game of golf.

ORANGE lives are directed, focused, intense, and connected. The 1994 Woodstock Concert offered cellular phone chargers and FAX services to keep the 'MEME-bearers in touch (though the BEIGE needs for water and toilets were less well met). Computerized diaries (when 'my people' are unavailable) help one to keep up with contacts and hectic schedules, but ORANGE thrives on the activity. Testing the limits brings on an adrenaline rush. If politicians in this zone lose, they rationalize it, learn from it, and re-enter the fray better candidates. Living is based on cost/benefit ratios, so paying one's dues and taking some hits is just part of it.

FLASH: Humans are resources, so '. . . to thine own self be true'

Away from public scrutiny appraisals are blunt, rather like the Nixon tapes. Criticism is cold-blooded and insensitive, but straightforward. When ORANGE goes, it does not go gently or submissively. One fights to win and stay on top, suffering ulcers, divorce, or a heart attack in the process.

There is superficial warmth for those who are useful, while they are useful, but **ORANGE** has more contacts than colleagues. Loyalty is based on utility, not obligation. To maximize its options **ORANGE** must maintain some distance, using understanding as a manipulative tool. There is open disdain for empathy since every person is expected to stand on his/her own feet in this world. What happens to others may be useful data, but one cannot become emotionally involved. Business is business. When people are no longer productive, they are cast aside, just as out-dated equipment is scrapped. It can be done without deliberate cruelty, but it will be done and the message will be clear.

Thus, interpersonal relations in heavily **ORANGE** enterprises are very tenuous. Trusting others is perceived as risky because **ORANGE** knows its own unpredictability and projects its own motives into others. Though they can give the appearance of caring, such people have difficulty focusing on someone other than the self. Everything turns back around to self interest, stored information to be used later. The more stress one feels, the more self-focused the behaviors become, sometimes to the point of manic desperation. There may even be internal espionage.

FLASH: Self-assurance comes with the territory

People with bright **ORANGE** in their profiles often appear masterful and forceful because they are accomplishing their goals. A healthy dose of this 'MEME is essential for start-ups and turn-arounds. It lends an air of self-confidence and 'positive thinking' which can be contagious and draw others onto the **ORANGE** band wagon. A great many sales seminars and corporate training packages are designed to pump up the **ORANGE** in people. If they experience some successes while listening to their own internal advertising it may be sufficient to alter their *Life Conditions* and consolidate long-term change on the Spiral. If there is no support, the 'shot in the mind' will fade quickly.

On the negative side, **ORANGE** can lack conscience, especially where important results are involved. They can be unscrupulous, justifying harms done to others as necessities that 'had to be done' or rationalizing them as 'actually for his/her own good.' Yet **ORANGE** is never purely ruthless as **RED** can be since it does not pay off in the long run. Repeat customers are best; cheat them badly and the word will spread. The people across the creek may come in handy later, so one burns as few bridges as possible. Emotional displays are controlled and monitored, since overt lust, ambition, or pride can turn others off. However, like the Singapore Yuppie in Chapter 2, the leopards show their spots with fellow **ORANGE**'s over drinks at a ferny watering hole or with a resounding 'YES!' in the bathroom after a courtroom victory.

ORANGE is equipped for independent operation. The thinking leads to entrepreneurial ventures by the loner who spreads the risk like an old-time wild-catter selling shares in an unproven oil field. The 'MEME's quest for novelty and improvements often drives social change and economic advancement. The arbitrageur (or any other wheeler-dealer) must have a healthy **ORANGE** understanding and an attorney who is even more skillful.

Decisions are based in cold, quantitative evaluation and calculation of probabilities. 'The facts, ma'am; nothing but the facts,' says **ORANGE**. One cannot look to others for support or advice as this is evidence of personal weakness and undermines the delusion of complete autonomy. All they want from others is their 'input' to be evaluated. Data must be gathered and processed to the accompaniment of myriad charts and graphs to enhance the odds of good decisions.

FLASH: Free-market, free-enterprise, and laissez-faire models are the favorites

Trickle-down economic theory is rooted in **ORANGE**. Each is responsible for him- or herself. The best will succeed and prosper. They, in turn, will use others to serve their ends, inevitably spreading the spoils downward. Eventually, even the least competent will get something because gravity, if nothing else, is in their favor. It draws memes which voice resentment at 'handout' social programs supporting people who do nothing to earn what they get. Work-fare, not entitlements, is the preferred safety net here. One invests in people; one does not give them charity. How this is done will be a huge issue in America as the number of middle-class niches is down-sized, health care needs increase, and the national Spiral is realigned in the next decade.

ORANGE/green: Exiting Phase

The Exiting range is still a self-centered way of existing, but the person is now feeling encroachments from others and their needs. **ORANGE/green** also introduces pangs of loneliness brought on by constant competition. The strategy of choice here is to keep others satisfied, in their places, and off one's back, yet just close enough to be of use when needed to get things done or for comfort on a 'dark and stormy night.' Teams can be useful sometimes.

This is the calm operator who succeeds when the odds are good and knows how to avoid bad deals and losing situations. The Teflon factor is high – problems that would devastate others slide right off. It is a common way of thinking for many younger contemporary politicians as leadership is leaving the hands of the World War II generation and passing to the Baby Boomers and their children. Just as the remarkably simple Cold War military context has become more complex, the Cold Warriors and their **BLUE/orange** and blue/ORANGE mindsets are yielding in insurgent GREEN as LC⁶ start to appear. It is now business as most unusual.

That is not to say that most human beings alive today are thinking at the upper end of the ORANGE band – we are not. But the prominent First-World leadership and emerging Second- and Third-World players have much more pragmatic, economic, multiplistic Peak ORANGE thinking in their Spirals than their BLUE/orange and blue/ORANGE predecessors. The GREEN ᵛMEME will gather strength next.

ORANGE/green thinking lets people meet-and-deal very successfully. They are not intimidated by complicated situations, though they may not perceive the full complexity at hand. They handle things, unruffle feathers, calm the waters, act as useful trouble-shooters, make a fine concierge, maitre d', or political campaign front-person. This the thinking of the 'dog robber' who can get whatever is needed as needed, yet leave everyone happy having been finagled into providing it. There is always a certain detachment and it is clear where the ultimate loyalties lie, but services are rendered smoothly and graciously. Victims of its crimes may not care to testify.

The superior talents (and confidence) of the person prevail. A characteristic of the entire ORANGE band is the sense of an unlimited self and limitless possibilities. People centered here are unconstrained by the harsher realities of being. Because of that optimism, they often read more into things than is there, turning 'maybes' into 'absolutelys' and 'somedays' into 'right nows.' When the dreams do not come to pass, their feelings are hurt and they become depressed, though it does not last long if the ORANGE is stronger than the GREEN. 'Pick yourself up, dust yourself off, and start all over again.'

Consciousness of feelings is beginning to increase at ORANGE/green, so this person becomes adroit at interpersonal maneuvers – today's consummate young politician. ORANGE/green polishes the skills of reading what is happening with others, assessing emotions, and making the right moves so they ask: 'How could she know so much about me? We just met, yet she could tell me what I was thinking before I said it.' These appraisals can be quite objective and often rather cold; but the outwardly displayed behavior which follows exudes warmth and camaraderie.

In learning the tricks of reading other people they also better understand how to manage their own images, controlling affect displays and giving the appearance of warmth and concern. However, because of the powerful pull of ORANGE control, they can instantly jerk back from involvement and turn off what seemed to be authentic interest. The demonstrations of warmth are still matters of controlled convenience. ORANGE/green may not have much time or attention for others when busy or distracted, often to the great surprise of those who thought they mattered more.

Those in the Exiting ORANGE/green zone dislike their new-found need for others (seeing it as a weakness), but recognize their importance in achieving objectives. By now one has learned how to use people and integrate them as resources for building mutual success. The hacker gangs now mugging the Internet are probably representative of this 'MEME profile, and the Closed version will find nothing wrong with showing how clever they are at the expense of AT&T or Citibank.

For example, this 'MEME set is common around the Olympic Village as teammates vie for medals against one another at the same time they root on behalf of the squad. When the **GREEN** component is too low, the overall teams are weakened as athletes try to undercut each other without compunction, focusing on **ORANGE** endorsements rather than sport. When a more proper balance is reached, though, the individuals works for personal best while supporting the team to be the top in the meet. It is the same image beauty contestants try to project as the runners-up are announced.

ORANGE/green genuinely wants to be 'the good guy' – virtuous, authentic, and sincere. Yet they have to work at being open and genuine; the affect displays often seem contrived and the self-disclosure forced. Offers of help are generally to assist others in meeting the **ORANGE/green** specifications (**ORANGE** knows it knows best) and to fit their schedules. Concrete decisions are often a struggle since what others think and want is beginning to matter. Polls, surveys, and discussions fill in the confidence gaps that would not have occurred to more sharply-defined Peak **ORANGE**. The foreign policy confusions and domestic wobbling of the Clinton administration are a superb case study of the **ORANGE/green** stack at work.

The very real desire to grow people and fix things is where the residual, well-meaning **ORANGE** control needs manifest themselves. In politics it guides efforts at social engineering – the ultimate laboratory – to grow whole classes of people and give them better health, welfare, and opportunities to contribute according to plans laid by 'the best and the brightest.' The **green** elements include attention to how people feel and a desire to be responsive to those feelings in the situation at hand. That leads to unfulfilled promises and an appearance (not necessarily deserved) of deceptiveness, especially by critics from **BLUE**.

Some **ORANGE/green** makes for a superb mentor in the corporate setting, a fine coach and a teacher who wants every child to excel. However, when the 'MEME set runs organizations there is still a distance between subordinate and superior. The warmth displays at **ORANGE/green** are conditional since people here still feel vulnerable and may become defensive when others know too much about them or delve into their 'private lives.' They need to retain an upper hand, and that often limits how fully committed others are willing to be in working with them. 'Let's all self-disclose our true inner feelings, and you may go first . . .'

ORANGE/green may selectively interpret the truth trying to keep everyone satisfied and compliant. When stories are challenged, they become confused and try to divert attention elsewhere. Another gambit is to play 'poor me' and focus on being misconstrued; the feelings can be quite genuine. Yet that produces a tone of angry disappointment when social schemes – sometimes politically correct for-profit – are thwarted or unappreciated. 'But we meant well; really we did. They just don't understand how good this would have been for them.' The frustration can become overwhelming.

In summation of the intelligences **ORANGE** adds, think about these forces the 'MEME adds to the Spiral:

- a capacity for detailed, disciplined, and focused problem resolution sequences as expressed in the scientific method
- a pragmatic sense that empowers individuals and groups to let go of myths, traditions, and beliefs, thus opening new possibilities within the inevitability of change
- an unquenchable thirst to explore, venture out, experience the novel, and to be the first to discover, invent or conquer the many 'hidden' worlds of knowledge
- a belief in human perfectibility through intelligent hard work and the constant testing of ideas
- a release of the competitive 'juices' that provide self-reinforcement for those who challenge the marketplace, athletic field, or political arena and seek to win the day

To its great credit, this 'MEME is the parent of modern times. It has brought liberation of individuals, technologies, and the willingness to explore ideas. However, it is also the source of the problematic *Life Conditions* that lead many to question whether government is working, how billions of humans can coexist with a reasonable quality of life, and if the planet can support the levels of consumption that characterize this age.

At its Exiting phase, guilt begins to reappear when the spotlight shifts from 'me' toward a 'me and thee' arrangement. Whether it is the **BLUE–GREEN** voice of the 'deep ecology' movement or the **PURPLE–GREEN** chants of the New Agers, the **ORANGE** 'MEME is being shouted down by a renewal of the Communal/Collective 'we' family. Through *Death of a Salesman* Arthur Miller forces his audience to question what 'work' is worth, what a life means, and what choices individuals and families can make to enrich the years they have left. Those kinds of questions lead to **LC**[6].

GREEN *HumanBond*
The Relativistic ᵛMEME

- **Explore the inner beings of self and others**
- **Promote a sense of community and unity**
- **Share society's resources among all**
- **Liberate humans from greed and dogma**
- **Reach decisions through consensus**
- **Refresh spirituality and bring harmony**

At the Core of GREEN – *Life Conditions*[6]:

'Life is for experiencing each moment. We can all come to understand who we are and how wondrous it is to be human if we will only accept that everyone is equal and important. All must share in the joy of togetherness and fulfillment. Each spirit is connected to all others in our community; every soul travels together. We are interdependent beings in search of love and involvement. The community grows by synergizing life forces; artificial divisions take away from everyone. There is an abiding order in the universe for those who are open to it. Bad attitudes and negative beliefs dissolve once we look inside each person and uncover the richness within. Peace and love for all.'

orange/GREEN: Entering Phase

The **GREEN** ᵛMEME is the climax of the First Tier of thinking systems, the culmination of these 'old brain,' subsistence-based modes of living. It is the result of both the successes and failures of the five ᵛMEMEs that have dominated until the last century or so. (As you will see, it is a step behind the level of complexity humanity needs to resolve twenty-first century problems but still represents quite a stretch for the vast majority of people alive today.)

GREEN awakens when BLUE and ORANGE ᵛMEMEs approach the end of their life cycles. The former traps minds in belief systems which are often rigid, intolerant, and full of dogmatic ideology. Pete Seger's old song, *Little Boxes* ('. . . full of ticky-tacky . . . all look just the same . . .'), assaults BLUE's absolutism with GREEN rejection of the brick-hard boundaries and regimentation this post-autonomy mind finds so stifling. While this ᵛMEME is an elaboration of the Communal/Collective family, the boxes are now much more elastic; the rules are fuzzy and walls are covered with roses. Their thorns only prick those who fail GREEN's communitarian tests by exhibiting too much independence and trying to climb out of niches assigned by the group.

As ORANGE weakens, many of those who have 'succeeded' start asking, to borrow from Miss Patty Page's song, 'Is that all there is?' Fancy homes, expensive cars, and material abundance may have been achieved, but at a significant price. As the GREEN ᵛMEME brightens, it illuminates the fact that there is still not parity among human beings. Many have more than they really need, while many more still do without. The glare of environmental fallout is also disturbing – the planet appears to have developed for the worse and residues of the mechanical/chemical age percolate everywhere. Divisive competitiveness makes peace of mind hard to find.

The person who has 'made it' through Peak ORANGE often does not feel genuine acceptance from others (and that begins to matter in the ORANGE/ green range); chickens may come home to roost after cut-throat competition lops off a few too many heads of those whose ghosts linger on; and manipulative strategies that felt so good are now accompanied by pangs of guilt. The children do not feel at home at home.

The rest who have not 'made it' begin to recognize basic inequity in the vertical hierarchy and want to see things level out so all can be 'have enoughs.' Most have read Karl Marx or know someone who has. The ᵛMEME builds interest in legislating behavior for the community's good and lending support to worthy causes that favor the downtrodden and helpless – 'sacrifice now to obtain now for self and others.'

When describing the temperament of the 'Entering orange/GREEN level, Graves called it 'the enticing way of life.' The person draws others unto the self for mutual benefit, anxious to please everyone and find success/prosperity for the group. The ᵛMEME mix is alive and well in organizations promoting animal welfare and advocating children's rights. It is the guiding principle of socially responsible co-ops and the political platform of many Scandinavian politicians.

Interpersonal skills are often at a peak because constructive, warm interaction is so integral to self-satisfaction. Intuition and insight are valuable commodities here, so individuals strive to polish skills like empathetic listening. In organizations moving through this range, 'human relations,' 'sensitivity,' 'diversity,' and 'cultural awareness' reading and training are often mandatory.

In the previous **ORANGE/green** zone others are resources to manipulate and use as necessary, but with kindest regards – aggressive entrepreneurism tempered with humanity. The 'hale fellow well met' gathers support like moths to flame, but there may be unpleasant surprises in store. With the intensified **green** at Entering **orange/GREEN** others are at less risk of being burned, but may instead have to fly in circles until exhausted because of a lack of direction. Now 'feelings' begin to replace the need for 'achievements' that so occupied heavier **ORANGE**'s attention and led to its sense of isolation and loneliness. Entrepreneurism is now tempered by humanity as LC^6 shift focus to the problems of inclusion, affiliation, and large-scale harmony. They grant the luxury of anti-materialism because the previous LC^1 through LC^5 are all now manageable, or so it seems.

On December 14, 1992, *The Wall Street Journal* printed an article entitled 'Business Books Emphasize the Spiritual.' The gist of the piece was that 'greed is out.' It went on to say, 'instead of comparing business to war, the operative metaphor in the new business guides is the corporation as family or tribe. Forget intimidation: hip managers are into "empowerment."' The *Journal* is identifying the **ORANGE** to **GREEN** transition in the business book market, if not in the business schools. Next comes love, acceptance, and spiritual transformations.

Literally thousands of private and public sector organizations are in the throes of **ORANGE/green** to **orange/GREEN** oscillations. From Ben & Jerry's Ice Cream and Apple Computer to the U.S. Army and the Dutch police, issues of lifestyles, organizational responsibility and citizenship, and the company/agency as extended family are occupying key decision makers' time. The bottom line, of necessity, includes much more than dollars; it must make sense once employees become assets to nurture instead of expenses to cut. How people feel about work (and each other *at* work) will join the parade right behind the quality and re-engineering bandwagons. Before teams can self-manage, they must first become teams; and that means 'the company' cannot be an adversary, nor 'the union' a warrior. Both must share common goals on common ground.

The individual in **orange/GREEN** is still entrepreneurial, but needs a circle of friends to join the business in a caring (but profitable!) confederation. Many creative start-ups have been initiated in **orange/GREEN** gatherings of odd ducks, only to flounder because the ducks refused to include a few **ORANGE** lone eagles in marketing and some **BLUE** homing pigeons to keep up with inventory and the accounts. At the extremes, interpersonal dynamics become the focus of the organization's 'culture' on the assumption that productivity follows harmony.

Yet Entering **orange/GREEN** is still unwilling to commit fully and 'let it all hang out.' The **orange** needs for control limit the openness and trust such a culture requires. Risks are to be taken with capital and concepts, not feelings. Instead of complete transparency, we find the jolly-good-fellow who takes pleasure in conviviality and 'meaningful' interaction, but keeps a couple of personal options open. This is the gregarious party animal (who happens to do estate planning) and the sales person who occasionally loses a commission because he or she actually does put the clients' welfare first. (Putting a more ORANGE spin on it, the short-term loss may lead to a long-term relationship that will generate gains if the customer has a strong BLUE or GREEN ᵛMEME active.)

The system is not all sweetness and light. Sometimes orange/GREEN milks good deeds to buy acceptance. You should also beware of 'Orange in Green clothing' – Peak ORANGE or even clever, well-coached RED who knows how to 'talk-the-talk' – that put on a GREEN facade to get something they want. Even when people are living authentically in the orange/GREEN range, they oscillate between 'us' and 'my own right-thinking mind' and you should be aware of which theme is in control during negotiations.

orange/GREEN replaces the certainties of BLUE truth and ORANGE tried-and-true-experience with relativism. With so many equally good possibilities, maybe none is invariably best. Perhaps everyone is right in her/ his own way, one time or another. It is this amorphous, context-sensitive aspect of GREEN which so disturbs clear-cut BLUE and impatient ORANGE – situational ethics, cultural relativism, and Outcome-Based Education (no grades, nobody fails), for example.

The soft edges of GREEN show up in language. Thoughts are modified, padded, and surrounded with verbose dialogue that leaves much room for reinterpretation, rather like the 'Hippie-talk' of the late 1960s or 'Beatnik' coffee house dialogue a decade earlier. Free speech must now be sensitive, aware, and respectful discourse using gender-neutral forms and without implying stereotypes or vertical distinction.

orange/GREEN has already done the Peak ORANGE materialism thing and found it wanting. Now the search is for that 'centeredness' waiting just around the pueblo that can bring real inner peace. One's own Individual/Elite mind is not enough, and the Higher Authority of BLUE is too cut-and-dried. With Communal/Collective spirituality returning, life begins to revolve around the unending quest for enlightenment from a metaphysical guide or practitioner of one healing art or another. New-age orange/GREEN psycho-shamans (and ORANGE marketing themselves as such) replace the PURPLE *curanderas* and medicine men who get lost in the world of individual enterprise; the Sweat Lodge now takes American Express. The use of 'mind-expanding' drugs is always an option in this urgency to explore altered consciousness and reach out and touch the universe. 'Better living through Chemistry' can be applied to karma.

When people are blocked in this zone, life often consists of a series of 'ah, ha!' experiences, awakenings, and growth steps that are, in fact, repetitious and even cyclic. orange/GREEN hops from guru to guru, from one peak experience to another, from one mystical path onto the next. While these enlightening adventures feel good for awhile, the person does not move on the Spiral. If their LC^6, some will begin to ask in quiet moments, 'Why can't I reach the light again?' For others, life in this zone can become a very fulfilling existence, rich with powerful turquoise jewelry, health foods, and well-built habitats for humanity. The ᵛMEMEs thrive in places like northern California; Boulder, Colorado; Auckland; and Amsterdam.

In organizations, you find emphasis on physical/psychological wellness programs (which decrease health care costs and increase productivity), self-managed teams (to let workers take more direct responsibility, reduce the need for supervisors, and convince employees top management believes they are trustworthy), and diversity/sensitivity training to help personnel recognize differences and reduce interpersonal problems. These efforts fail when they are conducted in **BLUE** terms – types of people based on race, gender, etc. – and without attention to how different people in those categories actually think.

When **orange/GREEN** programs work, 'cold' engineers may rediscover their humanity (and their children) and 'computer nerds' find how much they actually enjoy working with their colleagues. Gender equity becomes fact, not 'feminist' rhetoric. Police officers discover that the 'them' of the usual 'us versus them' split is a complex blend of personalities, world views, and needs. So long as these efforts do not attempt to undercut the essential, stabilizing **BLUE** – the belief in responsibility to a power beyond the self and its basic organizing principles – they can serve well.

In the extra-personal domain, **orange/GREEN** enhances the awareness of ecological systems. The mechanized success of **ORANGE** reduces biologic diversity as the 'fittest' take over without regard for long-range consequences and environmental contamination. 'A little pollution' is the price of successful competition and upping the **ORANGE** standard of living, said the Soviet nuclear establishment before Chernobyl. Taking a few controlled risks is necessary for improving what we have to make an even better future.

In response to the excesses of the **ORANGE** ᵛMEME the next LC^6 problems put regulating uncontrolled growth and protecting endangered living things high on the list. The awakening of the **GREEN** ᵛMEME puts ecology – the interconnections among plants, animals, humans, and place – on the front burner. The difficulties arise when **ORANGE** politicians negotiate the laws and **BLUE** turns their enforcement into a religion.

GREEN: Peak Phase

At the peak, **GREEN** is communitarian, egalitarian, and consensual. The person is energized and enthused by cooperative ventures. The human spirit is invigorated by association and enriched by sharing positive vibrations. As **ORANGE** individualistic needs dim further, the group takes on a life of its own. It is more open than the extended-family, kinship-dependent tribes of **PURPLE** and lacks the doctrinaire strictures of **BLUE**, but the Communal/Collective synergy is back full force, ready to flatten unfair **ORANGE** vertical pay scales and redistribute resources so those in need will never go without.

The workplace is team-oriented with much discussion and sharing of ideas and feelings. Everyone has an opportunity to speak and contribute. The short-term cost of **GREEN** decision-making is expenditure of considerable time and economic resources; but the initial 70% agreement it builds is augmented by a high degree of input and near 100% commitment to decisions once they are made. So long as reasonably intelligent and interested people with access to good information are involved, the process can be quite constructive.

GREEN FUZZY: Togetherness, harmony, and acceptance drive decisions

The group orientation of **GREEN** resolves the problems of isolation and loneliness that rise at the end of **ORANGE** and become so prominent in **LC⁶**. By abandoning the competitiveness and one-upmanship, at least within the immediate group, one reconnects with others in forming extended communities that offer support and meet the belonging needs that endure from **PURPLE**. Communes, 'liberal' religious orders, and volunteer health care agencies shelter the **GREEN** 'MEME. Though sometimes naive and tearful, it appears as youngsters take on social causes through church and school groups, helping the elderly, cleaning up the environment, or tutoring children younger than themselves. Often, the helper actually gains more than the helpee so long as open systems are involved.

FUZZY: Metaphysics and feelings begin to replace old scientific analysis

Spirituality returns on Entering **orange/GREEN** as non-denominational, non-sectarian 'unity.' Just as Einstein sought a unified theory that could rationalize Newton's physics and the sub-atomic world, **GREEN** seeks consolidation of the soul and the forces of nature through respect and even awe, but not mystical superstition or prescriptive rules. To paraphrase William James, one seeks harmony with the unseen order of things when this 'MEME is strong.

Thinking becomes mellower with the **ORANGE** components dimmed away, rather like a non-profit folk music festival. Anxiety is replaced with love, constraints are unlearned, and the doctrine of competitiveness yields to themes of sharing, understanding, appreciating, and tolerance. Only judgementalism may be judged harshly, for **GREEN** can be very rigid in its demands for 'open-mindedness' (on the group's egalitarian, homogenized terms, of course) and is quite willing to go to war for liberation of the oppressed and human rights. Unfortunately, in today's politics, the 'MEME's suggestions → protestations → sanctions → peace-keepers cycle often lacks a **BLUE** policy foundation or underlying **ORANGE** strategy. Like all of the First Tier 'MEMEs, **GREEN** can be quite dismissive of (or blind to) the rest of the Spiral in the belief that its way is the way, not a way.

FUZZY: Plenty of room for everyone

When this 'MEME does become prominent, gender roles are derigidified, glass ceilings opened, affirmative action plans are implemented, and social class distinctions blurred. Since **GREEN** authority lies within the group's mind, not with an external source, comparisons with others are less relevant; everyone is 'in it' together. Competition is between 'us' and other groups for benefits 'we' will then distribute, not individual acclaim.

What does it look like? Whereas **BLUE** leads to standardized, military-type uniforms (or Mao jackets, etc.) and **ORANGE** favors Armani and Donna Karan suits (or whatever is in fashion), **GREEN**'s outfits are un-tailored so as to make everyone feel comfortable and able to fit-in – natural fibres, authentic messages, tie-dyed with artful meaning. That does not imply there is not a set of norms at work; this is still a communal 'MEME and it may have little room for polyester, much less furs. However, those specifications are intended to foster togetherness and clarify separation from the consumptive excesses of **ORANGE**. Parodies of 'proper' attire may be designed to put **BLUE** authority in its place – tuxedo T-shirts, rock stars in military uniforms, and flag-print panties.

FUZZY: We, the people who share a common vision, have our weaknesses

GREEN is susceptible to group-think. The pressures to be supportive of collective decisions and actions can be extreme. The need to fit in and feel accepted may overwhelm the person's willingness to disagree – 'go along to get along' – and lead to moves which will be regretted when other 'MEMEs take over again.

Another vulnerability is collective guilt. Whereas **BLUE** feels guilt for personal transgressions against authority and the rules, **GREEN** feels it for short-comings of the group – a nation, a race, a company, an economic class, etc. Whatever the significant reference is, 'We have let them (the poor, the children, the battered women, the refugees, the at-risk youth, etc.) down.' If they have gumption and good **ORANGE** representation, reparations are in order. In the process, the sacrifice will make **GREEN** feel better. Some Japanese–Americans were paid for mistreatment during World War II. Groups of American Indians are suing to regain ownership of former tribal lands. A number of African-Americans propose recompense is due for slavery and the racial discrimination that followed.

In the corporate world, guilt appears during reductions in force when the community is being split apart. These times are often as painful for those who stay as those who go. Production suffers along with morale and discipline is difficult. Support groups, outplacement, retraining, and voluntary cutbacks help, but pain is a given.

Even in less stressful circumstances, extremes of **GREEN** lead to 'burn-out' in health care, law enforcement, and education. The pressures of caring can become overwhelming and people centered in heavy **GREEN** are at-risk for depression and suicide. When someone becomes frustrated because '. . . there is nothing I can do to help . . .' it is important for the group to step in, rotate the person to a different (less punishing) job, or implement peer counseling to process the feelings rather than allow them to bottle up and then explode. Public safety and the military have learned about the need for this in terms of traumatic stress; it is just as important in schools and business, especially when the **GREEN** ᵛMEME is active.

FUZZY: Communicating both content and feelings

On the positive side, this heightened empathy produces great customer relations in a retail business and bedside manner in health care. The coffee pot is always on and clients genuinely feel welcomed. From the pragmatic **ORANGE** perspective, some **GREEN** thinking is advantageous in 'reading' customers and preparing a sales presentation, although other ᵛMEMEs may be required to close the deal. It is sad how rarely healthy **GREEN** is found in the service industries and how quickly it is 'burned' when dealing with the harsh realities of Joan and John Q. Public, whether in the mall or hospital room. The comment that '. . . nice guys finish last . . .' is a cynical view of what happens when Communal/Collective ᵛMEMEs are 'eaten' by the self-expressive Individual/Elites.

Part of that sensation of warmth is the abundant communication in **GREEN** organizations – much chat, active (though not insidious) grapevines, and informal networking. On the down side, security can be a problem when everyone believes all have a right to know anything. While **ORANGE** enjoys debating to win and **BLUE** stands up for its beliefs, **GREEN** discussions dissolve conflict, build consensus, and enhance everybody's feelings of inclusion in the group. **GREEN** is low in dogmatism – many beliefs are quite acceptable and no single truth is 'it' for long – but high in rigidity. People in this range tolerate disagreement only so long as it is approached in **GREEN** ways, with gentility and through the collective. 'Come on strong,' act 'aggressive,' or sound mercenary and **GREEN** swells up indignantly, a phenomenon which shocks those naive enough to equate **GREEN**-ness with softness and unconditional love of everyone.

Other interesting traits related to this 'MEME include suggestibility, kindness, and consistency. **GREEN** shares both emotions and material goods, but participants in the transaction *must* belong to the group, commit to it, self-disclose, and contribute what they can. Those refusing to join in and accede to the group's norms are in trouble; freedom extends only so far as the group decides is appropriate. Go beyond and face censure, emotional punishment, and efforts to trigger guilt.

FUZZY: To bring diversity together into community

Whereas **BLUE** categorizes people into groups by ethnicity, age, gender, language, religion, etc. and **ORANGE** sorts people vertically according to socioeconomics and their status in some pecking order, **GREEN** believes in bringing diverse people together so long as they are willing to share in the common experience. The factors that produce discrimination for **BLUE** are used to balance and level by this 'MEME. Everyone is relative to the situation now, not their history or particular heritage. Their unique contributions – language usage, values, lifestyles – enhance the whole. As **GREEN** intensifies, so does the desire to level people out of classified hierarchies into clusters of equals with shared possibilities and few judgments. Sometimes the balancing is mandatory.

Individuals benefit through elevation of the group as a whole; society is bettered through collaboration of groups. Social safety nets, investment in people-oriented programs, and 'socialized' health care often run hand-in-hand with **GREEN** communitarianism. (President and Mrs Clinton badly misread the influence of the 'MEME when proposing national health care in 1994). Virtuous ideas run out of gas (and into red ink) when blocked by the 'MEME's finite competencies and easily mocked vulnerabilities. When problems like immigration controls arise, even more complex organizing principles are required to integrate and align resources to achieve effective results for all concerned. We will meet these at **YELLOW**.

All the talk of harmony and warmth can drop away quickly when other factions compete for the same group niche **GREEN** occupies. Just because the 'MEME is humanistic does not mean it is soft or a pushover. Just watch the voters in California. Because of its proximity to **ORANGE**, interest still lies with success, well-being, and accomplishment of good works, though not necessarily economic prosperity. While the overall good of humankind may be in the mission statement, the community of equals looks out for its own first. Even **GREEN** organizations have a deep imperative to survive.

FUZZY: The boundaries of tolerance and acceptance

The ᵛMEME is not wishy-washy, either, although its positions can be anywhere along the political spectrum. At the extremes, the unforgiving liberalism of 'political correctness' is just as stringent as rigid **BLUE** 'discrimination,' just as judgmental and self-righteous from the left instead of the right. Narrow **GREEN** excludes those who choose not to join the community, whatever the unifying principle might be. However, if one only expresses a desire to grow and raise one's consciousness, the ᵛMEME system will be tolerant of just about anything from insiders.

Like its cousin, **BLUE**, **GREEN** espouses a preference for the plain, not the fancy; it appreciates simplicity without the sacrificial sternness. The ᵛMEME wants enough to get the job done, but categorically rejects the displays of affluence and success so necessary to making **ORANGE** happy. These people enjoy making do with less and divesting themselves of materialistic encumbrances. Thoreau and other philosophers have written of the joys of minimalist living, just as many Peace Corps volunteers find **GREEN** fulfillment in giving up the trappings of the **ORANGE** First-World for enrichment in a more 'natural' existence that relies more on inner capacities than outer things.

Carried to the extremes, this reliance leads directly to the great **GREEN** delusion that each human can develop to the fullest, can maximize their being, and can reach a state of completeness much akin to Maslow's self-actualization. Whereas **ORANGE** is often guilty of the arrogant belief that 'I am far superior to thou,' the **GREEN** ᵛMEME builds a collective haughtiness that says 'Any one of us can be anything he/she chooses. We all have limitless potential. WE are number 1!'

If you care to believe that – and many people right now desperately do – so be it. Understand, though, that in terms of Spiral Dynamics you are denying that people have different capacities, reach their own limits, and that the range of possibilities for each one of us may not be the entire range but that portion of the range our unique *Life Conditions* have opened. And by doing that, you tell those who have not 'succeeded' by awakening their **GREEN** that there is something wrong and they need to get fixed, that they should have made it but did not. Perhaps they did and it is the critic who ought reconsider.

In this drive to grow people, **GREEN** often invests finite resources on underdogs and 'losing' causes (**ORANGE** tends to do the opposite and only invest in proven winners). The ᵛMEME attaches itself to 'special' cases with empathy for the needful, but sometimes at the expense of the apparently 'just average' ones who could excel with just a little bit more attention. Finding an appropriate balance between helping the needy reach a baseline and helping the normal become above average is an ongoing challenge for schools, domestic helping agencies, and investors of foreign aid funds.

Speaking of American economic assistance to the new South Africa and the percentage going to U.S. consultants working there, a state department official (with tongue slightly in cheek), remarked that '. . . those foreign aid dollars are coming back inside the [Baltimore/Washington] Beltway where they belong.' When **GREEN** is proposing that all sacrifice for a common benefit, be sure there is accountability and a concrete outcome. Far too many grand schemes turn into Black holes from which time and energy never merge, but which become self-perpetuating bureaucracies administered by **BLUE** and milked by **ORANGE**.

FUZZY: Relativity can be uncertain

Just as we cautioned about **ORANGE** in **GREEN** clothing earlier, be wary of **GREEN** talking **TURQUOISE**. **GREEN** thinkers are almost as inclined to grandiose self-appraisals of heightened consciousness as **ORANGE** is to its cleverness. But while **ORANGE** inflates competencies and intelligence – the resumé variables – **GREEN** imagines heightened awareness and contact with the higher plane of understanding – the 'oooh' factors. There can be a fine, ethereal detachment here as one relates to others through peer-defined enlightenment. While always speaking in terms of 'us, we, and our' level, this less than healthy form of **GREEN** looks down on anyone who does not share the ethereal interest or the lingo.

This spiritual confusion has led many mainstream **BLUE** American churches to scrambling about trying to build programs that reach the nouveau-**GREEN** who want experiences more than traditional sermonizing and threats or **ORANGE** entertainment and showmanship. While more traditionalist factions are vacillating in the **ORANGE–BLUE** zone and wondering what to do, another segment of the post-Yuppie movement is traveling from **ORANGE** toward **GREEN** fast. The 'community churches' that fit these ᵛMEMEs offer alternatives which fit LC^6, yet allow for some networking and moral anchors, as well. Their difficulty will be to design programs that can also reach LC^7 – a complex world where all of the ᵛMEMEs have the power to impact all the others at the same time the human population grows logarithmically and resources diminish. For many people, the rules of **BLUE** may actually link better with the principles of **YELLOW**.

FUZZY: To sacrifice self for love since everyone is beautiful, in their own way

When the **GREEN** ᵛMEME is dominant, being liked and accepted is more important than winning or material gain. Self-worth is strongly influenced by messages from one's social network. There are still forms of manipulation, but through collective guilt, withholding of affect, and control of inclusion by the group. In this range, whatever the community thinks is best, true, right, and proper. Its members accept each other unquestioningly, thus insuring reciprocal acceptance for themselves. There is great tolerance for differences (it keeps the group intact) and legitimizing of alternatives in lifestyle and behavior so long as they do not harm. Taken to extremes, this can foster excessive permissiveness and the absence of limits that has confused much of the Generation X – even the name is an unknown. But, then, 'Love means never having to say you're sorry.' Extremes of this ⱽMEME lead to the 'bleeding heart' mindset often charged against the 'social worker types' by police officers who prefer clear-cut **BLUE** versions of right and wrong.

Excessive **GREEN**, like any ⱽMEME that grows too much, produces a blind-spot. It leads, for example, to misunderstanding of **PURPLE**'s capacity for both healthy and negative behaviors – the romanticized myth of 'the noble savage' and films like Kevin Costner's charmingly **GREEN** *Dances with Wolves*. When viewing through **GREEN** filters, we deprive people of their right to a full human spectrum and paint them in false colors. The ⱽMEME's egalitarian homogenizing offers the false hope that 'there's no such thing as a bad boy' – only misunderstood, misguided youth. There is adamant refusal to accept that there may be brains 'broken' beyond repair by current treatments. On the other hand, when **GREEN** is too weak, hard-nosed punitiveness does not even consider giving second chances – 'Off with her head!' 'Three strikes and you're out!' Justice is available for the economically advantaged and proven True Believers, no one else.

Those disparities put **GREEN** at odds with doctrinaire **BLUE** because of differences in flexibility, easy access to right/wrong, and importance of feelings versus beliefs. Find someone with both healthy **BLUE** and **GREEN** and you have a genuinely caring person who is firmly anchored in strong beliefs, but may grant you the full and free expression of yours.

Prepare for some conflict with **ORANGE**, as well. People centered in **GREEN** can be disturbed both by their own **ORANGE** histories and those competitive, profit-seeking, self-satisfied associates still quite happy being there. The emerging role of this ⱽMEME in a free-enterprise, capitalistic, individual-oriented, LC^5-dominated society is going to be the best show around for the next few years. **ORANGE/green** President Bill and **orange/GREEN** Hillary Clinton are only the tip of a communitarian iceberg which will turn progressively **GREEN**-er.

GREEN/yellow: Exiting Phase

The move along the Spiral from Peak **GREEN** comes with doubts about the effectiveness of collectivism and a resurgence of the individuality that has been stifled within LC^6. The person begins to feel a surge of personal power from a mind that can reach out to the universe with or without hand holding inside the group. Positive relationships with others are important components of being, but not the purpose of it. Subsistence-level, First Tier concerns become less important as spirituality meets up with quantum mechanics.

The first disillusionment with **GREEN** begins as the pendulum swings the locus of control from outside (Communal/Collective) back within the Individual/Elite family. The first **LC**[7] questions arise about the cost of so much caring, both in terms of economics and human energy. In organizations, profitability and productivity drop while costs unexpectedly increase – entitlements come home to roost.

Societies in Exiting **orange/GREEN** begin to realize how expensive it is to provide for everyone without requiring some kind of contribution other than being 'present' for the handout. This really becomes apparent when easy immigration swells the rolls of needy. Most of the noble Great Society programs have not worked (**GREEN** ideas implemented by **ORANGE** and regulated by **BLUE**). Those who have tried socialism as their version of **GREEN** find it is not *the* answer either (usually **GREEN** implemented by **BLUE** and subsidized by **ORANGE**). Several northern European states are developmentally at this zone of the Spiral and will either be facing up to Second Tier problems or trying to handle regressions into avaricious **ORANGE**, hard-nosed **BLUE**, and tumultuous **RED** very soon. In this light it is important to remember that ᵛMEMEs do not exist in isolation, but in context of what has developed before. Large-scale change will occur simultaneously at multiple levels, and managing that kind of complexity is the hallmark of **LC**[7] problems ahead.

At this Exiting stage, one decides that time and resources can be used more effectively if the communal system is not so entrenched and entitled. Sometimes the business of **GREEN** helping entities is keeping the stake-holders of the agency – clients and servers alike – together in an enduring relationship. Individuals' goals are sometimes thwarted for the sake of group interests and they find themselves restrained by harmony.

If clumsily managed, attention to feelings and group process slows outputs. The tolerant fluidity of **GREEN** thinking also makes rapid, focused, hard-hitting responses to changing conditions difficult, especially when consensus must be found prior to action and anyone acting unilaterally risks rejection. Everyone must have their opportunity to participate before things happen; otherwise, there is resentment and more feathers to unruffle. Meanwhile, a skillful **ORANGE** competitor takes over the market.

In the **GREEN/yellow** zone the self begins to reassert its influence. The person again dares to say 'me' and 'I' as much as 'we' and 'our.' They begin looking outside the team/community at alternative ideas, finding relevance in other groups and competent individuals. If the freedom becomes dis-harmonizing, such a person will generally back off and return to the fold. Significant energy and/or profound problems are required to push them out of the comfort of the **GREEN** nest. In spite of the personal price that membership demands, it is worth while so long as **LC**[6] are strong.

The beginning of the end of this 'MEME's dominance is when the person begins (again) to get things done, and done well, all alone. The collective process just does not match up to the complexity of LC^7 issues because it consumes too much time and energy. The price of keeping everybody happy is untenably high; the cost of harmony sometimes too steep. The 'MEME filters the world to suit its definitions and abilities.

The person stepping out of the First Tier sees too much, from too many new angles to accept simplicity that is not here. With LC$^{1-6}$ now history, whole-Spiral judgments begin to replace **GREEN** relativism. The viability of both individual and group action increases, and the person's ability to handle simultaneous diversity and complexity also expands. A bit of disharmony becomes natural and one's tolerance for open contradictions grows. **GREEN/yellow** begins to express frustration and impatience at the group's needs, but still tries not to disrupt it. In addition to Scandinavia and the Netherlands, you can find these 'MEMEs alive and well in New Zealand, Canada, Switzerland, and even India.

Perhaps the most significant marker of the Exiting **GREEN/yellow** stage is the dropping away of fear. Life is life, after all. Tribal safety, raw power, salvation for all eternity, individual success, and the need to be accepted diminish in importance. Instead, there is growing curiosity about just being alive in an expansive universe. The person realizes how incredibly much there is to know and explore while accepting his or her own finite life. One begins to look at the group objectively, yet with concern. There is no deliberate rejection of belonging, but the need to be a part of something is fading. Bigger issues appear on the horizon that are beyond the scope of any community to handle within itself. A very different kind of thinking is about to emerge as the **YELLOW** 'MEME awakens the Second Tier of human existence.

Stepping Over to the Second Tier

The First Tier of human development, the 'action man' phase of the **BEIGE** through **GREEN** ᵛMEMEs, is the culmination of our primate nature. Watching the evening news, it sometimes seems we have inherited the breeze, not the wind. In spite of technological (read: tool-using) sophistication, our pecking orders, gender roles, political structures, and propensity toward violence still correlate remarkably well with those of our Earthly cohabitants.

The brightening of every new ᵛMEME is a major step in human development. But the **GREEN** to **YELLOW** transition is, as Graves called it, 'a momentous leap' which takes us over from the First Tier's Subsistence Levels to the Second Tier's Being levels. This is not just another step along the developmental staircase. The **GREEN** problems in LC^6 include those of all the previous worlds, LC$^{1, 2, 3, 4, \& 5}$ and often resonate with them. With LC^7, ᵛMEMEs almost start over, something like a musical theme repeated but in a different key. The Second Tier ᵛMEMEs are not caught up in the harmonics of the Subsistence levels; they can cooperate without singing along.

LC^7 introduces complexity beyond even the best First Tier thinking – the Humpty Dumpty Effect at work. Mega-organizations and mega-population masses exist because the subsistence problems are understood, if not fully under control. That introduces mega-problems that make these New Times which definitely call for New Thinking.

The perplexing issues and chaotic events in the last decades of this century are overwhelming the institutions and processes we have thus far developed. There are many crises – ecological, political, health care, race/ethnicity, economics, social – blinking on the radar scope for anyone who looks. Many people are arguing that Chicken Little was right; the ozone-depleted sky is falling. But as Graves declared: 'It [the **GREEN** system] must break down in order to free energy for the jump into the G–T [**YELLOW**] state, the first level of being. This is where the leading edge of man is today.'

When all the **GREEN** King's Horses and Men cannot fix Humpty Dumpty, a new perspective appears. It rides up like a knight who has seen the whole world, ready to find new interconnections and make a fresh synthesis. Bring on the new glue, tell Humpty Dumpty there is hope, and welcome to the world of the **YELLOW** 'MEME.

YELLOW *FlexFlow*
The Systemic 'MEME

- **Accept the inevitability of nature's flows and forms**
- **Focus on functionality, competence, flexibility, and spontaneity**
- **Find natural mix of conflicting 'truths' and 'uncertainties'**
- **Discovering personal freedom without harm to others or excesses of self-interest**
- **Experience fullness of living on an Earth of such diversity in multiple dimensions**
- **Demand integrative and open systems**

At the Core of YELLOW – *Life Conditions*[7]:

'Viability must be restored to a disordered world endangered by the cumulative effects of the first six systems on the earth's environment and populations. The purpose of living is to be independent within reason; knowledgeable so much as possible; and caring, so much as realistic. Yet I am my own person, accountable to myself, an island in an archipelago of other people. Continuing to develop along a natural pathway is more highly valued than striving to have or do. I am concerned for the world's conditions because of the impact they have on me as part of this living system.'

green/YELLOW: Entering Phase

On Entering **green/YELLOW** the quest for peace of mind continues, but it is no longer a singular objective. The interactive universe is becoming more intriguing than autonomy or even community. The order-seeking **GREEN** collectivism goes onto the shelf with the rest of the First Tier 'MEMEs, ready for use but no longer in control. Acceptance and harmony are peripheral to happiness. What others think is not critical, only interesting. Self-managed teams are means, not ends. The view through **YELLOW** glasses is clear.

At the Entering **green/YELLOW** range, other people's opinions still weigh heavily. Their input can sway decisions as much emotionally as rationally. But tempered individualism is also rising from the collective, now without confinement to **ORANGE** islands of independence or tough **RED** exploitiveness. This interdependence releases one to be as he or she chooses on personal terms, sometimes seeking inclusion and cooperating. If appropriate, however, the same person may become cold and ruthless as necessary.

With the shift toward Second Tier thinking the conceptual space of human beings is greater than the sum of all the previous levels combined with a 'logarithmic' (Graves' term) increase in degrees of behavioral freedom. Thus, when individuals or groups thinking through **YELLOW** are given a task, they generally get more and better results while expending less time and effort. They often approach the activity in surprising ways others would not even have considered. This is more than efficiency; it reflects the activation of thus-far uncommitted brain-power. Of course, the problems are also an order of magnitude more complex and dangerous.

Though it may sound like we are describing a new breed of human or meta-magical organization, the **YELLOW** 'MEME is latent in every normal brain. The point is that its power is awakened in only a few of us at this stage in our history because LC⁷s do not yet seem that sharp. Once outside the First Tier, ideas become multidimensional. People moving from **GREEN** toward **YELLOW** tolerate, even enjoy, paradoxes and uncertainties. As the group's magnetism weakens, there seem to be many plausible approaches to doing a thing – **BLUE**'s search for true meaning and purpose in life, **ORANGE**'s drive to excel, **RED**'s need for power and conquest, and the **PURPLE** urge to draw together in a protective circle. In their healthy forms, all contribute to maintaining the integrity of the Spiral. Few ideas are sacred; all are subject to review and upgrades to more functionality.

Dogmatism remains low as **YELLOW** brightens. But rigidity, a major problem for **GREEN** (in spite of its avowed liberality) extends into the Entering **green/YELLOW** range. The 'rightness' of the team is hard to abandon or deny. There are still shackles on diversity and individual freedom because of expectations that one tries to fit in to the collective's norms. These obligations are replaced by objective principles in Peak **YELLOW** and rigidity fades away.

YELLOW: Peak Phase

As **YELLOW** peaks, scales drop from our eyes enabling us to see, for the first time, the legitimacy of all of the human systems awakened to date. They are forms of human existence that have a right to be. The systems are seen as dynamic forces that, when healthy, contribute to the overall viability of the Spiral and, as a result, to the continuation of life itself.

The LC⁷s that awaken the **YELLOW** ᵛMEME echo **BEIGE**-like survival questions, but in the context of a fast-moving, information-laden, highly interactive world. The landscape is now strewn with the wreckage and glories of the first six human systems. **YELLOW** senses that successful human living in the First Tier has put everything in jeopardy. Yet the complex *Life Conditions* that jeopardize the very survival of species Homo sapiens are also opening unprecedented opportunities. Clearly, new societal priorities and modes of decision-making will be required in such a milieu. As we have tried to demonstrate in the first two sections of this book, New Times require New Thinking.

A FlexFlow Perspective

YELLOW generates a FlexFlow perspective. This view honors value system differences and facilitates the movement of people up and down the human Spiral. This produces a sense of stratification, a recognition of the layered dynamics of human systems operating within people and societies. If **PURPLE** is sick, it needs to be made well. If **RED** is running amuck, the raw energy must be channeled. If **BLUE** turns sour and becomes punitive, it must be reformed. Since many of our social 'messes' are caused by the interaction of people at different levels, such 'messes' can only be sorted out through the **YELLOW** complex of intelligences and resources.

YELLOW is 'flexible' in that it can enter the conceptual worlds of the first six systems and interact with them on their frequencies, speaking their psychological languages. **YELLOW** respects (while not necessarily agreeing with) their world views, modes of expression, and unique habits, customs, and cultures.

YELLOW is 'flowing' in that it is in touch with the natural evolutionary processes that appear to characterize our kind. Each system is seen as a next step, not the final one. As Graves remarked: 'each successive stage, wave, or level of existence is a state through which developing people pass on their way to other states of being.'

The **YELLOW** mind sees the ebbing and flowing of human systems all over the planet. These, rather than ethnic cores, cultural or national diversities, or even political structures, determine the interactions of peoples and societies. **YELLOW** gets behind the scenes in a hurry and acts directly on the deepest dynamics that are causing the problem. Much like the electricity company linemen who can restore power after a storm or the creative minds that, with a twist here and there, straighten out the Rubik's Cube, **YELLOW** thinking people are able to fix problems while others fret, manipulate, query higher authority, form study groups, or play theory games.

Of course, not everybody actually wants problems fixed in spite of what they claim. There are many variations on the struggle industry – racialism, sexism, the prison business, etc. – that depend on unresolved difficulties for their livelihoods. Actually getting at the root causes puts the solution providers out of work. When a First Tier 'MEME finds a niche that fits its interests and competencies, it will fight to keep that niche open, even though the overall Spiral may suffer in the process.

YELLOW's internal controls

The **YELLOW** 'MEME thinks and acts from an inner-directed core. The individual gyroscopes that enable the person to keep balance in a paradoxical world spin within the principled, knowledgeable self. Such people have strong ethical anchors of their own reasoned choosing, derived from many sources, but are not entrapped by rigid rules based in external dogma or mandates of authority. While they can readily admit to needing others to accomplish a task, they are not emotionally needful (as **GREEN** tends to be).

Graves observed the dropping away of the compulsions and anxieties (fear) from the previous levels, thus enhancing the person's ability to take a contemplative attitude and rationally appraise realities. As fear receded, the quantity and quality of good ideas and solutions to problems increased dramatically. With **YELLOW** active one avoids falling into the sink holes in any of the systems, from **ORANGE**'s unbridled ambition to **GREEN**'s naive altruism. The person is neither intimidated nor cavalier in the face of complexity. Rather, one develops confidence in the self-generated messages and instructions that emanate from one's core beliefs. And, the Spiral provides a reassuring pathway through turbulence and uncertainty.

YELLOW belongs in the family of systems that are expressive rather than sacrificial. As such, it will not, like the moth, fly into anybody's open flame. Do not expect it to sacrifice self on behalf of a commune, a tradition, your Truth, or humanity at large. There is no **YELLOW** sack cloth to go with guilt-laden ashes. It truly hears and responds to the beat of its own drummer. In doing so, it measures self against self rather than self against others. Instead of being isolated loners, though, **YELLOW** thinkers can function singly or in groups, based on the situation and output requirements. Ultimately, one interprets the world through a self-prism, making individual choices in a cafeteria of options and scenarios.

Such assessments flow from an idea of self that has matured beyond **RED** egocentrism or **ORANGE** hubris and autonomy. Think of it as positive or high self-esteem based on information as much as emotion. This enlightened self-acceptance acknowledges shortcomings and faults, and has even forgiven self for failings, but factors these distortions into the decision-making process. Such a person would even disqualify himself from participating in a critical decision if he was too full of internal emotional clutter around a person, issue or event.

Some Gravesian YELLOW Nuggets

- The Existence Ethic is the foundation stone for behavior since it is rooted in knowledge and reality.
- What is right yesterday may not be seen as right tomorrow.
- Some behavior that was wrong yesterday will always be wrong, just as some behavior that was right yesterday may or may not be right today.
- If it is realistic and appropriate to the circumstances to be happy, then it is good to be happy. If it is realistic to suffer, then suffering is proper behavior.
- If the situation calls for authoritarianism, then it is proper to be an authoritarian; and if the situation calls for democracy, one should be democratic. 'Good authority' that sets necessary limits is a lost art in many families and schools, having been confused with punitiveness, regimentation, and rigidity. At the same time, 'democracy' has almost been deified as the definitive, universal end-state model for decision-making, whether the active ᵛMEMEs in a group can handle it or not.
- Values come from the magnificence of existence rather than selfish or group interests. They are inherent within the nature of life itself – fundamental, natural law.

FLOW: YELLOW is open to learning at any time and from any source

While complex learning involves an array of higher-order thinking skills, it does not depend on raw IQ scores or formal education. Rather, it can be characterized by the knack of information gathering, the ability to access knowledge on multiple levels, the mental energy and discipline to carry through long-term tasks, and a sense of awe and playful delight with the new and novel.

Since **YELLOW** occupies a conceptual world of continuous change and variety, the capacities to observe cleanly and learn quickly are essential. A life-long interest in learning and experimentation is, therefore, a given. **YELLOW**-based thinkers will identify the level of Spiral complexity of the information to be learned and will activate the ᵛMEME-specific learning style that will access it. If that which is to be learned requires the patience, authoritarian climate, and self-denial inherent with **BLUE**, that system will be accessed. If information acquisition requires comparisons with others, then on turns **ORANGE**. If collaboration, then **GREEN** brightens.

These people will, likewise, activate any of the vast First Tier resources within themselves, ranging from fact recall to intuitive day dreams, in a deliberate Second Tier way. Obviously, they will break free from the bonds of the past and the expectations of others in generating fresh insights and new directions. Yet they will build upon the rich traditions and already-invented wheels from the past instead of rejecting them out of hand. You will not find much arrogance or smug self-satisfaction with this 'MEME's sphere.

YELLOW learns a remarkable amount when doing something, much of it peripheral to the task at hand and often suprising to friends and associates. 'How do you know that?' they will inquire. This virtual reality-type brain can explore many parallel versions of being, cross compare them, and select appropriate bits and pieces from each. YELLOW thinkers are adept at integrating complexity and finding clear pathways. Life is a mosaic of tiles without cement which can be rearranged to make the most appropriate picture of existence, at a given time.

FLOW: YELLOW thinkers rely on what's necessary, natural, and next

While the GREEN system is often full of idealism and human centered concerns, YELLOW may be abrupt in wanting 'to get on with it.' It does focus on what is necessary and has less interest participation in social amenities or interplay. YELLOW does penetrate to the core of an issue. When it is in a Closed condition, it appears uncaring if not downright ruthless. Healthier Open YELLOW will be more tolerant of needs from elsewhere on the Spiral – PURPLE's ceremonial greeting; RED's shakedown and arm wrestling; BLUE's agenda-setting and sign-in; ORANGE's handshakes and status jousting; and GREEN's hugs and warm, touchy-feely introductions.

When YELLOW thinking begins to move through an organization or community, you will notice the gradual disappearance of fancy offices, status symbols, hierarchies of privilege, or any of the adornments of authority or power. These changes are not driven by GREEN egalitarian, sacrificial motives. Instead, expressive functionality and 'who-knows-most-about-what' are the highly valued commodities, regardless of official credentials or power of the office. Less becomes more. Minimalist structures replace grandiose schemes and elegant simplicity beats ostentation whenever ORANGE yields control to YELLOW.

Authority in YELLOW is contextual. The best equipped and most capable gains authority, regardless of rank, tenure, or even feelings. Competence, knowledge, skills, and insight that match the needs at hand are the dominant factors. Again, what is 'natural' to the occasion is what will prevail. People begin to do more for themselves through an awakening of individual responsibility and personal autonomy. What is actually necessary to get the job done, or perform the task, or add value to a process become the primary concerns.

YELLOW is attracted to what is natural in contrast to what is artificial or contrived, the way things actually work, the most appropriate technology for the task, a symbolic preference for playing on real grass instead of plastic Astroturf. This is not a call for a lifestyle full of granola and berries or an exclusively L. L. Bean wardrobe. Plastic, a fast-food meal, and a Saville Row suit may all be appropriate at a given time, in a specific circumstance.

YELLOW understands the uniqueness of the conceptual and personal worlds each of the previous 'MEMEs creates. What is 'natural' for PURPLE in terms of rites, ritual, and mysticism will not be so for BLUE or ORANGE. Architectural preferences, acceptable living conditions, ways of learning, concepts of 'the family,' and even expressions of religion will vary because what is deemed to be 'natural.' This understanding gives rise to such familiar statements as 'different strokes for different folks,' 'different hypes for different types,' 'it takes all kinds,' and 'to each his own.'

YELLOW's objective is to find means of supplying adequacy so that other living systems do not suffer, so humanity does not suffer as a consequence, and so the individual can retain freedom to be as he or she chooses. YELLOW's evaluative plumb bob points to the life of the Spiral, keeping it healthy and evolving. This is personalized survival in the Global Village, a complex of coexisting realities all striving to occupy the unique niches each perceives to be important. What is 'natural' comes in all of the Spiral's colors – both singly and in various blends, mixtures and combinations.

YELLOW recognizes the inevitability of the unfolding sequence of human 'MEMEs as well as need to for controls of the value systems they produce. Think in terms of the deep sea diver. If he comes up too soon, he may get the bends, his blood may boil. If he comes up too slowly, he may well run out of air. Just as the ascending diver must pass through different stages of decompression, people must experience different human systems within a timed sequence of development.

FLOW: YELLOW thinkers display Second Tier lifestyle priorities and preoccupations

While it is unlikely all of the following characteristics will be recognizable in a single individual, these are some of the critical markers of the awakening of the 7th level 'MEME (YELLOW) in human development. When it is in charge, the person/group:

- is disinclined to spend much energy on perfunctory niceties *unless* they are important to others present;
- will not waste time on interpersonal gamesmanship or pointless interpretations or contrived layers of meaning or semantic trivia;
- values good content, clean information, open channels for finding out

more on their own terms, and an attitude of open questioning and discovery;

- favors appropriate technology, minimal consumption, and a deliberate effort to avoid waste and clutter;
- has no need for status, exhibitionism, or displays of power unless power is demanded by the *Life Conditions*;
- enjoys human appetites but does not become a compulsive slave to any of them;
- is concerned with the long run of time rather than his or her own life span or those of other humans;
- fully expresses anger, or even hostility, but the emotions are intellectually used rather than emotionally driven or manipulatively applied;
- sees life as an up-and-down journey from problem to solution, so both chaos and order are accepted as normal;
- replaces anything artificial or contrived with spontaneity, simplicity, and ethics that 'make sense';
- seeks after a variety of interests and will elect to do what he or she likes whether or not it is trendy, popular, or valued by others;
- cannot be coerced, bribed, or intimidated since there is no compulsion to control or desire to be controlled by others;
- will run the gamut of being gentle or ruthless, a conformist or nonconformist, based on the factors involved in a circumstance and the overall interests of life itself;
- locates his or her core motivational and evaluative systems within his- or herself, thus becoming relatively immune to external pressure or judgment.

FLOW: YELLOW engages a number of unique problem-resolution and decision-making processes that are both highly complex in design and remarkably simple in execution

People who are centered elsewhere along the Spiral are befuddled by **YELLOW**. To **PURPLE** they are virtually invisible. To **RED** they are strange, but sometimes fun to hang out with. To **BLUE** they appear inconsistent, disrespectful, and out-of-focus. To **ORANGE** they seem unwilling to commit themselves fully to achieving objectives. From the **GREEN** standpoint, they seem cool and reserved, intellectualizing emotions without joining wholeheartedly into the group experience.

Bright **YELLOW** people often prefer a low profile on the fringes of organizations. They announce their presence because of their uncanny skill at resolving complex issues. Their minds roam freely up and down past–present–future time lines. They may suggest a fresh, unthought of course of action. With a few twists and turns, they quickly sort out problematic puzzles. They employ a number of imaginative problem resolution mechanisms that engage people in systematic, disciplined, and solution-focused initiatives. Then, they may well disappear, leaving the celebrations and accolades to others. While they are drawn to interesting problems to address, they are just as likely to vanish when their personal interest wanes.

The **YELLOW** 'MEME's problem-solving tool kit includes several competencies:

Competency 1   **YELLOW** problem-solvers ride the explosive Spiral in search of major gaps, misfits, trigger points, natural flows and potential awakenings or regressions. **YELLOW** understands that profound change only occurs around serious problems of existence. Like a heat seeking missile, they are drawn to hot spots where the evolving crisis demands new insights. They realize many breakthrough ideas are forged within such crucibles. **YELLOW** thinkers are keenly aware of the Conditions for Change. They recognize that different solution packages are lined up along the Spiral. Each is designed specifically for that 'MEME range and may not be particularly useful or even workable elsewhere. This insight often causes **YELLOW** thinkers to pull back and let nature take its course. There are forces at work that we simply cannot manipulate, nor should we. Better to let them run their courses than create future problems through inappropriate and short-sighted interventions.

Much like Windows or OS/2 software packages, **YELLOW** thinkers can stitch together the interests of the often conflicting 'MEMEs so each continues to run independently together. **YELLOW** defines situations so as to make possible, though not to guarantee, the healthy coexistence of all of the systems. Free of First Tier compulsions – must haves, need tos, afraid ofs – **YELLOW** activists are uniquely qualified to remove blockages and smooth out flows between and among 'MEMEs. In short, **YELLOW** is able to move in and out of the various First Tier systems in order to (1) make them healthy and (2) show their connections with other systems on the Spiral.

Competency 2   **YELLOW** problem-solvers are adept at resolving paradoxes, creating abundance, and engineering Win:Win:Win outcomes. In resolving paradoxes, **YELLOW** can frame issues in such a way as to put conflicting ideas (or even the 'MEMEs that produce them) on the horns of a dilemma. The task, then, is to show how 'both and' is superior to a forced choice of 'either or.' The **ORANGE**-driven preoccupation with 'growth and progress' and **GREEN**'s concern with 'the needs of people' can certainly be resolved by seeking after a program based on 'prosperity through people.' The two can coexist in appropriate harmony.

In creating this abundance, **YELLOW** looks for ways to increase the range of options, available niches, maneuvering space, and expanded opportunities for each of the 'MEMEs. This may be essential if each of the systems is to be expressed in their healthy rather than destructive form. By 'abundance' we do not mean the materialistic splendor or conspicuous consumption defined through the **ORANGE** world view. Rather, we refer to the increase and subsequent distribution of whatever it takes for people 'to have enough' of what is needed at the various levels of human existence. Serious human conflicts often result from entities competing for a bigger slice of a diminishing pie. The search for sufficiency is a necessary stage in resolving complex social problems. Too often it is neglected in favor of highly competitive (if not aggressively violent) methods of redistribution.

Win:Win:Win is our way of saying in Spiral Dynamics that unless the greater good, the entire society, and the natural human Spiral are considered in negotiation, a simple and selfish win:win deal between only two parties will emerge. Such a narrow outcome will not produce positive results in the long term. As **YELLOW** increases, unions and management are forming liaisons that serve both AND the company AND the industry AND the market. Unfortunately, Republicans and Democrats, haves and have-nots, and even public and private sector entities are caught up in **ORANGE** win:lose and, at best, win:win solutions. If gridlock is to stop and developmental gaps to close, the third 'win' – the good of the spiral – must be factored into these equations. **YELLOW** thinking must turn on fast.

YELLOW: Exiting Phase

Within the 7th ᵛMEME's individualistic worldview, we are sensitive to differences, uniqueness, people at diverse levels, and chunks of this and that. We learn there are inevitable differences and we accumulate a great deal of knowledge and information about their origins, characteristics, and contours. We even begin to search for ways to integrate the entities, open up the flow of energy among them, and give each its full day in the sun. We rely heavily on 'the self' in this process, trusting in our own evaluative capacities. Much of the time, **YELLOW** will stand virtually alone, relying on the power of knowledge and information, not colleagues, in affirmation of the uniqueness of life.

Yet, as the Spiral zig zags once again between a focus on 'me' and 'us,' a new sense of community begins to replace individualism. **TURQUOISE**, the global collective of individuals, rises to enfold **YELLOW**, the information elites. It turns out that the great **YELLOW** questions cannot be answered – indeed, cannot even be adequately addressed – by lone human beings, no matter how much they know or how often they link up in cyberspace.

Other shifts occur and trend lines begin to form at this transition:

- Spirituality creeps back in among the likes of astrophysicists, advanced philosopher-thinkers, and high-order mathematicians.
- A heightened respect for the greater 'holistic' wisdom within systems as living organisms emerges.

- **YELLOW** concerns with 'what?' and 'how?' are supplanted with queries of 'why?' and 'who?'
- The search for universal causality and the means necessary to reorder the chaos of the world are revived.
- A sense of communitarian experiences resurfaces, but without the heavy emotional loadings of the **GREEN** group's grope.
- Knowledge develops a life of its own, suggesting that a focus on particles and entities will be replaced by an understanding of groups, fields, and waves.
- If the Universe began with a big bang, perhaps there was a consciousness that guided the pushing of the plunger that set it off.

16

The Second Tier, A Second Step

Remember the central theme of Spiral Dynamics. Environmental factors (Time, Place, Conditions and Circumstance) awaken systems within people and societies designed to cope with and adapt to those specific *Life Conditions*. Some individuals may have been born out of time. Their minds may be set for an age just beyond the horizons of most others. In the best of times, they are revered as prophets, pathfinders, and visionaries. In other ages they are imprisoned, burned-at-the-stake, or banished to crazy-land.

The end of this century is experiencing more than its fair share of predictions, omens, apocalyptic prophecies, and visions of cataclysmic end-times. Clearly, we are crossing a number of major technological and environmental thresholds during this generation. Any one of these crossings possesses the potential to detonate an evolutionary bomb which could totally change the direction of our kind. Such giant steps might include environmental crises, culture-shocks to our view of ourselves and the universe in which we live, plague-like pandemics, unpredicted effects of genetic engineering, or the still-possible triggering of a nuclear war.

In Graves' perspective, evolutionary 'bombs' have exploded on the planet at seven times previously. Early vibrations from the eighth blow-up, the release of the **TURQUOISE** world, are presently being felt. Once again here we are setting up the conditions for a major swing of the pendulum back toward the sacrifical/collective pole, the first time in the Second Tier.

When a new human form occurs, whether a new pattern of behavior or a new ᵛMEME, certain 'mutant' forms usually appear before the new 'habit' sticks. These may arise over a period of years or centuries. Eventually, a new critical mass must gather to ensure that almost everyone is doing it, or being it. Then the novel becomes the normal. At our present stage in human development, the **TURQUOISE** ᵛMEME is at an embryonic stage. While a few of our ancestors may have meditated over it for five thousand years, a clear and concise picture has still not emerged from the developing fluids of time. However, certain important 'holons' have become evident as this eighth 'MEME metabolizes in the mist and becomes a force to be reckoned with.

Holon is a Greek expression representing a 'whole' chunk. For example, a hologram ('the whole message') encodes information in such a way to create the illusion of a three-dimensional image when re-illuminated through a 'holographic' photo-plate.

TURQUOISE *GlobalView*
The Holistic 'MEME

- Blending and harmonizing a strong collective of individuals
- Focus on the good of all living entities as integrated systems
- Expanded use of human brain/mind tools and competencies
- Self is part of larger, conscious, spiritual whole that also serves self
- Global (and whole-Spiral!) networking seen as routine
- Acts for minimalist living so less actually is more

yellow/TURQUOISE: Entering Phase

The Entering **yellow/TURQUOISE** builds on the previous 'MEMEs' information and insight nets while shifting over into a more Communal/ Collective point of view. The problems **YELLOW** recognizes in **LC⁷** cannot be resolved by isolated individuals, no matter how much they know or learn. The huge amount of raw information calls for a renewal of order and collaborative synergy if it is going to be useful. That is one of the factors in **LC⁸** and the next problems to be solved. The Second Tier energies liberated with **YELLOW** have to be focused and carefully directed.

The awakening of these **TURQUOISE LC⁸**s – and we probably do not even recognize the most serious ones yet – presents challenges which are both complex and expansive. Joint activity across groups, factions, communities, and natures is necessary to gather enough human energy to find solutions of **TURQUOISE** complexity. A physicist might describe this as a holistic field theory, inferring that the behavior of any element in a universe immediately impacts all the others.

In the human universe the confederations are purpose-driven – not harmony-driven as at **GREEN**, dogma-centered as in **BLUE**, or linked by mystical forces and kinship as with **PURPLE**. This eighth 'MEME may well act with more urgency than **YELLOW** where doubts are raised but self-sacrifical investments of time and energy are difficult. Accentuated group contact is possible because **TURQUOISE** communities are conceptual, not just physical, and can function as well through microelectronic links and spiritual pacts as **ORANGE** does over donuts at Monday morning staff meetings.

Feelings and emotion come strongly back into play in **TURQUOISE**'s resurgent collectivism. This transition integrates feeling with knowing, and that appears to organize senses and capacities that become diluted in the mid-Spiral ranges because of dogmatic beliefs and reliance on artifice. This holistic theme is clear in contemporary medical practice, particularly in some of the alternative healing systems that seek to access the full range of mind, body, and environmental capacities for wellness. Although today's **ORANGE**-dominated 'age of discovery' medical establishment is reluctant to accept such 'unproven' (though often ancient) approaches, their upsurge in popularity (and, it seems, efficacy) should tell us something.

GREEN is always ready for holistic, organic, natural, and slightly mystical treatments in lieu of the cold technocracy of **ORANGE**. **TURQUOISE** is far beyond **GREEN**'s New Age chic and faddish spirituality. It seems that as one really comes to understand pain and bodily signals, the person routinely begins to have a new control over bodily processes, ranging from blood pressure to mental attitude. From the **TURQUOISE** perspective, there is nothing so mystical about mystics – a fact which disillusions **GREEN** no end.

YELLOW is also intrigued by the possibilities of alternative venues for consciousness and wants to learn about them. At the entrance to the **yellow/TURQUOISE** range, the mind/brain which nature has provided gets even more credit. A form of spirituality resurges here, but there is not an identifiable someone in active, deliberate control. Instead, a unifying force and set of guiding principles sets the course of the universe and gives the appearance of consciousness. Some choose an anthropomorphic view of this force, and that is fine. Others will recognize it through their efforts at denial. **GREEN** will try to weave it into their groups and **YELLOW** will question and explore the perspectives. The Graves theory predicts that yellow/**TURQUOISE** tries to learn what is while believing there is more than they shall ever see or know.

In this Entering, still 'mutant,' range one seeks to focus the brain/mind to energize actions. Business has a soul again, and the gaps between science and metaphysics close. This introduces a new sense of greater community with high expectations for everyone. As the **TURQUOISE** band brightens, people will start acting concretely on solutions to **YELLOW** questions and problems. Global Villagers will be busy folk concerned with issues like bringing Africa into the modern age without reproducing **ORANGE** pathologies, bringing healthy order into places like the former Yugoslavia and central Asia, retuning the South American Spiral, and closing the widening racial, educational, and economic schisms in the U.S. without the pathologies of world governance or an empowered United Nations.

TURQUOISE: Peak Phase

In **TURQUOISE**, one learns not only through observation and participation but through the experience of simply being. The person trusts intuition and instinct (reactivated at a new level from the earlier ᵛMEMEs), allowing the mind to process with both the conscious and unconscious selves as coparticipants. You will recognize that some of the out of body experiences – 'go toward the light' – people report may be sensory systems from deep within the Spiral restimulated a resonance with deep **PURPLE**. In this Second Tier ᵛMEME, we seem to reconnect with aspects of ourselves stifled or supplanted by powerful forces in the First Tier subsistence levels, while activating other untapped resources within our minds and brains.

As these deeper mental and spiritual capacities are awakened, people will take a great step in development. If the more fully utilized mind is layered over **YELLOW** and the rest of the Spiral, human beings will have a much wider range of new possibilities. Once again, these will not be better, nicer, or more intelligent creatures. What they (will) have is more expansiveness in thinking and a broader repertoire of behavioral options. That does not guarantee that they will be happy or virtuous, but they will be looking through a more powerful glass.

The Peak **TURQUOISE** ᵛMEME moves among previous systems in a fluid manner. That is, we believe, a central difference between the First Tier Subsistence and Second Tier Being series. More than **YELLOW**, this second step understands the fullness of the Spiral and uses its layers proactively and holistically since the Communal/Collective bank is bright. This helps adjustment to the confusing realities of our complicated world, what Graves called the 'existential dichotomies' that are just a natural part of the Second Tier.

HOLON: Everything flows with everything else in living systems

TURQUOISE views a world of interlinked causes and effects, interacting fields of energy, and levels of bonding and communicating most of us have yet to uncover. The ᵛMEME liberates a sense of living systems that mesh and blend, flowing in concert with each other. This is another order-seeking system, but the first one that searches for the macro view. 'Seeing-everything-at-once' before doing anything specific dominates the thinking process. Collective imperatives and mutual interdependencies reign supreme.

While **YELLOW** attempts to stitch together particles, people, functions, and nodes into networks and stratified levels, **TURQUOISE** detects the energy fields that engulf, billow around, and flow throughout naturally. **YELLOW** connects the dots while **TURQUOISE** fleshes in the 'art' of all of the colors and hues, and the picture comes alive. In terms of Spiral Dynamics, the **YELLOW** system gets its hands dirty dealing with the chaos. The **TURQUOISE** collective system steps back and creates the next form of order.

Handling these divergent but simultaneous realities is no great problem for **TURQUOISE**. If the dimensions are slightly apart, then bridge them. The person does not need to quantify and categorize events as much as experience being. They learn by becoming more fully there, not just studying about or feeling cozy with anything.

Another way to approach **TURQUOISE** complexity is through paradoxes. For example, factor together the desire for excellent health care to extend life, to lower costs of its delivery, to make it more widely available, yet maintain a population mass aligned with available resources. Or consider maximizing individual liberties while insuring the well-being of the community as a whole. Be fair to everyone in the school while helping the brightest to shine and the most challenged to grow. Build a highly profitable company that offers its employees superb benefits. Paradox construction and resolution is a good tool for tracking down the elegant, underlying order beneath **YELLOW**'s chaos. Without doubt, **TURQUOISE** will show us how to use diversity in new ways since it is the first time people fathom the complexity of the Spiral in terms of the good of the super-group, Homo sapiens.

HOLON: TURQUOISE embraces a global communitarian sense without attacking individuals' rights to be

Not to be mistaken with a New Age lexicon of pseudo-science and pseudo-mysticism, or a **GREEN** bond with only those people who share the same values, **TURQUOISE** defines a world community more broadly. In part, a Gaia view emerges, one that centers on life itself – all forms of life (not just humans). Every person, every creature, every species belongs. The planet itself is seen as a single ecosystem. Individuals are not separated; neither are national boundaries, ethinic peculiarities, nor elitist privileges allowed to divide people destructively.

Persons thinking with this ᵛMEME exist in relationship to collective other, not just the self. In **TURQUOISE** the 'I' is comfortably, but not needfully, integrated into the whole. One acts in conjunction with systems by observing and actively contributing systemic thinking. There is constant attention to more expansive implications and the unavoidability of connections among actions and actors. The shift from **yellow/TURQUOISE** into more centralized **TURQUOISE** seems to be from 'learning about . . .' and 'touching base with . . .' to becoming one merged into the many. This

Communal/Collective functioning both heightens sensory awareness and increases people's alertness to multiple dimensions of time and space (as the Aborigines and Hindus would instruct us).

TURQUOISE life consists of fractals, replications of the micro right through the macro. This is also the theology of TURQUOISE. The laws of nature that apply throughout the universe supplant the doctrinaire laws of BLUE or the interpersonal emotive links of GREEN. While TURQUOISE readily admits incomplete knowledge, it also has resurging faith that a grand unification is possible and that everything somehow connects to everything else.

To use a musical analogy, this is PURPLE revisited up an hectave. An interesting possibility in the repetition of that theme is global tribalism. Indeed, the frightening negative aspect of the pendulum's swing from YELLOW's knowing 'me' back toward a grander TURQUOISE 'we' is community division on a grand scale – the black, yellow, red, brown, and white races as blocs; residents of hemispheric or continental commons plotting like super-clans against rivals; or BLUE ideologies – religious, political, or both – forming in-group/out-group associations that bridge the oceans but seal out unbelievers. Such inter-factional conflicts could be catastrophic. They are serious enough now while using ORANGE technologies, much less YELLOW or TURQUOISE interconnections.

Just because the way of thinking includes more of the Spiral, that does not preclude destructive ideas and attachments. Humans always manifest their being in both healthy and unhealthy ways. In fact, one conceivable Problem of Existence that might foster the swing back toward a yet more complex 'I' system is the need for some centralized command-and-control to stop conflict among TURQUOISE megatribes. One would hope that compassion, altruism, and cooperative sharing would drive this CORAL ᵛMEME whenever it begins to take hold. That cannot be guaranteed, though, and the Entering phase might be pretty exciting.

HOLON: TURQUOISE discovers a new version of spirituality

In PURPLE one seeks to placate the animistic spirits, the entities that bring good fortune and bad. One hopes to join these spirits in a 'happy hunting ground.' In BLUE, spirituality is defined in terms of specific beliefs and truths, a code of conduct, and a contest with the forces of evil which will be settled in the end-time. In GREEN, the liberating power is ultimately within one's self, best explored with others in this humanistic context. The metaphysical realm is an adjunct to becoming more whole.

At TURQUOISE one stands in awe of the cosmic order, the creative forces that exist from the Big Bang to the smallest molecule. Elsewhere on the Spiral it takes the form of PURPLE's 'mother and father' figures,' RED's wielder of 'thunder-bolts-from-on-high,' BLUE's fair and just Scorekeeper,

ORANGE's master builder, GREEN's unity principle, and YELLOW's source of chaos.

TURQUOISE life experiences show that one can never know or understand all things. With this acceptance comes wonder, awe, reverence, humility, unity, and a refreshed value for simplicity. In this view, reality can be experienced, but never known. People functioning in this range avoid relationships where others try to dominate, but can provide direction when required in ways that are not personally domineering. It is easy for TURQUOISE to step away and contemplate, then re-enter refreshed with a new perspective. The person constantly monitors both self and situation as a participant-observer. The ego that drives the Subsistence layers is virtually nonexistent. 'Life is the most important thing there is; but my life is unimportant.'

HOLON: TURQUOISE's macro-view perspective translates into action in behalf of the whole Spiral and all its parts

One of the primary contributions that TURQUOISE makes to Spiral Dynamics is the macro- 'big picture' view it provides. Satellite eyes staring down from space can detect the flowing patterns of clouds and wind on the weather map. Earth's topography can be mapped, its crust can be penetrated with radar probes, and its vital signs can be assessed and measured. In the same sense, for example, TURQUOISE thinking allows community leaders to 'see' levels of interaction – both on the surface and below – they have never detected before. They can look at many dynamic forces before working on any single part of the community.

Corporate TURQUOISE thinkers detect the harmonics, the mystical forces, the chemical reactions, and the pervasive flow-states that permeate any organization – its people, brain syndicates, and marketplace. They can amass and process huge chunks of data in searching for the deepest trend lines and most subtle thought and energy patterns. While YELLOW adds more so-called 'left brain' logic into the Spiral Dynamics equation, TURQUOISE contributes a well-informed, cerebral and highly complex 'right-brain' processing mode to the mixture. Together, these constitue only the beginnings of the Second Tier and a commencement of a series of exciting new ^vMEMEs for generations to come.

SECTION 4

Global Order and Chaos on the Dynamic Spiral

This final section of *Spiral Dynamics* applies the Spiral Dynamics Tool Kit to large-scale systems analysis and change. Geopolitical shifts and transitions in the new world-wide markets make a lot more sense if you apply the principles of the Spiral.

> *Memes fan out across the planet carried by vigorously scheming hosts. These humans – out for idealism, gain, guts, or glory – spread the meme with vigor and enthusiasm that would have made Johnny Appleseed's fruit tree planting look lazy by comparison.*
> Howard Bloom, *The Lucifer Principle*,
> The Atlantic Monthly Press, New York, 1995, p. 171

I am not saying in this conception of adult behavior that one style of being, one form of human existence is inevitably and in all circumstances superior to or better than another form of human existence, another style of being.

What I am saying is that when one form of being is more congruent with the realities of existence, then it is the better form of living for those realities.

And what I am saying is that when one form of existence ceases to be functional for the realities of existence then some other form, either higher or lower in the hierarchy, is the better style of living.

I do suggest, however, and this I deeply believe is so, that for the overall welfare of total man's existence in this world, over the long run of time, higher levels are better than lower levels and that the prime good of any society's governing figures should be to promote human movement up the levels of human existence.

Clare W. Graves

17

Global Awakenings:
'New World Order' (and Chaos)

George Bush's hundred hour war in the Persian Gulf and Caesar-like triumphal parading through Washington, D.C. in 1991 became his twilight's last gleaming. He never recovered from the victory. In his speech announcing Operation Desert Storm he had claimed: 'We have before us the opportunity to forge, for ourselves and for future generations, a New World Order.'

That phrase – New World Order – not only became the butt of jokes but stoked paranoiac fears in the conspiracy-seeking ultra-right in his own homeland and a smoldering anti-colonialist backlash abroad. Fearful religious groups saw 'The Mark of the Beast' or sure signs of 'the Antichrist' afoot. Many Third Worlders were reminded of the threat of continued First-World imperialist hegemony and quaked. Later in that same year, President Bush softened the sentiment in an address before the United Nations General Assembly: 'In short, we seek a *pax universalis* built upon shared understanding.'

South African President Nelson Mandela used the same 'new world order' imagery in his speech before the U.S. Congress in 1994. He mandated what the rich nations should do for the poor and then closed his remarks with the command, 'Forward, March!'

In *The Next Century*, David Halberstam predicted just such a demand on the part of President Mandela when he warned: 'We now live in a world where the tensions are more likely to be North–South, white–nonwhite, rich–poor, developed–underdeveloped, educated–uneducated.' The political rhetoric and contrived groupings from Cold War days no longer suffice. In any case, they blinded us to the 'real' realities. Now is a time for something completely different, a framework universalis that gives a better understanding of us as Earthlings.

The Need for Spiral Wizards

James N. Rosenau, in *Turbulence in World Politics*, summarizes the state-of-the-planet that will challenge a new breed of Spiral Wizards to action:

> 'Doubtless every era seems chaotic to the people who live through it. And the last decades of the 20th century are no exception. It is as if Spaceship Earth daily encounters squalls, down draughts and wind shears as it careens into changing and uncharted realms of experience. Sometimes the evidence is furiously evident as thunderclouds of war gather or the lightning of crisis streaks across the global sky; but often the turbulence is of a clear-air kind, the havoc it wrecks unrecognized until after its challenges have been met or its damage done.'

To deal with these whirlwinds, Spiral Wizards-to-be ought first to do three things:

1 Activate **YELLOW** thinking in themselves and start looking for the **TURQUOISE** 'MEME. The solutions for First Tier problems can only be found in Second Tier approaches.
2 Stuff cotton in their ears to block out the false prophets of any Final State. So long as people live at different places along the developmental Spiral, their over-simplifications lead to dead ends. Also they should understand that they will be a serious threat to others' territory, turf, and social budget.
3 Review the Six Conditions for Change and decide which of the seven Variations on Change is appropriate. Geopolitical shifts involve simultaneous transitions among many 'MEMEs. What is good for one may be disaster for another.

If your goal is facilitating the change process, Spiral congruence is required. If the culture is more homogeneous and at lower levels of development, the goals must be specific, concrete (literally!) and immediate – the 'edifice complex.' If the culture is at higher levels, then more abstract, broader, and distant goals are viable. If it has powerful nodes both high and low, the goals must be dualistic – concrete and abstract, immediate and remote, spiritual and tangible. Whatever the case, change must be delivered through the level of existence of the population, in the psysho-social language they understand, not that preferred by the change agency or hired guns in public relations or communication.

- Spiral Wizards understand that the 'Butterfly Effect' applies to human affairs in the age of CNN and satellite phones. Seemingly isolated events can cascade quickly across the global electronic grid. There are no 'dark' continents as the glare of reporters' videocams illuminate connections throughout the globe. The 'primitivos' of Amazonas now have TV. There are plenty of fax machines in Nairobi, and a racist event in South Chicago will have repercussions in Soweto. In this post-information age, little flaps quickly become big winds.

- Like the orbiting Landsat's three-dimensional scans of Earthly terrain, you must image the movements of people up and down the Spiral. Survey psychosocial space for strata of turbulence and complexity of thinking.
- Look back in time to track the historic emergence and sequencing of 'MEMEs to help analyze why things are happening today so you can anticipate what is likely to come in the future.
- Try to see people as they are, not just as your filters would judge them. When scanning previous world orders, periodically stop to clean your lenses. Slip on 'their' colored glasses to see reality as 'they' do. We only see what we can see, not all that is there; so no wonder we revise history every time a new 'MEME awakens and rewrite the books through our new-found filters.

Geo 'MEMEs at the Meta-Plane

The norms and traits of culture are collections of Richard Dawkins' little memes – dress, icons, religious practices, mores, political forms, beliefs, attitudes, patterns, and structures. But cultures also have meta-'MEME profiles, just like individuals and organizations. Arthur Clarke, in *The Wall of Darkness*, writes of 'universes that drift like bubbles in the foam upon the River of Time.' When each 'MEME emerges and peaks, it claims to have reached the end of knowledge itself, an 'end of history.'

Yet, each new 'MEME universe has declined in the course of time only to be superseded by another. This cultural $_{awaken}$–rise–^{peak}–decline–$_{fall}$, then awaken anew cycle is triggered by many forces:

- assaults by alien cultures from the outside – economic, moral, political, religious, or physical invasions;
- emergence of startling new facts and ideas that undermine the 'fundamental' premises and ideology and expose us to renaissances and sea changes;
- sudden appearance of visionary or assertive leaders who recast and reframe everything into a new paradigm – saviors, demagogues, and prophets;
- eruption of simmering old problems that refuse to stay suppressed – ancient grudges artificially paved over by foreigners' roads and kept in temporary check with artificial boundaries surveyed by colonial despots or well-intentioned 'peace-keepers';
- decay from within as the elites feast on the spoils of success while failing to notice the rising tide of dangerous new problems that successful living generates;
- failure to cope adequately with or even abject denial of threatening new

Life Conditions that eventually overwhelm the society's active 'MEMEs' competencies.

Each emerging social universe is an interactive, Hollywood style moving picture instead of a still frame. In the closing scenes, the characters may 'live happily ever after,' be left in the shadows of doubt and uncertainty, find themselves 'tried in the balance and found wanting,' or succumb to the doom-and-gloom of a final apocalypse. The tone of the climax is set by the appropriateness of the linkage between *Life Conditions* and 'MEMEs. The point is that different people and societies are living out different movie scripts without realizing it.

In scanning the geopolitical currents, look for the following conditions:

- **FLASH-POINTS** – Crises caused (a) by collisions between different 'MEMEs vying for overlapping niches (like **PURPLE** and **ORANGE** in much of Africa) or (b) similar 'MEME profiles with mutually exclusive contents inside their structures (like Northern Ireland, Bosnia–Herzegovina, India/Pakistan, and the West Bank.)
- **HOT-SPOTS** – Areas bubbling beneath the surface that could soon erupt explosively. Inner-city conditions of overcrowded urban centers worldwide; have-not states envying wealthy neighbors; have-a-lot nations still exploiting others; and unresolved **PURPLE**, **RED**, and **BLUE** disputes from tens to hundreds of years old can trigger boil-overs.
- **DIASPORAS** – The dispersal, spread, and/or migration of people with shared little memes and 'MEMEs over the various continents. This is evident in the Jewish diaspora, overseas Chinese, Europeans' 'discovery' of the Americas, a growing Mother Africa society, and the spread of militant Islam in North Africa. The decline of national boundaries and ease of movement will result in formation of global megatribes. The forces of **BLUE** and **ORANGE** are on the move right now. These will locate alternative capitals in cyberspace, ethnic homelands, hemispheric centers, or neo-tribal gathering places based on the interests of the 'MEME.
- **REGRESSIONS** – An entity in a down-shift phase as it spirals down in response to worsening *Life Conditions* because of ineffectual systems-within. The Balkans, Rwanda, Tajikistan, and parts of Uganda are examples, though every nation is susceptible to these steps back and even dangerous free-falls.
- **HARMONICS** – Simultaneous movement of two or more 'MEME systems in which a powerful theme liberates energy in several places on the Spiral. The First-World shift toward **TURQUOISE** may resonate with the Third-World move to **BLUE**. Both tracks would be characterized by authoritarian mandates and collective actions. The upsurge of **ORANGE** in the Second-World creates sympathetic vibrations into more **RED** and perhaps even some **YELLOW**.

- **CUTTING-EDGES** – The first flash of new 'MEMEs. The fiery plumes of several Spiral colors can appear across the planet at any time. Cutting-edges that cannot harmonize or integrate either clash or erupt like a psychological geyser in producing Flash-Points.
- **GRID-LOCK** – A stalemate, holdup, or blockage where systems are forced to be static while *Life Conditions* change. Sometimes a function of Arrested or Closed 'MEME stacks, Grid-Lock may also result from *Life Conditions* that present nearly insurmountable barriers, overwhelming problems, or belief contents that are fixated. If the 'MEME stack is Open or only somewhat Arrested, the Grid-Lock can become the pressure cooker for a Hot-Spot.

Different World Orders at Different Times

Spiral Dynamics identifies eight 'MEME-based scenarios in the movie script of human development with the ninth being written. No one knows the true distribution of these forces along the world's population curve, but consider the spread in the following chart. Feel free to modify the percentages – these are only guesswork – but recognize the relative power of the **BLUE** and **ORANGE** 'MEMEs in setting policy and distributing global perks.

Themes of history's screen play are myriad. Such concepts as Germany's *lebensraum*, Japan's 'co-prosperity sphere,' Francis Fukuyama's 'last man,' G. W. F. Hegel's 'liberal state,' Karl Marx's 'communist society,' Max Weber's 'Protestant ethic,' Talcott Parson's 'evolutionary universal,' Herbert Spencer's 'social Darwinism,' Gerhard Lenski's 'technological evolutionism,' Marvin Harris's 'evolutionary materialism,' Immanuel Wallerstein's 'world-system,' and, of course, George Bush's 'new world order' populate the shelves of the Spiral Library. The search for what Fukuyama calls the 'MECHANISM' – that which explains the direction of history – has been endless and fruitless. If Spiral theory holds, it will continue to be so.

The bookends of change for each universe are periods of dissonance, chaos, and turbulence. Each jerky step leads to a stumble, recovery, and then another step. The patterns are not determined by linear time or the oscillations of cycles. Rather, the entire process is driven by the laws of Spiral Dynamics – back and forth and up and down and round and round at once. Critical masses form, become fixed, then weaken, fracture, and finally dissipate.

The Plumb Line and the Globe

Hang your plumb bob on the moon so it points to Earth. Finding what makes living healthier for *Homo sapiens* and other living things is the job to be done. Align from that point over any piece of geography, culture, community,

'MEME Color	System	Explanation of 'world order' where system is 'cutting edge' in the late twentieth century	Estimated		
			% of people?	% of power?	% of usage?
BEIGE	Semi-Stone Age	Natural order and natural law prevail	0.1%	0%	.01%
PURPLE	Tribal	Mystical spirits, good and bad, swarm Earth leaving blessings, curses, and spells which determine events. The spirits exist in ancestors and bond 'the people' in supportive relationships. Kinship and lineage establish political links. Liaisons form across tribes by marriage.	10%	1%	1%
RED	Exploitative	Big Spirits, dragons, beasts, and powerful people (chieftains) dominate, set boundaries, punish, and reward according to their whims. Feudal lords protect underlings in exchange for obedience and labor. Pacts of convenience to expand influence and control. Control and expansion of turf.	20%	5%	5%
BLUE	Authoritarian	The unfathomable System, Truth, or Force rules the universe, sets human destiny and limitations, prescribes what is 'right' and 'wrong,' gives meaning and purpose to human existence, and rewards the faithful. Treaties, doctrinal alliances, and borders. Diplomacy and sectarianism.	40%	30%	10%

ORANGE	Entrepreneurial	The world is a rational and well-oiled machine that has inner workings and secrets that can be learned, mastered, and manipulated. The laws of science rule politics, the economy (invisible hand), and human events. The world is a chessboard on which games are being played as winners gain pre-eminence and perks over losers. Marketplace partners, strategic alliances.	30%	50%	75%
GREEN	Communitarian	Each entity in human populations or in the meta-physical realm is unique, yet belongs to the same cosmic community and should be seen relative to the field of equals. The bonding impulse within everything and dispersed everywhere rules the world. Human rights issues, collectivism, and reciprocality.	10%	15%	10%
YELLOW	Systemic	The prevailing world order is a function of (a) the existence of different realities and (b) the inevitable patterns of movement up and down a dynamic spiral in response to the problems of human existence. The command and control center facilitates the emergence of entities through levels of increasing complexity.	1%	5%	5%
TURQUOISE	Holistic	Universal forces permeate all forms of life, energy, and existence, ordering their movement, changes, and patterns. Preservation of eternal truths and forces of the cosmos.	0.1%	1%	1%

village, or organization. Design an **X** Template like that for any entity in addressing the ᵛMEME-related issues, gaps, and opportunities.

Recognize the What and Why of Physical Boundaries

Archaeologists identify different civilizations as they dig down through strata of Earth and cultural artifacts. As we slice through the psychological ᵛMEME layers, recognize how each draws its physical boundaries and stakes out its territory. Many geopolitical conflicts are turf battles over which group of human beings with their ᵛMEMEs and cultural screenplays gets to be dominant. Note how each ᵛMEME defines space and boundaries:

- **TURQUOISE:** *the functional needs of life on Earth*
  What life needs supersedes any special, natural, ethnic or parochial groupings. Man-made boundaries, as such, will fade. Such criteria as land and resources utilization and natural geological forms and structures will establish human limits and habitation patterns along with other forms of life sharing the planet.
- **YELLOW:** *whichever level(s) on the Spiral are active in a given situation*
  Different needs are legitimized so long as boundary conflicts, border disputes, and proprietary clashes do not endanger the health of the Spiral itself. Some conflict between and among the different levels (see below) is inherent and inevitable.
- **GREEN:** *open space that meets the needs of people coming together in a greater sense of community and mutual caring*
  Nationalistic divisions and private ownership of resources are viewed as artificial contrivances to keep people apart. The whole human race is seen as a single family living together on 'the Commons' which should be shared for the good of all.
- **ORANGE:** *spheres of economic influence and individual ownership*
  Limits are adjusted by mercantile and imperialistic interests, negotiated contracts, economic/political alliances, diplomatic compromise, commodity-based cartels, and trade agreements. Boundary lines are drawn and redrawn to suit contemporary financial needs and political expediency.
- **BLUE:** *the Higher Power assigns different people to different lands*
  The rightful places for habitation are properly surveyed, documented for history, picket fenced, and then defended as holy and permanent. May become national borders protected by treaties and compacts, markers and armies. 'God gave this land to us.'
- **RED:** *where the big 'me' leaves his or her personal mark*
  These are the areas of conquest over which the PowerGod, Chieftain, King, Queen, or feudal lord reigns. The limits are set by how far the elites can extend fear and wield control. Boundaries endure in direct relation to

the strength to enforce them. Dangers exist beyond those boundaries – murderous warlords, fierce dragons, and rival ranchers with shotguns.

- **PURPLE:** *where the spirits and the ancestors walked*
  Defined by myth and legend, this is the 'sacred ground' where the ancient ones lived, died, and are buried. The limits are of sight-lines and walking distance. Marked by symbols and defined in oral tradition carried in the collective memories of people – this tree, that river, over the next mountain peak, and up and down the valley. The land beyond is fearful and foreboding since evil spirits and competing tribes threaten harm.
- **BEIGE:** *the current place occupied by the band*
  The people migrate throughout the world as they know it. The space is available to all, owned by none.

GEOcurrents Flowing Over the Planet

This section will illustrate the large-scale impact of 'MEMEs with (a) an example of the Spiral Arrested by politics, (b) three great GEOcurrents, and (c) two sub-currents that actually generate most of the newspaper headlines and media reports today.

The Spiral Arrested by a Cold War

The forty-year Cold War locked two ideologies in a pitched and expensive battle in the **BLUE** to **ORANGE** transition. One side proclaimed Communism; the other worshipped capitalism. Large parts of the world's Spiral were locked into dichotomy – us or them. Both sides wanted to 'win' the right to spread their respective memes, both little ones and big 'MEMEs, over the planet.

Karl Marx was a secular theologian who replaced a belief in the spiritual hereafter with a soaring faith in the ultimate and inevitable secular victory of the proletariat on Earth. The 'theology' of atheistic materialism does not dignify the individual and has a depressing final state view. The locus of control is blocked in the cool, ordered, Sacrificial Spiral systems. Typically, a few **RED–ORANGE** elites take covert control and live quite well while talking up 'the people.'

Adam Smith couched his faith in the marketplace beneath an umbrella of monotheistic religion and rewards to come. The locus of control was in the warm, chaotic, Expressive bands of the Spiral. The advantage these thinking systems offer is a hopeful future for liberated, risk-taking individuals. The **ORANGE** elites justify their prerogatives as 'God's will,' 'divine right,' 'nature's way,' and other **BLUE** rationales.

The conflict between these -isms became a holy war, pitting Western ideology and materialism against a Marxist–Leninist version of a better world. Both views shared the same **RED–BLUE–ORANGE** belief container, though in different ratios. As such conflicts do, this had the effect of arresting the Spiral's movement. The Cold War laid down a sheet of ice that artificially covered the hot ethnic cores, nationalistic surges, and revenge-driven revolutions. The two philosophies competed around the globe buying 'hearts and minds' and fought through surrogates. Third-World societies fell prey to strong-armed dictators who were financed by economic and military aid from the 'super-powers' trying to buy off short-term allies. In the end, it became clear that the Western view produced greater complexity in thinking and superior weapons systems, as well.

The Harmonics from the world-wide bipolar confrontation resonated within many countries in the form of two-party competitive structures: one 'liberal,' the other 'conservative' (in the American usage of these stereotypes). Those designated as too liberal were charged with being communists. Those ordained as too conservative were classified as 'fascists.' Arrested thinkers adopted this polar model as *the* model for governance. Many still do and that denies the complexity of the Spiral.

GEOcurrent 1: **RED–BLUE** *(Nationalism, Ideology, and Ethnicity)* The presently nonaligned, developing 'have-not' societies (with heavily **PURPLE** and **RED** population masses), along with the super-rich have-a-lot desert kingdoms are either moving into or are Arrested (for now) in the **RED–BLUE** range.

The term 'Third World' was first coined in 1955 at the Bandung conference in a meeting of the nonaligned nations. The free market, multiparty societies were named 'First World'; the socialist systems with command economies were designated 'Second World.' Actually, to students of Spiral Dynamics, First World means the presence of **ORANGE** with: (a) an achievement-oriented work ethic – Puritan, Confucian, etc.; (b) an analytical reasoning capacity allied to competence with measured time; and (c) a drive for materialistic excellence and individual success among a burgeoning middle class.

'Second World' is more of a Peak **BLUE** authoritarian conduit, designed to purge **RED** anarchy and replace it with dutiful, obeisant, categorical authoritarianism and heavily Sacrificial thinking. In Spiral terms, 'Third World' implies radical divisions between the very rich and the very poor with little or no middle class, more **PURPLE** ethnic concerns, and a **BLUE** future. The **RED** PowerGods still dominate in a world filled with superstitions, clan or tribal conflicts, and periods of lawlessness and social implosions. A 'Fourth World' element, largely children, is more in the **BEIGE** and **PURPLE** survival mode.

It is important to consider these designations as thinking components rather than just socioeconomic conditions. There are First-World elements in

Third-World countries and Third-World components in the First-World. The question is one of proportions and influence, not categories.

As **RED–BLUE** pulsates, HOT-SPOTS, FLASH-POINTS, and even REGRESSIONS will impact First-World societies. There will be even more occurrences of violence in struggling Third-World environments moving toward Second-World status. Here are a few examples:

Africa – African **PURPLE** and **RED** cores were trapped within artificial **BLUE** national boundaries imposed by colonial Europeans. The developmental short-circuits led to further exploitation, even when accompanied by deceptive songs of national liberation, on-time trains, and the pretense of multiparty democracy in a Third World *milieu*. The results have been catastrophic:

- a succession of military coups (also an issue in much of South America);
- major civil wars in Mozambique, Zaire, Nigeria, Angola, Uganda, Ethiopia, Sudan, Mali, and Liberia;
- near-genocidal ethnic strife in Rwanda and Burundi;
- brutal despots in Uganda, the Central African Republic, Somalia, and Ethiopia;
- one-party states, nepotism, mismanagement, corruption and a siphoning off of overseas financial assistance into the Swiss bank accounts of small ruling elites;
- calamitous neglect and destruction of natural resources, including wildlife.

Much of Africa (and the Third World) has yet to experience the agrarian revolution, a positive move through the **BLUE** Second-World conduit. This must occur before the **ORANGE** free-market and multiparty democratic packages can take root. A top level executive from the African Development Bank in the Ivory Coast once asked us: 'Why don't we Africans [speaking of the African employees who worked in his bank] have a work ethic? We seem to have no sense of discipline, no time consciousness?'

We explained that it is not a function of being African; that is racialism. Instead, his complaint was about the lack of an active **BLUE** work ethic, **BLUE** discipline, and **BLUE** time sense. Because of the prevailing *Life Conditions* in much of Africa, the **BLUE** system has yet to be fully awakened. It has been hindered by the persistence of **BEIGE, PURPLE,** and **RED** and the historic failure of colonial powers – both deliberate and not – to resolve their problems with congruent **BLUE**.

Some form of Second-World Pan-Africanism might well be more useful than attempts to build separate national identities at this stage while the First-World thinking component is still small. A Second-World **BLUE** passage would build the base for First-World **ORANGE** instead of **RED** exploitation. While the particular rendition of **BLUE** that fits best is open to question, virtually the same thing can be said for much of the South American continent.

MID-EAST – The Middle East (what wonderful Eurocentrism!) continues to boil and bubble as tribes, empires, and other **PURPLE** feudal residues from the breakup of the Ottoman Empire percolate just beneath the sand. Overlay this turbulence with the impact of **ORANGE** Western imperialistic ventures, competing **red/BLUE** religious zealots striving to protect 'their' respective holy places, and the enticements from windfall oil money. No wonder the region is so full of explosive geocurrents.

BLUE exists in the form of Muslim prescriptions and **PURPLE** in one-party (or extended family) feudal authoritarianism. Despite the youth who visit the West or obtain university degrees from 'liberal' institutions around the world, much of the region continues to be Arrested or Closed in heavy **BLUE/red**. Those people with awakening **ORANGE** or **GREEN** would see limits on 'human rights' and constraints on the roles open to women. For others with more congruent Spiral profiles (and who share the beliefs contents), this is a proper way of being. There is a great GAMMA potential in the region because those with awakening **ORANGE** or **GREEN** are unlikely to wait for liberation much longer while the **RED/blue** faction will fight for a more rigid *status quo*. The former group is restless in eastern Europe; the latter may be found in the U.S. if militant Islam, for example, should become malignant.

While much of Israel's political thinking has evolved more of an **ORANGE**, even **ORANGE/green**, secular free-market driven society, the bulk of indigenous Arab societies have not made that transition. Conflicts occur on the vertical (between and among levels on the Spiral) dimension as well as between -isms, tribes, and empires on the horizontal plane. Some of the region's difficulties are First-World **ORANGE** versus Second-World **BLUE** and even Third-World **RED** and **PURPLE**. Others are derived from close-minded True Believers who insist on their -ism or else.

First Tier negotiation experts or conflict management teams, especially with Peak **ORANGE** and even **GREEN** world views, often make things worse instead of better in Second- or Third-World contexts such as the Mid-East. Like leadership, arbitration has to function within a half-step or so of the base 'MEMEs. The continual threat of a Jihad-like mobilization in an Arab nation or a counter-Jihad pre-preemptive strike by Israel keep the **BLUE–RED** geocurrent turbulent. There will be 'wars and rumors of wars' so long as well-armed societies in the **RED** to **BLUE** band prevail.

Until this **RED** to **BLUE** blockage is released, and a positive and stabilized non-punitive **BLUE** emerges, the shift into a pragmatic and non-ideological **ORANGE** cannot occur. The region may spawn any number of Saddam Husseins or other demagogues who exploit their own religious beliefs, anti-U.S. sentiments, or Babylon-type promises of a return to grandeur and glory.

These human time bombs tick within every country in the region, threatening both their neighbors and their present governmental structures.

SINGAPORE – The power of the **BLUE** system in dealing with strong **PURPLE** and **RED** elements while creating a Second-World transition stage for the emergence of **ORANGE** thinking can be seen in Singapore. Long an object of curiosity and criticism for its unique blend of open economics, social engineering, and authoritarian politics, this island republic is the smallest and most successful of Asia's rapidly developing 'Little Dragons.' (The others are South Korea, Taiwan, and Hong Kong until 1997, then we shall see.)

The extraordinary reliance on an ethos of honesty and a Confucian work ethic came from the country's founding leader, Lee Kwan Yew. Lee's legacy continues in the form of strict rules for decency and order, harsh punishments for 'improper' behavior, the mandated recognition of Singapore's five ethnic groupings through public holidays and festivals, and a sense of communal sacrifice reinforced by national youth service and other forms of patriotism. Yet, the economic model is of a decidedly free-market orientation. Savings, discipline, hard work, and education are highly valued. The *Life Conditions* that lead to this sacrificial-prosperity thinking in economics and politics are heightened by (1) Singapore's potentially volatile ethnic mixtures and (2) the fear of her bigger neighbors.

While each society must craft its own unique political, economic, and social order, Singapore is an excellent example of the use of 'soft' **BLUE** authoritarianism to bring order out of Third-World chaos. The same applies to inner-cities where Third-World components are escalating in First-World countries and appropriate transitions back from the cutting edge are essential.

Meeting the social order and personal achievement needs of citizens will force Singapore to search for ways to open the valves, allowing more individual freedom. Many young executives are chaffing at the high levels of conformity demanded in Singapore and the restriction of political dissent. Successful living at **BLUE** will awaken more Peak **ORANGE, GREEN, YELLOW,** and **TURQUOISE.**

GEOcurrent 2: **BLUE–ORANGE** *Free-Market and Multiparty Democracy*
One thing is certain. The rest of the developing world will not be able to access the same level of materialistic consumption that today's Western societies have committed and enjoyed. Our natural resources are finite. Earth cannot sustain a population at the same level that characterizes First-World societies. Yet remember that **ORANGE** is essentially a thinking system, a quest to improve, enhance, and seek after 'the best' among many options. It is not necessarily conspicuous consumption or expensive life-styles, *per se.* The expression of the **ORANGE** 'MEME in non-Westernized, less Eurocentric societies could be quite different from what one sees in New York, Paris, or even Tokyo.

Such terms as 'privatize,' 'deregulate,' or the replacement of a command economy with 'free-market' principles punctuate the airwaves, newsprint, and serious conversation among **ORANGE**-thinking government planners and academics. Consultants have descended on South and Central America plying their **ORANGE** wares. Experts from Harvard, the University of Chicago, the Department of the Treasury, and former Reagan staffers have flooded into the former Soviet Union with an array of shock treatments designed to pull the collapsed socialist economy into the First World twentieth century. Will these manipulative initiatives work? Can the American system be transplanted into Eastern European (much less African or South American) societies intact? Not unless they tend to the Spiral.

RUSSIA – Russia and her former Soviet neighbors are struggling to cast off, virtually overnight, the legacy of a thousand years of **RED** Empires and **BLUE/red** authoritarian regimes. There is no broad tradition of individual rights, entrepreneurial initiatives, or open international relations. As the seven-decade experiment with a forced **BLUE** command economy controlled by a few **RED** elites lies in ruins, anarchy and anomie lurk around the corner. Runaway inflation, mass unemployment, and a growing tide of lawlessness are real threats to the infant 'democracy.'

Though he intellectualized about Change of the 5th and 6th Variations, Gorbachev was operationally locked into either Change 1st or 2nd, personally unable to break free of the **BLUE/orange** Communist shackles which he had begun to dismantle. Ill equipped to handle quantum shifts of the 7th Variation, he continued to vacillate and was displaced by Boris Yeltsin who gained attention by flamboyant **RED** – the executive branch fired tank rounds at the legislative – but spoke the language of **blue/ORANGE**. Like Gorbachev, Yeltsin appeared to understand that Change was urgently needed for individuals and institutions, but he could only comprehend the 3rd or 5th Variation.

As of this writing, the regressive **RED/blue** debacle in Chechnya has proven him shaky on even how to get that done. The dislocations of millions of former Soviet citizens prove that **PURPLE**, even **BEIGE** problems still endure in central Asia. When **ORANGE** appears, it is accompanied by so much **RED** that Vertical Change is not feasible. The leadership forms that rise to fit these disarrayed ᵛMEMEs are troubling, and the strict **BLUE** backlash that may then result to restore balance is even more dangerous. The fact that no leader of a Lee Kwan Yew's capacity appears to be on the cold Russian horizon opens the possibility of the emergence of a **RED/blue** -driven dictator from the wings or a resurgence of old hard-line **red/BLUE** authoritarianism.

Before Russia and the other former Soviet states can consider a move into the 'democratic' **ORANGE** band on the Spiral, a new, healthier, **BLUE** stabilizing force must first be in place. Otherwise, Westernized free-market thinking and constructive individualism cannot grow, even if they germinate. Optimistic but disciplined **BLUE/orange** American models from the 1950s and even the 1890s are more in phase with the developmental stages of Russians than the popular U.S. methods of the 1980s and 1990s which consulting ᵛMEME Wizards so gleefully hauled over. Spiral Wizards recognize that Russia's period of reconstruction needs its Carnegie's, Ford's, and Rockefeller's before meeting the Trump's, Smith's, and Eisner's.

JAPAN – The success of the Pacific Rim countries in general and Japan in particular is due in large part to the sacrificial thinking strain that permeates the Confucian-based cultural monoliths. The same impulse translates into a strong, patriotic urge and sense of national identity. Companies show a similar penchant for collective thinking and action resulting in relatively non-hierarchical organizations and a general sharing of profits and perks.

Indeed, American reporters were deeply touched as the citizens of Kobe responded with stoic discipline and dignity, expressing grief without self-pity after the catastrophic earthquake of January 1995. Less impressive was the delay in relief efforts as the Communal ᵛMEMEs worked for consensus in the absence of fast-responding Individual ᵛMEME-based disaster command and controls. Both aspects of this catastrophe illustrate power of the Sacrifice-self ᵛMEMEs in Japanese culture.

There is evidence, though, that sacrificial values are being challenged by expressive ones, primarily by the youth. As lifetime job guarantees lessen, and materialistic needs of Japanese citizens are met, demands for more personal freedom, leisure time, and career alternatives for their children will challenge the old order. That will resonate in a harmonic upsurge in **RED** organized crime and violence that **BLUE**-thinking Japanese will not understand. Taichi Sakaiya, one of Japan's leading social philosophers, notes in his book, *The Knowledge-Value Revolution*:

> 'But Japan's giant corporations, having long lived with the system of collective cooperation between business and government bureaucracy, are sorely lacking the imagination needed to develop new concepts. The government is, if anything, actually working to suppress efforts to develop new thinking.' (p. 349, Translated by George Fields and William Marsh, Kodansha International, Tokyo, New York, London, 1991.)

CHINA – China belongs in a separate class because of its mammoth size and lengthy history. The move into **ORANGE** structures cannot occur until an open **BLUE** system is in place (as opposed to Arrested Maoist **red/BLUE**), the basic needs of people have been met (and they nearly are), the rate of population growth is under control (and they are working on it although the means are often horrific), and the emergence of an affluent middle class is possible. As China gains control of Peak **ORANGE** Hong Kong, we will be able to assess whether the monolithic, authoritarian system is giving way to individual freedoms and private initiative yet or not. If it is, the stage may well be set for a new GEOcurrent as mainland and overseas Chinese launch a post-diaspora global **ORANGE** enterprise of huge proportions. China's difficulties in signing on to President Clinton's human rights agenda is a function of its dominant 'MEMEs. Clare Graves often said: 'We should help a country to become what is next for it to become so it can take yet another step toward a more complex version of democracy.'

BRAZIL – With a stabilized currency and a growing understanding of interdependence, this major chunk of the South American continent is at a transition from Second/Third-World Status into First-World influence. Like South Africa, Brazil is a Spiral microcosm of humanity. The nation includes peoples close to the **BEIGE** zone at one extreme and others leading First-World technologies at the other. In between is a middle class of potential 'have-enoughs' that is about to spring into the global marketplace and balance a Pan-American trade zone. A great asset for Brazil is the way in which its diverse population seems able to tap the strengths of the Spiral's zones without putting the 'MEMEs into adversarial win–lose conflicts.

If the urgent needs of the 'have-nots' and 'can-nots' are finally addressed with adequate health care, nutrition, education, and law and order, the Brazilian sleeping giant can awaken within a decade. While a few indigenous 'have-a-lots' might not relish the idea of wider distribution of economic power, social influences are already reshaping the nation. Because of its remarkably wide 'MEME blend, the new form has the potential of modeling a First-World entrance that respects the healthy aspects of all 'MEMEs without the missteps that Eurocentric cultures have made thus far.

The Third GEOcurrent: From Ethnic Cores to Megatribes

The planet's social structuring has begun shifting from a state-centric world of international politics to an autonomous multicentric one. In this new world ordering, racial, ethnic, social, religious and political sub-groupings are weakening the long-standing structures based on national boundaries, economic spheres of interest, and multinational alliances. More insular city-states like Barcelona, Saò Paulo, Brussels, Nizhni Novgorod, Mexico City, and even Atlanta will rise as besieged and increasingly irrelevant nationalistic boundaries soften. In *Power Shift*, Alvin Toffler referred to these entities as 'mosaics.' Joel Kotkin describes this new global trend as 'The road to Cosmopolis.' Kotkin notes that:

> '. . . global tribes combine a strong sense of a common origin and shared values, quintessential tribal characteristics, with two critical factors for success in the modern world: geographic dispersion and a belief in scientific progress.' (p. 4, *Tribes*, New York, Random House, 1993)

In other words, these entities transcend national boundaries and will not be represented in regional alliances or the present United Nations. Just as city-states will thrive in the post-Cold War world, so will these unique human groupings that rise from a common **PURPLE** base and resonate up the Spiral into more complex forms. Kotkin identifies five principle 'global tribes' – the Jewish, Anglo–American, Japanese, Chinese, and Indian. All five have powerful vertical psychological 'MEME stacks that foster unique interests and identities.

Many other global tribes have existed historically or are presently growing over Earth's surface. One must take a magic carpet ride to detect them since their dispersed pieces are scattered on virtually every continent, island, ocean, and in the air. New global tribes are forming around Islamic and African Diaspora's led by the African–American power peak. In religion, the Mormons (Church of Jesus Christ of Latter-day Saints) are rapidly becoming a global tribe because of their aggressive missionary work and solid **purple/ BLUE/ORANGE** foundation in Utah.

Kotkin's five major global tribes, along with the growing list of others, can best be defined in terms of the Spiral colors. The composition of their 'MEME Stacks will shape their relative power, variety, exclusivity, and adaptability. Their vulnerability to collapse will differ widely and which will exist fifty years from now is unknowable. As they move into the **GREEN, YELLOW**, and **TURQUOISE** ranges the hard edges tend to drop away since definitions of the human race as a single organism replace unique versions based on national origin, skin color, beliefs, or blood lines. These great 'MEMEs lurk behind such terms as traditional or conservative, progressive, reformed, liberal, orthodox, labor, or modern. The stress, strain, and fault lines in the human terrain ahead may well follow the value systems of global tribes. The next world order will be characterized more by them and world cities than the national boundaries that presently divide people on maps of the planet. They will profoundly impact the future of the human species in the mosaic of a twenty-first century cosmopolis.

Two Kinds of GEO-Subcurrents

You will also want to look for two minor sub-currents. Their relative impacts are a function of the success of the major currents in capturing more individuals and groups within their mainstreams. To observe the first, you need to scout the backwaters, cut-off stretches, and stagnant pools. To find the second, go up-stream to where the future comes from, search for the headwaters and explore the watershed that will feed tomorrow's flow.

Regressive Sub-currents: Backwaters and Isolated Bends Whole societies can literally implode or come unglued. Large segments of a culture can be bogged down in lower levels of functioning. These down-Spiral stagnations or REGRESSIONS often lead right into the GAMMA trap. Certainly Sudan,

Haiti, and Ethiopia qualify, as does the former Yugoslavia. The cultures of the Maya and Aztecs lost prime and virtually disappeared, victims of inadequate food supples, Spanish horsemen and smallpox. A number of South and Central American states are still at-risk today.

There is no guarantee that any society can either maintain equilibrium or move to greater complexity. Plagues, natural catastrophes, internal conflict, invasions from outsiders, or any other major disruption of *Life Conditions* may lift an entity out of a main current and regress it to a stagnant backwater. 'MEMEs will tend to move into alignment, whether 'up' or 'down' the Spiral.

Emergent Sub-currents: Headwaters of Entering Systems   While many prominent issues hover around the two main currents, **RED** to **BLUE** and **BLUE** to **ORANGE**, you will detect pockets of **GREEN**, **YELLOW**, and **TURQUOISE** at global, national, and local levels.

The drive into Europe 1992, with its circle of twelve stars as the logo, resulted in the election of a **GREEN**-leaning European Parliament. Ironically, the Green Party has gained in political strength over the last decade, indicating an interest in development beyond materialism toward inclusion of other human and ecological factors.

The new European community has been sidetracked by the revival of **BLUE** fears in member countries ranging from Germany's Skinheads and France's rebelling farmers to Denmark's desire to keep her unique culture unique. Margaret Thatcher's 'Hail Britannia' sentiments were well known, especially when it came to currency, autonomy, and culture. In addition, unresolved **PURPLE** and **RED** issues in the Balkans put the whole thing in some jeopardy.

Scandinavia was known for its early excursions in the **GREEN** world with communitarian values and high taxes, though Sweden is in a temporary downshift caused by economic problems. Canada's **GREEN** resulted in an elaborate national health insurance plan and a heightened sensitivity to the separatists demands of the Inuit in the Northwest and the French–Canadians in Quebec. A hemisphere away, The Netherlands continues to struggle with **GREEN** social conscience, **ORANGE** economic constraints, and an influx of predominantly **BLUE, RED,** and even **PURPLE** thinking immigrants.

As we discussed in Section 3, elements of **YELLOW** and **TURQUOISE** thinking are appearing at the top of societal peaks as **ORANGE** and **GREEN** solutions fail and fade, requiring the emergence of new expressive-elite (**YELLOW**) and sacrificial-collective (**TURQUOISE**) ranges of existence. Watch for them in northern Europe and Canada.

Macro-Managing the Planet

Now you are starting to understand the global system in Spiral terms and to recognize the **YELLOW** and **TURQUOISE** Problems of Existence our unique *Life Conditions* (the Times, Place, Conditions, and Circumstances) present. More than anything else, certainly more than cyclical theory or political predictions, these Second Tier forces will shape that next world order or disorder. No wonder so many people continue to seek the simpler life within Cycleland.

The post-Cold War planet is literally alive with spinning Spirals, some free-standing, others locked in deadly competition. Others are trapped behind unnatural boundaries. We have various nation-states based on their ethnic composition. Some are relatively pure forms (Germany and Botswana); others have made internal peace among the ethnic and linguistic cores (Switzerland and Singapore); while many others are ethnic Hotspots or Flashpoints (South Africa, Kenya, Mexico, India, and the United States).

Global-tribes are expanding rapidly within the vacuum left by the fall of the Berlin Wall. No doubt these eruptions will challenge the maps drawn when **BLUE/ORANGE** national boundaries were firm and fixed. How does one 'draw' the Jewish global tribe? The Chinese one? The one flowing out of Islamic fundamentalism? Will national boundaries really matter?

Europe's Catalans, Scots, and Lombards are talking independence. Even California is discussing splitting into three parts and Texans joke about the state constitution which keeps the secession option open. World-cities are hotly contesting with each other for prime global events with the attendant TV coverage, corporate headquarters relocations, and high profile athletic teams. Border cities such as Laredo (Texas) have become binational entities with culture, families, cash, and commerce flowing in both directions as transmigration patterns obliterate traditional borders. Other cities are regressing into backwaters, resulting in inner-city cesspools and uncontrolled, violent gang warfare. No wonder Australian filmmaker George Miller's *The Road Warrior*, depicting modern day versions of Visigoths and Vandals riding around the outback on Harley-Davidson's and dune buggies, was so alarming.

As first sensed when we could finally look at the Earth from the Moon, we are, as Archibald MacLeish noted, 'riders on the Earth, together.' What choices do we have as global citizens? One option is that we simply let things be, let nature take its course. The fittest on the Spiral, or the fittest Spiral, will survive. Shall we let the Code of the Spiral's **RED** system prevail? Or allow the societies with the finest technology to dominate – the **ORANGE** ᵛMEME *über alles*?

Yet, as we approach Second Tier ᵛMEME systems, the transition from Subsistence to levels of Being, we may be developing the knowledge to participate in our own evolutionary history. If so, what courses of action are available to us?

What if we were to gather some Spiral Wizards on the magic carpet and activate the Z GEOtemplate's Command Intelligences? We would ask them to design a Spiral-based global straegy. To do so they must go through the discipline and precision inherent in the *Streams* process at the whole-Earth level. Forget about imposing solution packages from one society onto another unless their *Life Conditions* are similar. Then they would craft a GEOtemplate structure for each societal entity, realizing it will need to change and shift as Conditions alter in either direction.

Alert the U.N. to the activity of the Spiral Wizards! Get reporters from CNN to televise the proceedings! Force the gathered Wizards to keep their eyes on the prize – the health of global sub-Spirals and the human Spiral itself. Two conditions must be met:

1   *Spirals are healthy when each of the ^{v}MEMEs is being expressed in its positive version.*

    'Good authority' is necessary when people travel the **RED** to **BLUE** GEOcurrent, yet zealotry-driven ideologies and militant holy wars of any kind are destructive to the Spiral. 'The good life' pursued in the **BLUE** to **ORANGE** GEOcurrent need not be heavily materialistic with polluted rivers, poisonous air, or wasteful consumers. Here is the basic question Wizards always ask: 'Will the expression of a given ^{v}MEME add to or take from the life of the Spiral itself?' In other words, will other ^{v}MEMEs in different ranges remain free to express themselves and develop along their trajectories?

2   *A human Spiral is healthy when avenues are open for movement on toward the more complex bands of thinking.*

    Blockages for any reason cause the Spiral to stagnate or even implode. People begin to feel like helium-filled balloons trapped under a ceiling, particularly onerous when it is of glass. As you recall, we term this the GAMMA Trap in Chapter 4. The trap must be unlocked and barriers cracked before the Spiral becomes affirmatively active.

Structures on the Y GEOtemplate:

Note the index of political and economic packages on the matrix below. These are tools of the **Y** GEOtemplate. Spiral Wizards must understand (a) the nature of each package and (b) how and when to introduce each into specific situations. It makes no sense at all to debate between or among the various models. The only question should be 'what are the Problems and *Life Conditions?*'

Each political and economic package is congruent with specific ranges on the Spiral. Attempts to force too great a complexity on an emerging society will make things worse, not better. Those who wish to introduce less complexity than appropriate into a situation waste critical time, resources, and energy. A sensible host society should be incensed by such paternalistic attitudes.

For Spiral Wizards to influence the shift from one set of ^{v}MEMEs to what is next on the Spiral, they must see that the exact steps each social system must

Political and Economic Matrix

vMEME	`Democracy is . . .	Political Form . . .	
BEIGE	No concept of governance	Band	Little exchange. Eat when hungry. Few possessions
PURPLE	What` our people' decide to do. Announced by the chief and guided by elders and spirits	Tribe (clans councils and lineage connections)	Mutual reciprocity and barter. Chief distributes based on need through kinship.
RED	Whatever the Big Boss says it is.` Power to the people` means to Boss and chosen few.	Empire (dictatorial perhaps `corrupt` autocratic strong arm tactics)	Feudal distribution system where the rich elites get richer the poor get poorer.
BLUE	Justice and fairness for the right, good people who follow rules and traditions.	Authoritarian (one-party rule government control)	Basic standard of living will be raised through hard work, discipline, and savings
ORANGE	Give-and-take pluralistic politics within a check-and-balance game of economics.	Enterprise (multi party states, bills of rights)	Free market-driven process where the 'invisible hand' of economy sets pay, price, perks
GREEN	Everybody shares equally in making consensus decisions to care for` we the people'	Communitarian (social democracy, equal rights/results)	Communally-based distribution meets human needs before any benefit from excess or profit
YELLOW	Process of integrating the majority of interests in expediting flows up the Spiral	Integrated Structures (stratified systems in Spiral intelligence)	Simultaneous value-added moves throughout Spiral for higher quality of being to next steps
TURQUOISE	Macro management of all life forms toward common good in response to macro problems	Holistic (whole- Earth networks and interconnections)	Earth's resources and learning distributed by need, not want, so all can survive with enough

navigate are introduced in the proper sequence. There is no evidence that an entity can leap over or bypass these developmental stages without leaving weak spots and engendering problems for the future.

Peace-keeping or starvation-preventive initiatives, such as those in Somalia and Haiti, initially require a healthy **RED** Peace Lord package that can counter or overwhelm the **RED** warlords. This provides the essential leadership to stabilize the environment and neutralize destructive forces. It may be necessary in some form for the restabilization of Russia if predatory violence escalates.

African societies, for the most part, have not been ready for **ORANGE** free-market systems, much less the **GREEN** social democracy versions. They tend to drown in the complexity. As Clare Graves observed, 'the transitions from tribalism to democracy must first pass through autocracy.' In our Spiral language, **PURPLE** and **RED** must establish **BLUE** 'good authority' physical and mental infrastructures before **ORANGE** enterprise movements can sprout. The future of the Third World first requires a passage through the **BLUE** conduit of Second World before enjoying the fruits of First-World existence. Only then can the middle class be developed and empowered.

Any Third-World society (or Third-World components in First- and Second-World environments) seeking to escape a colonial or despotic past must take certain initial steps to fill the gaps in the developmental staircase. In *Who Prospers: How Cultural Values Shape Economic and Political Success*, Lawrence E. Harrison identifies the common components in those societies that have 'prospered' (escaped Third-World conditions, excessively authoritarian structures, and stagnant economies) in contrast to those which have not. In Gravesian language, Harrison's 'prospering' is a function of awakened **BLUE/ORANGE**: the emergence of a Puritan-Confucian-Islamic-type work ethic; the values associated with individual initiative; a relatively free and open economic system; educational opportunities; a stable society in terms of law and order; and respect for personal rights and property. Again, watch Brazil for a case study in the coming decade.

Generally, efforts to impose **ORANGE** 'enterprise zones' over Third World LCs in the U.S. and elsewhere will fail until the **BLUE** base has been built and the **RED** Problems and barriers contained. Without the **BLUE** foundation, resources are wasted, the aspiring people 'fail' once again, and situations get worse. The debate between supply-side, trickle-down theories and those who advocate pump-priming bubble-up approaches are, as we have said, highly misleading. Both have to be integrated and meshed in specific ratios to spark human development. The exact proportions are determined by the location of the group and its leadership on the Spiral itself.

Instead of advocating either government spending or individual initiatives to stimulate development, consider the ^{V}MEME profiles of the elites and the nature of the collective systems in place. **RED** must be contained by a government imposed or theocratic law-and-order regimen. **ORANGE** must be monitored through a 'play within the rules' form of administration as individuals compete. **PURPLE** needs the embellishment of organizing purposeful **BLUE** before risk-taking entrepreneurial behavior can ever blossom. **BLUE** needs exposure to 'the invisible hand' of free-market initiatives and entrepreneurial opportunities of **ORANGE**. In turn, **ORANGE** impulses must be tempered by **GREEN** concerns for the environment and human rights. It takes **YELLOW** to manage the **Z** GEOtemplate intelligences which can coordinate this complicated process as living moves towards the Second Tier.

Macro-Managing Change of the 7th Variation

Multiple 'MEMEs Simultaneously in Transition throughout a Society

What kinds of initiatives should Spiral Wizards recommend in macro-managing societies that are passing through multiple 'MEME ranges on the Spiral simultaneously? What do you do when all three GEOcurrents are flowing strongly at once, all demanding pre-eminence and access to a country's resources? Such are the conditions facing such global microcosms as South Africa and Brazil.

When entities contain such a diverse mix of 'MEMEs and value systems, the models will need to accommodate those vertical levels by managing at the Core Intelligence of the Spiral's spine. For example, **BLUE** authoritarian needs can be meshed with **ORANGE** expansionistic systems so long as there is a fair value exchange between the two and both are kept Open for movement. In other cases, an entire array of 'MEMEs can be managed concurrently when they remain in their positive as opposed to negative versions, thus keeping the Spiral itself alive and vibrant.

The South African Microcosm

To most people the issues in South Africa have been about racial oppression and *apartheid*. In our view, the real conflicts have to do with major collisions and restrictions of 'MEMEs. Today, South Africans of all races must jointly manage the strong Third- to Second- World developmental sequence while, at the same time, preserving and enhancing the much smaller First-World component. If the center of gravity were to shift from the **BLUE/ORANGE** to the **RED-BLUE** 'black majority rule' position, the largely white First-World component will wither and die. Unfortunately, that has been the traditional African pattern. On the other hand, if the European/Afrikaner-dominated First-World infrastructure continues to dominate, the wealth will be transferred to **ORANGE** in the form of expensive homes, elegant motor cars, high-rise office buildings, and shopping centers for the predominantly, but no longer exclusively, white elites. Little will actually trickle down to **PURPLE** where needs are greater to defuse the smouldering **RED**.

We were able to resolve that paradox by describing a **YELLOW** thinking strategy to South African leadership, one that places the two critical masses into a synergistic rather than mutually exclusive arrangement. New South Africans will now have to create a political and economic package that can deal with their unique circumstances. In so doing, they may well uncover the models necessary to manage the diversity of the planet itself. (For more details on the nature of this strategy, see *The Crucible: Forging South Africa's Future*, Don Edward Beck and Graham Linscott, New Paradigm Press, 1991.)

South Africa is not alone in this complexity, only the first to gain global prominence. Brazil shares many of the microcosmic aspects on a different continent. Racialism, have/have-not, and know/know-not gaps are major concerns there, too. Disparities among Fourth through First-World components endure in Brazilian society where . . .

> '. . . during the era of slavery there had been bridges between the white and the black communities. After 1888 [when slavery was abolished] . . . society stabilized and closed its ranks. The upper classes became acutely conscious of everything that separated the white man from the black man . . . Skin color, once 'forgotten,' now established an unbreakable divide between rich and poor. Unsuccessful whites were lumped together with blacks . . . Everywhere there was racism and everywhere it was denied . . . In relations between individuals, the imperatives of humility, obedience, and fidelity were even stronger than they had been during the time of slavery.' Mattoso, (Katia M. de Queriós, *To Be a Slave in Brazil*, New Brunswick, New Jersey, Rutgers University Press, 1986.)

Once again, the issue is the Spiral, not race or ethnicity. **RED, BLUE**, and **ORANGE** take precedence over black, brown, or white when we become serious about positive human development.

The Next Global Order?

Clearly, the world will be a dangerous place for some time to come, perhaps more dangerous than it has ever been. There are far too many deficits in terms of access to human rights, comforts and lifestyles. Neither basic standard of living nor an enhanced quality of life can be guaranteed to anyone. Competitive niches will continue to open and close to various groups on the planet. Some niches will be enriched, while others will be characterized by bare levels of human subsistence. What needs to happen and how?

Power elites, economic spheres of influence, individual nations and large global tribes will have to negotiate new relationships or the natural turbulence coming from the inevitable conflict could well block human movement up the

Spiral. There are no guarantees about our future, after all. A little money buys a great deal of technological power right now, and our knowledge sometimes exceeds our wisdom.

The world community, acting through a successor to the U.N. or some new and more effective whole-Earth entity should build a catalogue of tailored resources, packages, personnel, and programs that could be dispatched into specific circumstances to address the needs of people at diverse levels on the Spiral. Teams of highly trained and competent professionals (who are also Spiral Wizards) could act quickly in addressing great issues through the most appropriate means, preempting deadly conflicts and health disasters with peaceful intent. Most of what is needed is known; we just lack good ways to apply it. With **YELLOW** and **TURQUOISE** active, all would be equipped to act locally and plan globally while acting globally and planning locally at the same time.

Twenty years ago Clare Graves noted in 'Human Nature Prepares for a Momentous Leap':

'The present moment finds our society attempting to negotiate the most difficult, but at the same time the most exciting, transition the human race has faced to date. It is not merely a transition to a new level of existence but the start of a new 'movement' in the symphony of human history. The future offers us, basically, three possibilities:

(1) Most gruesome is the chance that we might fail to stabilize our world and, through successive catastrophes regress as far back as the Ik tribe has.

(2) Only slightly less frightening is the vision of fixation in the D-Q/E-R/F-S [**BLUE-ORANGE-GREEN**] societal complex. This might resemble George Orwell's *1984*, with its tyrannical, manipulative government glossed over by a veneer of humanitarian-sounding double-think and moralistic rationalization, and is a very real possibility in the next decades.

(3) The last possibility is that we could emerge into the G-T [**YELLOW**] level and proceed toward stabilizing our world so that all life can continue. If we succeed in the last alternative, we will find ourselves in a very different world from what we know now and we will find ourselves thinking in a very different way.'

(*The Futurist*, April 1974)

We may have help from outside. Tautatis, a large asteroid that swings around the sun in a lopsided orbit, was first spotted by a French astronomer in 1934. It is large enough to leave quite a mark on planet Earth. In December 1992 it missed us by only 2.2 million miles. Phew! In 2005 it will pass within a bare million miles, darned close by astronomical standards. It will swing by several more times in the next few decades. The last time a large asteroid hit Earth, the dinosaurs supposedly had a very bad day. Astronomers now predict that Tautatis might give the human race an equally bad day as soon as 2069. No one could go home again.

What would happen to the species Homo sapiens if in 2050 we decided that

Tautatis actually were on a collision course and we had only 19 years before the crunch? What would we or our children or their children do? How would that wake-up call impact the human Spiral? New realities? New priorities? Even different mind-forms? What if NASA or some other agency listening to the heavens for radio signals from intelligent beings finds one before 2069? What would we do then, knowing that we are not alone? Ask for help? Wave bye, bye?

Perhaps the greater question is, 'Who shall we choose to become by then?' Humanity is facing up to some hard truths. We have some powerful choices to make. Many will be political, some religious, and others educational. All will be predicated on the Spiral, whether we recognize it at the time or not. A little knowledge is a dangerous thing, but ignorance is worse. If you are now awakening to Spiral Dynamics, you hold the handle of a versatile tool. Merge it into your wisdom and other insights. Then use it wisely and well.

Resources for Spiral Wizards

A Wizard's Tool Kit – Including Books, Theories, and Ideas

These authors, theories, models and concepts have special relevance to different ᵛMEMEs, the process whereby ᵛMEMEs are awakened, and how different 'MEMEs' spheres can best be led, managed, educated, and accommodated. While a few will be familiar classics, we have tried to introduce some newer works that are not part of the stock bibliographies of 'business books.' You will find them sorted into appropriate Wizard's Library stacks, though you may wish to do some rearranging and will, no doubt, have your own models, mentors, and gurus to add to your tool kit.

Some ᵛMEME-Specific Tools

The **BEIGE** *ᵛMEME – survival senses and deep brain systems*
Jean Auel's anthropological fiction (*Clan of the Cave Bear*, etc.).
The literature of development and early childhood such as the work of Jean Piaget.
Medical models for helping Alzheimers sufferers, schizophrenia, autism.

The **PURPLE** *ᵛMEME – animistic beliefs, tribal orders, harmony, and superstitions*
Aveni, Anthony, *Conversing with the Planets: How Science and Myth Invented the Cosmos*, Times Books, London, 1992.
Calvin, William H., *How the Shaman Stole the Moon: In Search of Ancient Prophet-scientists from Stonehenge to the Grand Canyon*, Bantam, New York, 1991.
Campbell, Joseph, *Masks of God*, and other works on mythology and religion.
Fraser, James G., *The Golden Bough: A Study in Comparative Religion*, 1890.
Moore, Robert and Douglas Gillette, *The Magician Within: Accessing the Shaman in the Male Psyche*, Avon Books, New York, 1993.
Morris, Desmond and Peter Marsh, *Tribes*, Gibbs-Smith Books, Salt Lake City, 1988.
Narratives and personal explorations with native peoples' healers and spiritual guides.
Wesselman, Hank, *Spiritwalker: Messages from the Future*, Bantam Books, New York, 1995.

The **RED** *ᵛMEME – egocentric personalities, empire structures, power-centered leadership approaches*
Behavorism – Positive Reinforcement and Control

Tough Love
Positive Discipline
Colonial Management
Leadership Secrets of Attila the Hun
Hands-on-training
'Street smart' behaviors
Carry the biggest stick
Old-time *La Cosa Nostra*

Moore, Robert and Douglas Gillette, *King, Warrior, Magician, and Lover: Rediscovering the Archetypes of the Mature Masculine*, Harper, San Francisco, 1991.
Moore & Gillette, *The King Within*, Willard Morrow, New York, 1992.
Shay, Jonathan, *Achilles in Vietnam: Combat Trauma and the Undoing of Character*, Atheneum, New York, 1994.
The literature of 'at-risk' youth intervention.
Applications of Lawrence Kohlberg's 'Levels of Moral Reasoning' framework, especially in the prison setting.

The **BLUE** *ᵛMEME – moral compasses and authoritarian structures*
Systematic Thinking
Moral Education – Boy and Girl Scouts
Behavorism – Negative Reinforcement and punishments
Seniority-based Systems
Basic 'Plan, Control, and Do' Training
Governance by theocracy or the state as god-surrogate
Fundamentalisms in religious, secular, and political arenas
Traditional military and paramilitary chains-of-command
'Spare the rod, spoil the child'

Bellah, Robert Wn., et al. *The Good Society*, Alfred A. Knopf, New York, 1991.
Bennet, William, *The Book of Virtues*.
Johnson, Mark, *Moral Imagination*, The University of Chicago Press, Chicago, 1993.
Murchison, William, *Reclaiming Morality in America*, Thomas Nelson, Nashville, 1994.
Wilson, James Q., *The Moral Sense*, The Free Press, New York, 1993.
Wrong, Dennis H., *The Problem of Order: What Unites and Divides Society*, The Free Press, New York, 1994.

The **ORANGE** *ᵛMEME – enterprise structures, success-driven leadership*
Managerial Grid (Blake & Mouton)
Achievement Motivation (McClellan)
Management by Objectives
Zig Ziglar – 'See you at the Top'
Strategic Planning
SBOs – Strategic Business Units
Situational Management
The 'Excellence' of Tom Peters
Ken Blanchard's *One Minute Manager*
Privatization as *the* solution.

Andreas, Steve and Charles Faulkner (Eds.), *NLP: The New Technology of Achievement*, William Morrow, New York, 1994.

D'Aveni, Richard A., *Managing the Dynamics of Strategic Maneuvering*, The Free Press, New York, 1994.

de Geus, Arie, Peter Schwartz, and Piere Vack approach: 'Scenarios.'

Florman, Samuel C., *Blaming Technology: The Irrational Search for Scapegoats*, St. Martin's Press, New York, 1981.

Kotkin, Joel, *Tribes: How Race, Religion and Identity Determine Success in the New Global Economy*, Random House, New York, 1993.

Maccoby, Michael, *The Gamesman: The New Corporate Leaders*, Simon & Schuster, 1976.

Seligman, Martin E. P., *Learned Optimism*, Alfred A. Knopf, New York, 1991.

The **GREEN** ᵛ*MEME – community structures, consensus-driven leadership*
Sensitivity Training
E.S.T. and Esalen
Wellness Programs
Quality Circles
Interpersonal skills development
Conflict management programs
Theory X and Y
Maintenance, Motivation, and Hygenic Factors

Autry, James A., *Love & Profit*, William Morrow, New York, 1991.

Baldwin, Christina, *Calling the Circle*, Swan-Raven & Co., Newberg (OR), 1994.

Berger, Peter L., *The Capitalist Revolution*, Basic Books, New York, 1986.

Berman, Morris, *The Reenchantment of the World*, Bantam, New York, 1984.

Bernstein, Richard, *Dictatorship of Virtue: Multiculturalism and the Battle for America's Future*, Alfred Knoph, New York, 1994.

Bruckner, Pascal, *The Tears of the White Man: Compassion as Contempt*, The Free Press, New York, 1983.

Capra, Fritjof and Charlene Spretnak, *Green Politics: The Global Promise*, W. P. Dutton, Inc., New York, 1984.

D Quinn Mills' 'Cluster Organizations'

Etzioni, Amitai, *The Spirit of Community: Rights, Responsibilities, and the Communitarian Agenda*, Crown Publishers, New York, 1993.

Farrell, Larry C., *Searching for the Spirit of Enterprise*, Dutton, New York, 1993.

Freeman, R. Edward and Daniel R. Gilbert, Jr., *Corporate Strategy and The Search for Ethics*, Prentice Hall, Englewood Cliffs, 1988.

Henry, William A., III, *In Defense of Elitism*, Doubleday, New York, 1994.

Nair, Keshavan, *A Higher Standard of Leadership*, San Francisco, Barrett-Koehler Publishers, 1994.

Magnet, Myron, *The Dream and the Nightmare: The Sixties' Legacy to the Underclass*, William Morrow and Company, New York, 1993.

O'Toole, James, *The Executive's Compass*, Oxford University Press, New York, 1993.

Ozaki, Robert, *Human Capitalism*, Kodansha International, Tokyo, 1991.

Paepke, C. Owen, *The Evolution of Progress: The End of Economic Growth and the Beginning of Human Transformations*, Random House, 1993.

Peck, M. Scott, *A World Waiting to be Born: Civility Rediscovered*, Bantam, 1993.
Postman, Neil, *Technopoly: The Surrender of Culture to Technology*, Alfred Knopf, New York, 1992.
Redfield, James, *The Celestine Prophecy*, Time Warner, New York, 1993.
Roger T. Harrison's concept of 'Attunement'

The YELLOW ᵗMEME – *integrated structures, systems-systemic leadership*
Model-builders:
D. Keith Denton – *Horizonal Management*
Peter Senge – *The Learning Company*
Charles Handy – *The Age of Unreason*
Charles Hampden-Turner – *Paradox Resolution*
Elliott Jaques – *The Requisite Organization*
Russ Ackoff – *Architecturally Designed Solutions*
James Brian Quinn – *Intelligent Enterprise*

Erikson, Kai, *A New Species of Trouble: Explorations in Disaster, Trauma, and Community*, Norton, New York, 1991.
Fuller, R. Buckminster, *Critical Path*, St. Martin's Press, 1981.
Goldsmith, Edward, *The Way: An Ecological World-view*, Shambala, Boston, 1992.
Penrose, Roger, *The Emperor's New Mind: Concerning Computers, Minds and the Laws of Physics*, Oxford University Press, Oxford, 1989.
Pinchot, Gifford & Elizabeth, *The End of Bureaucracy & the Rise of the Intelligent Organization*, Berrett-Koehler Publishers, San Francisco, 1993.
von Bertalanffy, Ludwig, *Perspectives on General System Theory*, George Braziller, New York, 1975.
Wired Magazine and the journals of the 'Information Age'

The TURQUOISE ᵗMEME – *ecological thinking and holistic structures*
Barrow, John D., *Theories of Everything: The Quest for Ultimate Explanations*, Clarendon Press, Oxford, 1991.
Boulding, Kenneth, *The World as a Total System*, Sage Publications, London, 1985.
Crick, Francis, *The Astonishing Hypothesis: The Scientific Search for the Soul*, Charles Scribners, New York, 1994.
Hall, Stephen S., *Mapping the Next Millennium*, Vintage Books, New York, 1993.
Harman, W. with J. Clark (eds.), *New Metaphysical Foundations of Modern Science*, Institute of Noetic Sciences, Sausalito, CA, 1994.
Kelly, Kevin, *Out of Control: The rise of Neobiological Civilizations*, Addison-Wesley, Reading, Mass, 1995.
Quinn, Daniel, *Ishmael*, Bantam/Turner, New York, 1992.
Sheldrake, Rupert, *The Presence of the Past: Morphic Resonance and the Habits of Nature*, Times Books, New York, 1988.
—— , *The Rebirth of Nature: The Greening of Science and God*, Bantam Books, New York, 1991.
Stock, Gregory, *Metaman: The Merging of Humans and Machines into a Global Superorganism*, Simon & Schuster, New York, 1993.
Talbot, Michael, *The Holographic Universe*, HarperCollins, New York, 1991.

On Life Conditions – Times, Place, Problems, and Circumstances

Colinvaux, Paul, *The Fates of Nations: A Biological Theory of History*, Simon & Schuster, New York, 1980.

Crawford, Michael & David Marsh, *The Driving Force: Food, Evolution and the Future*, Heinemann, London, 1989.

Edgerton, Robert B., *Sick Societies: Challenging the Myth of Primitive Harmony*, The Free Press, New York, 1992.

Gallagher, Winfred, *The Power of Place: How Our Surroundings Shape Our Thoughts, Emotions, and Actions*, Poseidon Press, New York, 1993.

Harrison, Lawrence E., *Who Prospers: How Cultural Values Shape Economic and Political Success*, Basic Books, New York, 1992.

Hobhose, Henry, *Forces of Change: An Unorthodox View of History*, Little Brown and Company, New York, 1989.

Jacoabs, Jane, *Systems of Survival: A Dialogue on the Moral Foundations of Commerce and Politics*, Random House, New York, 1992.

Nikiforuk, Andrew, *The Fourth Horseman: a Short History of Epidemics, Plagues and Other Scourges*, The Fourth Estate, London, 1991.

Reader, John, *Man on Earth*, University of Texas Press, Austin, 1988.

Schama, Simon, *Landscape and Memory*, Alfred A. Knopf, New York, 1995.

Schreinder, Samuel A., Jr., *Cycles*, Donald I. Fine, New York, 1990.

Thomas, Lewis, *The Fragile Species*, Charles Schribner's Sons, New York, 1992.

Weatherford, Jack, *Savages and Civilization: Who Will Survive?*, Crown Publishers, New York, 1994.

On How the Mind Makes a ᵛMEME

Bloom, Howard, *The Lucifer Principle*, The Atlantic Monthly Press, New York, 1995.

Bodmer, Walter, and Robin McKie, *The Book of Man: The Quest to Discover our Genetic Heritage*, Little Brown & Company, London, 1994.

Brodie, Richard, *Virus of the Mind*, Integral Press, Seattle, 1995.

Claxton, Guy, *Noises from the Darkroom: The Science and Mystery of the Mind*, Aquarian, London, 1994.

Csikszentmihalyi, Mihaly, *The Evolving Self: A Psychology for the Third Millennium*, HarperCollins, New York, 1993.

D'Souza, Dinesh, *The End of Racism*, The Free Press, New York, 1995.

Davis, Philip J., *Spirals from Theodorus to Chaos*, A. K. Peters, Wellesley, MA, 1993.

Dawkins, Richard, *The Extended Phenotype*, Oxford University Press, Oxford, 1982.

——, *The Selfish Gene*, New Edition, Oxford University Press, Oxford, 1989.

Dennett, Daniel C., *Darwin's Dangerous Idea: Evolution and the Meanings of Life*, Simon & Schuster, New York, 1995.

Donald, Merlin, *Origins of the Modern Mind: Three Stages in the Evolution of Culture and Cognition*, Harvard University Press, Cambridge, 1991.

Dozier, Rush W., Jr., *Codes of Evolution*, Crown Publishers, New York, 1992.

Edelman, Gerald M., *Bright Air, Brilliant Fire: On the Matter of the Mind*, Basic Books, New York, 1992.

Gazzaniga, Michael S., *Nature's Mind: The Biological Roots of Thinking, Emotions, Sexuality, Language, and Intelligences*, Basic Books, New York, 1992.

Harth, Erich, *Dawn of a Millennium: Beyond Evolution and Culture*, Penguin, New York, 1990.

——, *The Creative Loop: How the Brain Makes a Mind*, Addison-Wesley Publishing Company, Reading, Massachusetts, 1993.

Hundert, Edward M., *Lessons from Optical Illusion*, Harvard University Press, Cambridge, MA, 1995.

Kevles, Daniel J., *In the Name of Eugenics: Genetics and the Uses of Human Heredity*, Harvard University Press, Cambridge, MA, 1995.

Kingdon, Jonathan, *Self-made Man: Human Evolution from Eden to Extinction*, John Wiley & Sons, New York, 1993.

McKenna, Terence, and Dennis McKenna, *The Invisible Landscape: Mind Hallucinogens and the I Ching*, Harper, San Francisco, 1975.

Murphy, Michael, *The Future of the Body: Explorations into the Further Evolution of Human Nature*, Jeremy P. Tarcher, 1992.

Penrose, Roger, *Shadows of the Mind*, Vintage, London, 1994. (First published by Oxford University Press, 1994.)

Plotkin, Henry, *Darwin Machines and the Nature of Knowledge*, Harvard University Press, Cambridge, MA, 1994.

Pollack, Robert, *Signs of Life: The Language and Meanings of DNA*, Houghton Mifflin, Boston, 1994.

Scott, Alwyn, *Stairway to the Mind*, Springer-Verlag, New York, 1995.

Volk, Tyler, *Metapatterns: Across Time, Space, and Mind*, Columbia University Press, New York, 1995.

Wills, Christopher, *Exons, Introns, and Talking Genes*, Basic Books, New York, 1991.

——, *The Runaway Brain: The Evolution of Human Uniqueness*, Basic Books, New York, 1993.

——, *The Wisdom of the Genes*, Oxford University Press, Oxford, 1991.

Spiral-based Thinking and Evolutionary Flows

Abraham, Ralph, *Chaos, Gaia, Eros: A Chaos Pioneer Uncovers the Three Great Streams of History*, Harper, San Francisco, 1994.

Allman, William F., *The Stone Age Present*, Simon & Schuster, New York, 1994.

Barlow, Connie, (ed.), *Evolution Extended: Biological Debates on the Meaning of Life*, The MIT Press, Cambridge, 1994.

Calvin, William H., *The River that Flows Uphill: A Journey from the Big Bang to the Big Brain*, Macmillan, New York, 1986.

Carlsen, Mary Baird, *Meaning–Making: Therapeutic Processes in Adult Development*, W. W. Norton, London, 1988.

Cavalli-Sforza, Luigi Luca and Francesco, *The Great Human Diasporas: The History of Diversity and Evolution*, Addison-Wesley Helix Books, New York, 1995.

Chilton, Stephen, *Grounding Political Development*, Rienner, Boulder, 1991.

Corning, Peter A., *The Synergism Hypothesis*, McGraw-Hill, New York, 1983.

Diamond, Jared, *The Third Chimpanzee: The Evolution and Future of the Human Animal*, HarperCollins, New York, 1992.

Eisler, Riane, *The Chalice & the Blade*, Harper & Row, San Francisco, 1987.

Eldredge, Niles, *Time Frames: The Rethinking of Darwinian Evolution and the Theory of Punctuated Equilibria*, Simon & Schuster, New York.

Elgin, Duane, *Awaking Earth: Exploring the Evolution of Human Culture and Consciousness*, William Morrow, New York, 1993.

Fagan, Brian M., *The Journey from Eden: The Peopling of Our World*, Thames and Hudson, London, 1990.

Fowler, James W., *Stages of Faith: The Psychology of Human Development and the Quest for Meaning*, Harper, San Francisco, 1981.

Gardner, Howard, *Frames of Mind: Theories of Multiple Intelligences*, Basic Books, New York, 1983.

———, *Creating Minds*, Basic Books, New York, 1993.

Habermas, Jurgen, *The Theory of Communicative Action*, Beacon Press, Boston, 1987.

Harman, Willis and John Hormann, *Creative Work: The Constructive Role of Business in a Transforming Society*, Knowledge Systems, 1990.

Hawkins, Gerald S., *Mindsteps to the Cosmos*, Harper & Row, New York, 1983.

Hoogvelt, Nkie M., *The Sociology of Developing Societies*, Macmillan, London, 1982.

Kegan, Robert, *The Evolving Self: Problem and Process in Human Development*, Harvard University Press, Cambridge, 1982.

Land, George, and Beth Jarman, *Break-Point and Beyond*, Harper Business, New York, 1992.

Leonard, George B., *The Transformation: A Guide to the Inevitable Changes in Humankind*, Tarcher, Los Angeles, 1972.

Mayr, Ernst, *Toward a New Philosophy of Biology*, Harvard, Cambridge, 1988.

Miller, Jamer Grier, *Living Systems*, McGraw-Hill, New York, 1987.

Munitz, J. K., *Theories of the Universe: From Babylonian Myth to Modern Science*, Free Press, New York, 1957.

Parsons, Talcott, *The Social System*, Routledge & Kegan Paul, Ltd., London, 1951.

Pearce, Joseph Chilton, *Evolution's End*, Harper, San Francisco, 1992.

Salk, Jonas, *The Survival of the Wisest*, Harper & Row, New York, 1973.

Sanderson, Stephen K., *Social Evolutionism*, Blackwell, Oxford, 1990.

Saszlo, Ervin, *Evolution: The Grand Synthesis*, Shambhala, Boston & London, 1987.

Schmookler, Andrew Bard, *The Parable of the Tribes: The Problem of Power in Social Evolution*, University of California Press, Berkeley, 1984.

Sklair, Leslie, *Sociology of the Global System*, Harvester, New York, 1991.

Skolimowski, Henry, *The Participatory Mind*, Penguin, New York, 1994.

Swimme, Brian & Thomas Berry, *The Universe Story: From the Primordial Flaring Forth to the Ecozoic Era*, Harper, San Francisco, 1992.

Taylor, Gordon Rattray, *The Evolution Mystery*, Secker and Warburg, London, 1983.

Toffler, Alvin, *PowerShift*, Bantam, New York, 1991.

———, *Future Shock*,

———, *The Third Wave*,

———, *War and Peace in the Global Village*

Volk, Tyler, *Metapatterns: Across Time, Space, and Mind*, Columbia University Press, New York, 1995.

Wilber, Ken, *The Holographic Paradigm*, Shambhala, Boulder & London, 1982.
——, *Up From Eden: A Transpersonal View of Human Evolution*, Anchor Press, New York, 1981.
Wright, Robert, *The Moral Animal: The New Science of Evolutionary Psychology*, Pantheon, New York, 1994.

Resources for the Spiral's Streams and Templates

Adizes, Ichak, *Corporate Lifecycles*, Prentice Hall, New York, 1988.
Araoz, Daniel L., & William S. Sutton, *Reengineering Yourself: A Blueprint for Personal Success in the New Corporate Culture*, Bob Adams, Holbrook, Mass., 1994.
Badaracco, Joseph L., Jr., *The Knowledge Link*, Harvard Business School Press, Boston, 1991.
Band, William A., *Touchstones: Ten New Ideas Revolutionizing Business*, John Wiley & Sons, New York, 1994.
Beckhard, Richard, and Wendy Pritchard, *Changing the Essence: The Art of Creating and Leading Fundamental Change in Organizations*, Jossey-Bass, San Francisco, 1992.
Champy, James, *Reengineering Management*, Harper Business, New York, 1994.
Cohen, William A., and Nurit Cohen, *The Paranoid Corporation*, American Management Association, New York, 1993.
Conner, Daryl R., *Managing at the Speed of Change*, Villard Books, New York, 1993.
Covey, Stephen, et al., *First Things First*, Simon & Schuster, 1994.
——, *Principled Leadership*, Simon & Schuster.
——, *The 7 Habits of Highly Effective People*, Simon & Schuster, 1989.
Denton, D. Keith, *Horizontal Management: Beyond Total Customer Satisfaction*, Lexington Books, New York, 1991.
Depree, Max, *Leadership as an Art*, Dell Publishing, New York, 1989.
Goodstein, Leonard D., et al., *Applied Strategic Planning: A Comprehensive Guide*, McGraw-Hill, New York, 1993.
Hammer, Michael & James Champy, *Reengineering the Corporation*, Harper Business, New York, 1993.
Hampden-Turner, Charles, *Creating Corporate Culture: From Discord to Harmony*, Addison-Wesley, Reading, Mass., 1990.
Handy, Charles, *The Age of Unreason*, Harvard Business School Press, Boston, 1989.
Heifetz, Michael L., *Leading Change, Overcoming Chaos*, Ten Speed Press, Berkeley, California, 1993.
Imparato, Nicholas, and Oren Harari, *Jumping the Curve: Innovation and Strategic Choice in the Age of Transition*, Jossey-Bass, San Francisco, 1994.
Jaques, Elliott, and Stephen D. Clement, *Executive Leadership: A Practical Guide to Managing Complexity*, Blackwell, London, 1994.
Karasek, Robert, and Tores Theorell, *Healthy Work: Stress, Productivity, and the Reconstruction of Working Life*, Basic Books, New York, 1990.
Katzenback, Jon R., and Douglas K. Smith, *The Wisdom of Teams: Creating the High Performance Organization*, Harvard Business School Press, Boston, 1993.
Lawler III, Edward E., *The Ultimate Advantage: Creating the High Involvement Organization*, Jossey-Bass, 1992.

Lipnack, Jessica, & Jeffrey Stamps, *Age of the Network: Organizing Principles for the 21st Century*, Oliver Wright Publications, Essex Junction, VT, 1994.

McCarthy, J. Allan, *The Transition Equation*, Lexington Books, New York, 1995.

Makridakis, Spyros G., *Forecasting, Planning and Strategy for the 21st Century*, The Free Press, New York, 1990.

Meyer, Christopher, *Fast Cycle Time: How to Align Purpose, Strategy, and Structure for Speed*, The Free Press, New York, 1993.

Morris, Langdon, *Managing the Evolving Corporation*, Van Nostrand Reinhold, New York, 1995.

Neuhauser Peg C., *Tribal Warfare in Organizations*, Harper Business, New York, 1988.

Pascale, Richard Tanner, *Managing on the Edge*, Touchstone, New York, 1990.

Quinn, James Brian, *Intelligent Enterprise*, The Free Press, New York, 1992.

Savage, Charles M., *5th Generation Management: Integrating Enterprises through Human Networking*, Digital Press, Boston, 1990.

Schrage, Michael, *Shared Minds: The New Technologies of Collaboration*, Random House, New York, 1990.

Semler, Ricardo, *Maverick: The Success Story Behind the World's Most Unusual Workplace*, Warner Books, New York, 1993.

Sproull, Lee, and Sara Kiesler, *Connections: New Ways of Working in the Networked Organization*, The MIT Press, Cambridge, 1991.

Treach, Michael, & Fred Wiersema, *Discipline of Market Leaders*.

Vaill, Peter B., *Managing as a Performing Art*, Jossey-Bass, San Francisco, 1991.

Wheatley, Margaret J., *Leadership and the New Science*, Barrett-Koehler Publishers, San Francisco, 1992.

On Global Forces Impacting Spiral Dynamics

Adler, Mortimer J., *Haves Without Have-Nots*, Macmillan, New York, 1991.

Bauer, P. T., *Equality, the Third World, and Economic Delusion*, Harvard University Press, Cambridge, 1981.

Black, Jan Knippers, *Development in Theory & Practice: Bridging the Gap*, Westview, Boulder, 1991.

Cetrob, Marvin, and Owen Davies, *Crystal Globe: The Haves and Have-Nots of the New World Order*, New York, St. Martin's Press, 1991.

De Soto, Hernando, *The Other Path: The Invisible Revolution in the Third World*, Harper & Row, New York, 1989.

Fukuyama, Francis, *The End of History and the Last Man*, The Free Press, New York, 1992.

Hampden-Turner, Charles, and Alfons Trompenaars, *The Seven Cultures of Capitalism*, Currency/Doubleday, New York, 1993.

Inglehart, Ronald, *Culture Shift in Advanced Industrial Society*, Princeton University Press, Princeton, 1990.

Kennedy, Paul, *Preparing for the Twenty-first Century*, Random House, New York, 1993.

———, *The Rise and Fall of the Great Powers*, Random House, New York, 1986.

Reich, Robert B., *The Work of Nations: Preparing Ourselves for the 21st Century Capitalism*, Alfred A. Knopf, 1991.

Roxborough, Ian, *Theories of Underdevelopment*, Macmillan, London, 1981.

MEMEs	Characteristics	Decision making	Education
PURPLE *Safety*	Mystical spirits, signs Safe clans and nests Powerful elders Our people vs. them	Custom and tradition Elders' counsel Signs or the shaman Clan gets the spoils	Paternalistic teachers Rituals and routines Passive learners Family-like learning
RED *Power*	Raw power displays Immediate pleasure Unrestrained by guilt Colorful and creative	Tough-one dictates What gets respect What feels good now Powerful grab spoils	Rewards for learning Tough-love tactics Work on respect Controlled freedom
BLUE *Truth*	Only one right way Purpose in causes Guilt in consequences Sacrifice for honor	Orders from authority Do right, obey rules Adhere to tradition Righteous earn spoils	Truth from authority Traditional stair steps Moralistic lessons Punishment for errors
ORANGE *Prosperity*	Competes for success Goal-oriented drives Change to progress Material gain/perks	Bottom-line results Test options for best Consult experts Successful win spoils	Experiments to win High-tech, high status How to win niches Mentors and guides
GREEN *Communitarian*	Seeks inner peace Everybody is equal Everything is relative Harmony in the group	Reach consensus All must collaborate Accept any input Communal spoils	To explore feelings Shared experiences Social development Learn cooperation
YELLOW *Systemic*	Big picture views Integrative structures Naturalness of chaos Inevitability of change	Highly principled Knowledge centered Resolved paradoxes Competent get spoils	Becomes self-directed Whole-day package Tuned to interests Non-rigid structure
TURQUOISE *Holistic*	Scans the macro Synergy of all life Safe, orderly world Restore harmony	Blend natural flows Look up/downstream Plan for long range Life gets spoils	Access to world Blend feelings & tech Bring past to life Maximize the brain

HEALTHY COMMUNITIES . . .'
alignment, and integration of . . .

Family	Community	Life space
Extended kinships	Respects folk ways	Old country ways
Rites of passage	Honors ethnicity	Focus on subsistence
Strict role relations	Lets group be itself	Fearful and mystical
Protects bloodline	Guards magic places	Full of spirit beings
Gang-like battles	Predators in control	Unconstrained
Builds us–them walls	Danger to outsiders	Might makes right
Tests of worthiness	Forms fiefdoms	Winners and dead losers
Struggles with system	Turf wars and vendettas	Attention-seeking
Seat of truths and values	Peace-and-quiet	Law abiding citizen
Proper places for all	Cautious and careful	Places for everybody
Codes of conduct	Tidy, green, and neat	Seeks peace of mind
Teaches moral ways	Born into society	Rewards to come
Upwardly mobile	Caters to prosperous	Wants to prosper now
Demands attention	Displays affluence	Competition always
High expectations	Buys into society	Leverages influence
Image conscious	Security for the elite	Seeks material things
Grouping of equals	Social safety-nets	Thrives on belonging
Participative activity	'Politically correct'	Needs acceptance
Highly accepting	Open for insiders	Sacrifice feels good
All feelings processed	Invests in itself	Renews spirituality
Shifting roles	Does more with less	Life is learning
Expects competence	Appropriate techs.	Intrigued by process
Takes each as is	Power is dispersed	Freedom just to be
Information base	Integrated systems	Rarely fearful
Global awareness	Interconnected	Belong to universe
Grows consciousness	Highly diversified	Fit into chain of being
Broad interest ranges	Not isolationist	Do something here
Seeks outreach	Information rich	As one with life-force

Communicating through ^vMEMEs on the Spiral

^{v}MEME	Appropriate sourcing	Elements of appropriate message design
BEIGE	Caretaker Provider	Biologic senses – touch, taste, smell, see, hear Physical contact rather than symbols
PURPLE	Caring chieftain Shaman or elders From within tribe/clan group From spirit realm From word of ancestors Traditional ways	Traditional rites, rituals, ceremonies Includes mystical elements and superstitions Appeals to extended family, harmony and safety Recognizes blood-bonds, the folk, group Familiar metaphors, drawings, and emblems Minimal reliance on written language
RED	Person with recognized power Straight-talking Boss One with something to offer Respected (feared) other Proven tough entity	Demonstrate 'What's in it for me, now?' Offer 'Immediate gratification if . . .' Challenges and appeals to machismo/strength Heroic status and legendary potential Flashy, to-the-point, unambiguous, strong Simple language and fiery images/graphics
BLUE	Rightful proper authority Higher authority in the Way Down the chain-of-command According to the book's rules Person with position power Revered Truth keepers	Duty, honor, country images of discipline Self-sacrifice for higher cause and purpose Appeal to traditions and established norms Use class-consciousness and knowing one's place Propriety, righteousness, and responsibilities Insure future rewards and delayed gratification Assuage guilt with correct consequences

ORANGE	One's own right-thinking mind	Appeal to competitive advantage and leverage
	Successful mentors and models	Success motivations and achieving abundance
	Credible professionals	Bigger, better, newer, faster, more popular
	Prosperous elite contacts	Citations of experts and selected authorities
	Advantageous to the self	Experimental data and tried-and-true experience
	Based in proven experience	Profit, productivity, quality, results, win
	Findings of science	Demonstrate as best of several options
GREEN	Consensual community norms	Enhance belonging, sharing, harmony of groups
	Enlightened friend/colleague	Sensitive to human issues and care for others
	Outcome of participation	Expand awareness and understanding of inner self
	Resultant of enlightenment	Symbols of equity, humanity and bonding
	Observation of events	Gentle language along with nature imagery
	Participative decision	Build trust, openness, exploration, passages
	Team's collective findings	Real people and authentic emotional displays
YELLOW	Any information source	Interactive, relevant media, self-accessible
	May adopt **BEIGE** thru **GREEN**	Functional 'lean' information without fluff
	Competent, more knowing person	The facts, the feelings and the instincts
	Relevant, more useful data	Big picture, total systems, integrations
	Merge hard sources and hunches	Connect data across fields for holistic view
	Conscious and unconscious mind	Adapt, mesh, blend, access, sense, gather
	Disregards status or prestige	Self-connecting to systems and others usefully
TURQUOISE	Experience of discovery	Multidimensional chunks of insight
	Learning in communal network	Use multi-tiered consciousness to access
	Holistic conception of reality	Renewed spirituality and sacrifice to whole
	Any being in **TURQUOISE** sphere	Ecological interdependency and interconnections
	Systems across the planet	Macro (global) solutions to macro problems
	Resonance with First Tier	Community beyond nationalities or partisanship
		High-tech and high-touch for experiential knowing